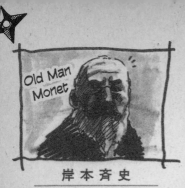

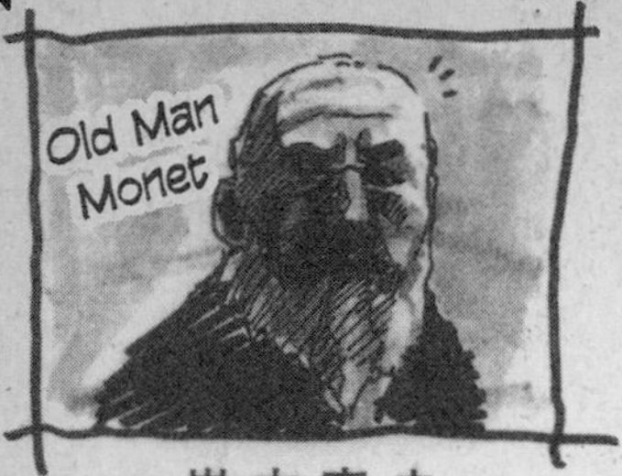
Old Man Monet

岸本斉史

One day, after I bought a book for background research, I noticed it had a special feature on the artist Claude Monet. I actually have very little interest in paintings and painters, but ever since my student days, I loved the grand old man Monet—I went to exhibits of his work and owned several books of his paintings. I envy Monet because, although in his later years he was virtually blind, he kept on painting right up until his death, and was able always to paint whatever he wanted. I would love to keep drawing whatever I want for the rest of my own life, too.

—Masashi Kishimoto, 2001

Author/artist Masashi Kishimoto was born in 1974 in rural Okayama Prefecture, Japan. After spending time in art college, he won the Hop Step Award for new manga artists with his manga **Karakuri** (Mechanism). Kishimoto decided to base his next story on traditional Japanese culture. His first version of **Naruto**, drawn in 1997, was a one-shot story about fox spirits; his final version, which debuted in **Weekly Shonen Jump** in 1999, quickly became the most popular ninja manga in Japan.

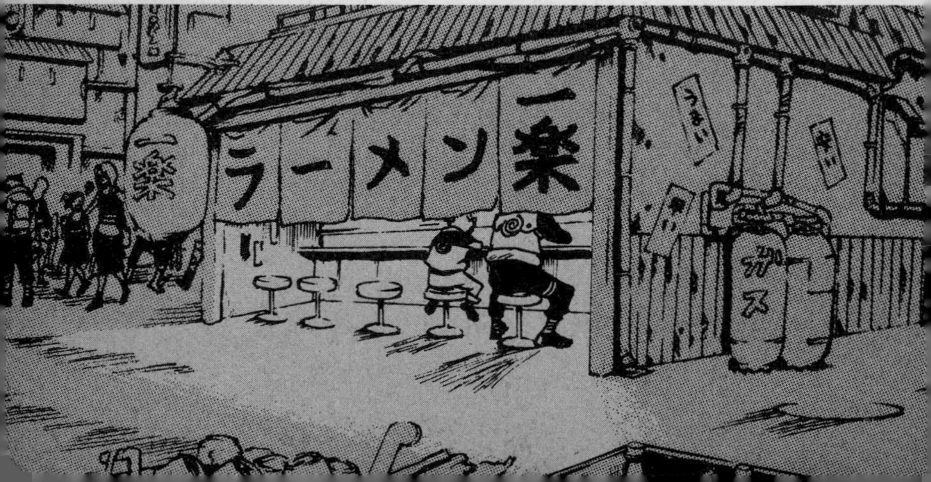
ラーメン一楽

NARUTO VOL. 9
The SHONEN JUMP Manga Edition

This manga contains material that was originally published in
English in **SHONEN JUMP** #36-38. Artwork in the magazine
may have been slightly altered from that presented here.

STORY AND ART BY MASASHI KISHIMOTO

English Adaptation/Jo Duffy
Translation/Mari Morimoto
Touch-up Art & Lettering/Heidi Szykowny
Additional Touch-up/Josh Simpson
Design/Sean Lee
Editor/Frances E. Wall

Editor in Chief, Books/Alvin Lu
Editor in Chief, Magazines/Marc Weidenbaum
VP of Publishing Licensing/Rika Inouye
VP of Sales/Gonzalo Ferreyra
Sr. VP of Marketing/Liza Coppola
Publisher/Hyoe Narita

Printed in the U.S.A.

Published by VIZ Media, LLC
P.O. Box 77010
San Francisco, CA 94107

SHONEN JUMP Manga Edition
10 9 8 7 6
First printing, March 2006
Sixth printing, April 2008

www.viz.com

THE WORLD'S
MOST POPULAR MANGA

www.shonenjump.com

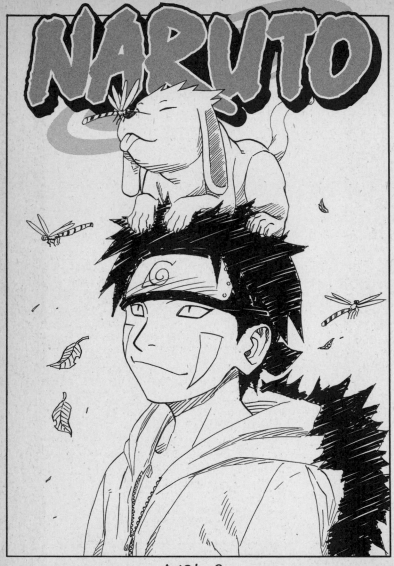

SHONEN JUMP MANGA EDITION

NARUTO

VOL. 9
TURNING THE TABLES
STORY AND ART BY
MASASHI KISHIMOTO

SAKURA サクラ

Smart and studious, Sakura is the brightest of Naruto's classmates, but she's constantly distracted by her crush on Sasuke. Her goal: to win Sasuke's heart!

NARUTO ナルト

When Naruto was born, a destructive fox spirit was imprisoned inside his body. Spurned by the older villagers, he's grown into an attention-seeking trouble-maker. His goal: to become the village's next *Hokage*.

SASUKE サスケ

The top student in Naruto's class, Sasuke comes from the prestigious Uchiha clan. His goal: to get revenge on a mysterious person who wronged him in the past.

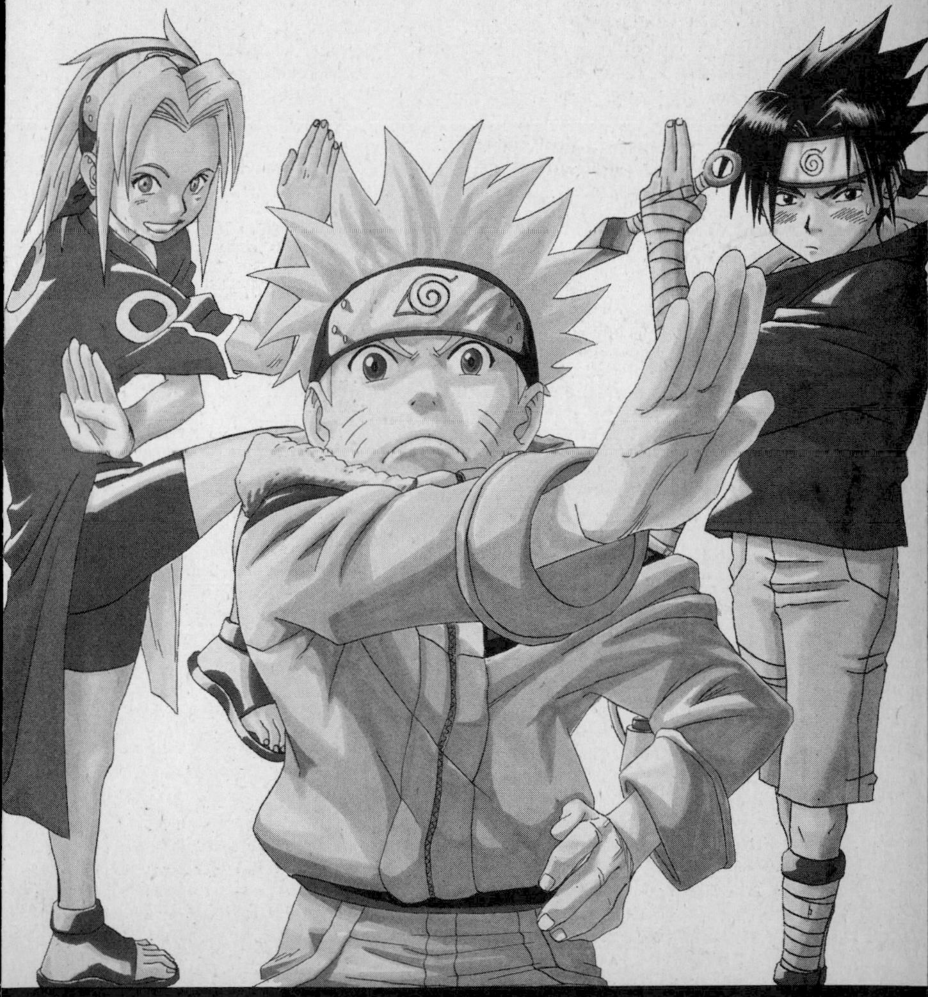

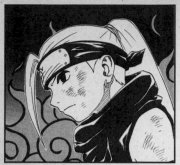

Yamanaka Ino 山中いの

Though Ino and Sakura were once close friends, their bitter rivalry for Sasuke's affection has turned them against each other.

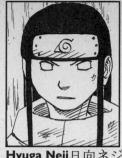

Hyuga Neji 日向ネジ

Neji shares many traits with Hinata, including the all-seeing Byakugan eye. But what is their relationship?

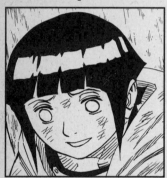

Hyuga Hinata 日向ヒナタ

This shy young kunoichi (female ninja) has a monster crush on Naruto.

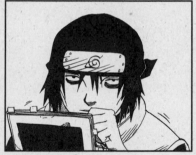

Gekko Hayate 月光ハヤテ

As the proctor of the third portion of the exam, Hayate has the job of stepping in and stopping any fight where there's a clear winner...to prevent unnecessary bloodshed.

THE STORY SO FAR...

Twelve years ago, a destructive nine-tailed fox spirit attacked the ninja village of Konohagakure. The *Hokage*, or village champion, defeated the fox by sealing its soul into the body of a baby boy. Now that boy, Uzumaki Naruto, has grown up to become a ninja-in-training, learning the art of *ninjutsu* with his classmates Sakura and Sasuke.

Naruto, Sasuke and Sakura (along with six other teams of student ninja) have moved on to the third portion of the Chûnin (Journeyman Ninja) Selection Exam—a series of no-holds-barred, one-on-one bouts that begin with a set of preliminary matches. As the preliminaries continue, Sakura faces off against her rival, Ino! Although strategic taunting by Sakura seems to have sent her opponent over the edge, Ino craftily distracts Sakura long enough to trap her into succumbing to the Mind Transfer Technique (Shintenshin no Jutsu), Ino's signature move! With Sakura under her control, Ino has all but won the match...or has she?!

CONTENTS

NUMBER 73:	A DECLARATION OF DEFEAT...?!	7
NUMBER 74:	THE SIXTH ROUND MATCH, AND THEN...!!	27
NUMBER 75:	NARUTO'S COMING-OF-AGE...!!	47
NUMBER 76:	KIBA TURNS THE TABLES... ...AND SO DOES NARUTO?!	67
NUMBER 77:	NARUTO'S CLEVER SCHEME!!	87
NUMBER 78:	NEJI AND HINATA	105
NUMBER 79:	THE HYUGA CLAN	123
NUMBER 80:	THE OUTER LIMITS	143
NUMBER 81:	GAARA VERSUS...	163
PREVIEWS		182

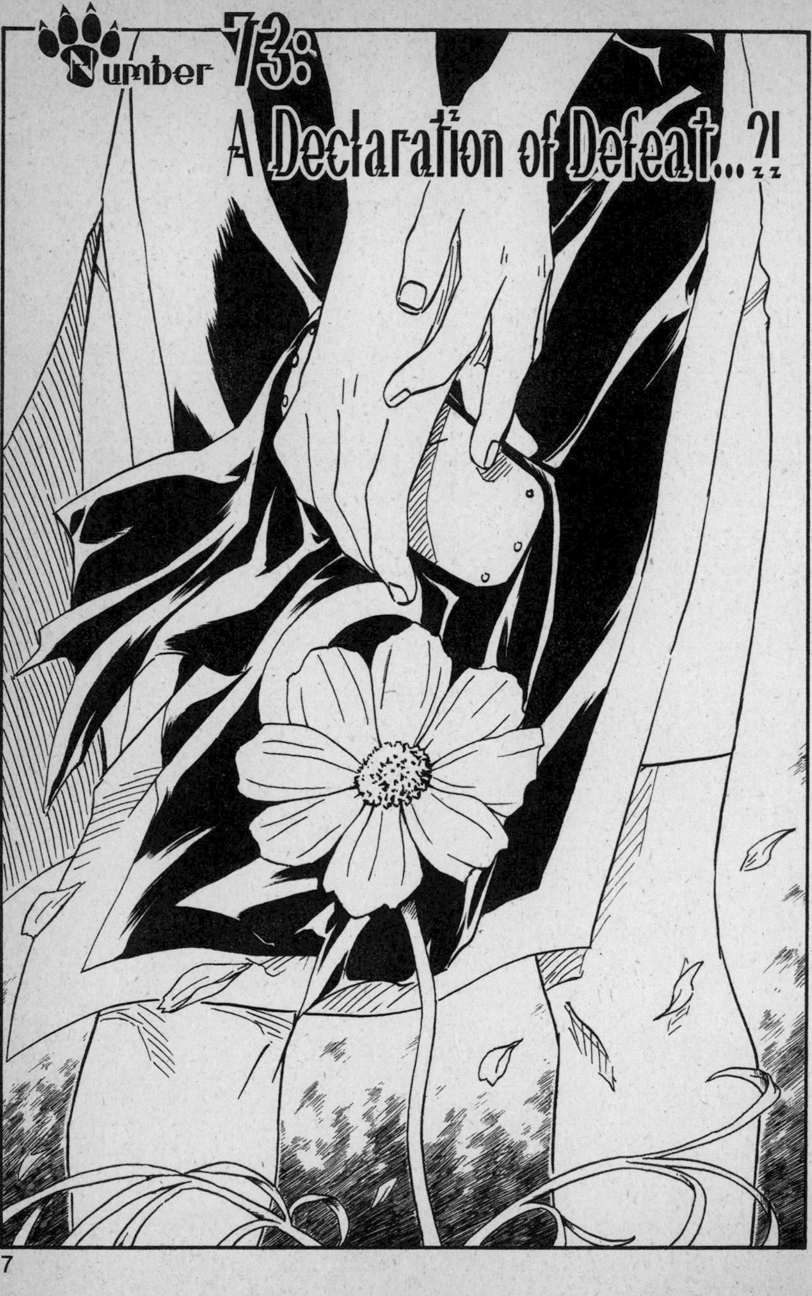
Number 73:
A Declaration of Defeat...?!

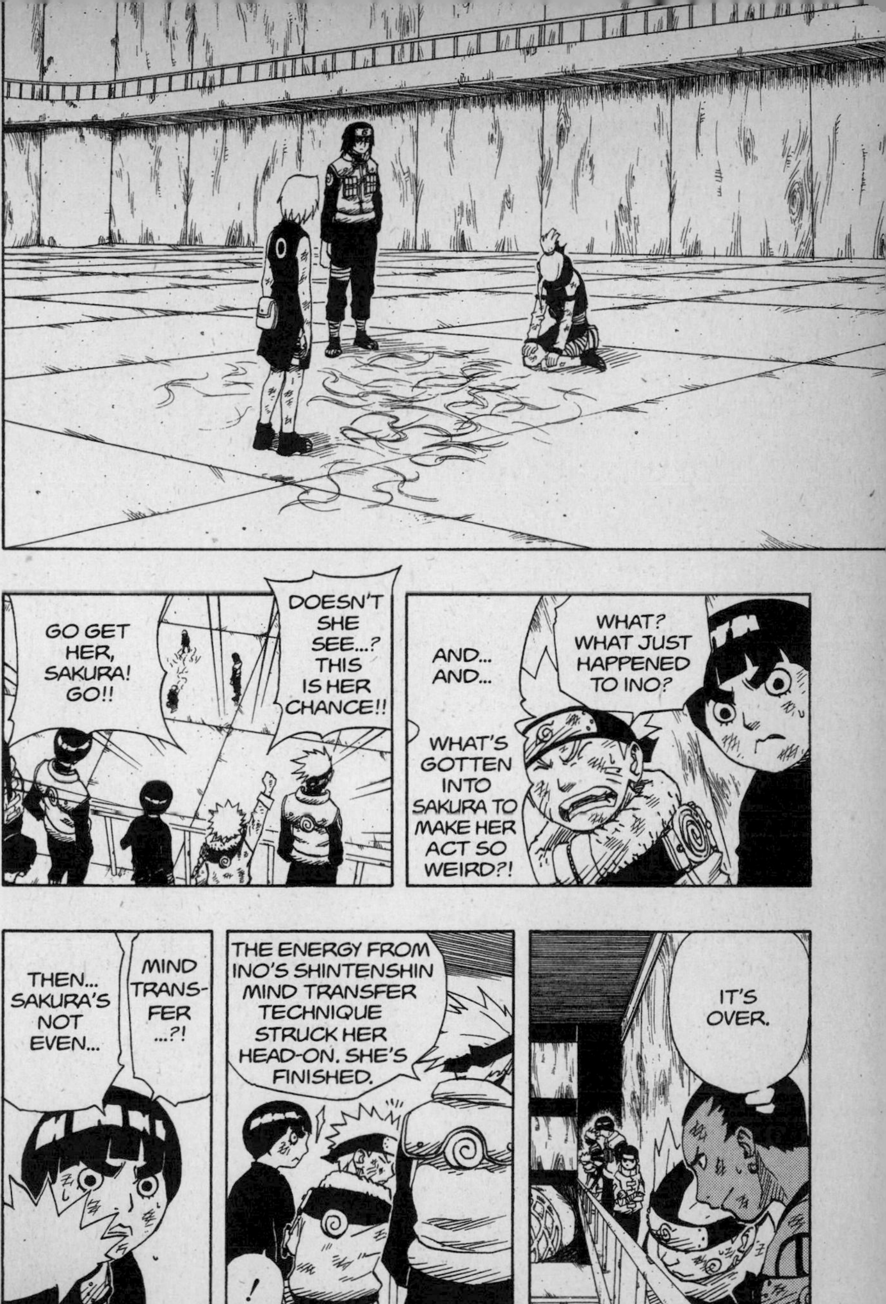
WHAT? WHAT JUST HAPPENED TO INO?
AND... AND...
WHAT'S GOTTEN INTO SAKURA TO MAKE HER ACT SO WEIRD?!
DOESN'T SHE SEE...? THIS IS HER CHANCE!!
GO GET HER, SAKURA! GO!!
IT'S OVER.
THE ENERGY FROM INO'S SHINTENSHIN MIND TRANSFER TECHNIQUE STRUCK HER HEAD-ON. SHE'S FINISHED.
!
MIND TRANS-FER ...?!
THEN... SAKURA'S NOT EVEN...

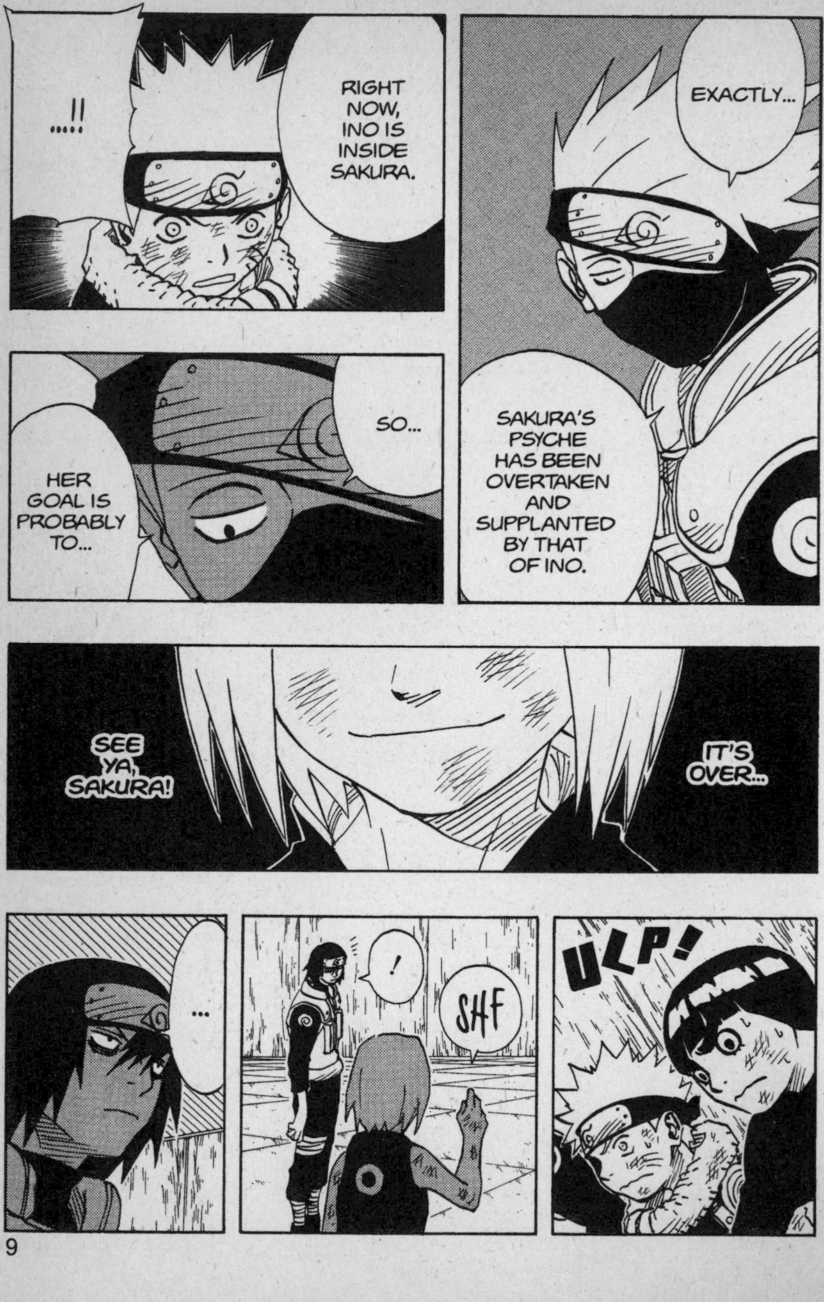
EXACTLY...
SAKURA'S PSYCHE HAS BEEN OVERTAKEN AND SUPPLANTED BY THAT OF INO.
RIGHT NOW, INO IS INSIDE SAKURA.
......!!
SO...
HER GOAL IS PROBABLY TO...
IT'S OVER...
SEE YA, SAKURA!
ULP!
!
SHF
...

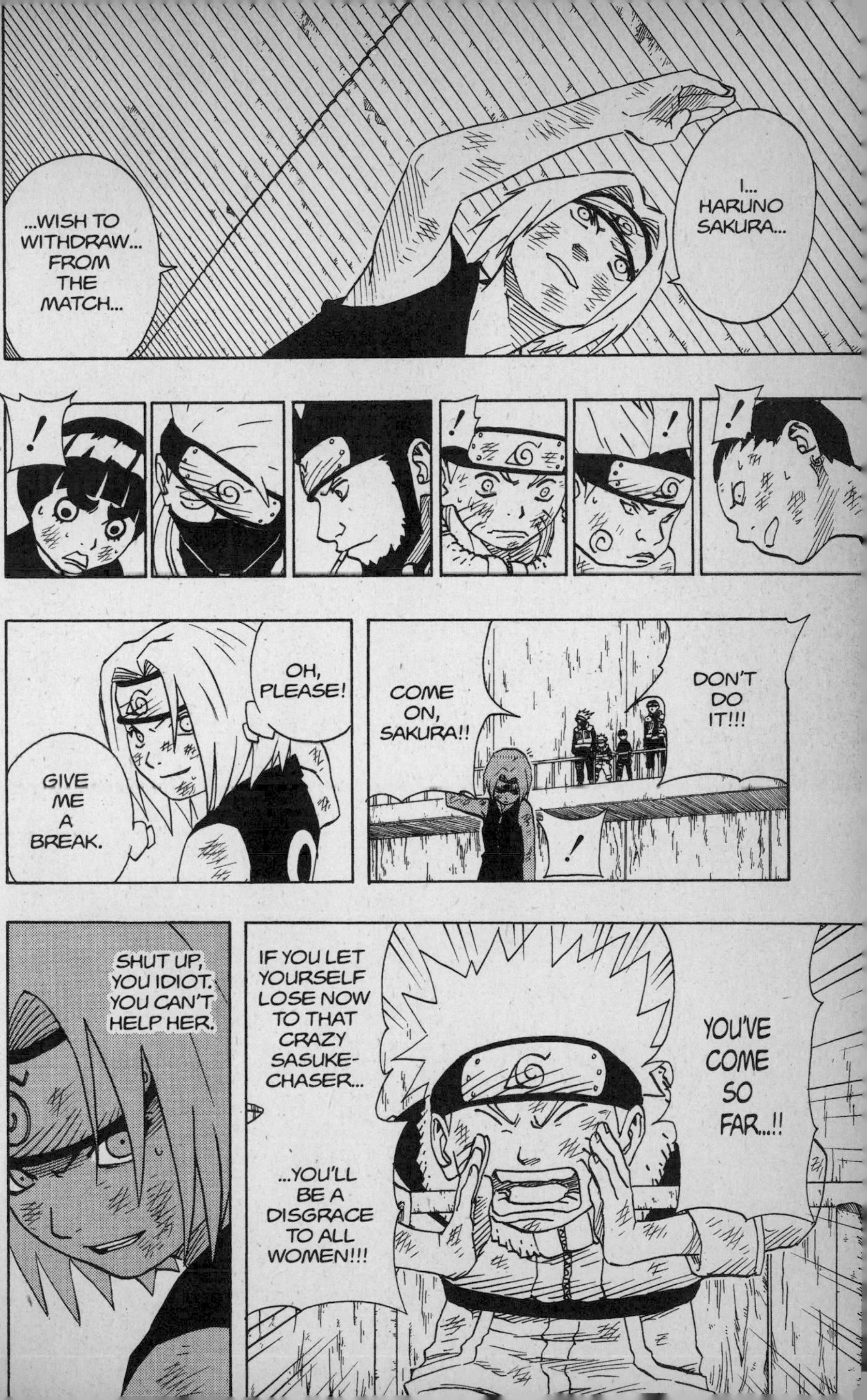
I... HARUNO SAKURA...
...WISH TO WITHDRAW... FROM THE MATCH...
!
!
!
!
!
!
DON'T DO IT!!!
COME ON, SAKURA!!
!
OH, PLEASE!
GIVE ME A BREAK.
YOU'VE COME SO FAR...!!
IF YOU LET YOURSELF LOSE NOW TO THAT CRAZY SASUKE-CHASER...
...YOU'LL BE A DISGRACE TO ALL WOMEN!!!
SHUT UP, YOU IDIOT. YOU CAN'T HELP HER.

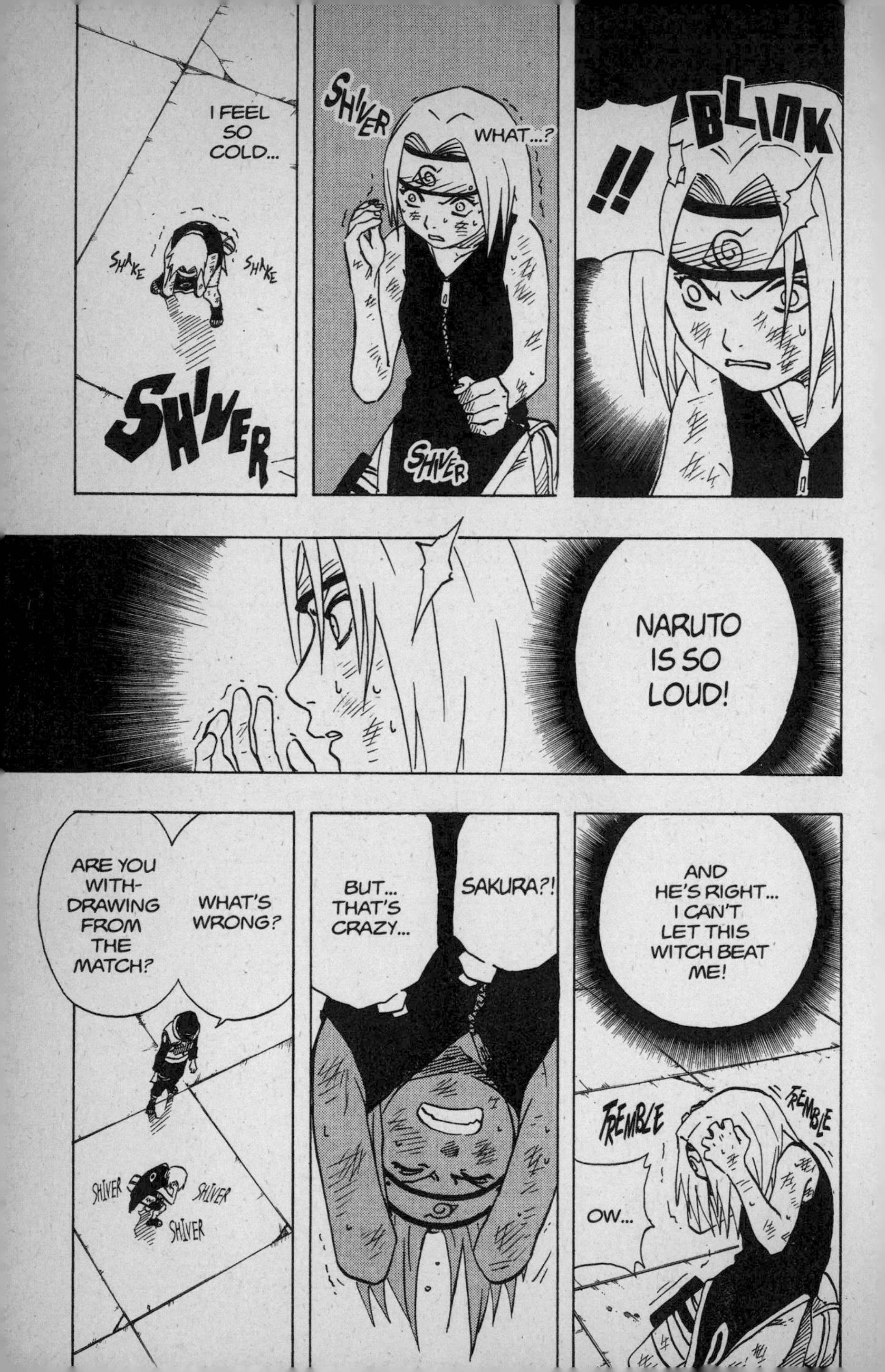
BLINK
!!
SHIVER
WHAT...?
SHIVER
I FEEL SO COLD...
SHAKE
SHAKE
SHIVER
NARUTO IS SO LOUD!
AND HE'S RIGHT... I CAN'T LET THIS WITCH BEAT ME!
TREMBLE
TREMBLE
OW...
SAKURA?!
BUT... THAT'S CRAZY...
WHAT'S WRONG?
ARE YOU WITH-DRAWING FROM THE MATCH?
SHIVER
SHIVER
SHIVER

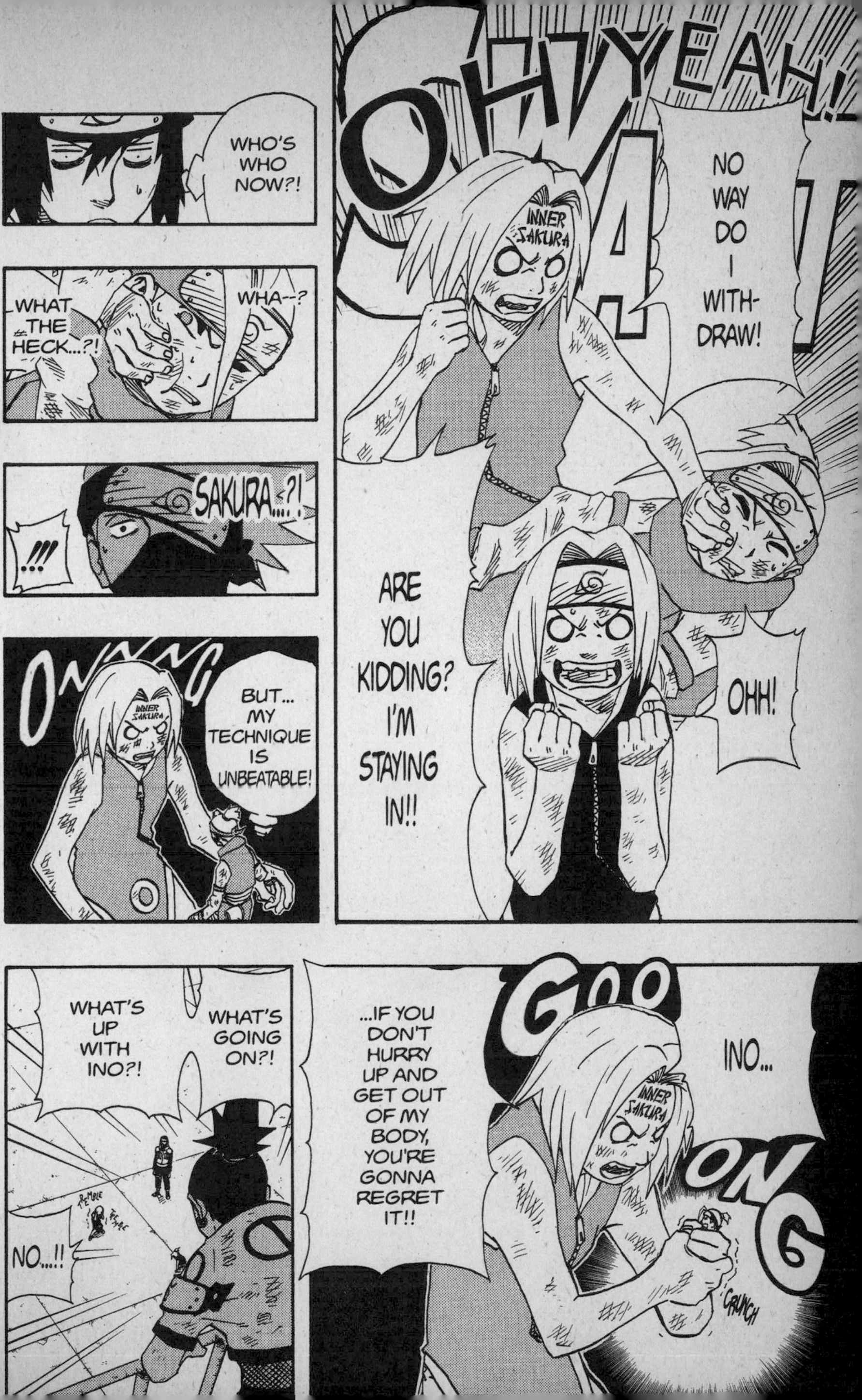
OH YEAH!!
NO WAY DO I WITHDRAW!
ARE YOU KIDDING? I'M STAYING IN!!
OHH!
WHO'S WHO NOW?!
WHA--?
WHAT THE HECK...?!
SAKURA...?!
!!!
ONNNG
BUT... MY TECHNIQUE IS UNBEATABLE!
GOOONG
INO...
...IF YOU DON'T HURRY UP AND GET OUT OF MY BODY, YOU'RE GONNA REGRET IT!!
CRUNCH
WHAT'S GOING ON?!
WHAT'S UP WITH INO?!
NO...!!

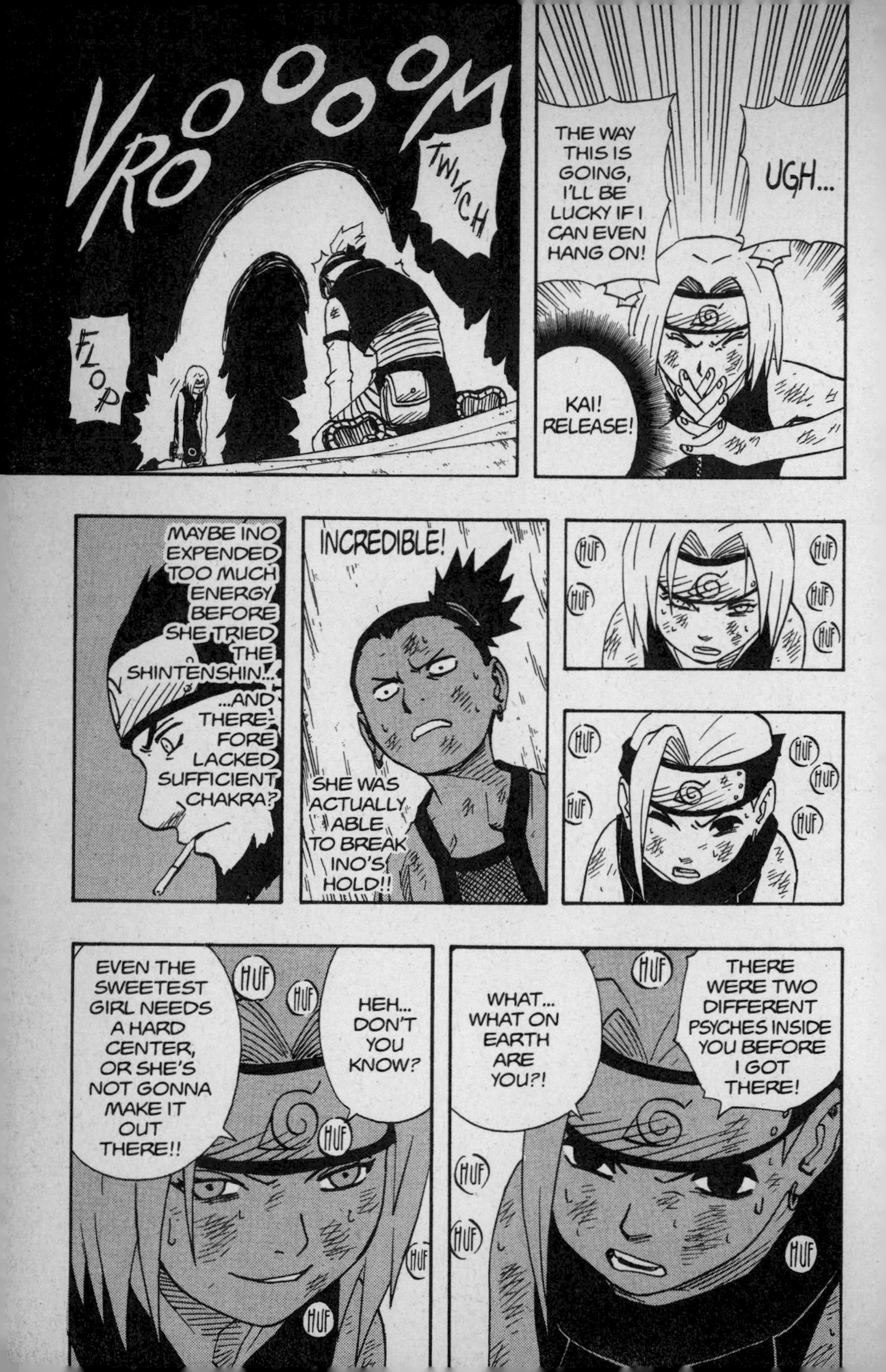
THE WAY THIS IS GOING, I'LL BE LUCKY IF I CAN EVEN HANG ON!
UGH...
KAI! RELEASE!
VROOOOOM
TWITCH
FLOP
HUF HUF HUF HUF HUF
HUF HUF HUF HUF HUF
INCREDIBLE!
SHE WAS ACTUALLY ABLE TO BREAK INO'S HOLD!!
MAYBE INO EXPENDED TOO MUCH ENERGY BEFORE SHE TRIED THE SHINTENSHIN...
...AND THEREFORE LACKED SUFFICIENT CHAKRA?
HUF
THERE WERE TWO DIFFERENT PSYCHES INSIDE YOU BEFORE I GOT THERE!
WHAT... WHAT ON EARTH ARE YOU?!
HUF HUF HUF
HEH... DON'T YOU KNOW?
HUF HUF
EVEN THE SWEETEST GIRL NEEDS A HARD CENTER, OR SHE'S NOT GONNA MAKE IT OUT THERE!!
HUF HUF HUF

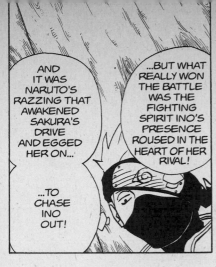

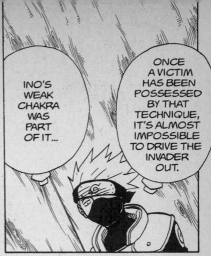

ONCE A VICTIM HAS BEEN POSSESSED BY THAT TECHNIQUE, IT'S ALMOST IMPOSSIBLE TO DRIVE THE INVADER OUT.
INO'S WEAK CHAKRA WAS PART OF IT...
...BUT WHAT REALLY WON THE BATTLE WAS THE FIGHTING SPIRIT INO'S PRESENCE ROUSED IN THE HEART OF HER RIVAL!
AND IT WAS NARUTO'S RAZZING THAT AWAKENED SAKURA'S DRIVE AND EGGED HER ON...
...TO CHASE INO OUT!
HUF HUF HUF
IT'S REALLY NOT SO STRANGE. LIKE NARUTO, SAKURA POSSESSES A HEART THAT CANNOT BEAR TO BE BEATEN.
AT THIS POINT, THOUGH, I DOUBT WHETHER EITHER COMBATANT HAS MUCH CHAKRA LEFT...
HUF HUF HUF HUF HUF
HUF HUF HUF HUF HUF HUF
THIS IS IT...
HUF HUF HUF HUF
TAK TAK

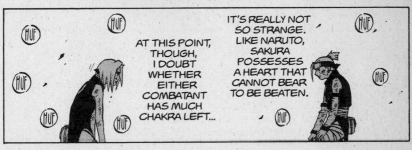

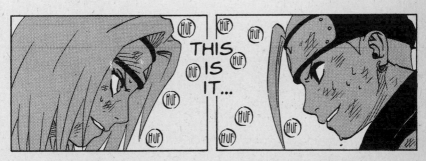

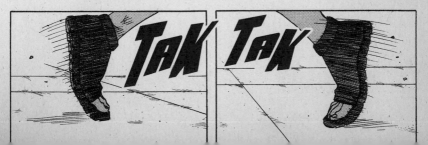

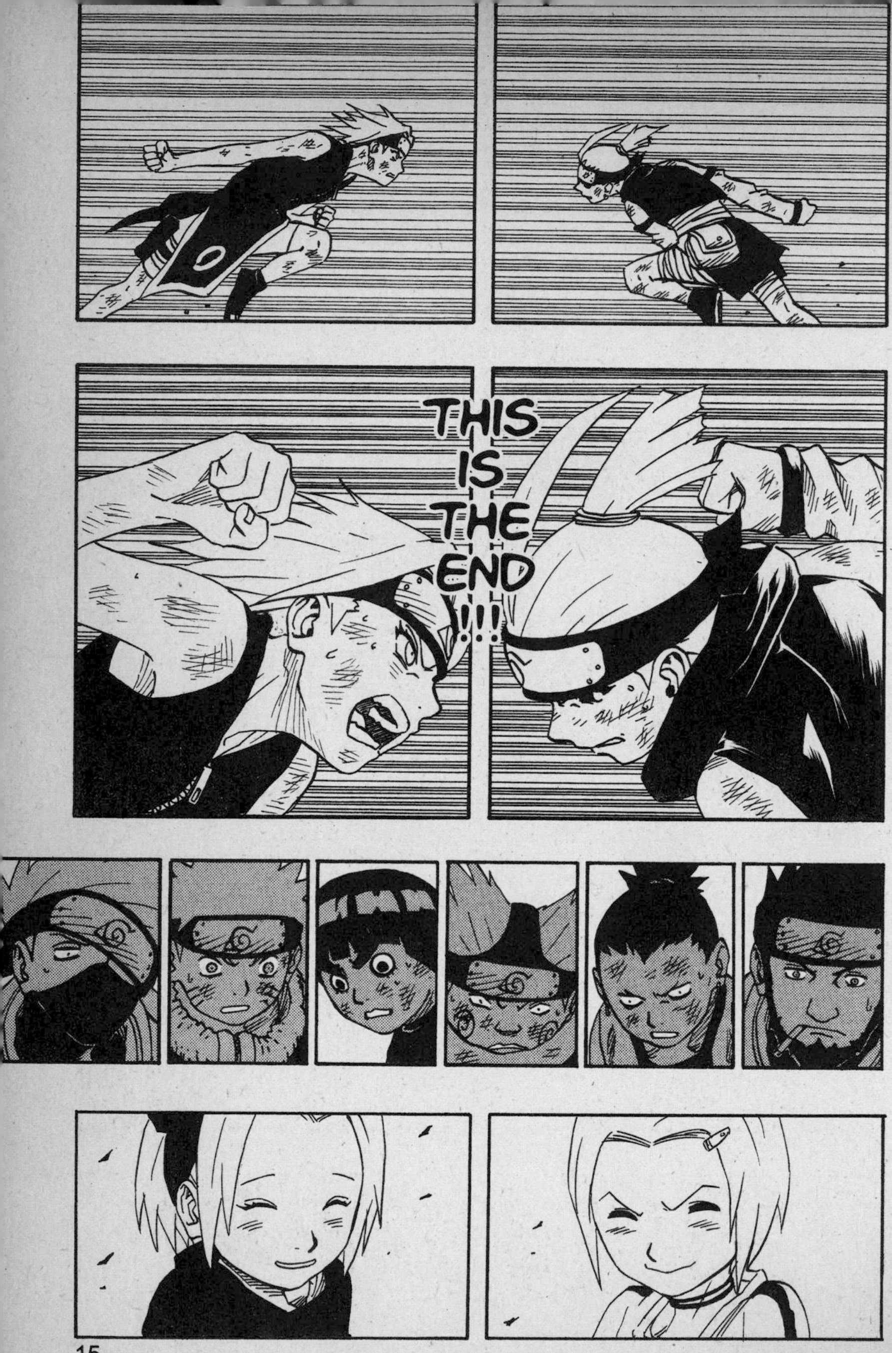
THIS IS THE END!!!

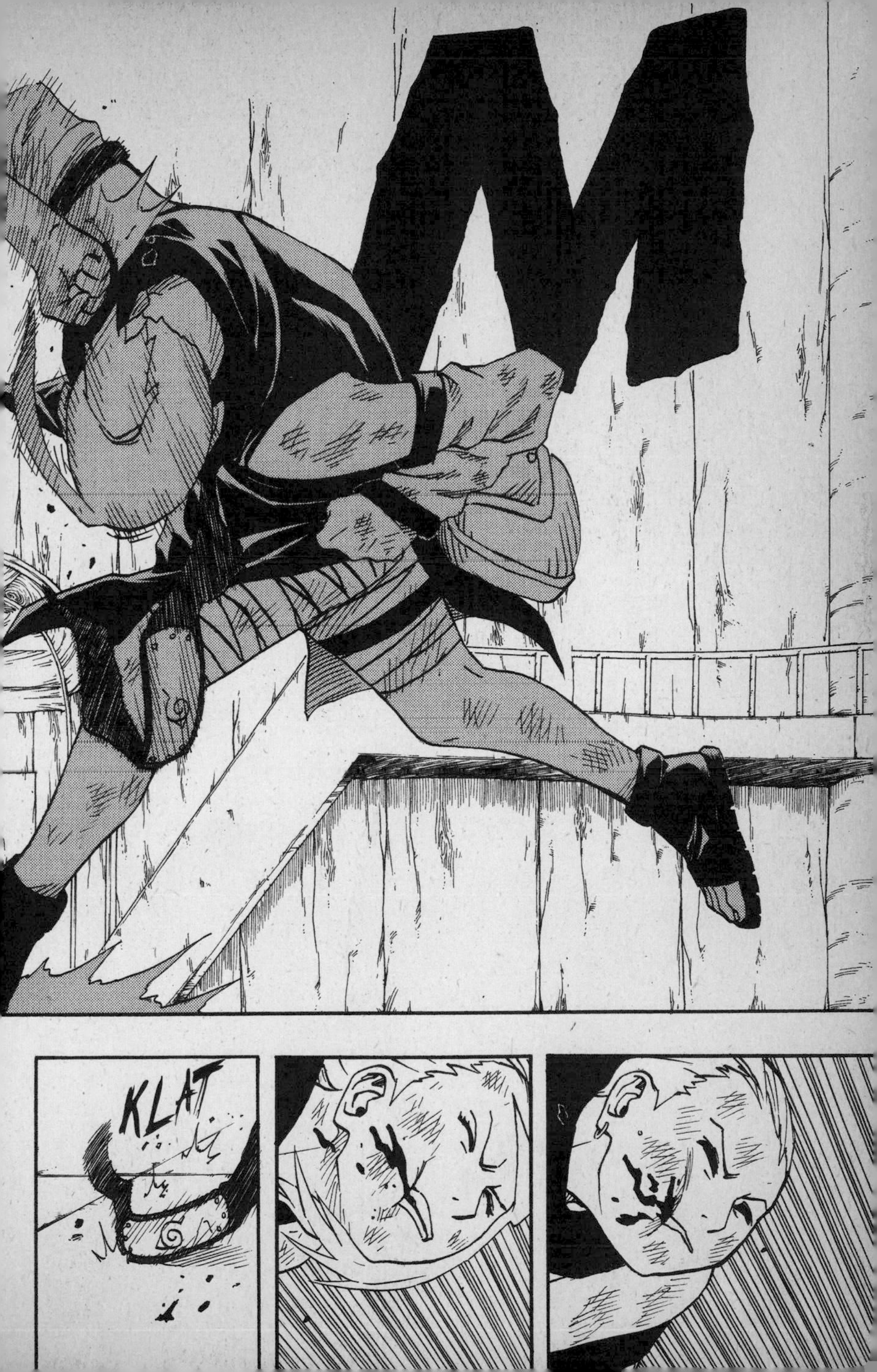
KLAT

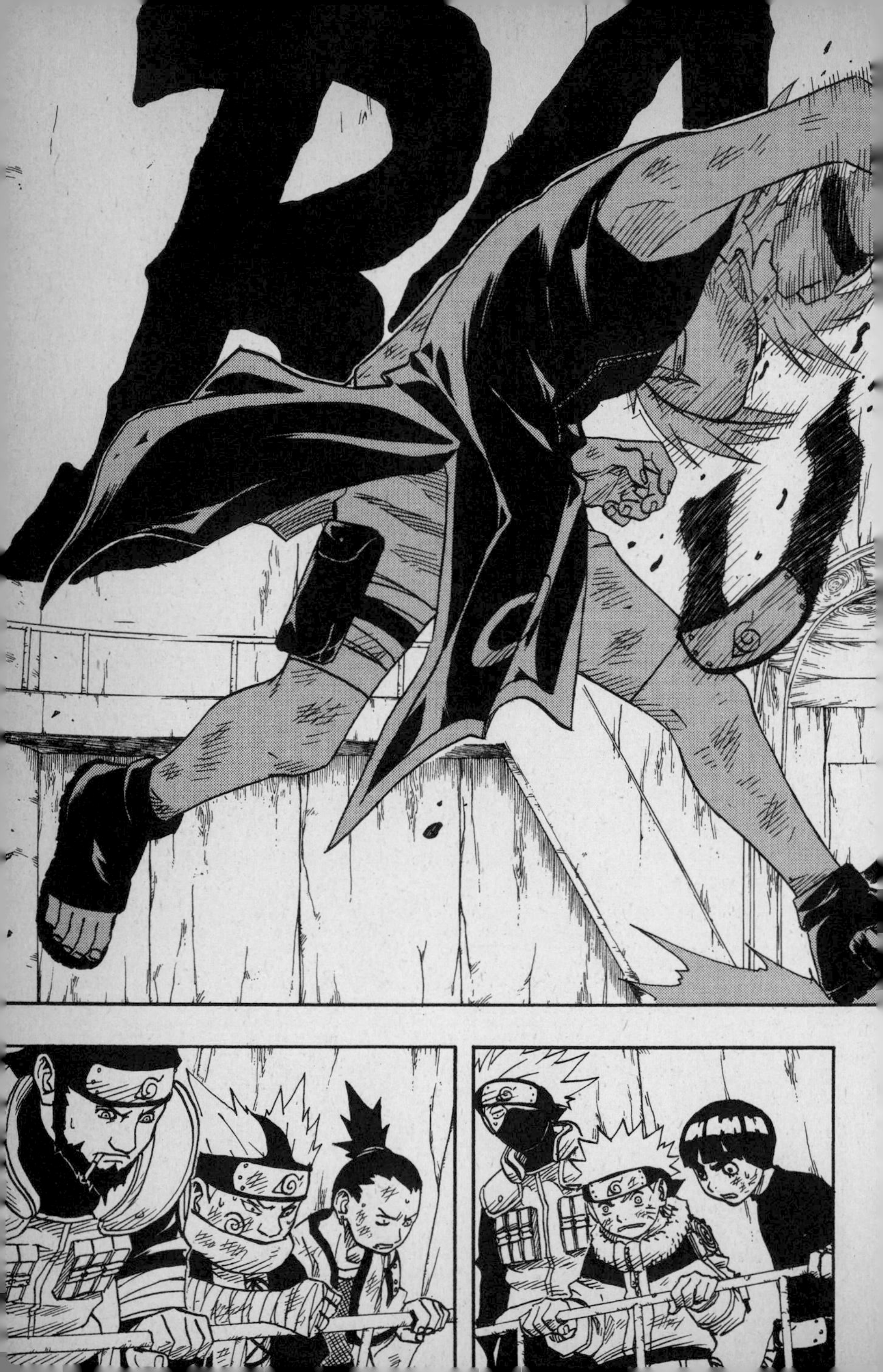
BA

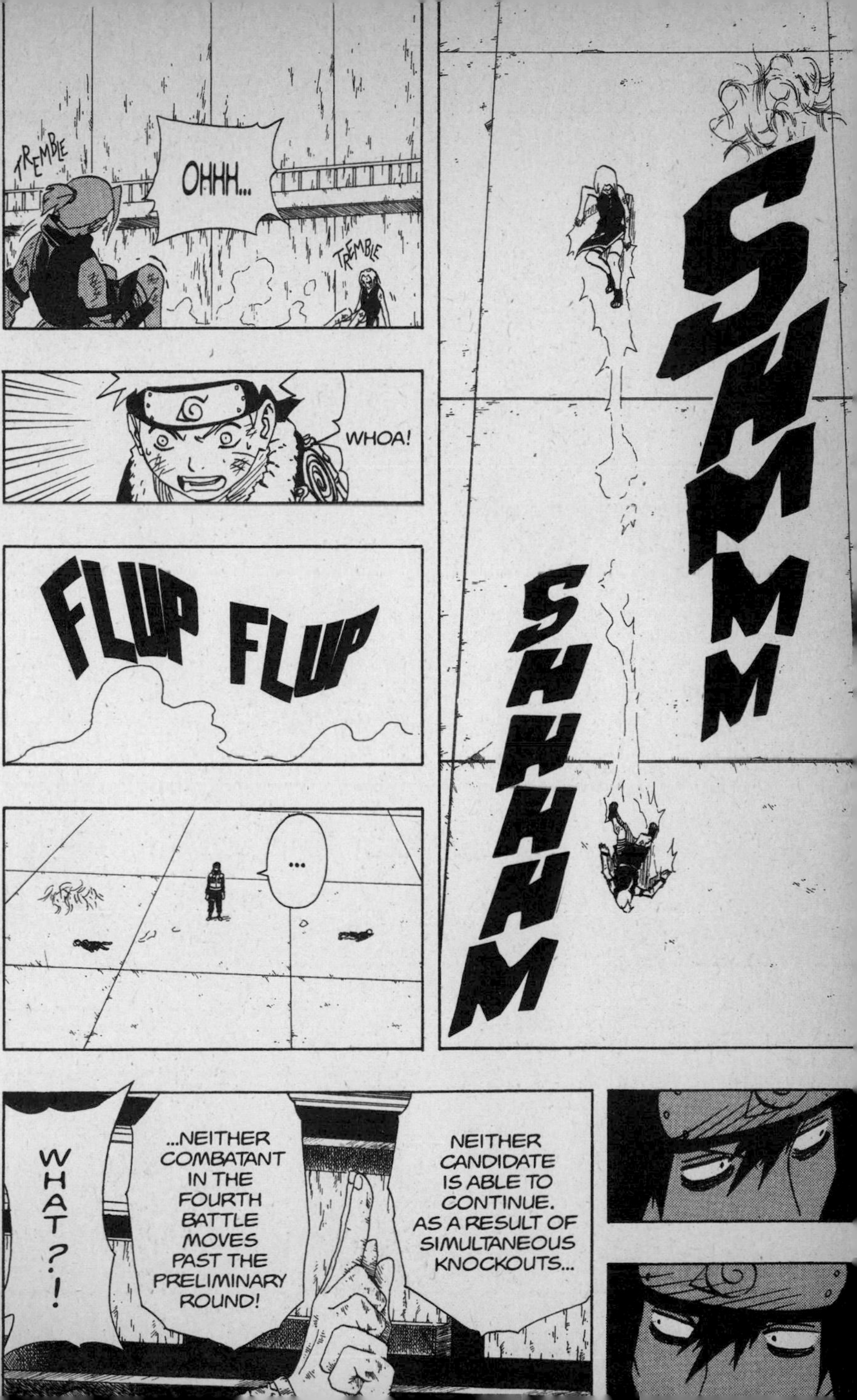
SHMMM
SHHHHM
OHHH...
TREMBLE
TREMBLE
WHOA!
FLUP FLUP
...
NEITHER CANDIDATE IS ABLE TO CONTINUE. AS A RESULT OF SIMULTANEOUS KNOCKOUTS...
...NEITHER COMBATANT IN THE FOURTH BATTLE MOVES PAST THE PRELIMINARY ROUND!
WHAT?!

READ THIS WAY

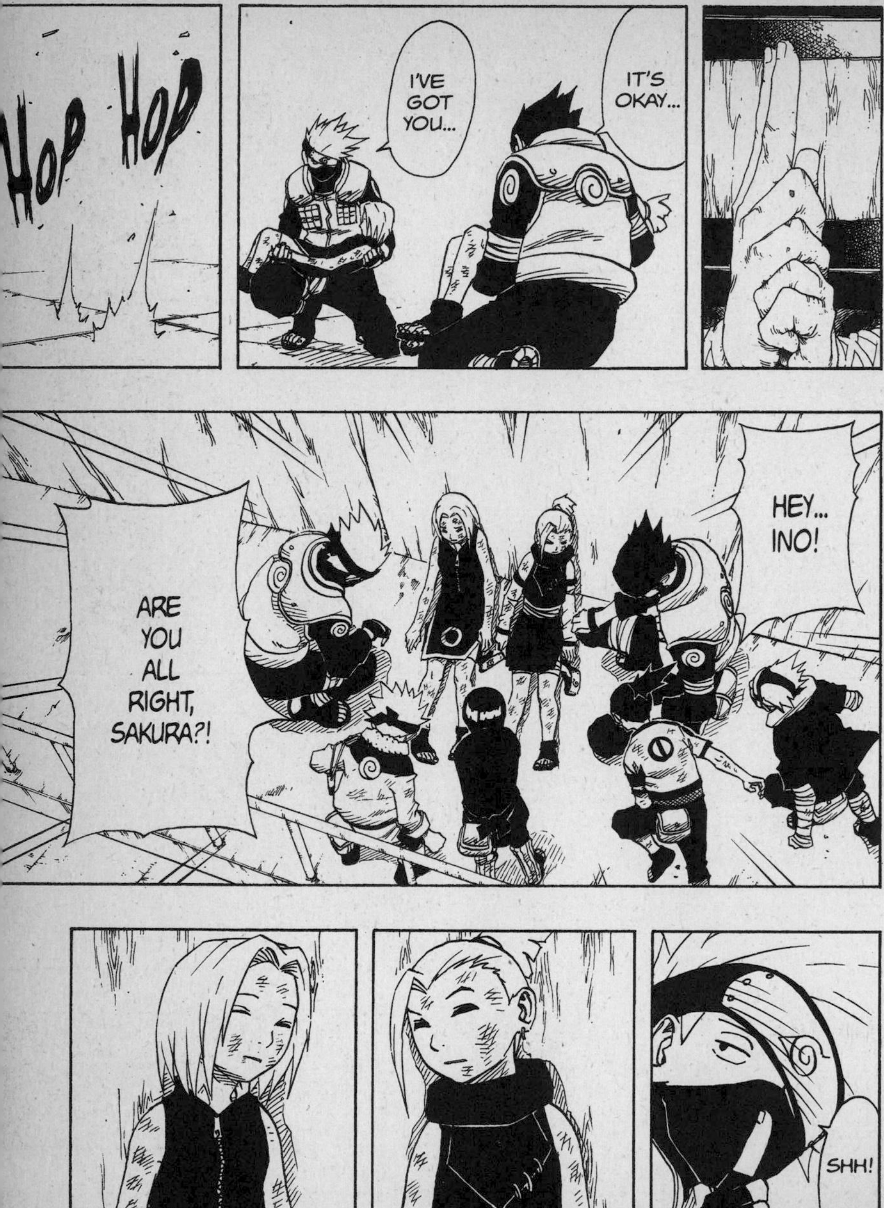
IT'S OKAY...
I'VE GOT YOU...
HOP HOP
HEY... INO!
ARE YOU ALL RIGHT, SAKURA?!
SHH!

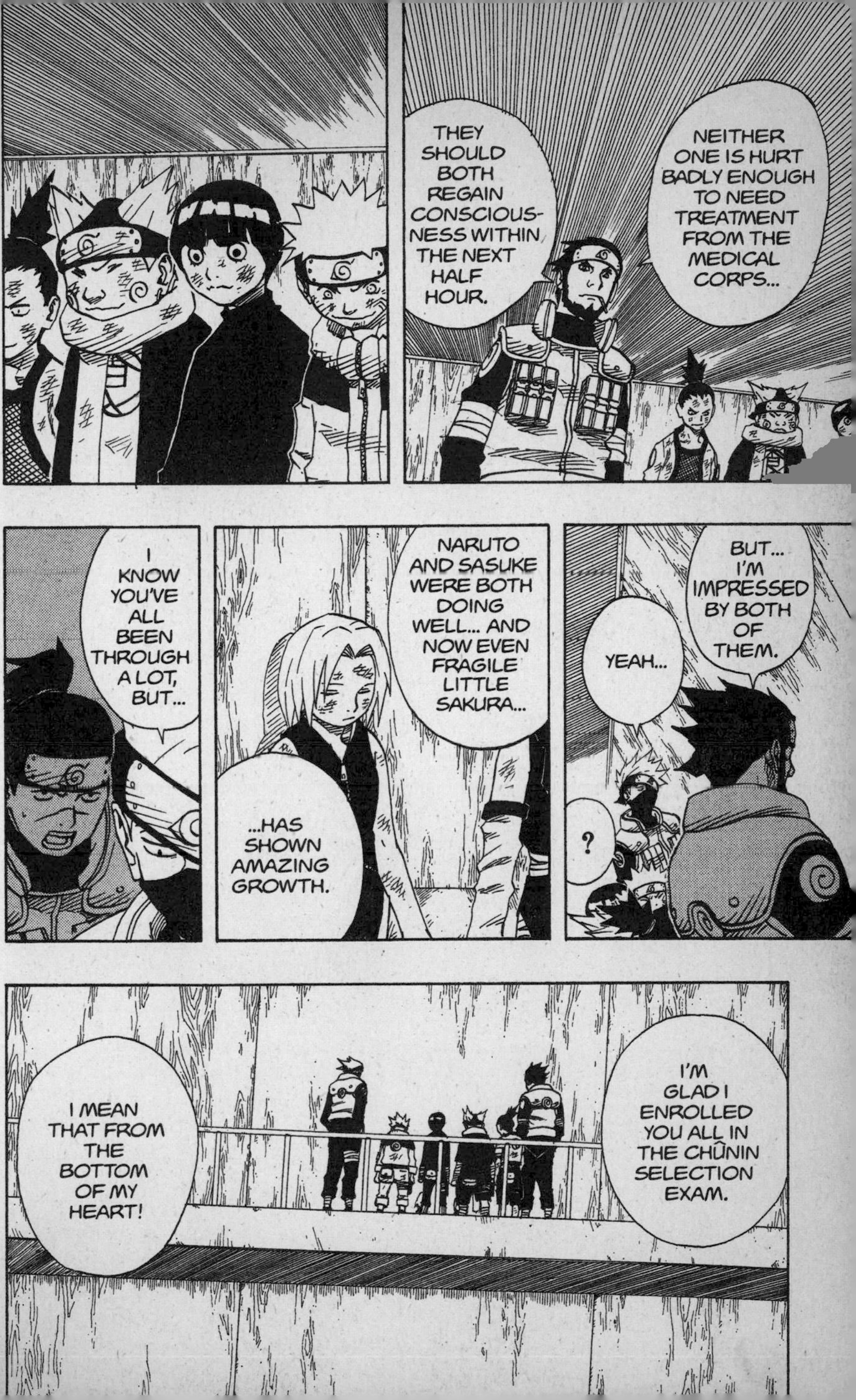
NEITHER ONE IS HURT BADLY ENOUGH TO NEED TREATMENT FROM THE MEDICAL CORPS...
THEY SHOULD BOTH REGAIN CONSCIOUS-NESS WITHIN THE NEXT HALF HOUR.
BUT... I'M IMPRESSED BY BOTH OF THEM.
YEAH...
?
NARUTO AND SASUKE WERE BOTH DOING WELL... AND NOW EVEN FRAGILE LITTLE SAKURA...
...HAS SHOWN AMAZING GROWTH.
I KNOW YOU'VE ALL BEEN THROUGH A LOT, BUT...
I'M GLAD I ENROLLED YOU ALL IN THE CHŪNIN SELECTION EXAM.
I MEAN THAT FROM THE BOTTOM OF MY HEART!

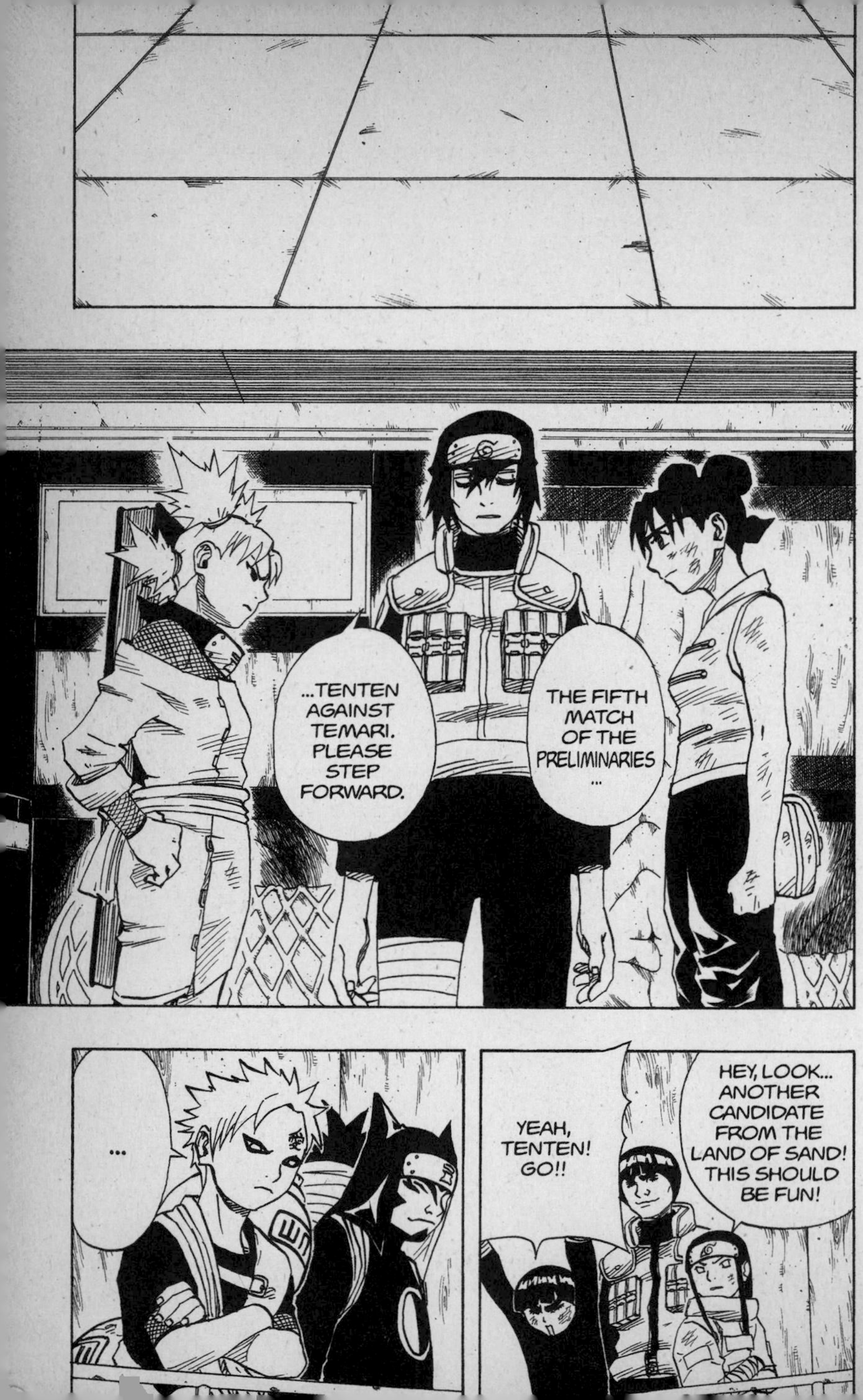
THE FIFTH MATCH OF THE PRELIMINARIES ...
...TENTEN AGAINST TEMARI. PLEASE STEP FORWARD.
HEY, LOOK... ANOTHER CANDIDATE FROM THE LAND OF SAND! THIS SHOULD BE FUN!
YEAH, TENTEN! GO!!
...

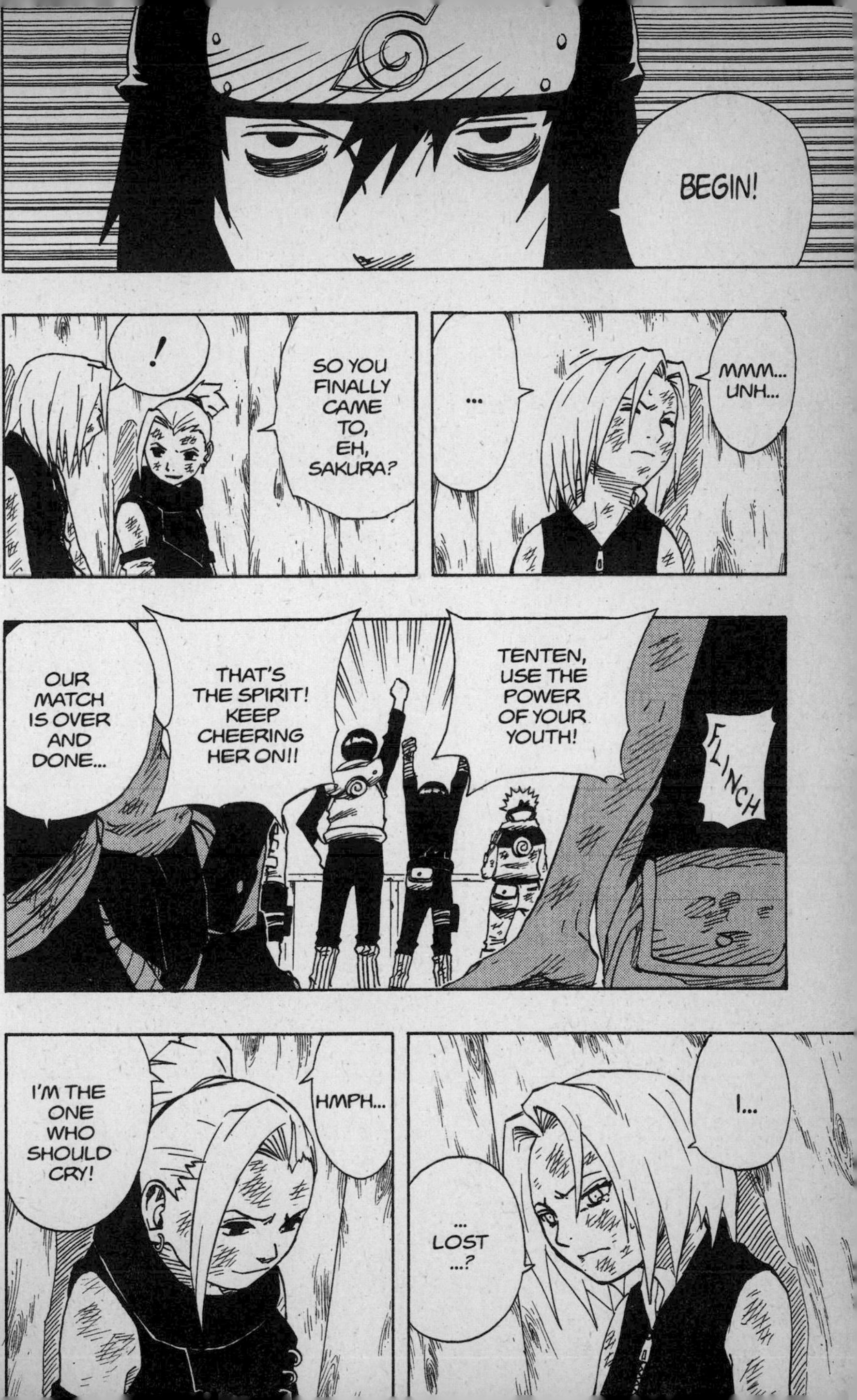
BEGIN!
MMM... UNH...
...
SO YOU FINALLY CAME TO, EH, SAKURA?
!
FLINCH
TENTEN, USE THE POWER OF YOUR YOUTH!
THAT'S THE SPIRIT! KEEP CHEERING HER ON!!
OUR MATCH IS OVER AND DONE...
I...
... LOST ...?
HMPH...
I'M THE ONE WHO SHOULD CRY!

READ THIS WAY

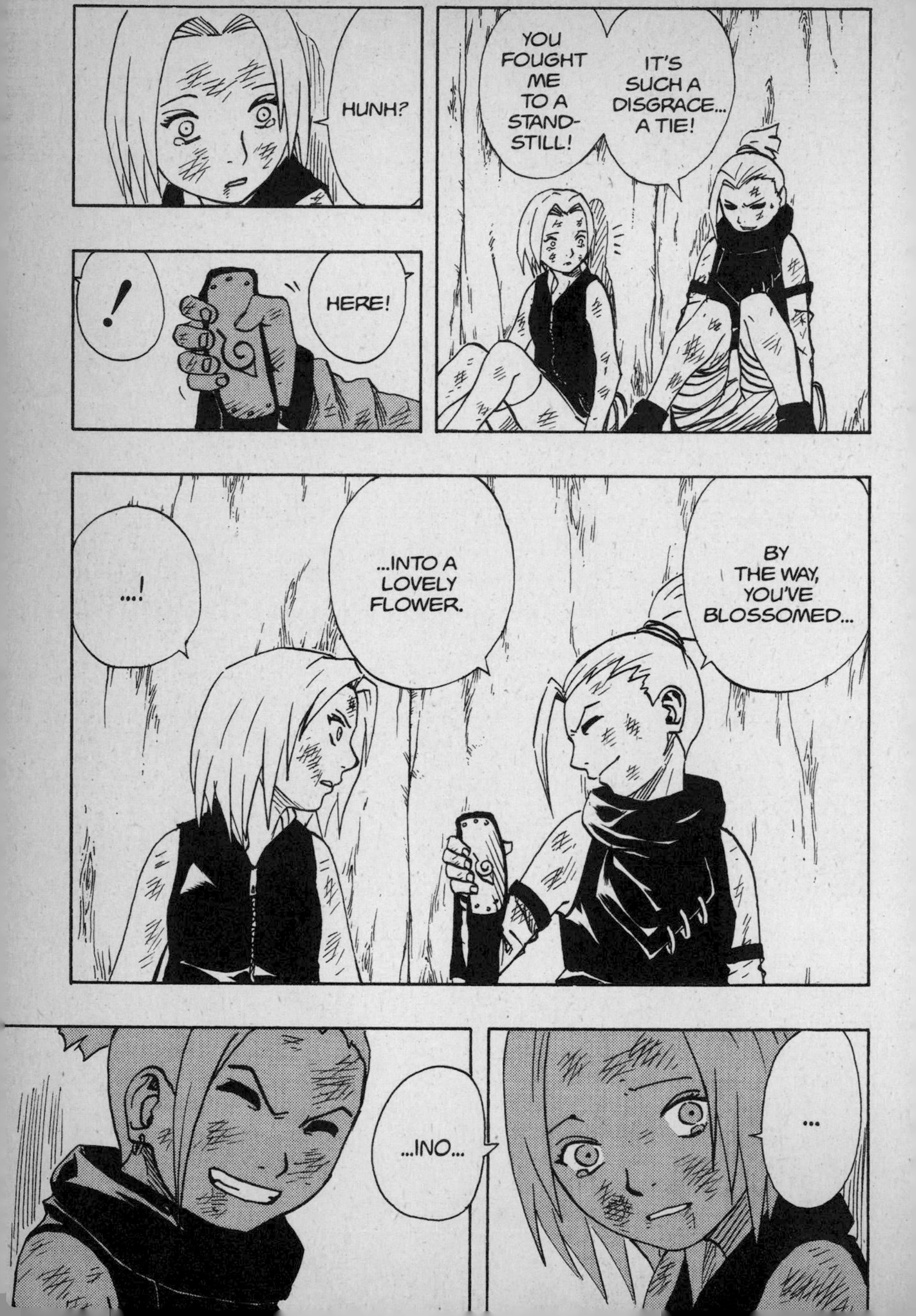
IT'S SUCH A DISGRACE... A TIE!
YOU FOUGHT ME TO A STAND-STILL!
HUNH?
HERE!
!
BY THE WAY, YOU'VE BLOSSOMED...
...INTO A LOVELY FLOWER.
...!
...
...INO...

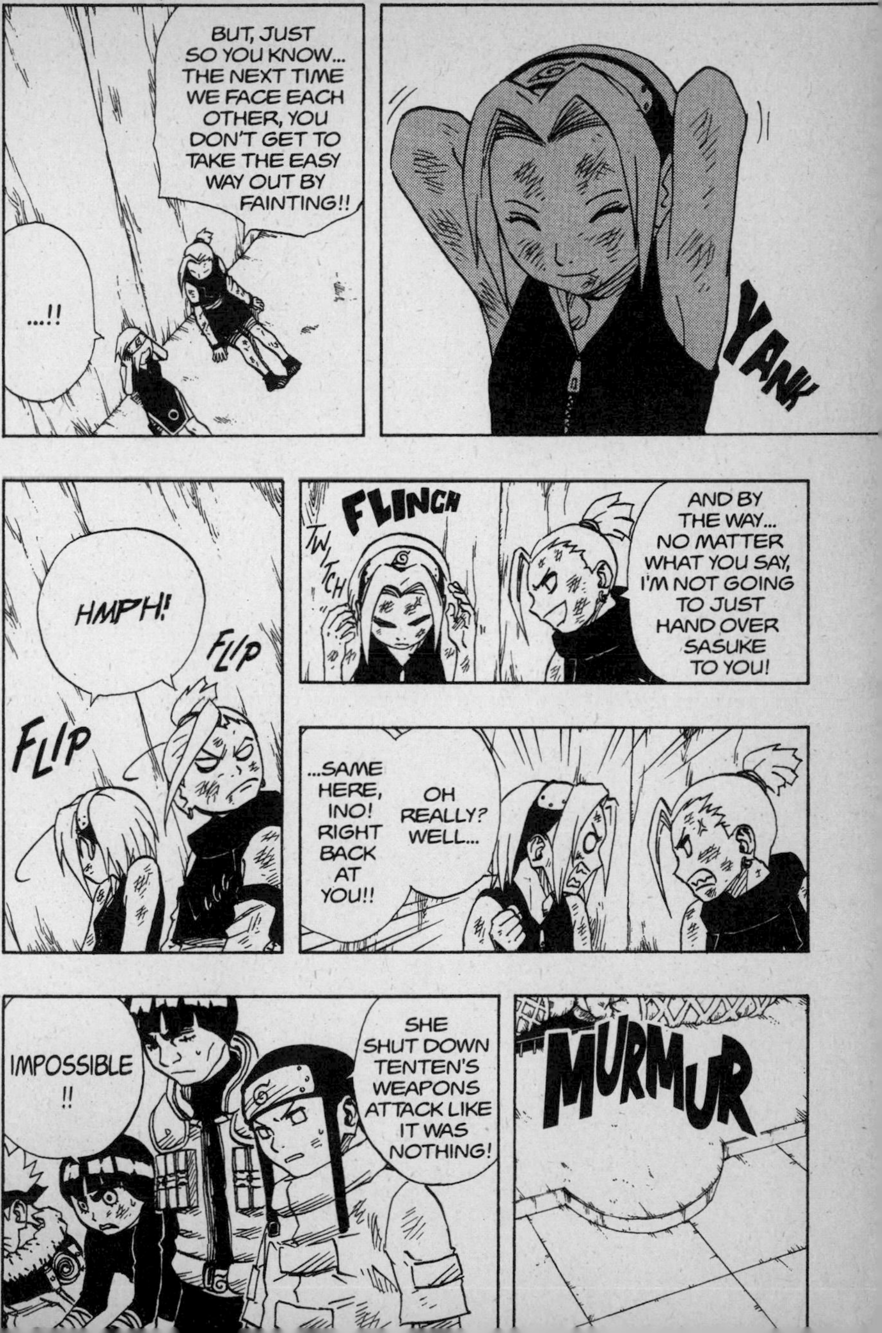
YANK
BUT, JUST SO YOU KNOW... THE NEXT TIME WE FACE EACH OTHER, YOU DON'T GET TO TAKE THE EASY WAY OUT BY FAINTING!!
...!!
AND BY THE WAY... NO MATTER WHAT YOU SAY, I'M NOT GOING TO JUST HAND OVER SASUKE TO YOU!
FLINCH
TWITCH
OH REALLY? WELL...
...SAME HERE, INO! RIGHT BACK AT YOU!!
HMPH!
FLIP
FLIP
MURMUR
SHE SHUT DOWN TENTEN'S WEAPONS ATTACK LIKE IT WAS NOTHING!
IMPOSSIBLE !!

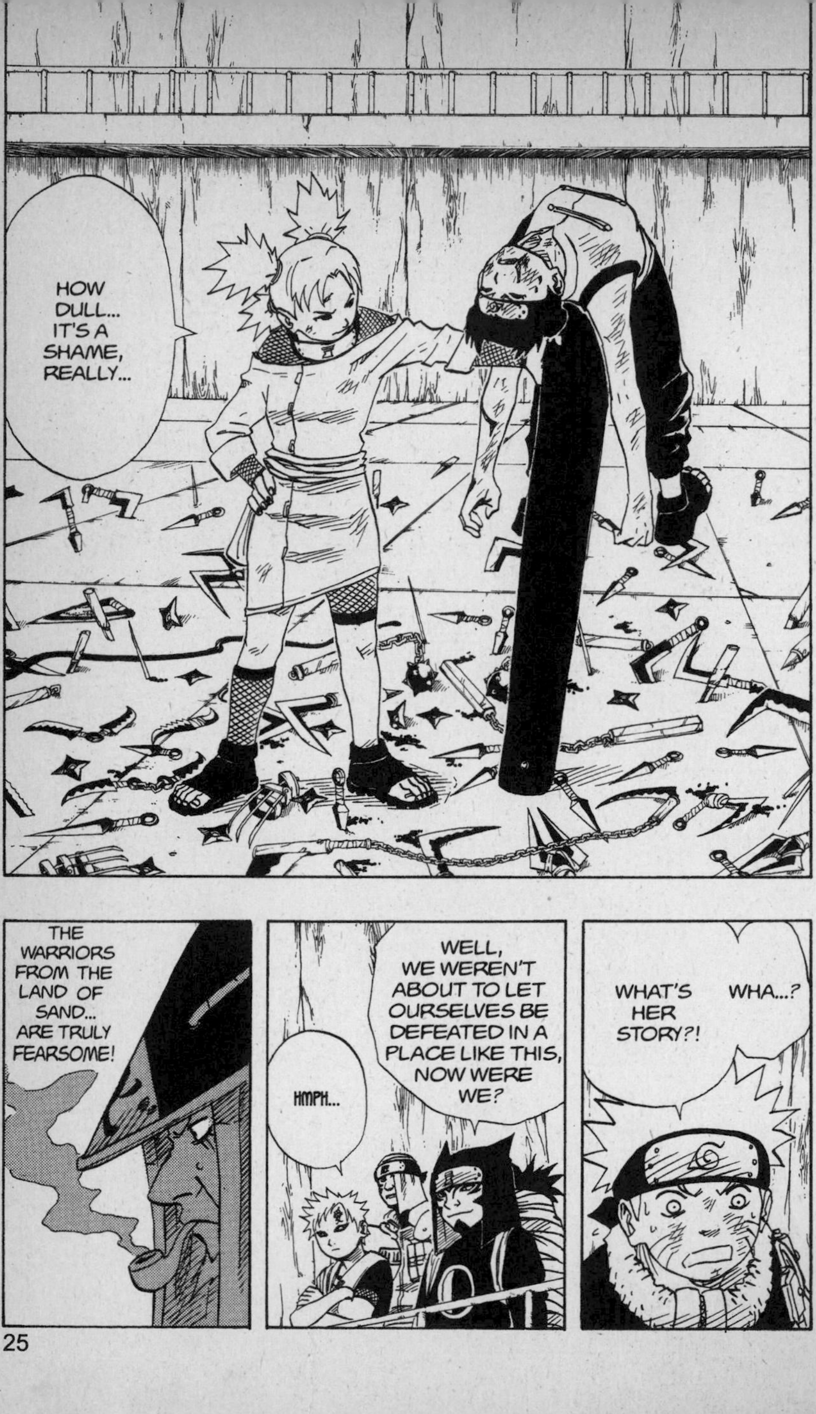
HOW DULL... IT'S A SHAME, REALLY...
WHA...?
WHAT'S HER STORY?!
WELL, WE WEREN'T ABOUT TO LET OURSELVES BE DEFEATED IN A PLACE LIKE THIS, NOW WERE WE?
HMPH...
THE WARRIORS FROM THE LAND OF SAND... ARE TRULY FEARSOME!

THE WORLD OF KISHIMOTO MASASHI
MY PERSONAL HISTORY, PART 8

I PLAYED SOFTBALL FOR A WHILE IN ELEMENTARY SCHOOL,
AND WHEN I ENTERED MIDDLE SCHOOL, I DECIDED TO JOIN
THE BASEBALL CLUB. MY YOUNGER TWIN WAS INTO BASEBALL
AS WELL, SO WE JOINED THE CLUB TOGETHER. THIS WAS
WHEN THE BASEBALL ANIME *TOUCH* WAS A MONSTER
SUCCESS ALL OVER JAPAN. IT WAS CREATED BY MITSURU
ADACHI, AND WAS A STORY ABOUT TWIN BROTHERS WHO
JOIN A BASEBALL CLUB. IN THE END, THE YOUNGER
BROTHER DIES, AND THE OLDER ONE IS INSPIRED TO REALLY
STEP UP AND DO A GREAT JOB FOR HIS BROTHER'S SAKE.
THE IDEALISM OF THAT THEME APPEALED TO ME
TREMENDOUSLY AT THE TIME.

AS AN ADOLESCENT, I GOT A LITTLE CONFUSED AND
DECIDED THAT THE STORYLINE IN *TOUCH* TRULY REFLECTED
MY OWN LIFE, SO I BOUGHT AND VORACIOUSLY CONSUMED
THE MANGA SERIES AS WELL AS THE ANIMATION. BUT MY
PASSION FOR IT COMPLETELY COOLED DOWN WHEN MY
LITTLE BROTHER RUDELY TOLD ME, "OUR BASEBALL
CLUB REQUIRES YOU SHAVE YOUR HEAD TO *GORINGARI*
STANDARDS -- NO HAIR LONGER THAN A MILLIMETER...
AND BY THE WAY, FOOL, WE BOTH SUCK AT BASEBALL." I HAD
TO ADMIT HE WAS RIGHT, SO I SWITCHED MY ALLEGIANCE
TO ANOTHER MANGA CALLED *MEIMON DAISAN YAKYUUBU* --
"THE GLORIOUS #3 BASEBALL CLUB" AND CONVERTED
TO THE ASUNARO CAMP -- THE ADMIRERS OF THAT
SERIES' MAIN CHARACTER, ASUNARO.

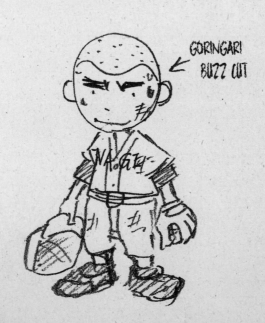

GORINGARI
BUZZ CUT

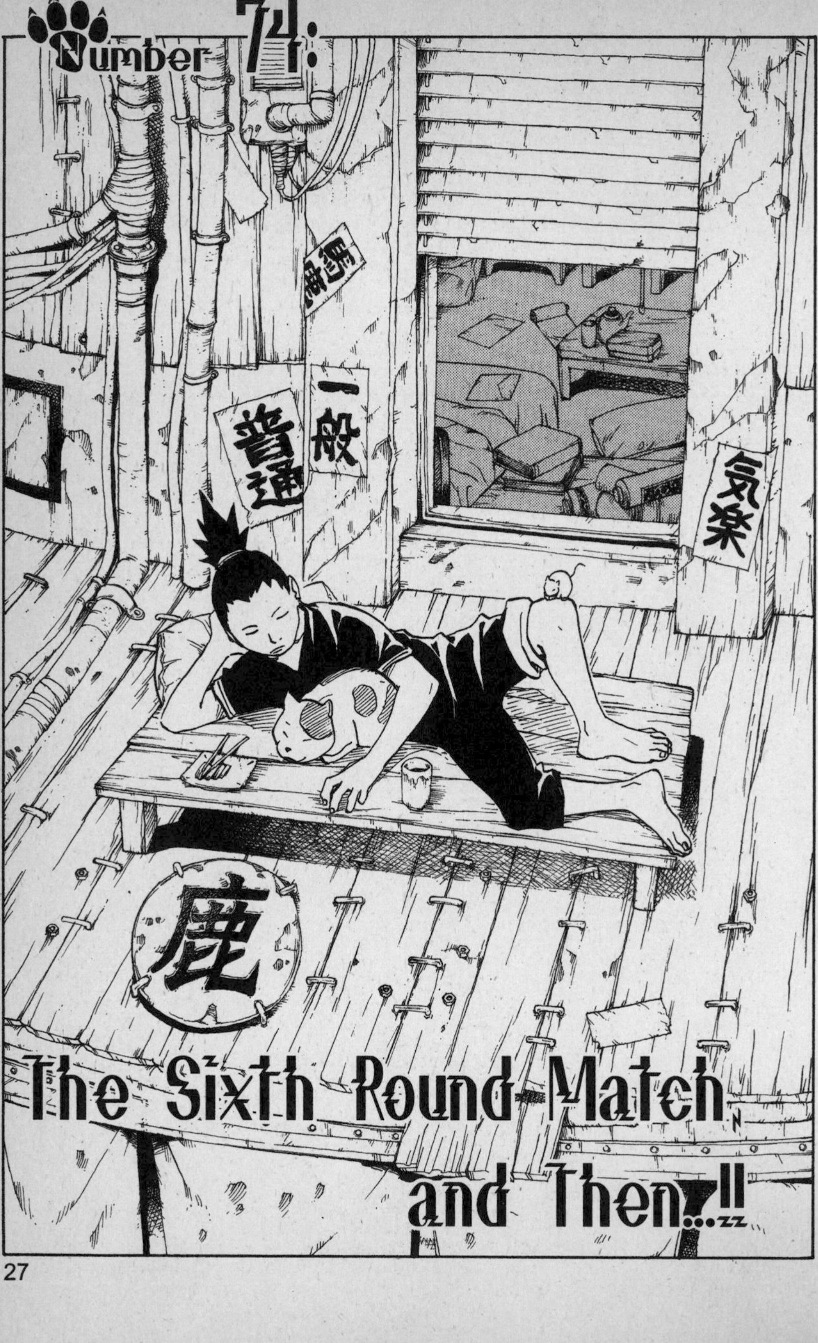
Number 74:
The Sixth Round Match and Then...!!
馬鹿
一般
普通
気楽
鹿

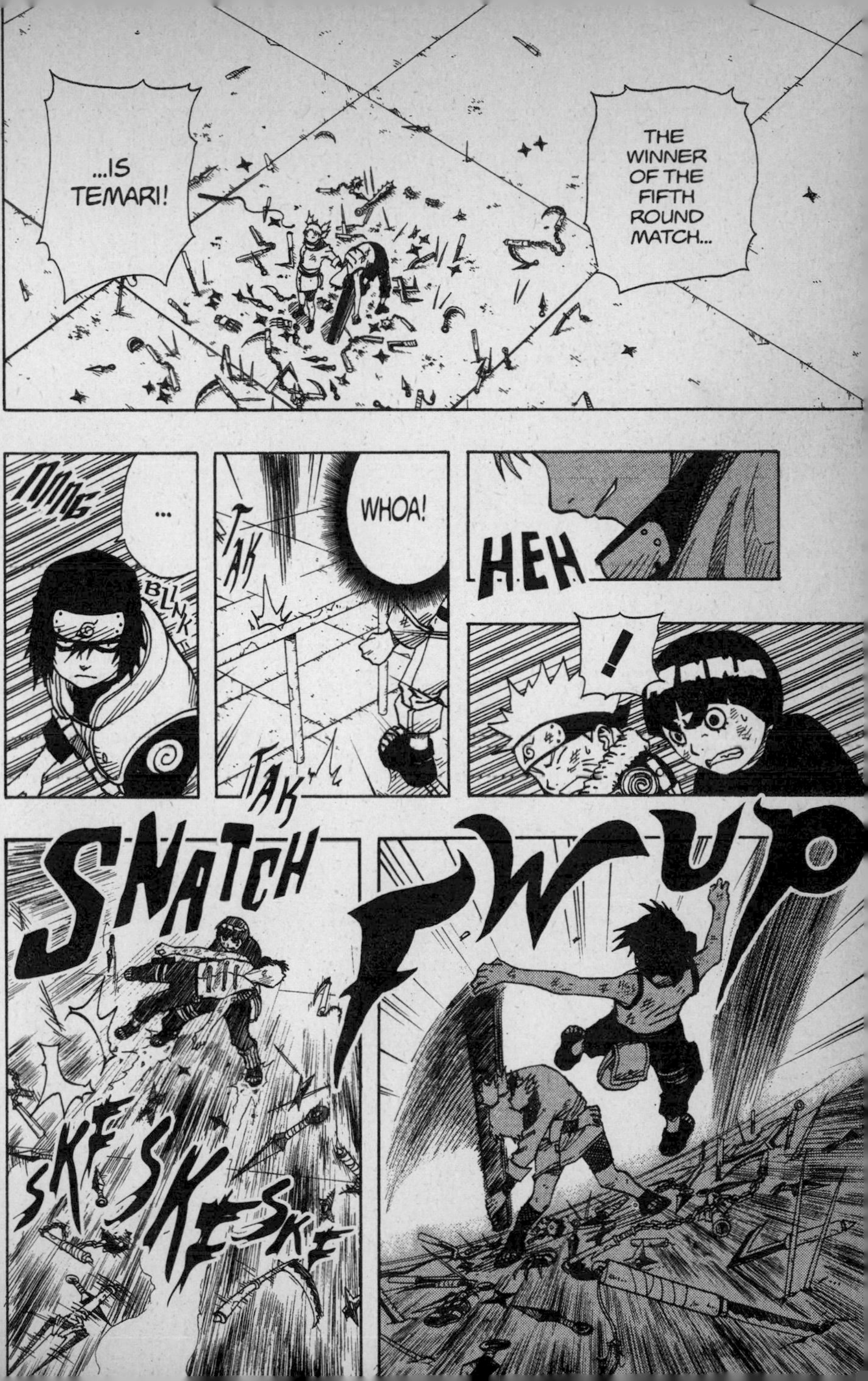
THE WINNER OF THE FIFTH ROUND MATCH...
...IS TEMARI!
HEH
!
WHOA!
TAK
TAK
...
BLINK
FWUP
SNATCH
SKE
SKE
SKE

READ THIS WAY

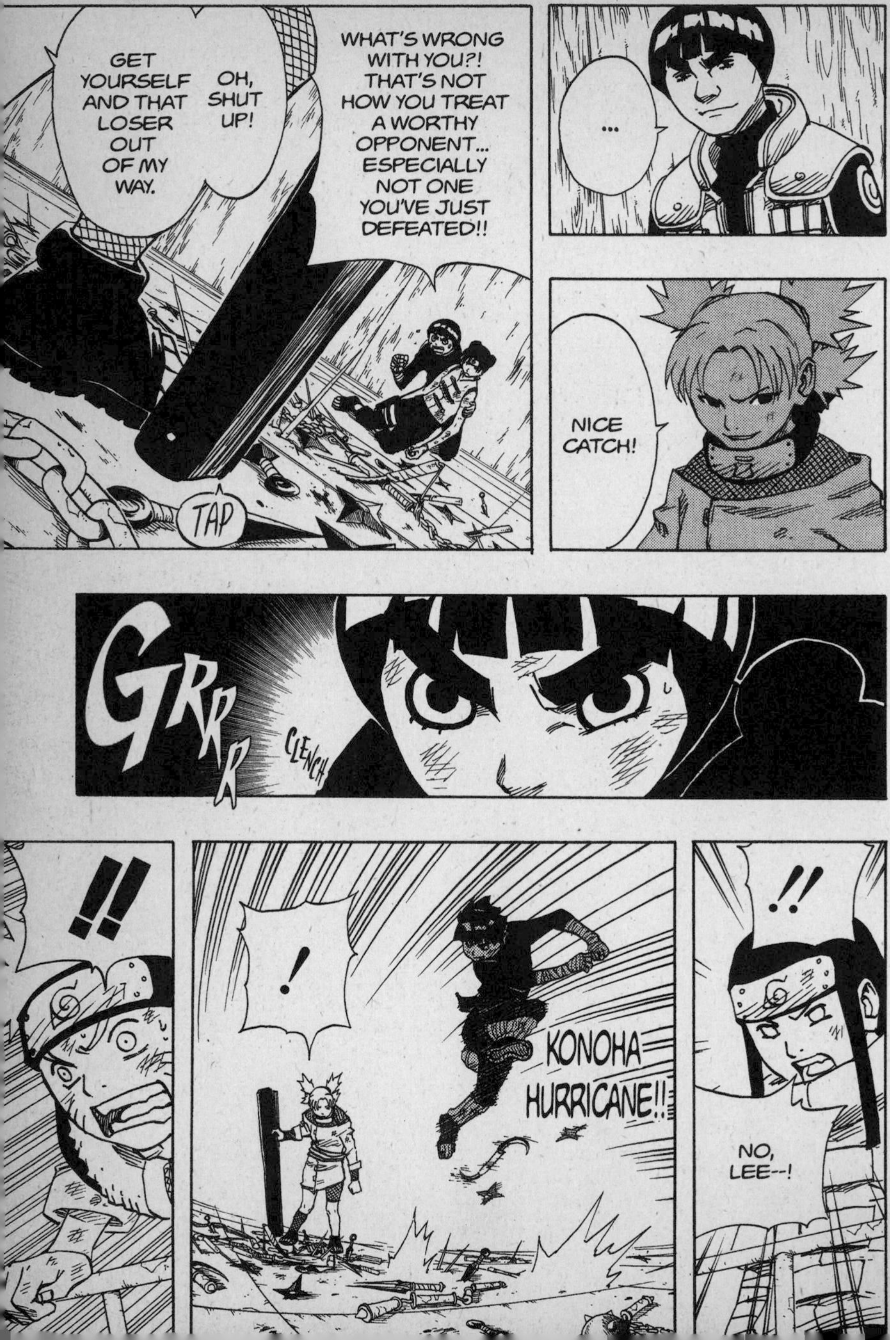
...
NICE CATCH!
WHAT'S WRONG WITH YOU?! THAT'S NOT HOW YOU TREAT A WORTHY OPPONENT... ESPECIALLY NOT ONE YOU'VE JUST DEFEATED!!
OH, SHUT UP!
GET YOURSELF AND THAT LOSER OUT OF MY WAY.
TAP
GRRR
CLENCH
!!
NO, LEE--!
!
KONOHA HURRICANE!!
!!

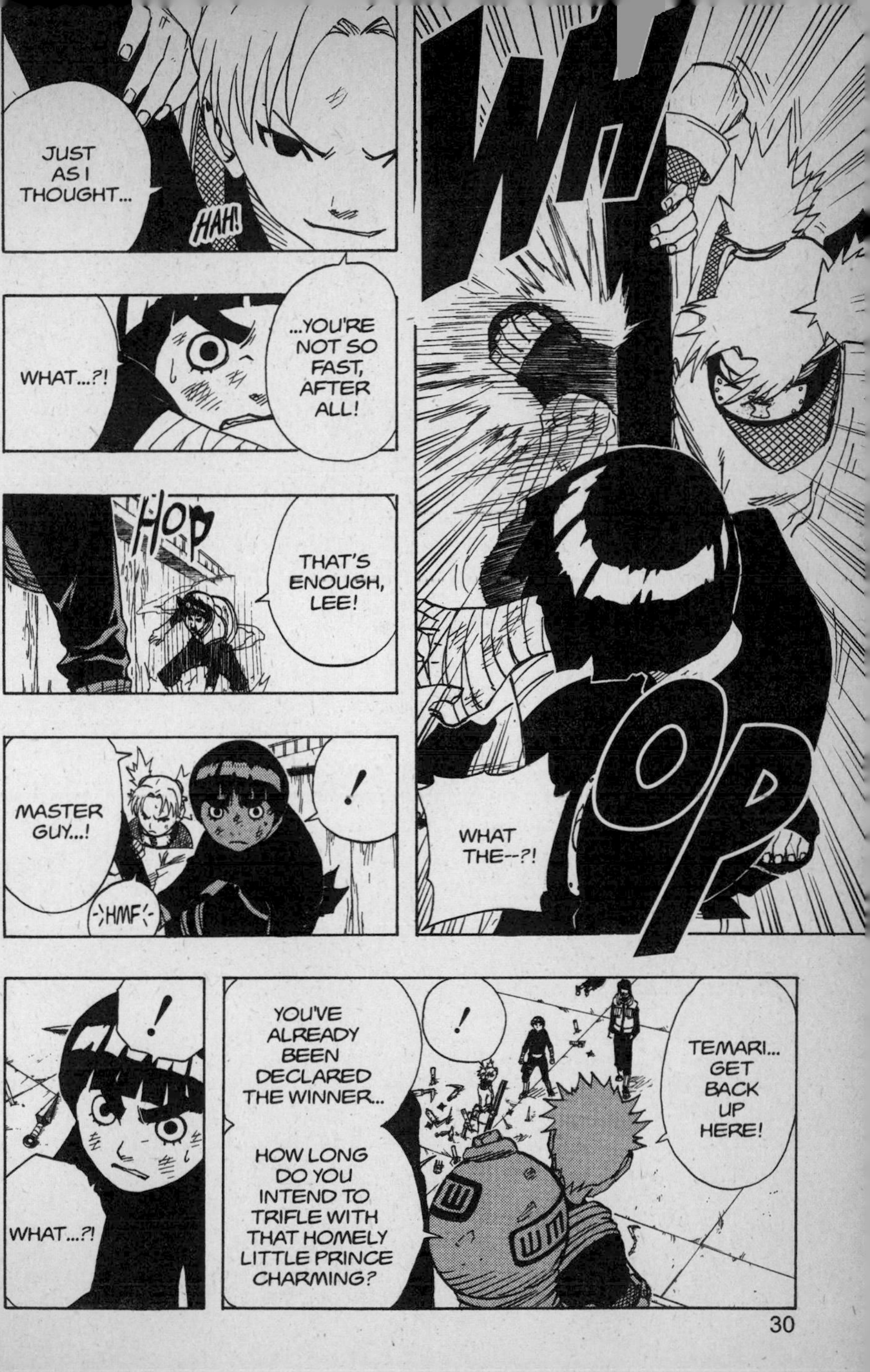
WH
OP
WHAT THE--?!
JUST AS I THOUGHT...
HAH!
...YOU'RE NOT SO FAST, AFTER ALL!
WHAT...?!
HOP
THAT'S ENOUGH, LEE!
!
MASTER GUY...!
HMF
TEMARI... GET BACK UP HERE!
!
YOU'VE ALREADY BEEN DECLARED THE WINNER...
HOW LONG DO YOU INTEND TO TRIFLE WITH THAT HOMELY LITTLE PRINCE CHARMING?
!
WHAT...?!

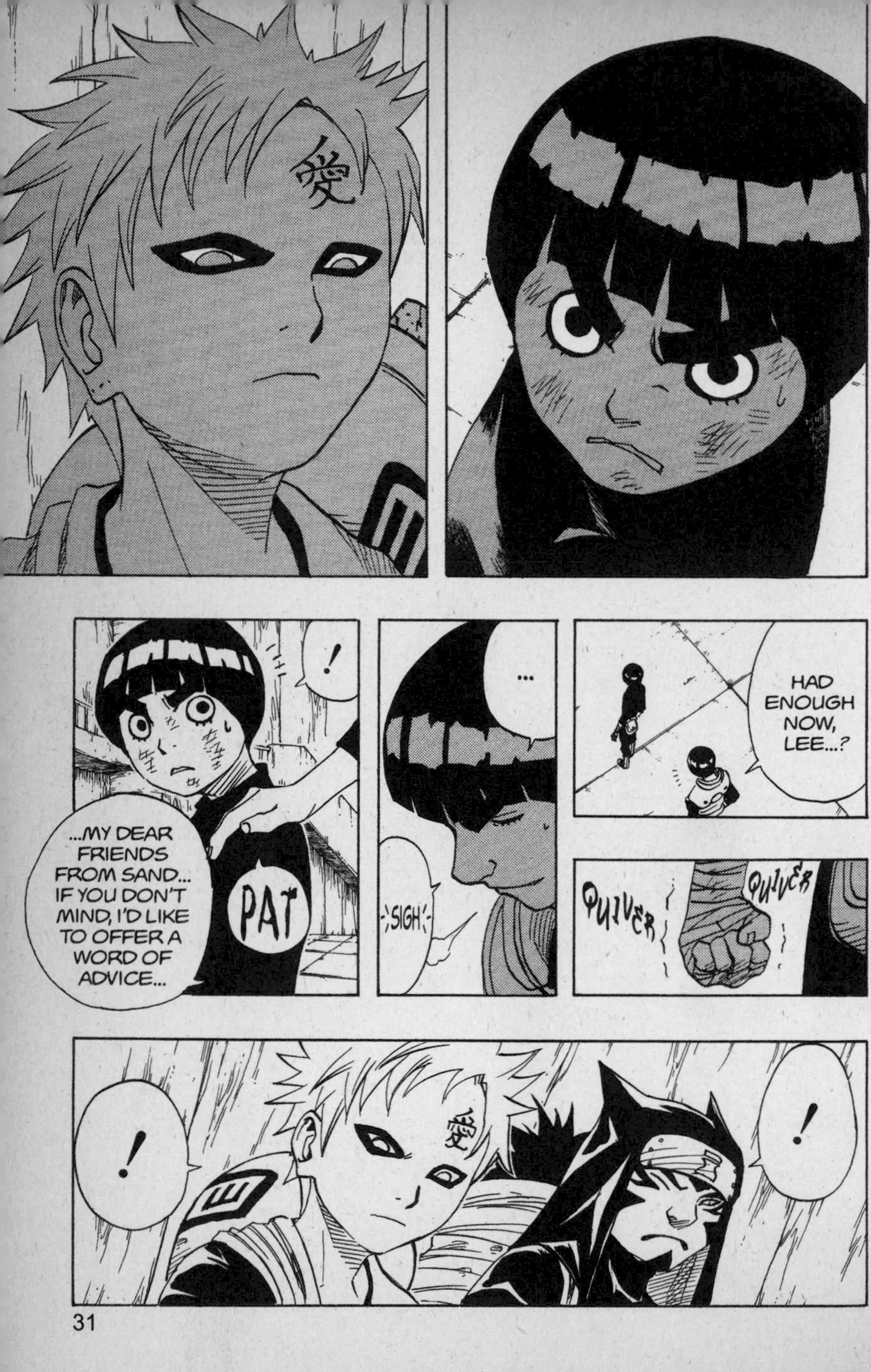
HAD ENOUGH NOW, LEE...?
QUIVER
QUIVER
...
SIGH
!
...MY DEAR FRIENDS FROM SAND... IF YOU DON'T MIND, I'D LIKE TO OFFER A WORD OF ADVICE...
PAT
!
!

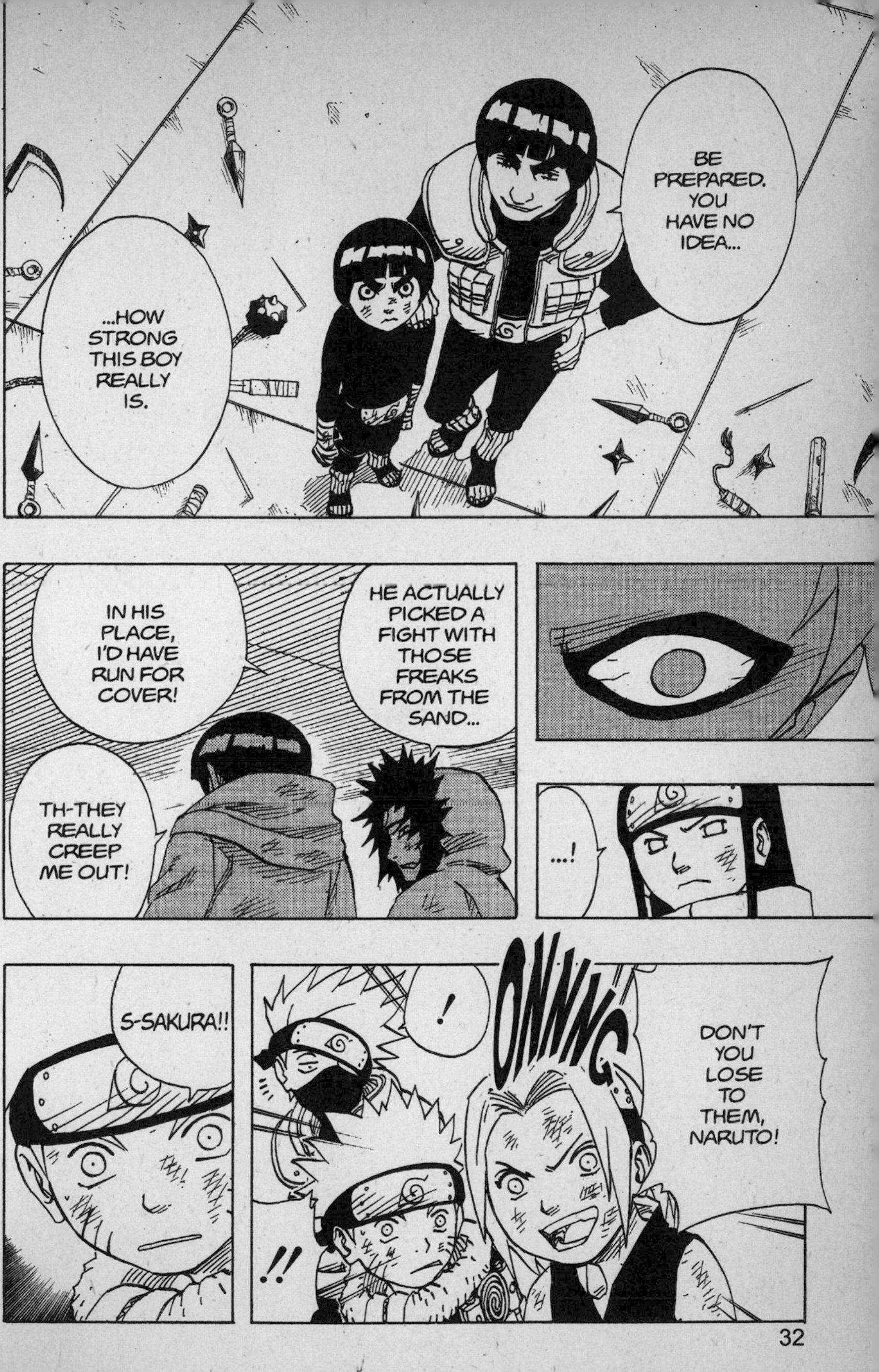
BE PREPARED. YOU HAVE NO IDEA...
...HOW STRONG THIS BOY REALLY IS.
...!
HE ACTUALLY PICKED A FIGHT WITH THOSE FREAKS FROM THE SAND...
IN HIS PLACE, I'D HAVE RUN FOR COVER!
TH-THEY REALLY CREEP ME OUT!
DON'T YOU LOSE TO THEM, NARUTO!
!
!!
S-SAKURA!!

READ THIS WAY

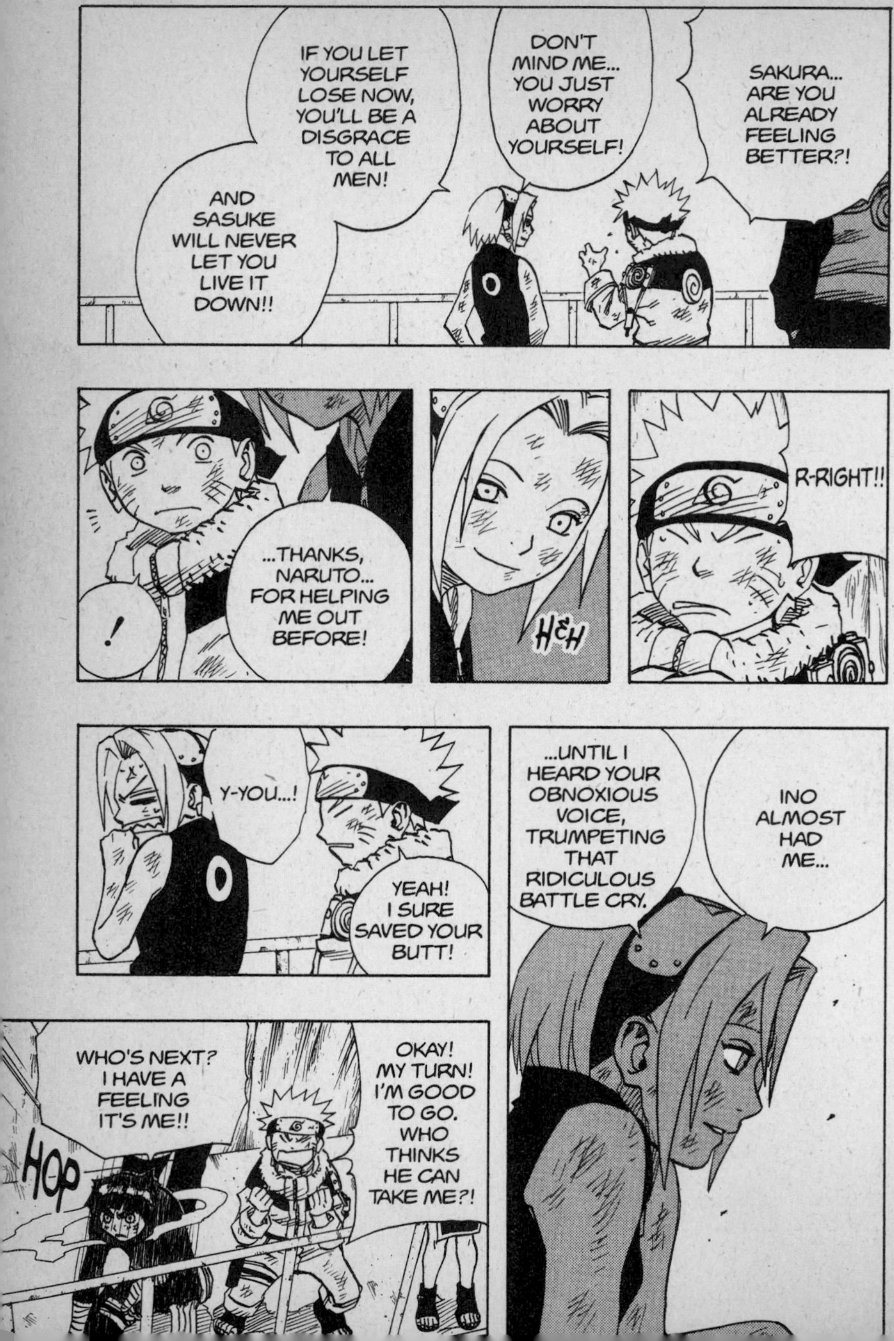
SAKURA... ARE YOU ALREADY FEELING BETTER?!
DON'T MIND ME... YOU JUST WORRY ABOUT YOURSELF!
IF YOU LET YOURSELF LOSE NOW, YOU'LL BE A DISGRACE TO ALL MEN!
AND SASUKE WILL NEVER LET YOU LIVE IT DOWN!!
R-RIGHT!!
HEH
...THANKS, NARUTO... FOR HELPING ME OUT BEFORE!
!
INO ALMOST HAD ME...
...UNTIL I HEARD YOUR OBNOXIOUS VOICE, TRUMPETING THAT RIDICULOUS BATTLE CRY.
Y-YOU...!
YEAH! I SURE SAVED YOUR BUTT!
OKAY! MY TURN! I'M GOOD TO GO. WHO THINKS HE CAN TAKE ME?!
WHO'S NEXT? I HAVE A FEELING IT'S ME!!
HOP

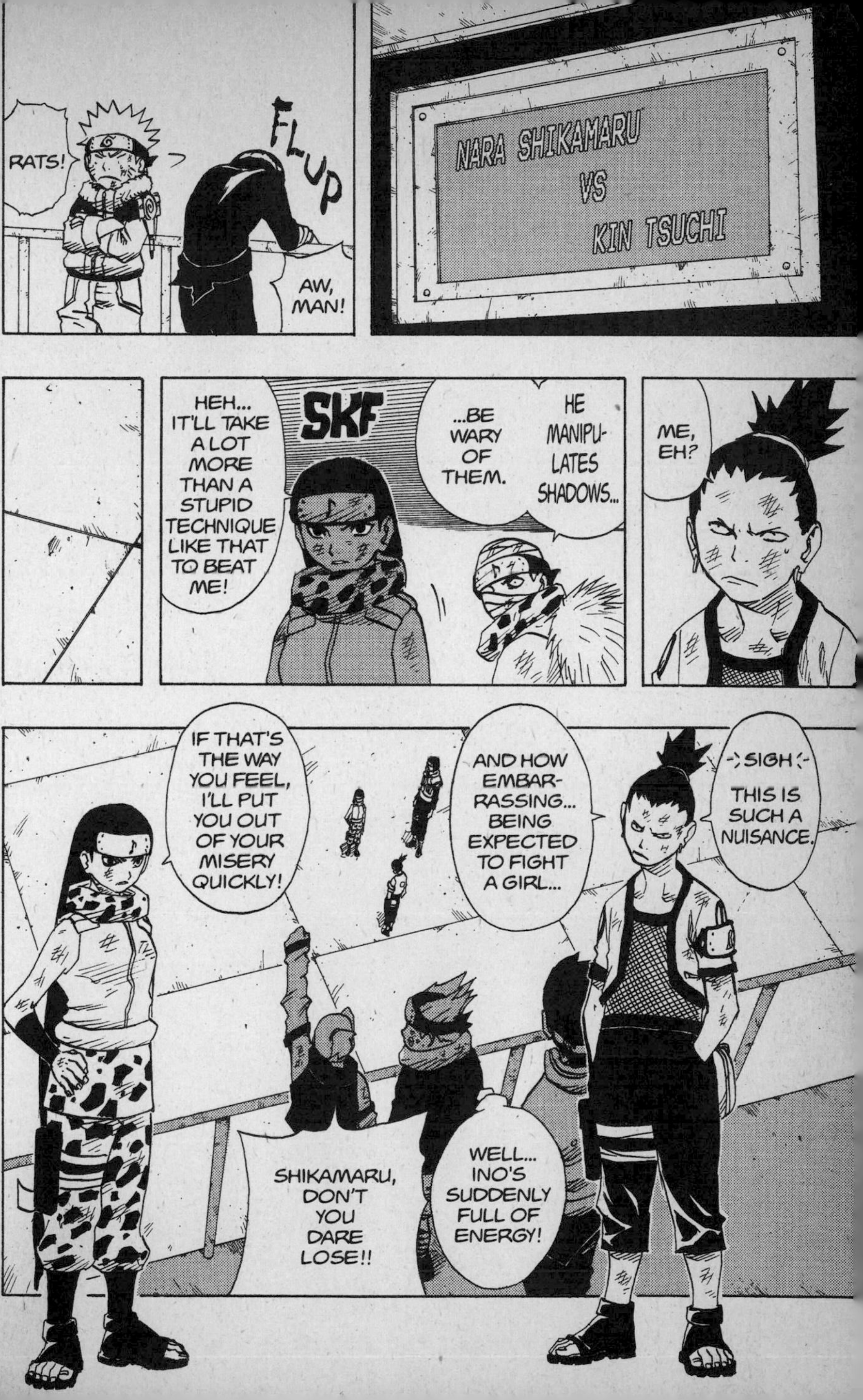
NARA SHIKAMARU VS KIN TSUCHI
FLUP
RATS!
AW, MAN!
ME, EH?
HE MANIPULATES SHADOWS...
...BE WARY OF THEM.
SKF
HEH... IT'LL TAKE A LOT MORE THAN A STUPID TECHNIQUE LIKE THAT TO BEAT ME!
-SIGH- THIS IS SUCH A NUISANCE.
AND HOW EMBARRASSING... BEING EXPECTED TO FIGHT A GIRL...
IF THAT'S THE WAY YOU FEEL, I'LL PUT YOU OUT OF YOUR MISERY QUICKLY!
WELL... INO'S SUDDENLY FULL OF ENERGY!
SHIKAMARU, DON'T YOU DARE LOSE!!

READ THIS WAY

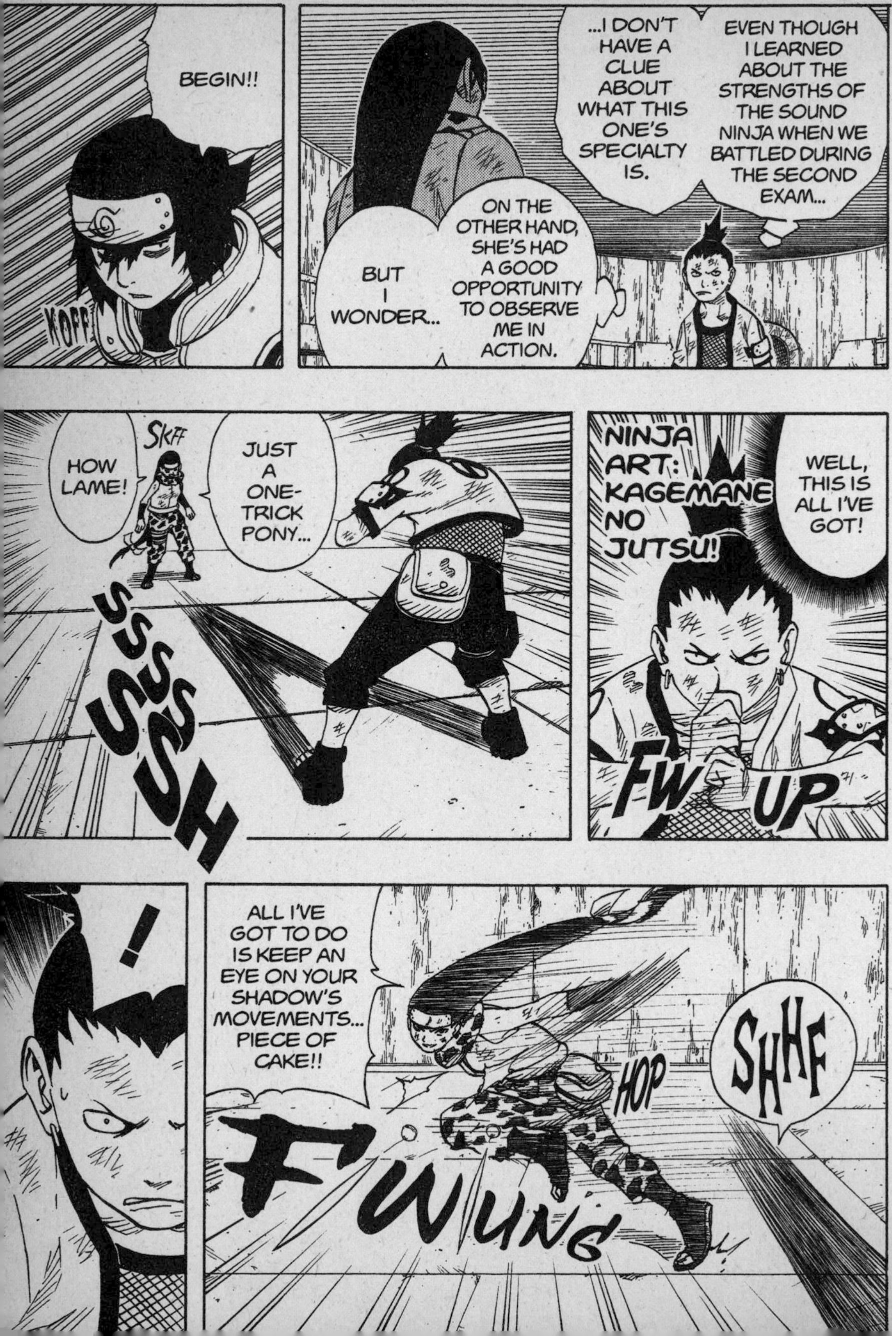
EVEN THOUGH I LEARNED ABOUT THE STRENGTHS OF THE SOUND NINJA WHEN WE BATTLED DURING THE SECOND EXAM...
...I DON'T HAVE A CLUE ABOUT WHAT THIS ONE'S SPECIALTY IS.
ON THE OTHER HAND, SHE'S HAD A GOOD OPPORTUNITY TO OBSERVE ME IN ACTION.
BUT I WONDER...
BEGIN!!
KOFF
WELL, THIS IS ALL I'VE GOT!
NINJA ART: KAGEMANE NO JUTSU!
FW UP
JUST A ONE-TRICK PONY...
HOW LAME!
SKFF
SSSSSH
SHHF
ALL I'VE GOT TO DO IS KEEP AN EYE ON YOUR SHADOW'S MOVEMENTS... PIECE OF CAKE!!
HOP
FWUNG
!

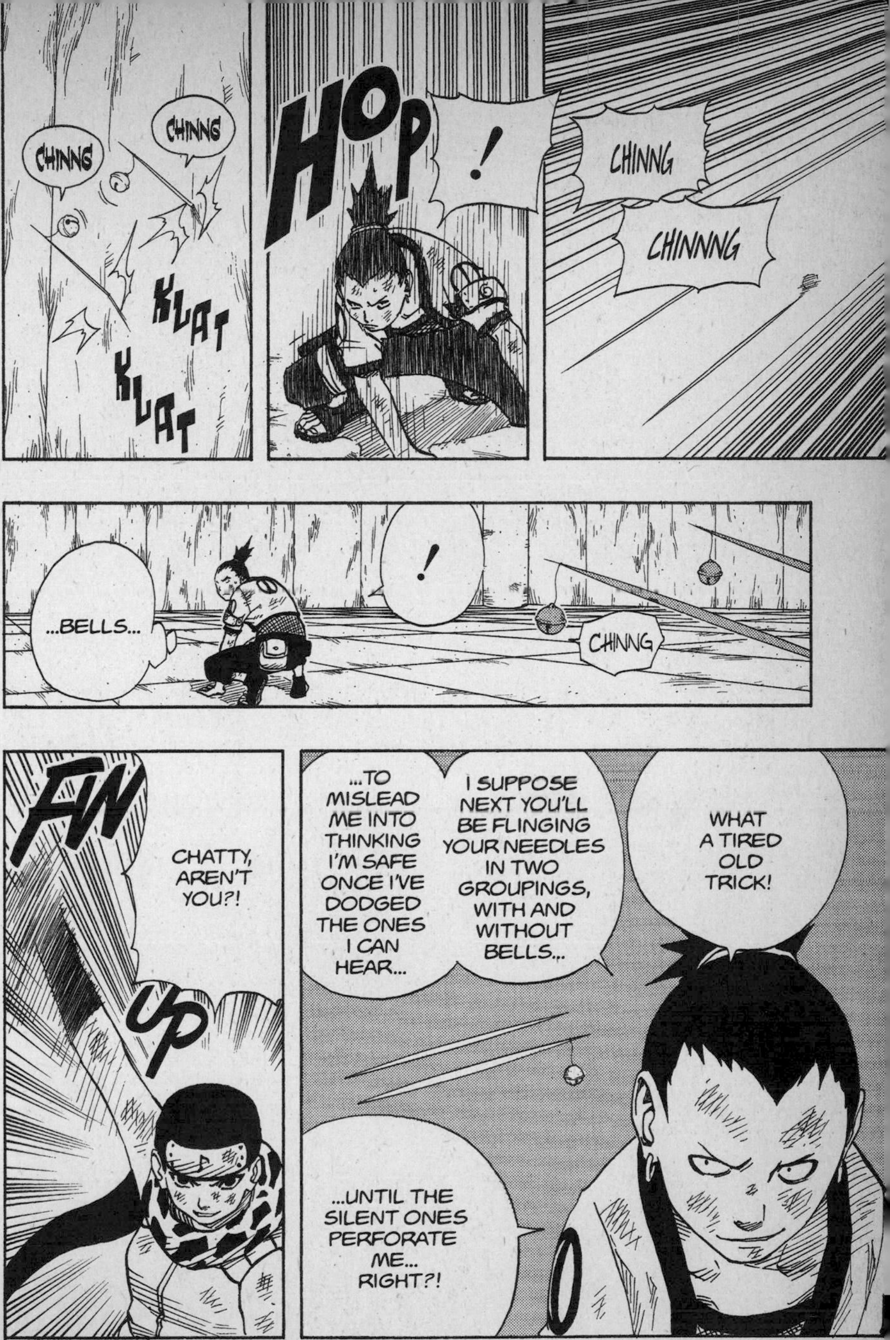
CHINNG
CHINNNG
HOP
!
CHINNG
CHINNG
KLAT
KLAT
CHINNG
!
...BELLS...
WHAT A TIRED OLD TRICK!
I SUPPOSE NEXT YOU'LL BE FLINGING YOUR NEEDLES IN TWO GROUPINGS, WITH AND WITHOUT BELLS...
...TO MISLEAD ME INTO THINKING I'M SAFE ONCE I'VE DODGED THE ONES I CAN HEAR...
...UNTIL THE SILENT ONES PERFORATE ME... RIGHT?!
FW
UP
CHATTY, AREN'T YOU?!

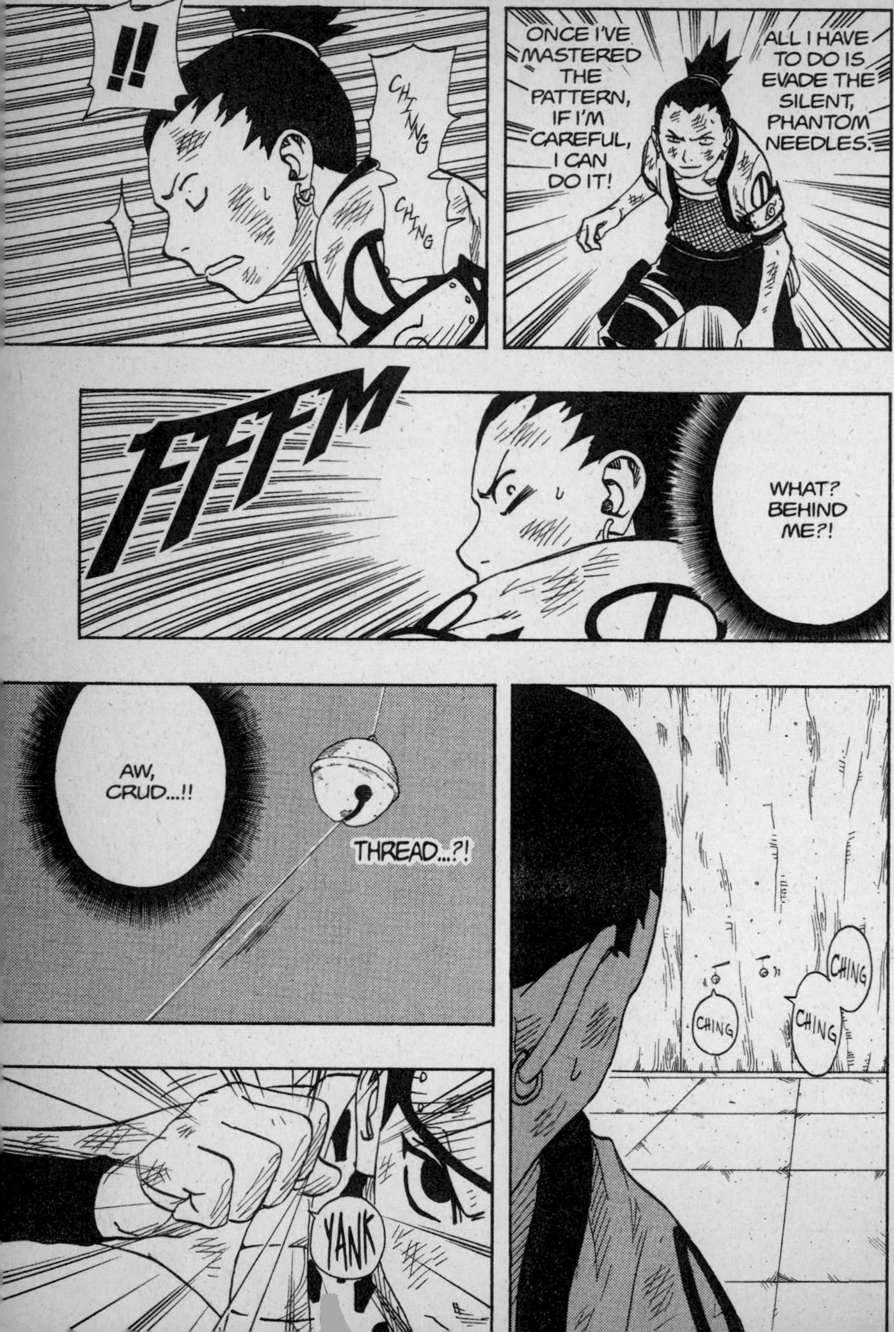
ALL I HAVE TO DO IS EVADE THE SILENT, PHANTOM NEEDLES.
ONCE I'VE MASTERED THE PATTERN, IF I'M CAREFUL, I CAN DO IT!
!!
CHINNNG
CHING
WHAT? BEHIND ME?!
FFFM
CHING
CHING
CHING
AW, CRUD...!!
THREAD...?!
YANK

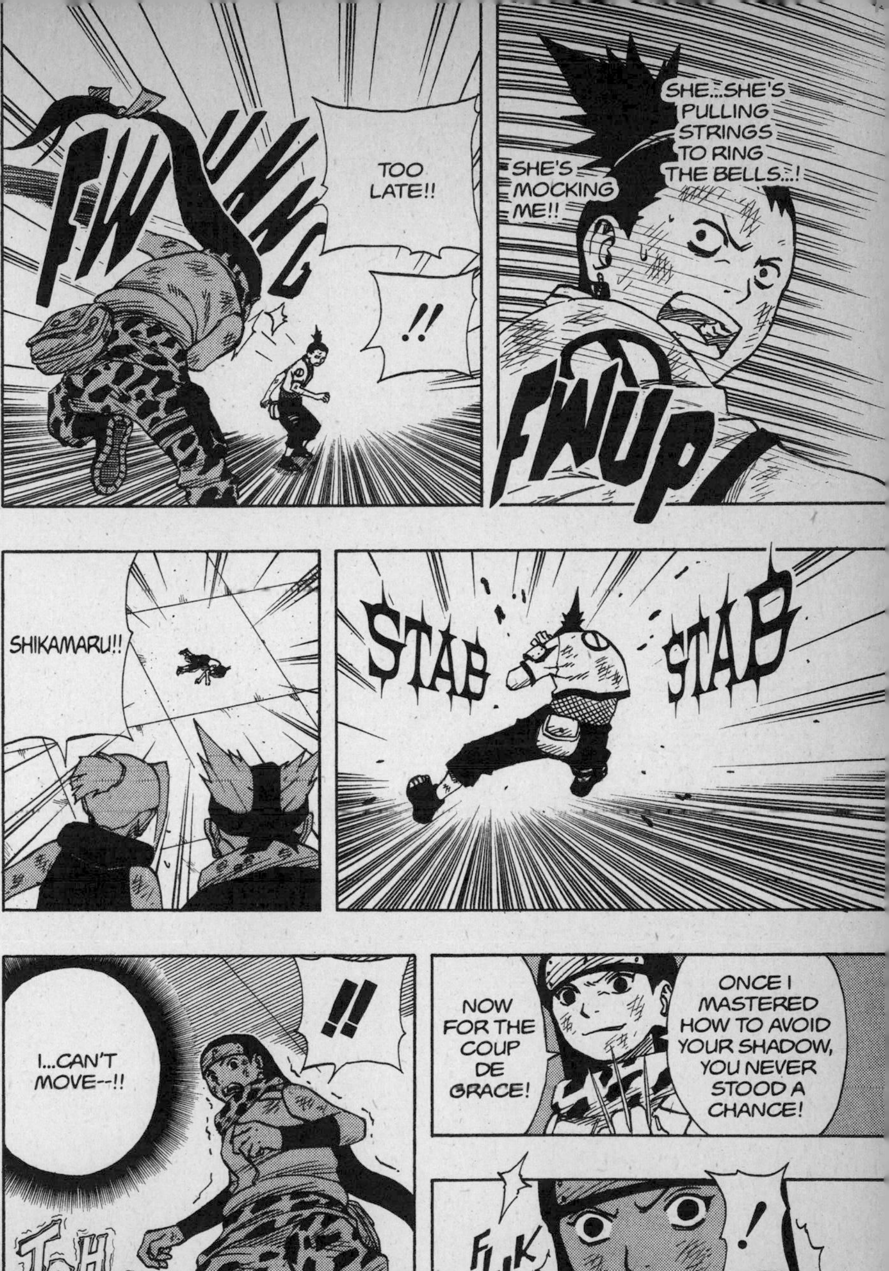
SHE...SHE'S PULLING STRINGS TO RING THE BELLS...!
SHE'S MOCKING ME!!
FWUP
TOO LATE!!
!!
FWUNG
STAB STAB
SHIKAMARU!!
ONCE I MASTERED HOW TO AVOID YOUR SHADOW, YOU NEVER STOOD A CHANCE!
NOW FOR THE COUP DE GRACE!
!
FLIK
!!
I...CAN'T MOVE--!!
TCHGK

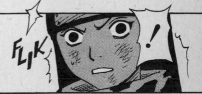

READ THIS WAY

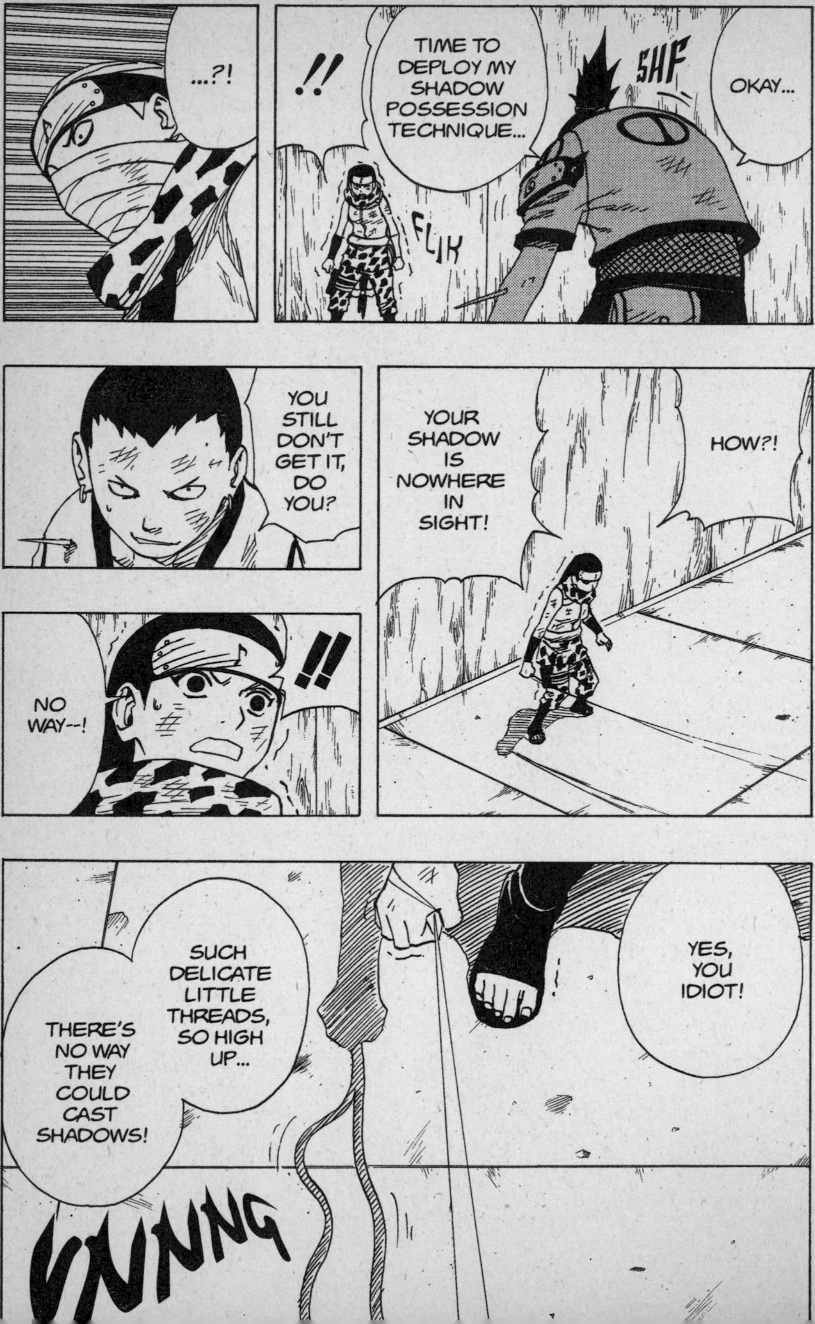
OKAY...
SHF
TIME TO DEPLOY MY SHADOW POSSESSION TECHNIQUE...
!!
FLIK
...?!
HOW?!
YOUR SHADOW IS NOWHERE IN SIGHT!
YOU STILL DON'T GET IT, DO YOU?
!!
NO WAY--!
YES, YOU IDIOT!
SUCH DELICATE LITTLE THREADS, SO HIGH UP...
THERE'S NO WAY THEY COULD CAST SHADOWS!
VUNNG

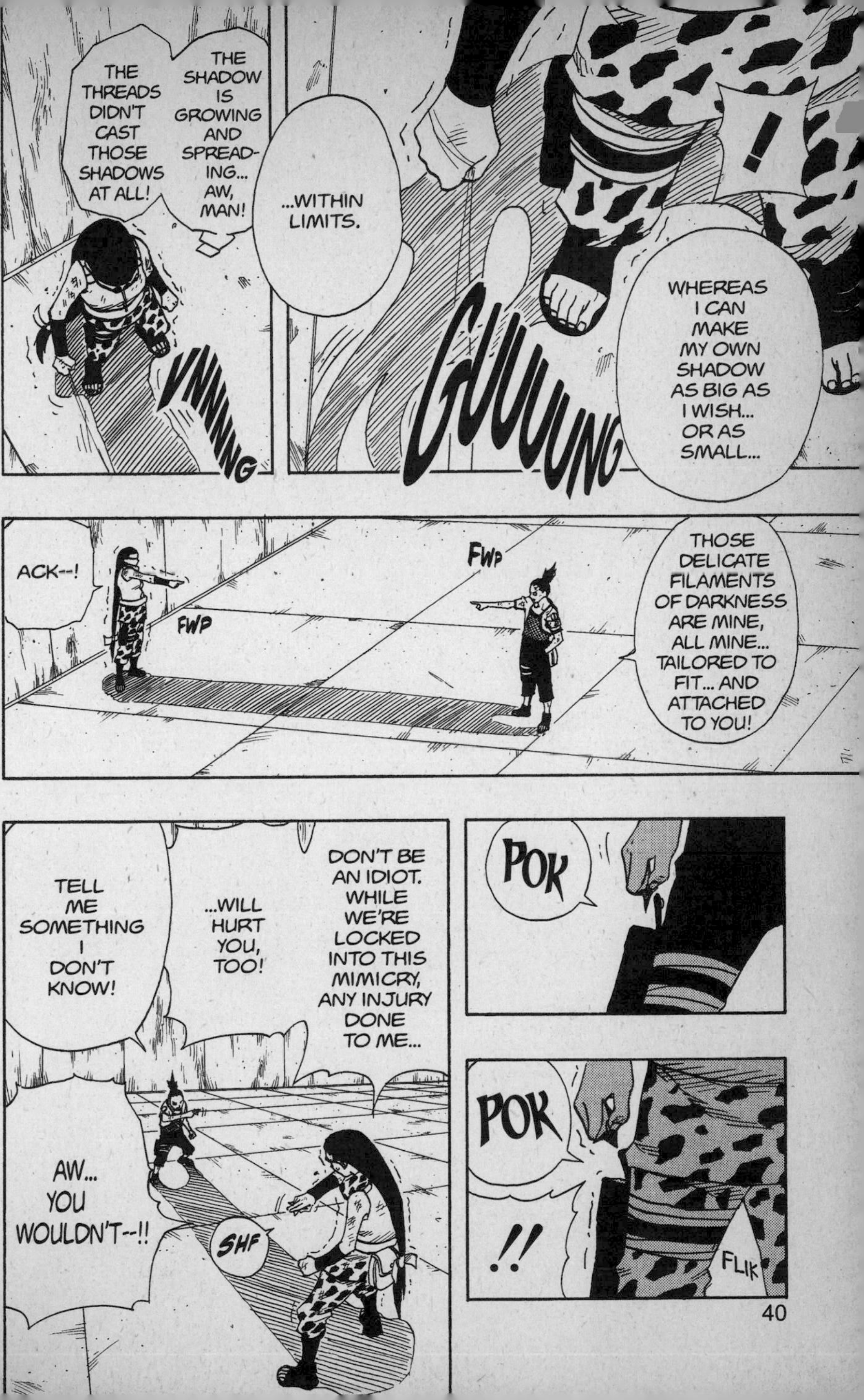
!
WHEREAS I CAN MAKE MY OWN SHADOW AS BIG AS I WISH... OR AS SMALL...
GUUUUNG
...WITHIN LIMITS.
THE SHADOW IS GROWING AND SPREADING... AW, MAN!
THE THREADS DIDN'T CAST THOSE SHADOWS AT ALL!
VNNNNG
THOSE DELICATE FILAMENTS OF DARKNESS ARE MINE, ALL MINE... TAILORED TO FIT... AND ATTACHED TO YOU!
FWP
FWP
ACK--!
POK
POK
!!
FLIK
DON'T BE AN IDIOT. WHILE WE'RE LOCKED INTO THIS MIMICRY, ANY INJURY DONE TO ME...
...WILL HURT YOU, TOO!
TELL ME SOMETHING I DON'T KNOW!
AW... YOU WOULDN'T--!!
SHF

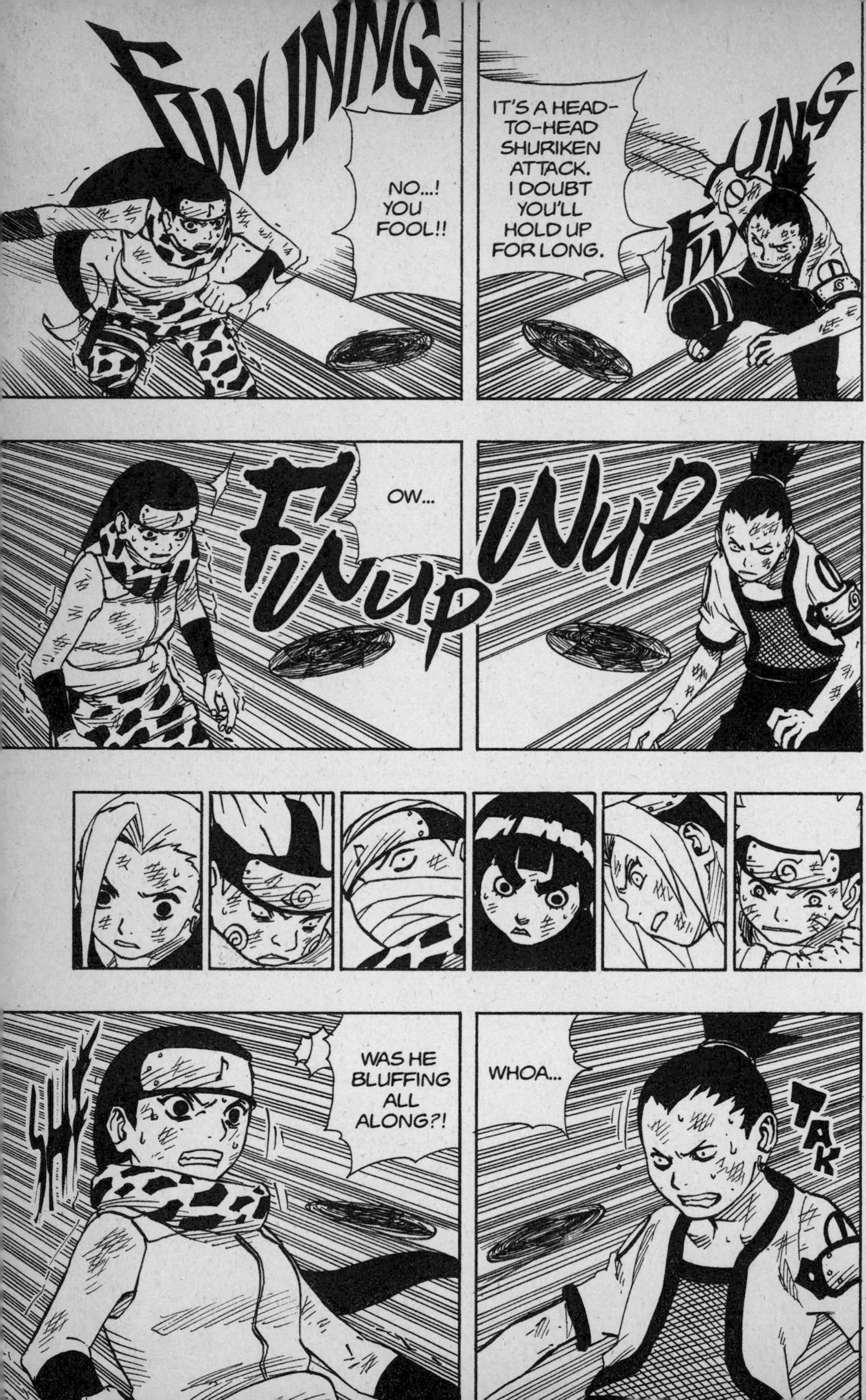
IT'S A HEAD-TO-HEAD SHURIKEN ATTACK. I DOUBT YOU'LL HOLD UP FOR LONG.
FWUNNG
NO...! YOU FOOL!!
WUP
FWUP
OW...
WHOA...
TAK
WAS HE BLUFFING ALL ALONG?!

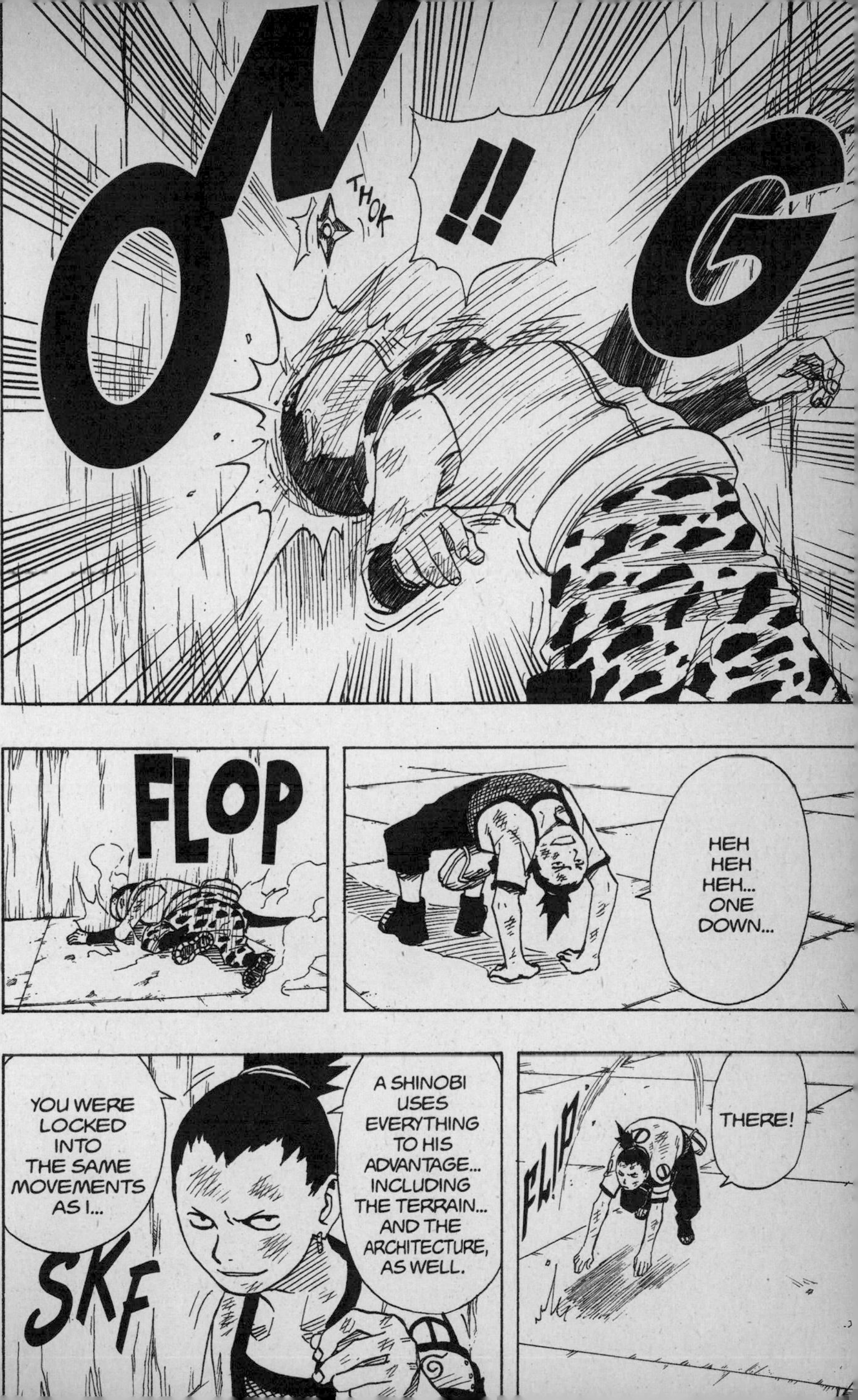
THOK
ON!!G
HEH HEH HEH... ONE DOWN...
FLOP
THERE!
FLIP
A SHINOBI USES EVERYTHING TO HIS ADVANTAGE... INCLUDING THE TERRAIN... AND THE ARCHITECTURE, AS WELL.
YOU WERE LOCKED INTO THE SAME MOVEMENTS AS I...
SKF

READ THIS WAY

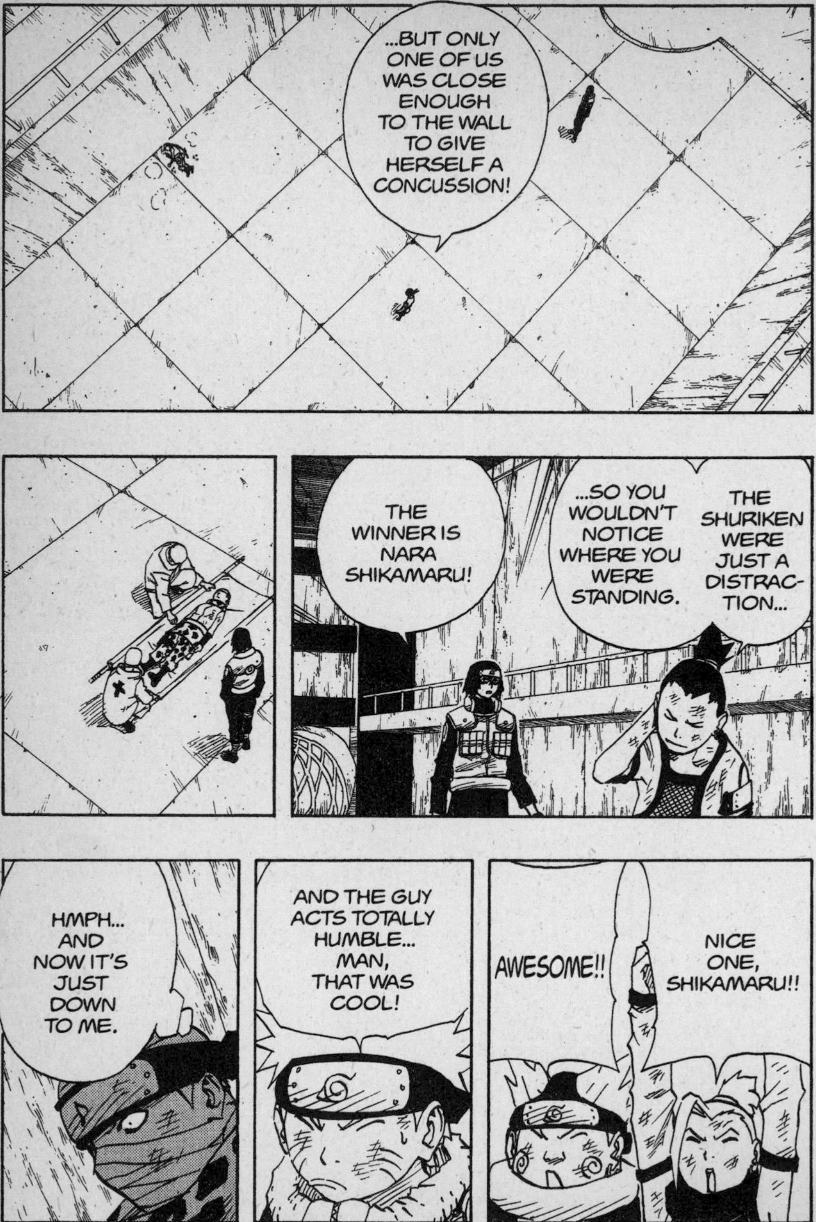

...BUT ONLY ONE OF US WAS CLOSE ENOUGH TO THE WALL TO GIVE HERSELF A CONCUSSION!
THE SHURIKEN WERE JUST A DISTRACTION...
...SO YOU WOULDN'T NOTICE WHERE YOU WERE STANDING.
THE WINNER IS NARA SHIKAMARU!
NICE ONE, SHIKAMARU!!
AWESOME!!
AND THE GUY ACTS TOTALLY HUMBLE... MAN, THAT WAS COOL!
HMPH... AND NOW IT'S JUST DOWN TO ME.

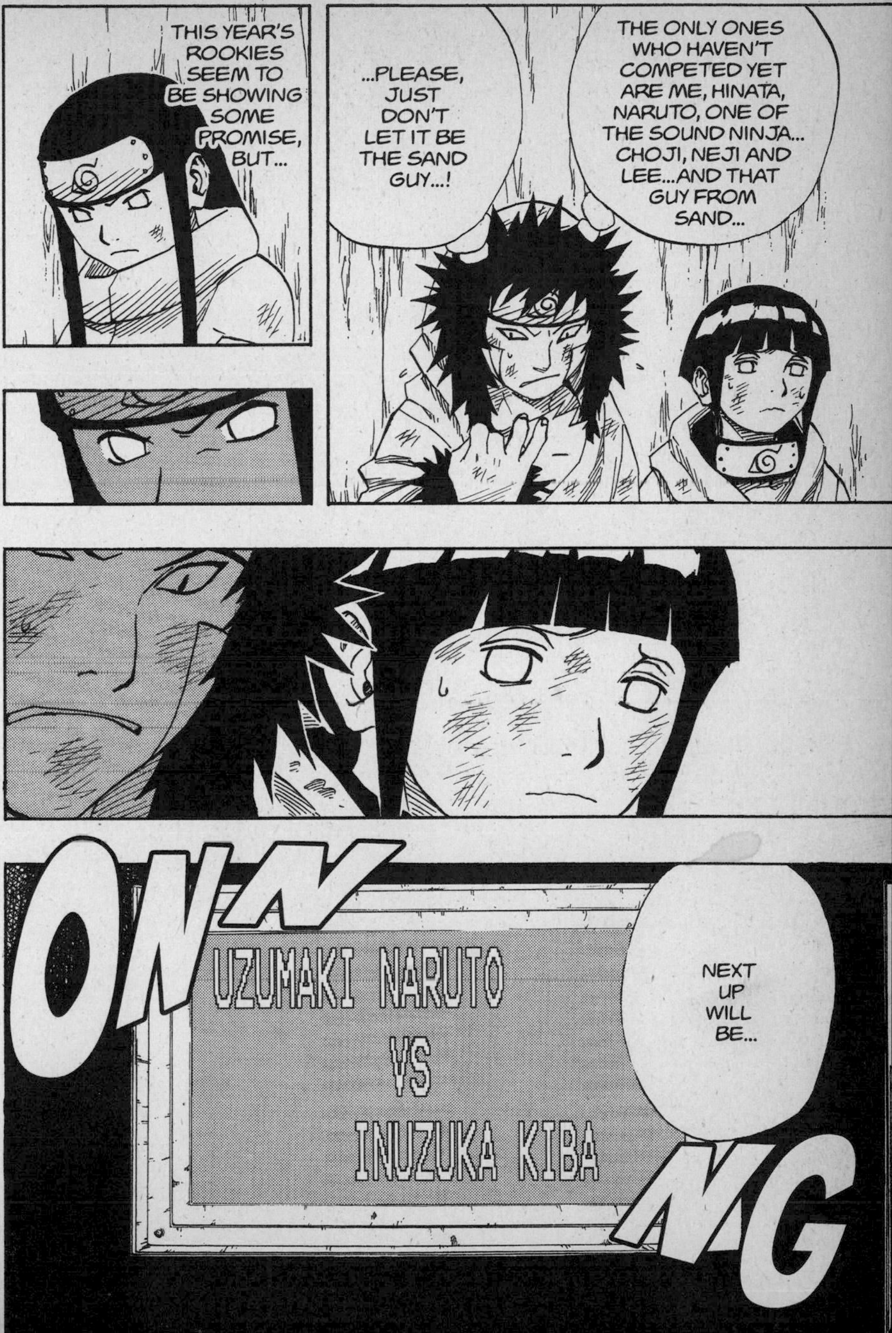
THE ONLY ONES WHO HAVEN'T COMPETED YET ARE ME, HINATA, NARUTO, ONE OF THE SOUND NINJA... CHOJI, NEJI AND LEE...AND THAT GUY FROM SAND...
...PLEASE, JUST DON'T LET IT BE THE SAND GUY...!
THIS YEAR'S ROOKIES SEEM TO BE SHOWING SOME PROMISE, BUT...
NEXT UP WILL BE...
UZUMAKI NARUTO VS INUZUKA KIBA
ONN
NG

READ THIS WAY

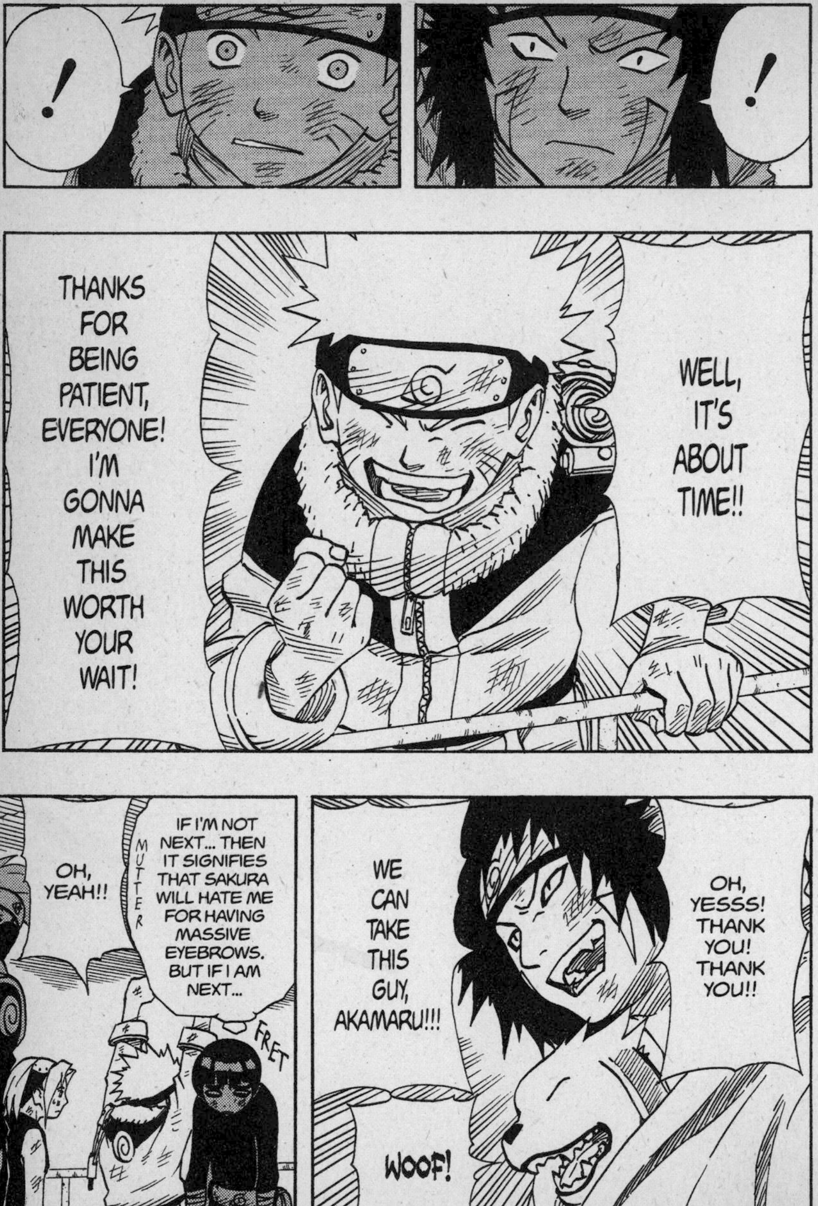
!
!
WELL, IT'S ABOUT TIME!!
THANKS FOR BEING PATIENT, EVERYONE! I'M GONNA MAKE THIS WORTH YOUR WAIT!
OH, YESSS! THANK YOU! THANK YOU!!
WE CAN TAKE THIS GUY, AKAMARU!!!
WOOF!
IF I'M NOT NEXT... THEN IT SIGNIFIES THAT SAKURA WILL HATE ME FOR HAVING MASSIVE EYEBROWS. BUT IF I AM NEXT...
MUTTER
FRET
OH, YEAH!!

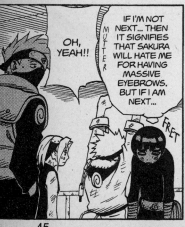

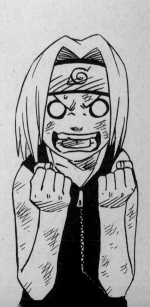

Number 75: Naruto's Coming-of-Age...!!

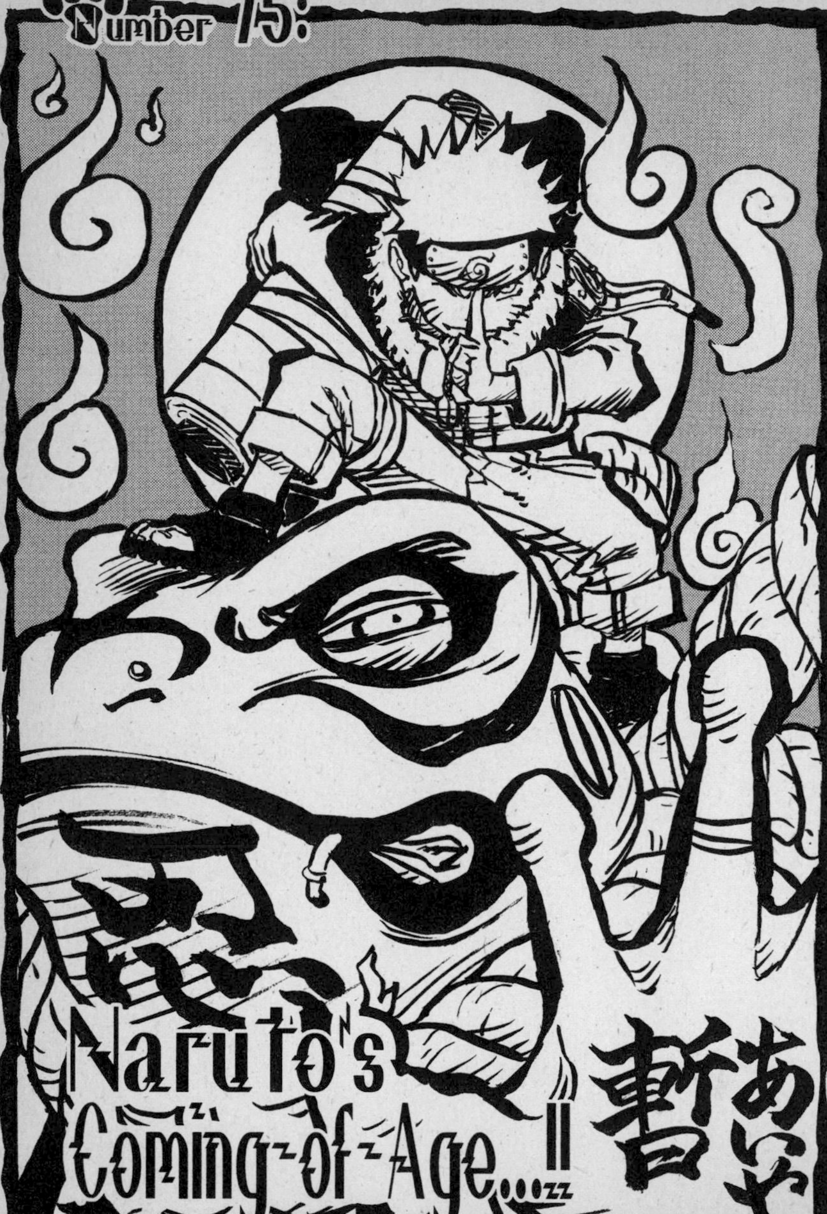

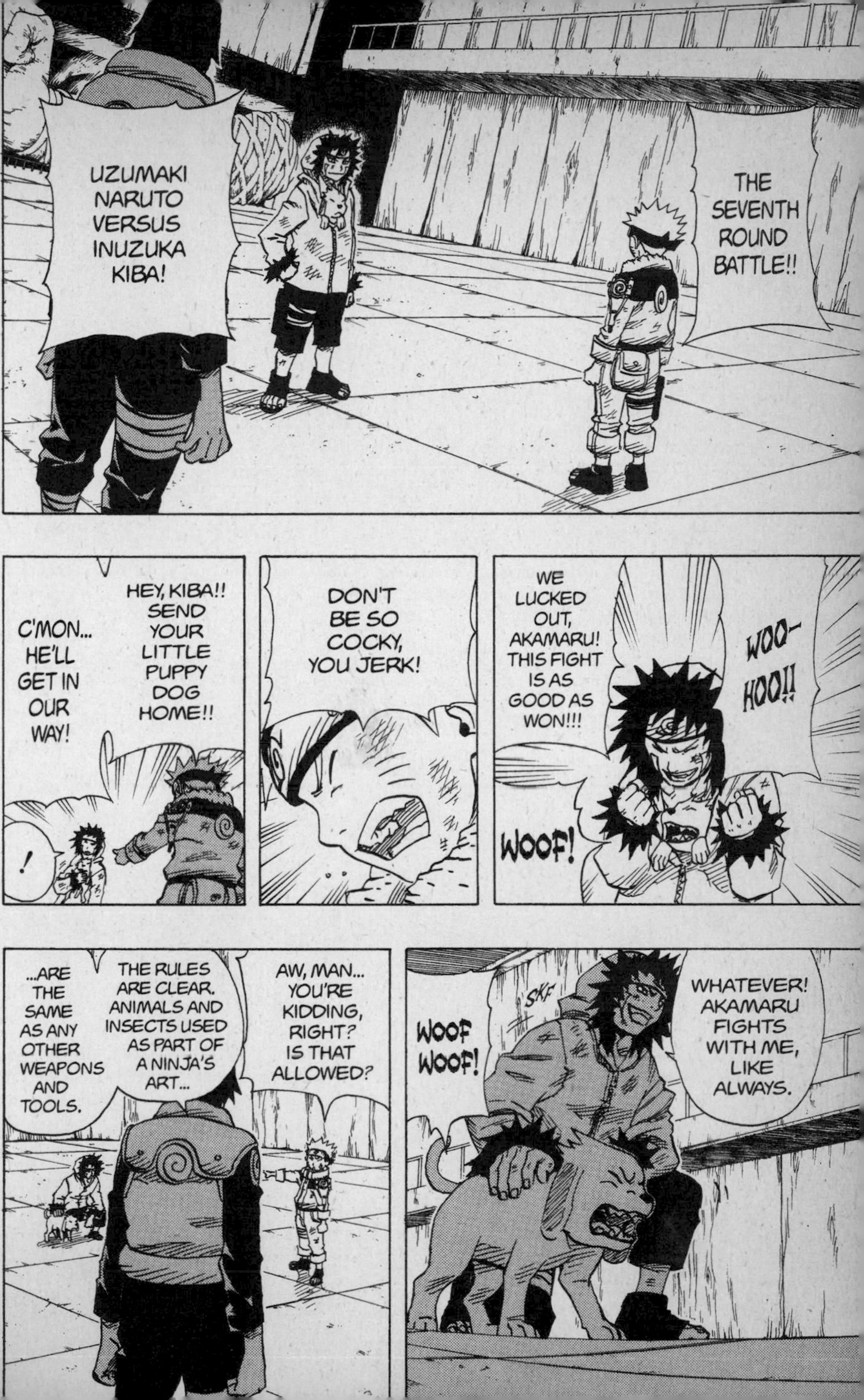
THE SEVENTH ROUND BATTLE!!
UZUMAKI NARUTO VERSUS INUZUKA KIBA!
WE LUCKED OUT, AKAMARU! THIS FIGHT IS AS GOOD AS WON!!!
WOO-HOO!!
WOOF!
DON'T BE SO COCKY, YOU JERK!
HEY, KIBA!! SEND YOUR LITTLE PUPPY DOG HOME!!
C'MON... HE'LL GET IN OUR WAY!
!
WHATEVER! AKAMARU FIGHTS WITH ME, LIKE ALWAYS.
SKF
WOOF WOOF!
AW, MAN... YOU'RE KIDDING, RIGHT? IS THAT ALLOWED?
THE RULES ARE CLEAR. ANIMALS AND INSECTS USED AS PART OF A NINJA'S ART...
...ARE THE SAME AS ANY OTHER WEAPONS AND TOOLS.

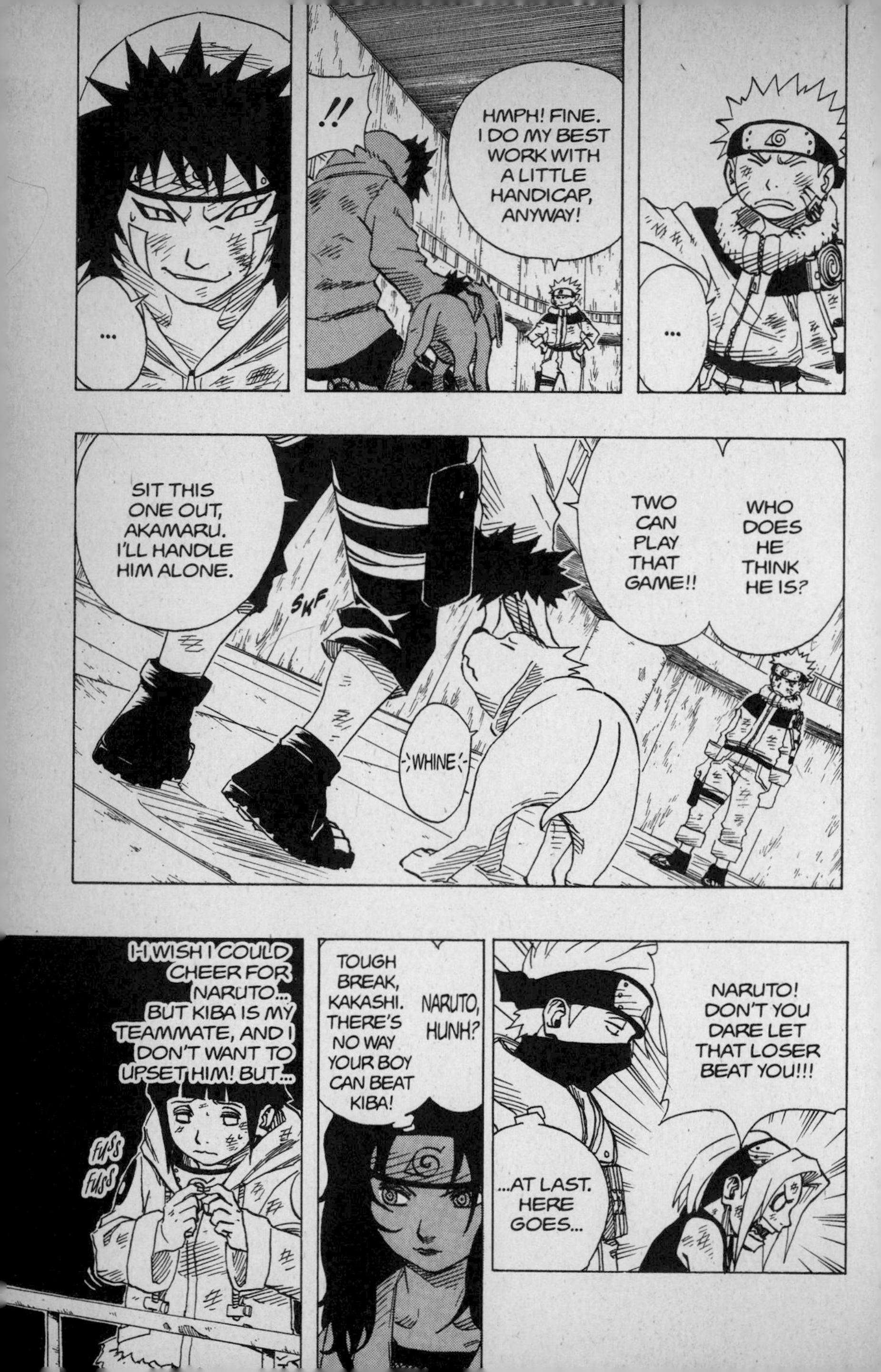
...
HMPH! FINE. I DO MY BEST WORK WITH A LITTLE HANDICAP, ANYWAY!
!!
...
WHO DOES HE THINK HE IS?
TWO CAN PLAY THAT GAME!!
SIT THIS ONE OUT, AKAMARU. I'LL HANDLE HIM ALONE.
SKF
WHINE
NARUTO! DON'T YOU DARE LET THAT LOSER BEAT YOU!!!
...AT LAST. HERE GOES...
NARUTO, HUNH?
TOUGH BREAK, KAKASHI. THERE'S NO WAY YOUR BOY CAN BEAT KIBA!
I-I WISH I COULD CHEER FOR NARUTO... BUT KIBA IS MY TEAMMATE, AND I DON'T WANT TO UPSET HIM! BUT...
FUSS FUSS

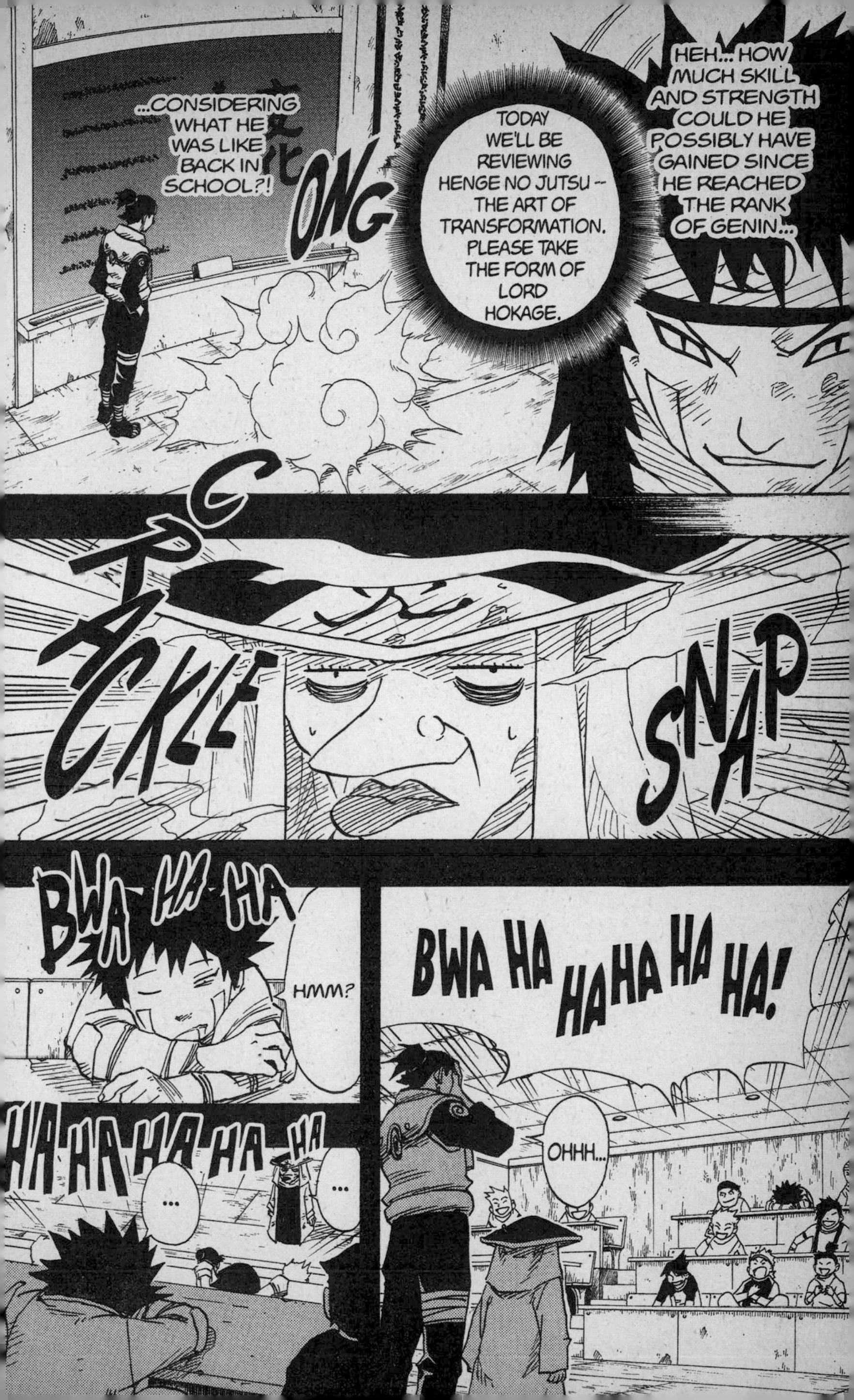
HEH... HOW MUCH SKILL AND STRENGTH COULD HE POSSIBLY HAVE GAINED SINCE HE REACHED THE RANK OF GENIN...
TODAY WE'LL BE REVIEWING HENGE NO JUTSU -- THE ART OF TRANSFORMATION. PLEASE TAKE THE FORM OF LORD HOKAGE.
ONG
...CONSIDERING WHAT HE WAS LIKE BACK IN SCHOOL?!
SNAP
CRACKLE
BWA HA HAHA HA HA HA!
OHHH...
BWA HA HA
HMM?
HA HA HA HA HA HA
...
...

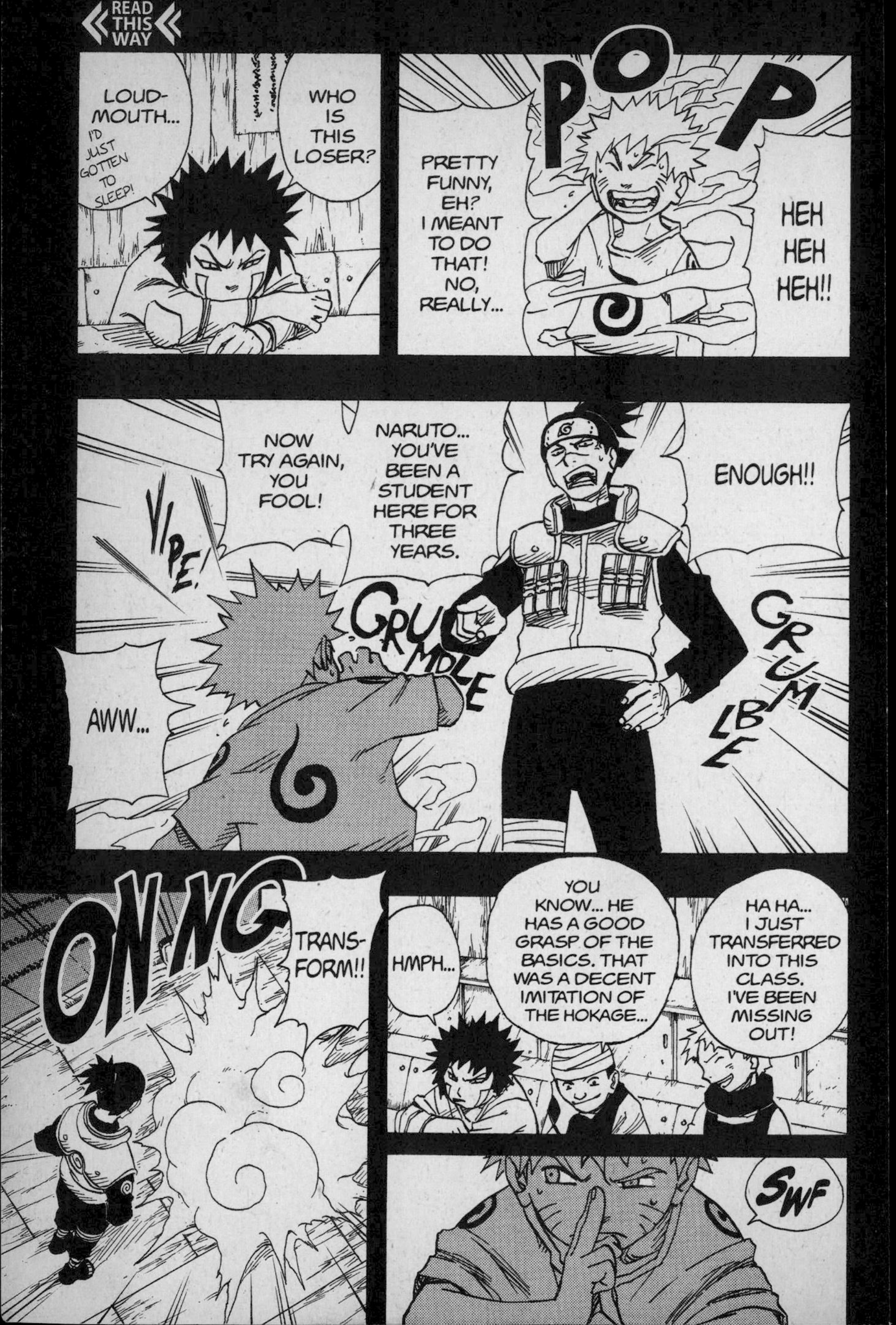
READ THIS WAY
POP
PRETTY FUNNY, EH? I MEANT TO DO THAT! NO, REALLY...
HEH HEH HEH!!
WHO IS THIS LOSER?
LOUD-MOUTH...
I'D JUST GOTTEN TO SLEEP!
ENOUGH!!
NARUTO... YOU'VE BEEN A STUDENT HERE FOR THREE YEARS.
NOW TRY AGAIN, YOU FOOL!
YIPE!
GRUMBLE
GRUMBLE
AWW...
HA HA... I JUST TRANSFERRED INTO THIS CLASS. I'VE BEEN MISSING OUT!
YOU KNOW... HE HAS A GOOD GRASP OF THE BASICS. THAT WAS A DECENT IMITATION OF THE HOKAGE...
HMPH...
SWF
TRANS-FORM!!
ONNG

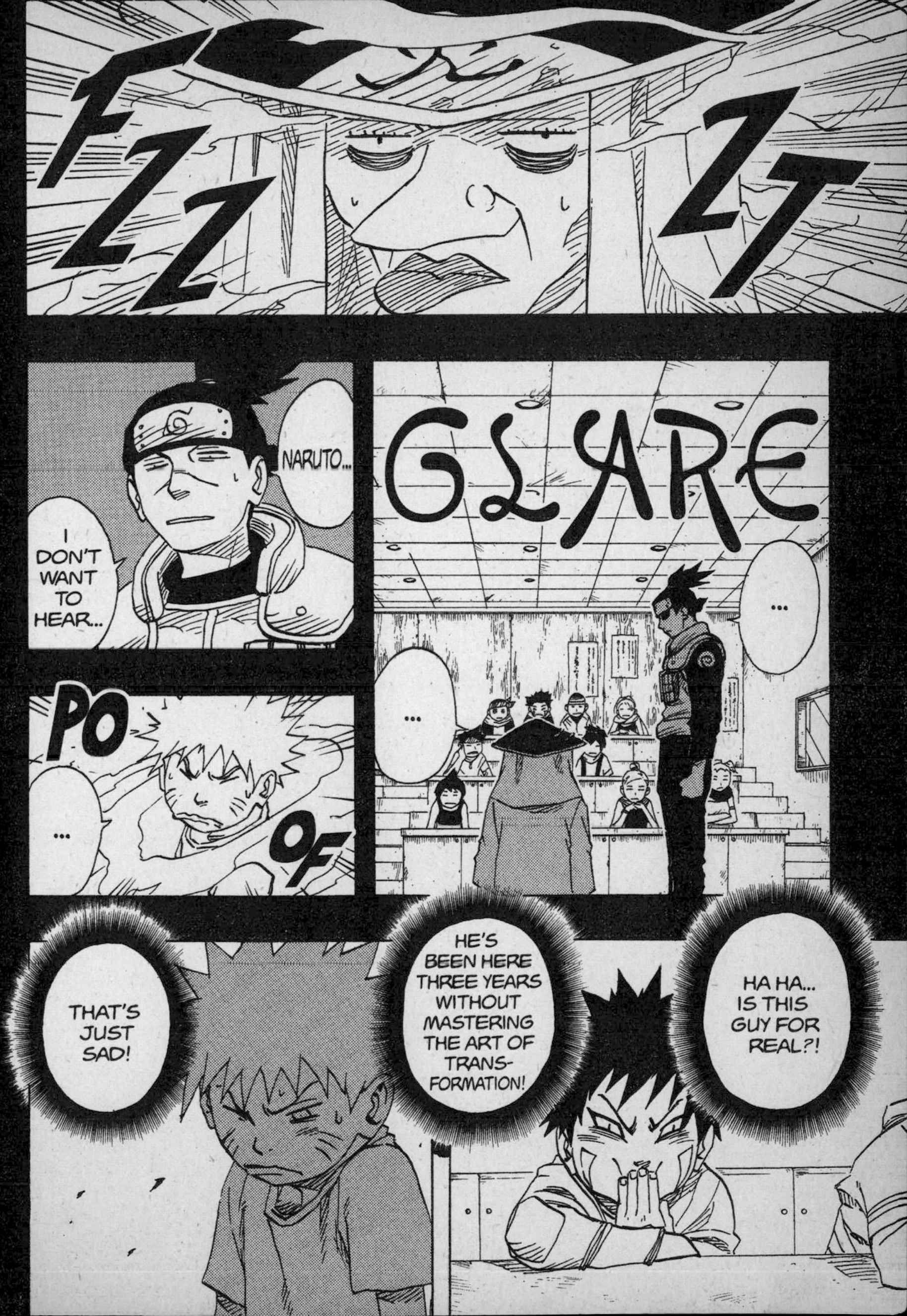
FZZZT
GLARE
...
...
NARUTO...
I DON'T WANT TO HEAR...
POOF
...
HA HA... IS THIS GUY FOR REAL?!
HE'S BEEN HERE THREE YEARS WITHOUT MASTERING THE ART OF TRANS-FORMATION!
THAT'S JUST SAD!

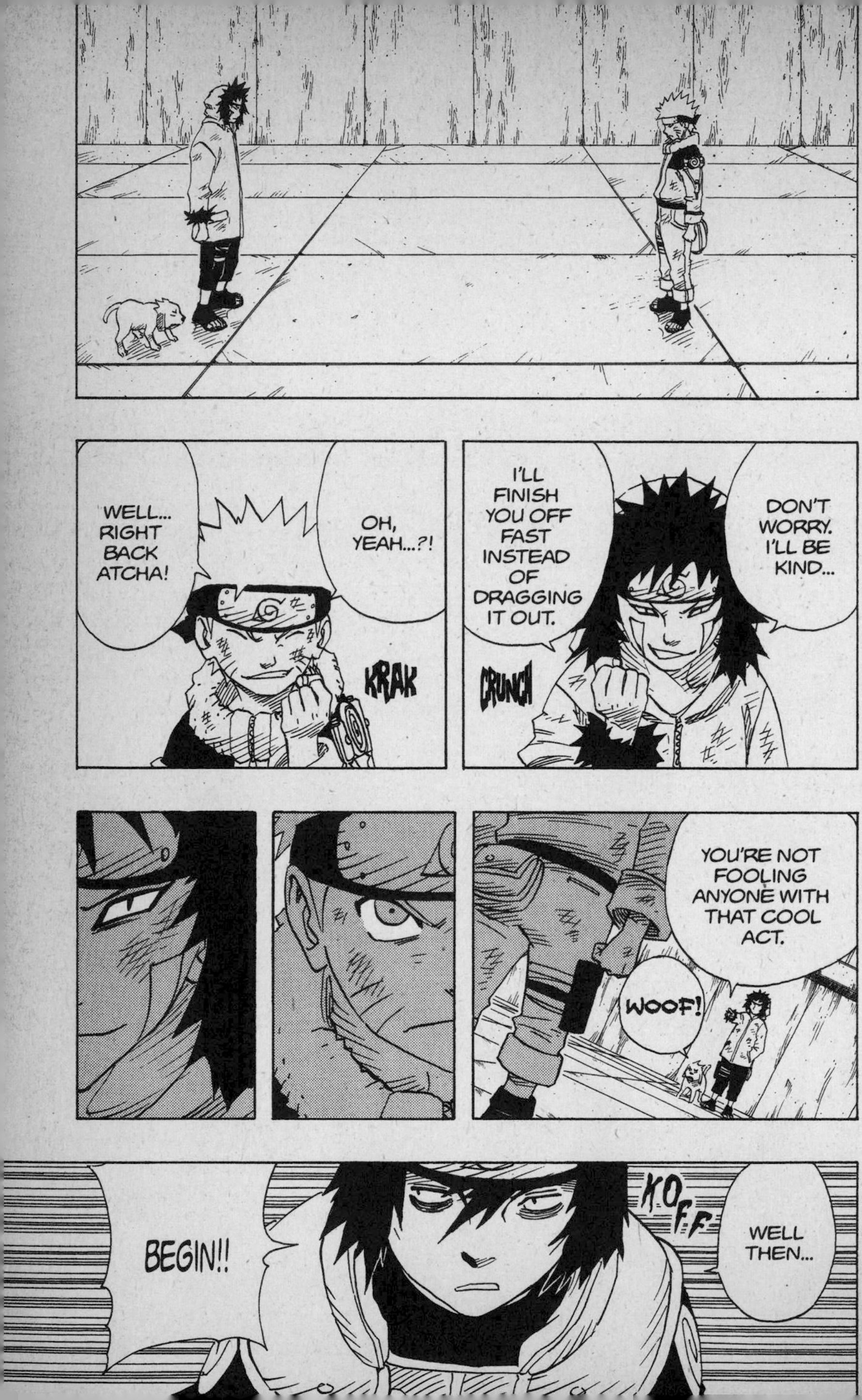
DON'T WORRY. I'LL BE KIND...
I'LL FINISH YOU OFF FAST INSTEAD OF DRAGGING IT OUT.
CRUNCH
OH, YEAH...?!
WELL... RIGHT BACK ATCHA!
KRAK
YOU'RE NOT FOOLING ANYONE WITH THAT COOL ACT.
WOOF!
KOFF
WELL THEN...
BEGIN!!

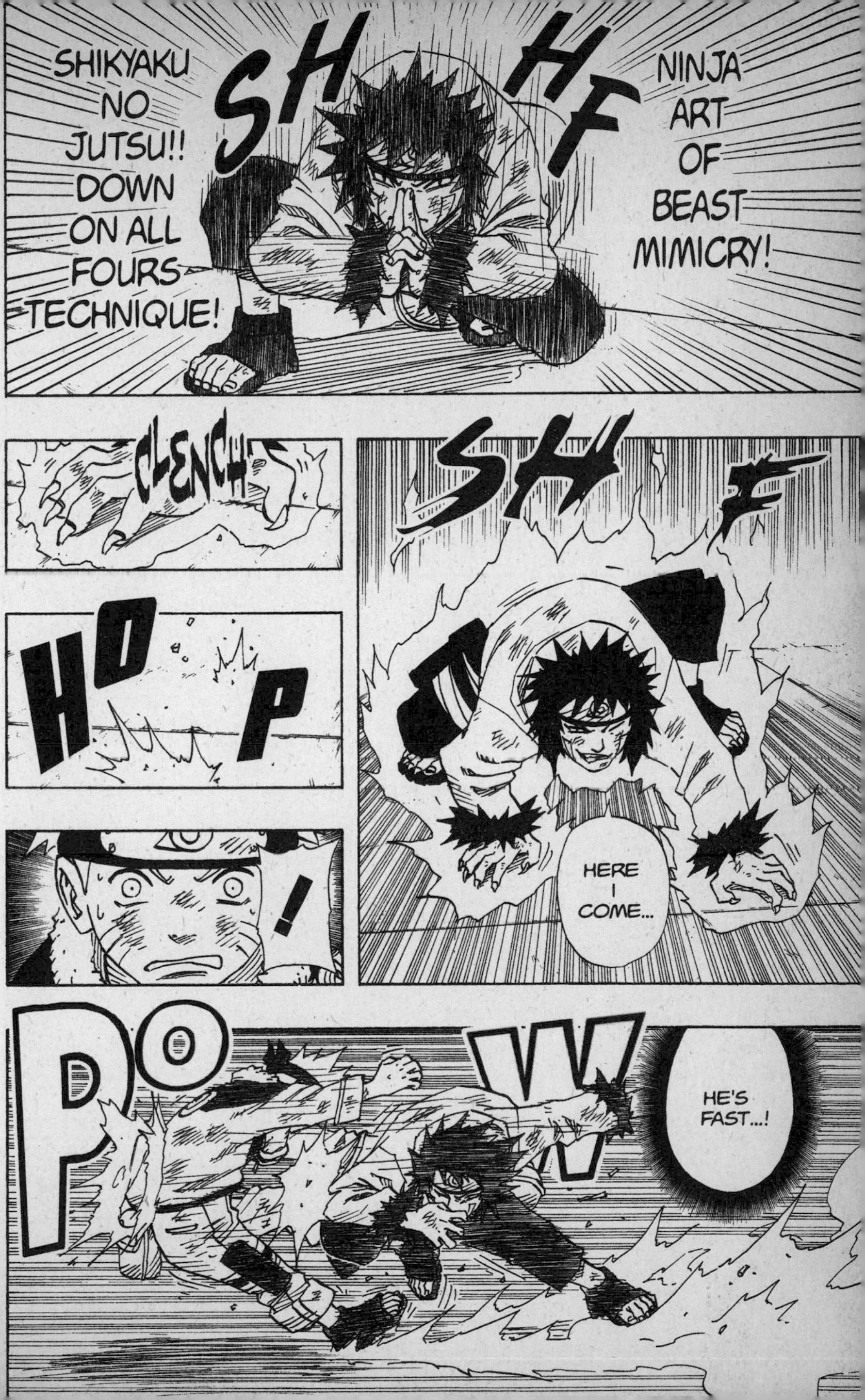
NINJA ART OF BEAST MIMICRY!
SHHF
SHIKYAKU NO JUTSU!! DOWN ON ALL FOURS TECHNIQUE!
SHHF
HERE I COME...
CLENCH
HOP
!
HE'S FAST...!
POW

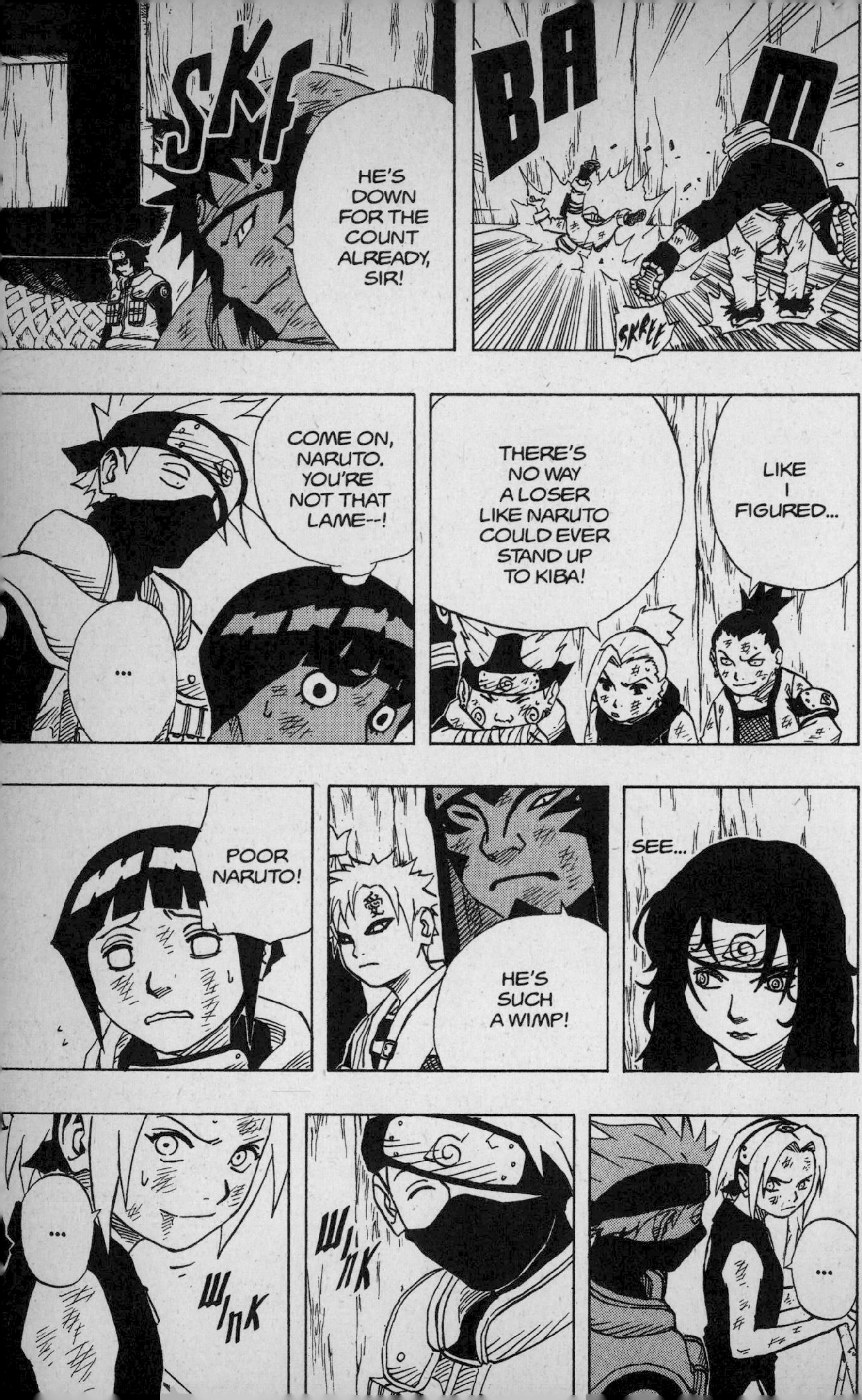
BAM
SKREE
SKF
HE'S DOWN FOR THE COUNT ALREADY, SIR!
LIKE I FIGURED...
THERE'S NO WAY A LOSER LIKE NARUTO COULD EVER STAND UP TO KIBA!
COME ON, NARUTO. YOU'RE NOT THAT LAME--!
...
SEE...
HE'S SUCH A WIMP!
POOR NARUTO!
...
WINK
...
WINK

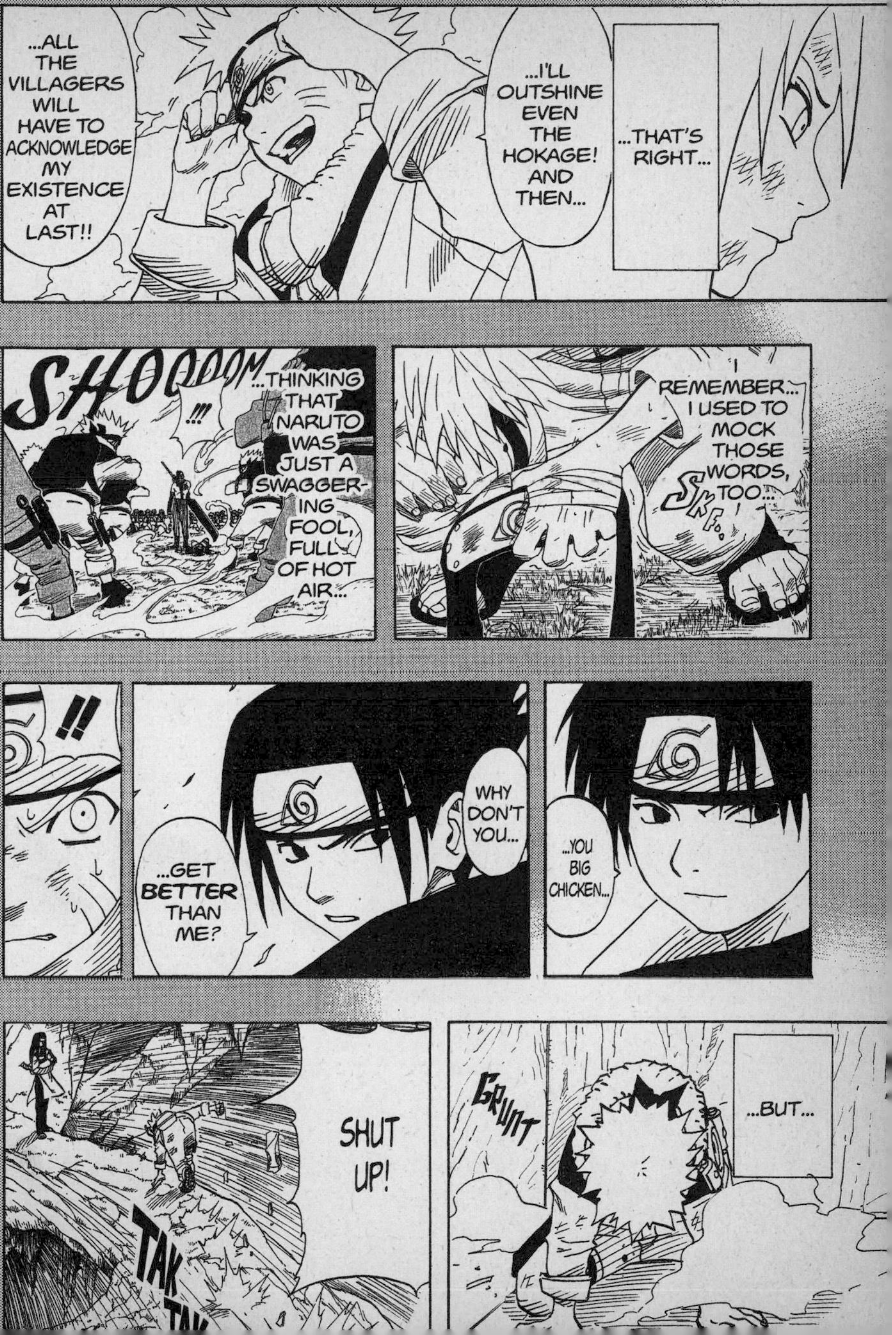
...THAT'S RIGHT...
...I'LL OUTSHINE EVEN THE HOKAGE! AND THEN...
...ALL THE VILLAGERS WILL HAVE TO ACKNOWLEDGE MY EXISTENCE AT LAST!!
I REMEMBER... I USED TO MOCK THOSE WORDS, TOO...
SKF...
...THINKING THAT NARUTO WAS JUST A SWAGGERING FOOL, FULL OF HOT AIR...
!!!
SHOOOOM
...YOU BIG CHICKEN...
WHY DON'T YOU...
...GET BETTER THAN ME?
!!
...BUT...
GRUNT
SHUT UP!
TAK TAK

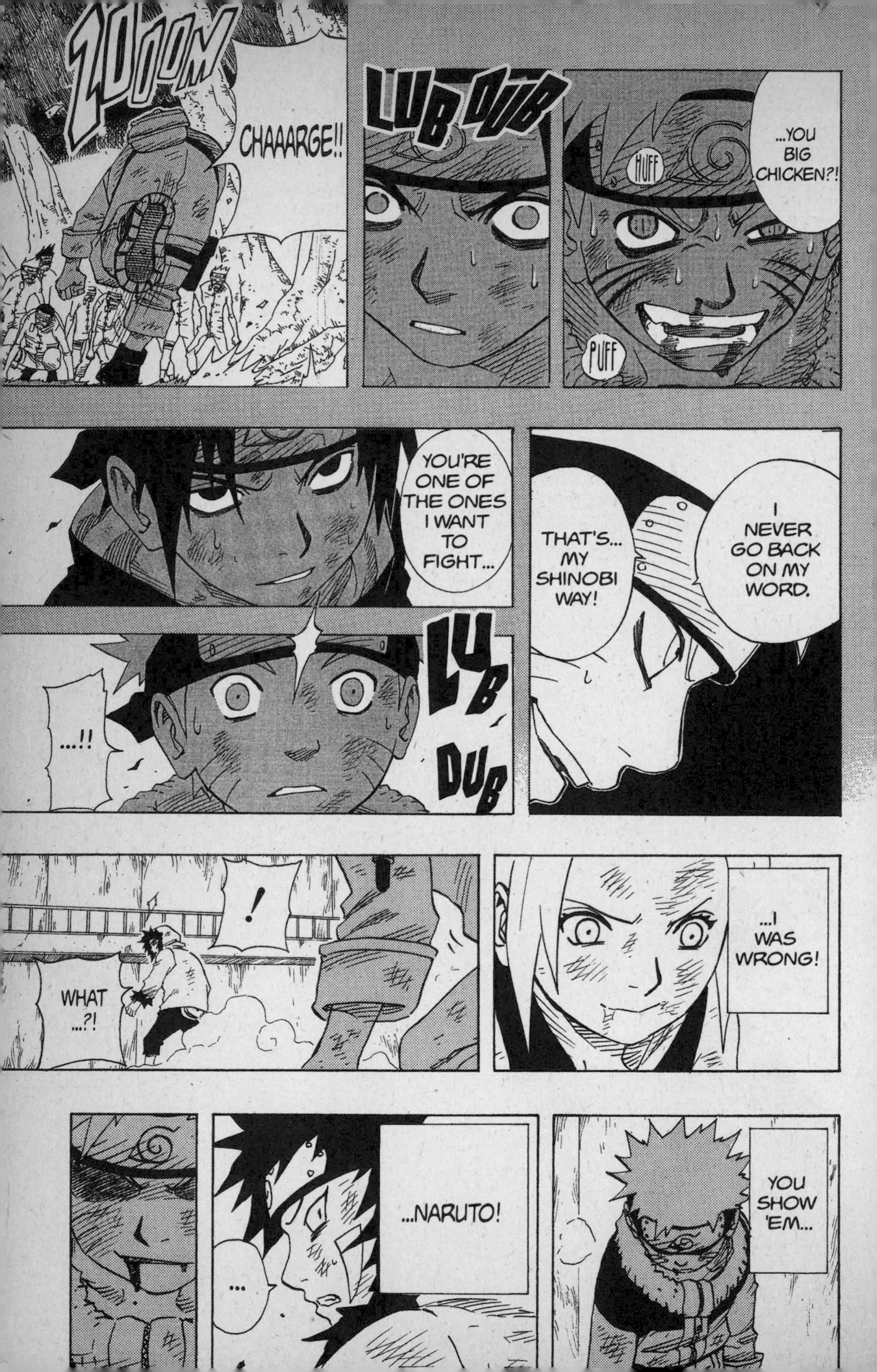
...YOU BIG CHICKEN?!
HUFF
PUFF
LUB DUB
ZOOOM
CHAAARGE!!
I NEVER GO BACK ON MY WORD.
THAT'S... MY SHINOBI WAY!
YOU'RE ONE OF THE ONES I WANT TO FIGHT...
LUB DUB
...!!
...I WAS WRONG!
!
WHAT ...?!
YOU SHOW 'EM...
...NARUTO!
...

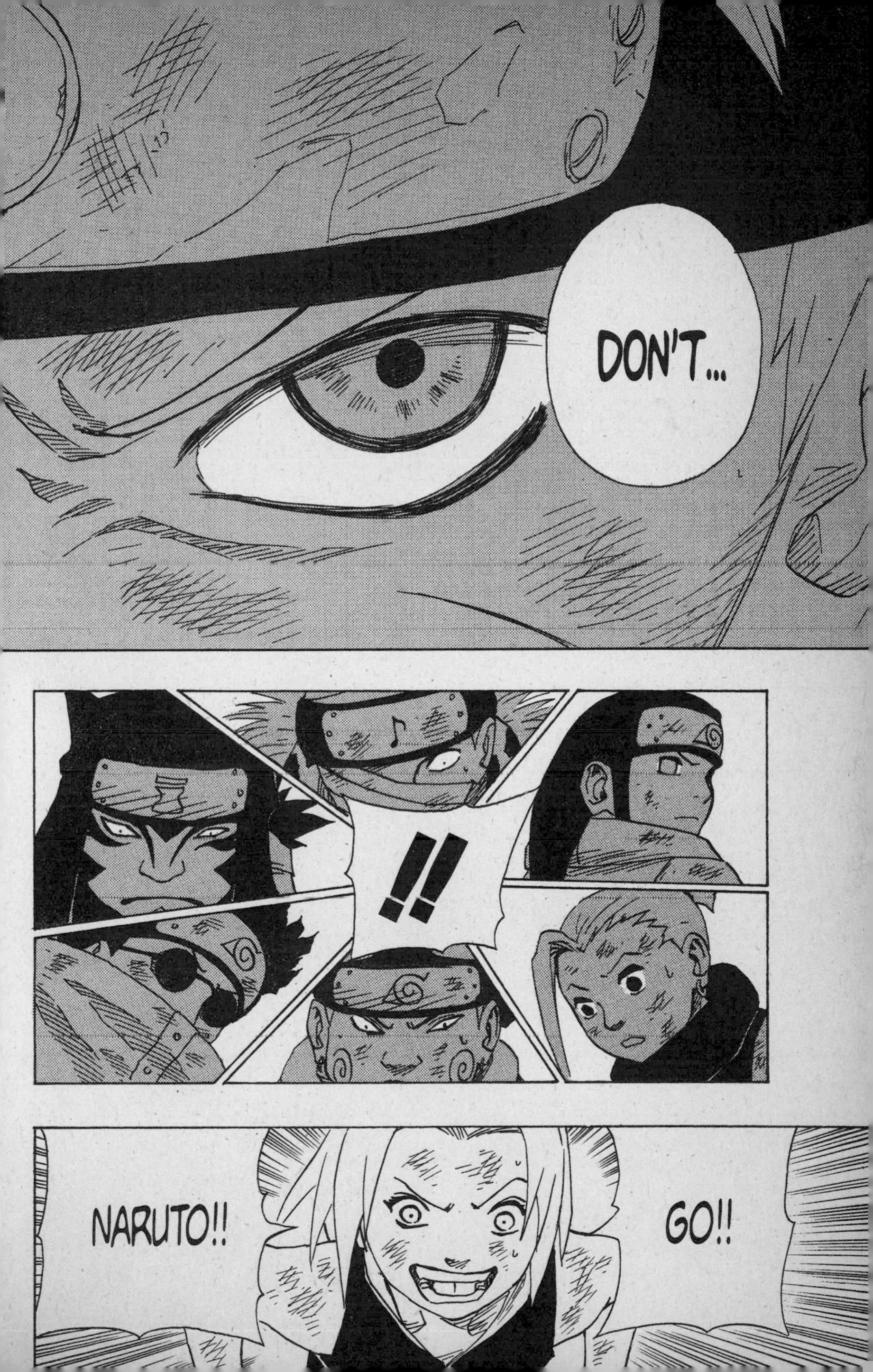
DON'T...
!!
GO!!
NARUTO!!

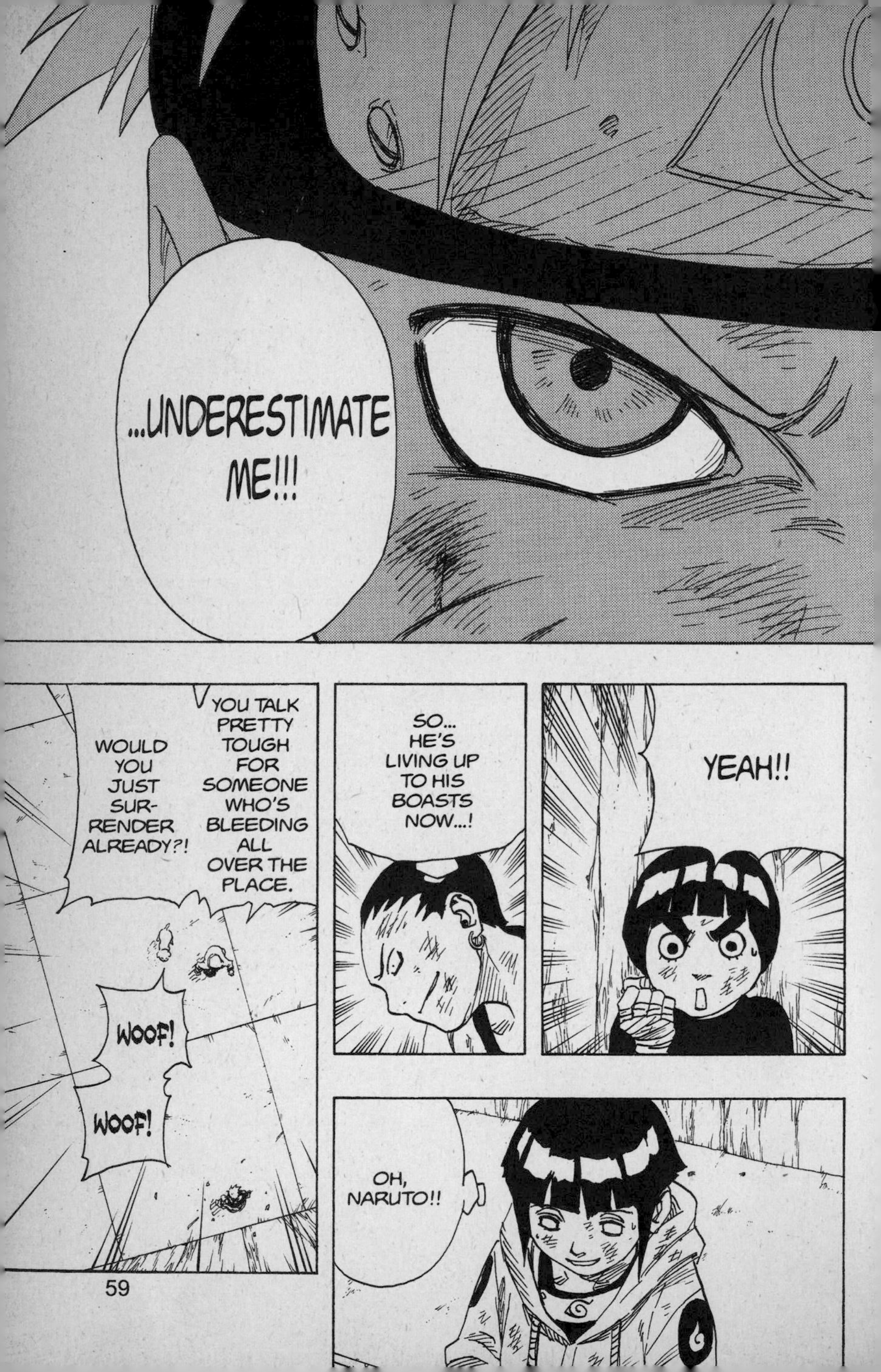
...UNDERESTIMATE ME!!!
YEAH!!
SO... HE'S LIVING UP TO HIS BOASTS NOW...!
OH, NARUTO!!
YOU TALK PRETTY TOUGH FOR SOMEONE WHO'S BLEEDING ALL OVER THE PLACE.
WOULD YOU JUST SUR-RENDER ALREADY?!
WOOF!
WOOF!

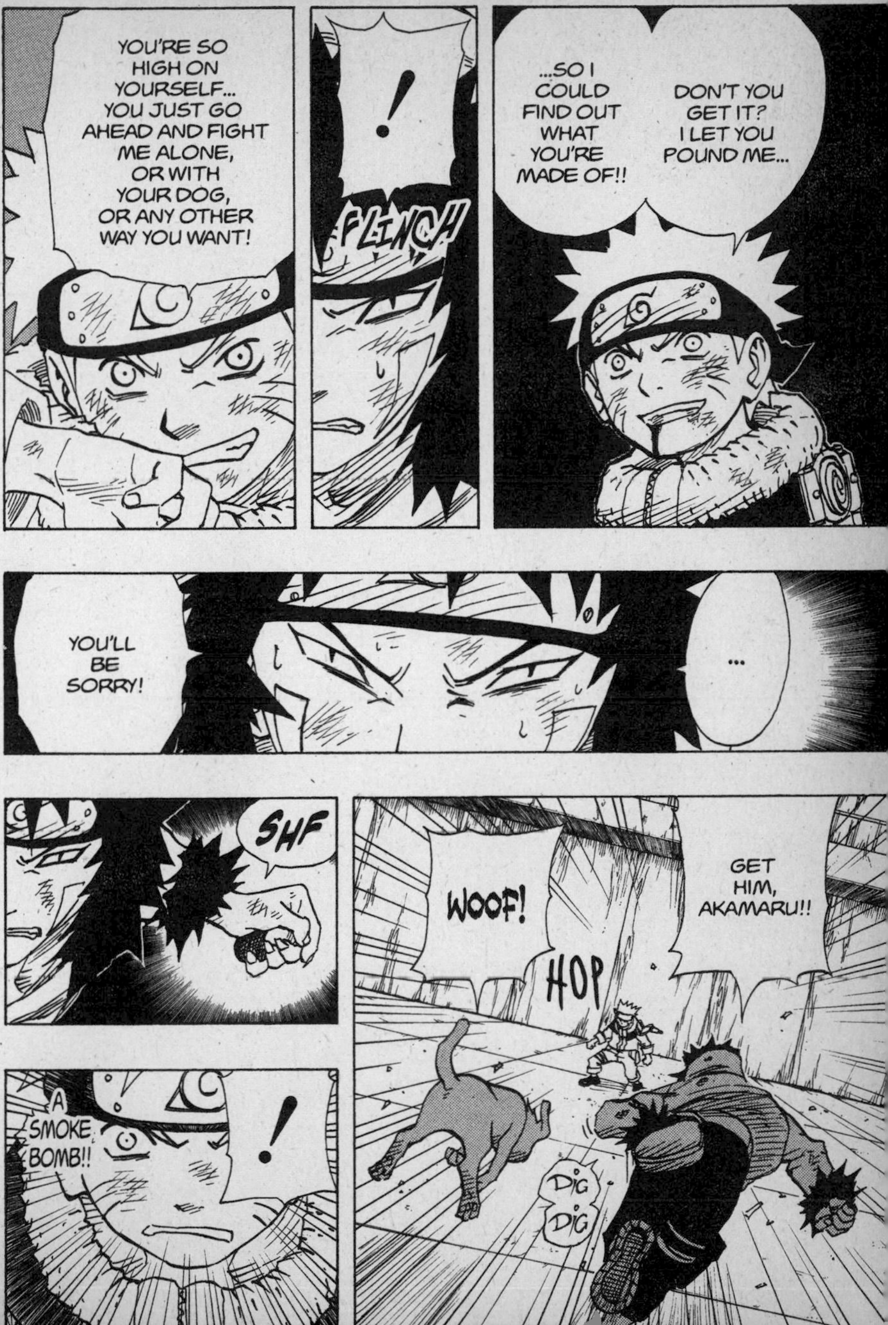
DON'T YOU GET IT? I LET YOU POUND ME...
...SO I COULD FIND OUT WHAT YOU'RE MADE OF!!
!
FLINCH
YOU'RE SO HIGH ON YOURSELF... YOU JUST GO AHEAD AND FIGHT ME ALONE, OR WITH YOUR DOG, OR ANY OTHER WAY YOU WANT!
...
YOU'LL BE SORRY!
GET HIM, AKAMARU!!
WOOF!
HOP
DIG DIG
SHF
!
A SMOKE BOMB!!

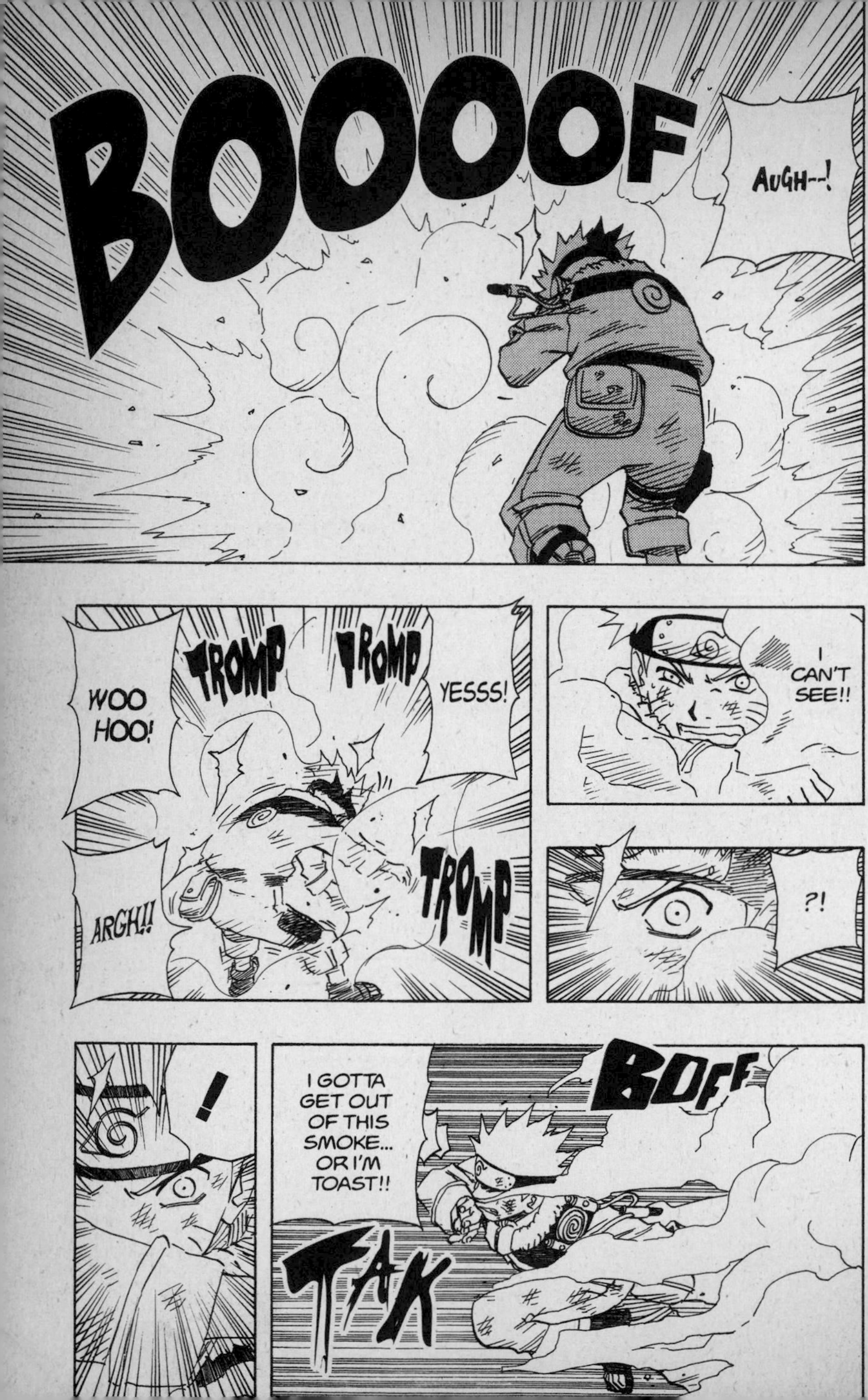

AUGH--!
BOOOOF
I CAN'T SEE!!
?!
YESSS!
TROMP
TROMP
WOO HOO!
TROMP
ARGH!!
BOFF
I GOTTA GET OUT OF THIS SMOKE... OR I'M TOAST!!
TAK
!

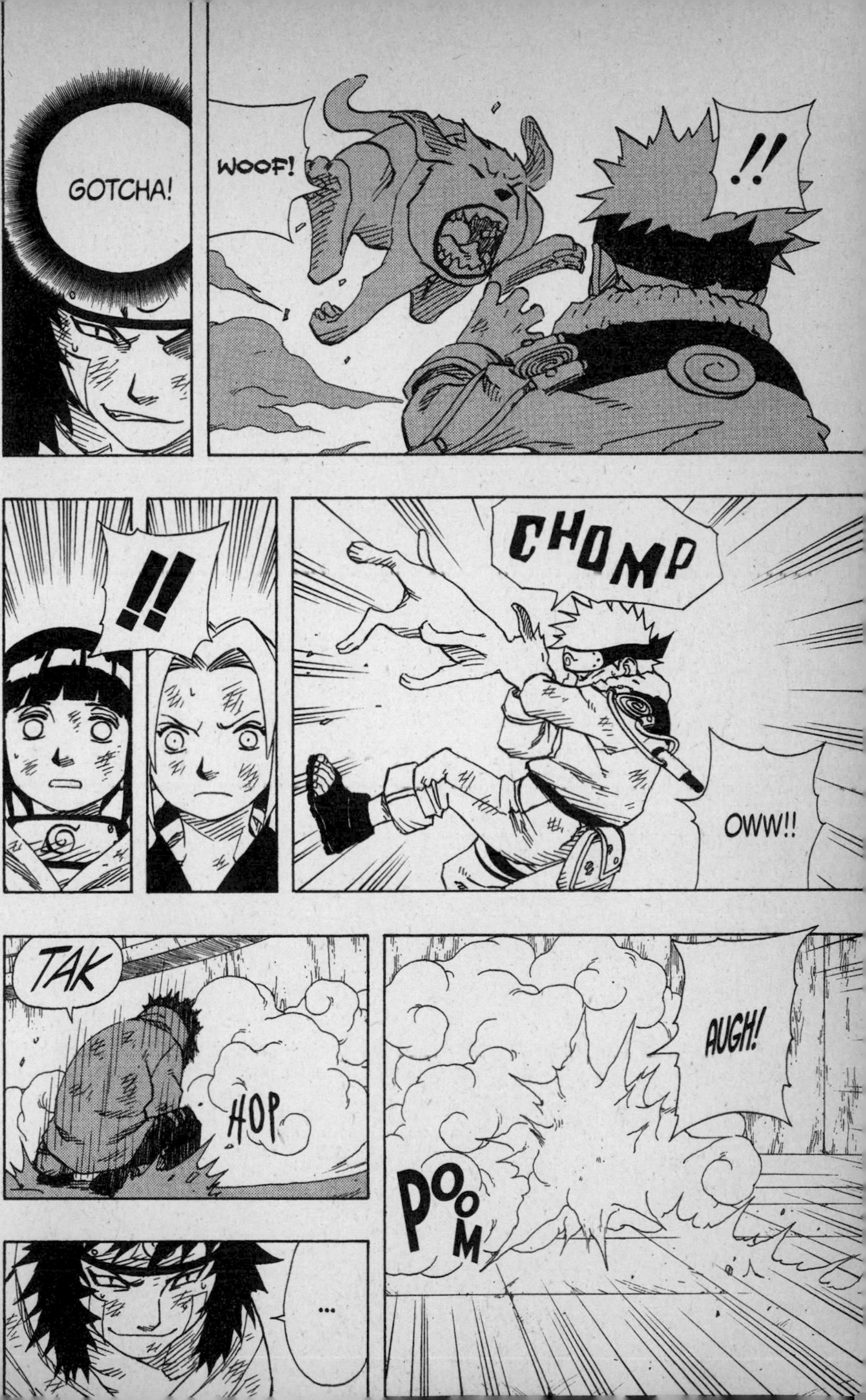
!!
WOOF!
GOTCHA!
CHOMP
OWW!!
!!
AUGH!
POOM
TAK
HOP
...

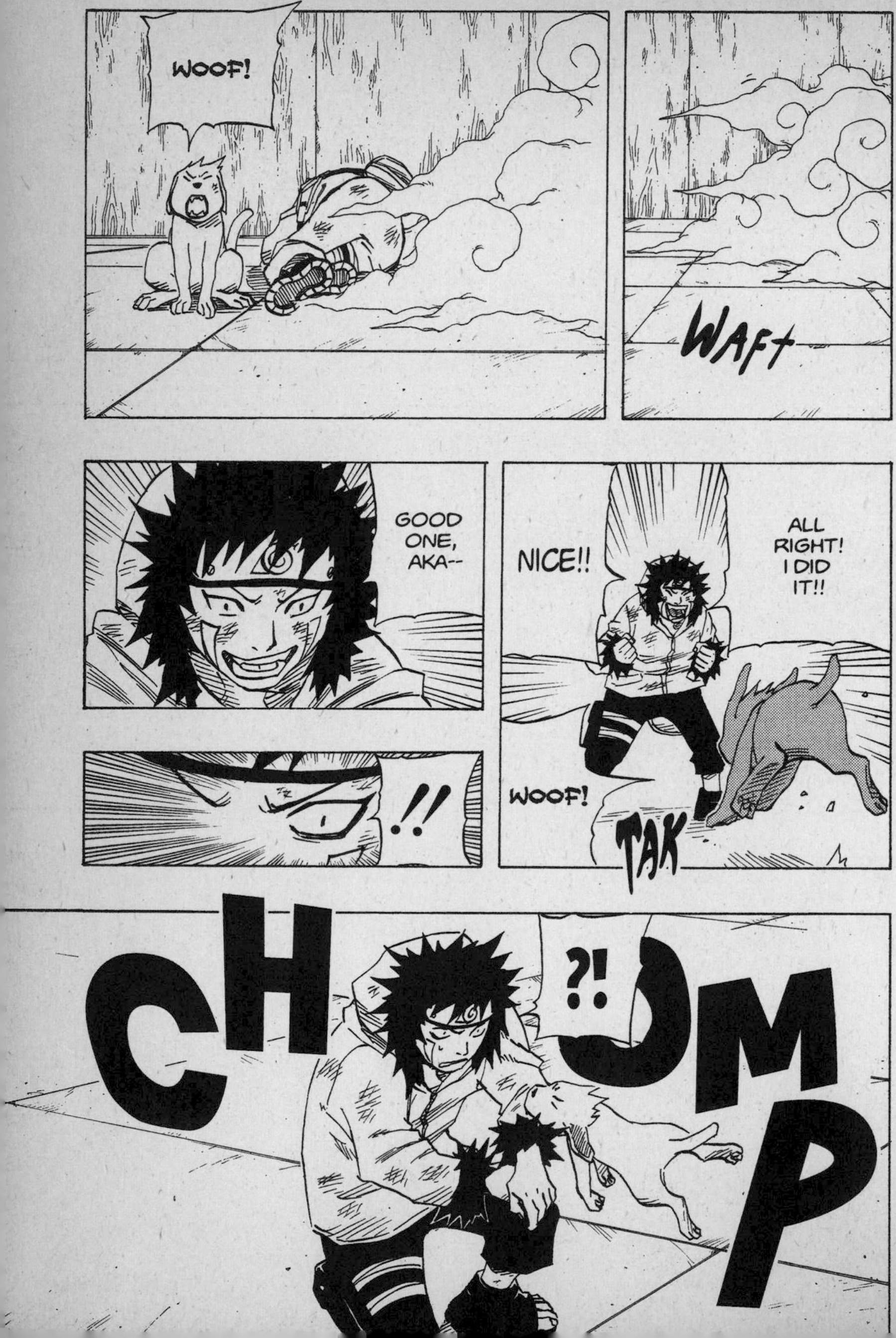
WAFT
WOOF!
ALL RIGHT! I DID IT!!
NICE!!
WOOF!
TAK
GOOD ONE, AKA--
!!
?!
CHOMP

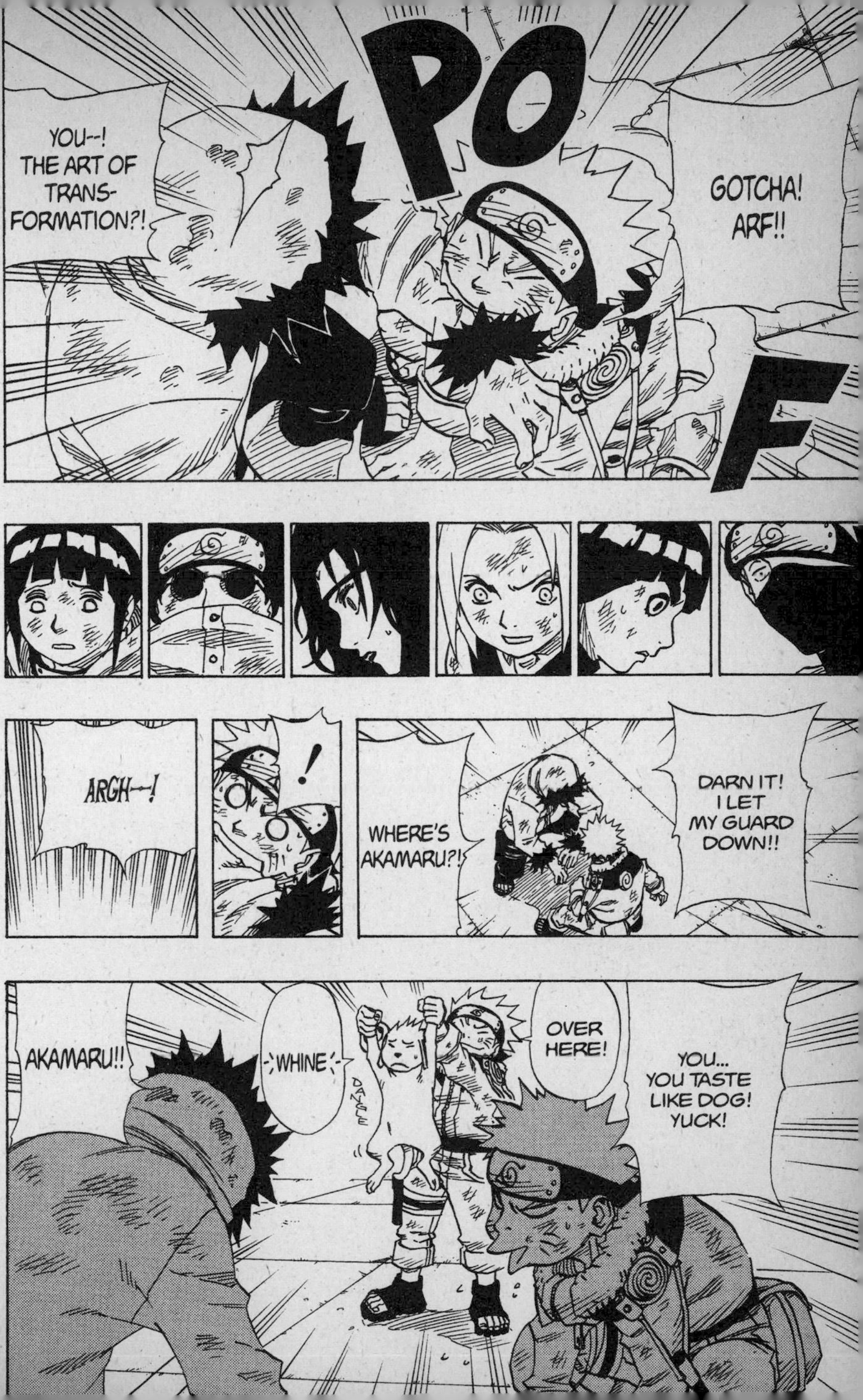
PO
F
GOTCHA! ARF!!
YOU--! THE ART OF TRANSFORMATION?!
DARN IT! I LET MY GUARD DOWN!!
WHERE'S AKAMARU?!
!
ARGH--!
YOU... YOU TASTE LIKE DOG! YUCK!
OVER HERE!
DANGLE
WHINE
AKAMARU!!

READ THIS WAY

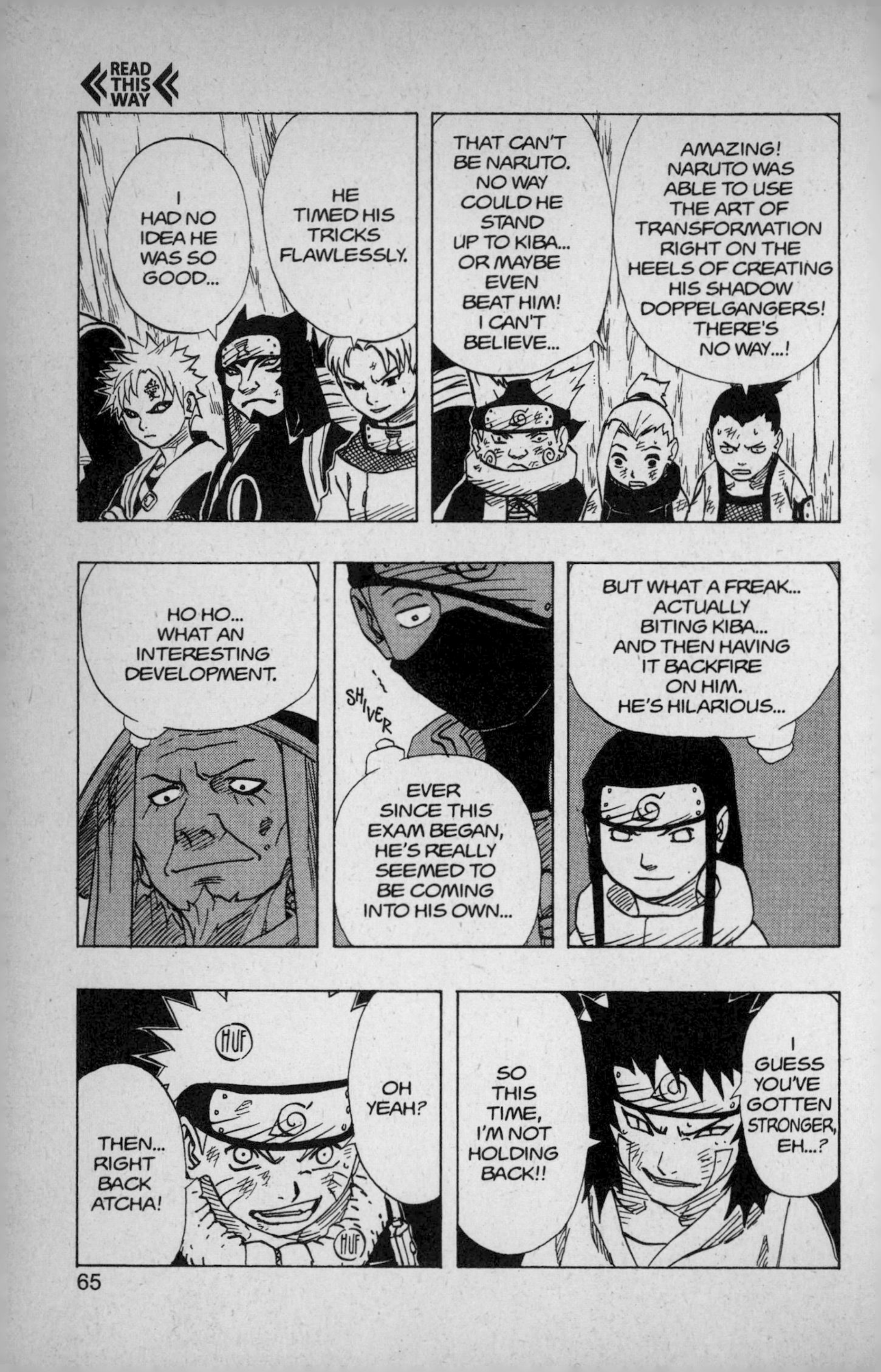
AMAZING! NARUTO WAS ABLE TO USE THE ART OF TRANSFORMATION RIGHT ON THE HEELS OF CREATING HIS SHADOW DOPPELGANGERS! THERE'S NO WAY...!
THAT CAN'T BE NARUTO. NO WAY COULD HE STAND UP TO KIBA... OR MAYBE EVEN BEAT HIM! I CAN'T BELIEVE...
HE TIMED HIS TRICKS FLAWLESSLY.
I HAD NO IDEA HE WAS SO GOOD...
BUT WHAT A FREAK... ACTUALLY BITING KIBA... AND THEN HAVING IT BACKFIRE ON HIM. HE'S HILARIOUS...
SHIVER
EVER SINCE THIS EXAM BEGAN, HE'S REALLY SEEMED TO BE COMING INTO HIS OWN...
HO HO... WHAT AN INTERESTING DEVELOPMENT.
I GUESS YOU'VE GOTTEN STRONGER, EH...?
SO THIS TIME, I'M NOT HOLDING BACK!!
HUF
OH YEAH?
THEN... RIGHT BACK ATCHA!
HUF

THE WORLD OF KISHIMOTO MASASHI
MY PERSONAL HISTORY, PART 9

FOR ME, JUNIOR HIGH SCHOOL WAS ALL ABOUT BASEBALL,
AND DURING EVERY SUMMER VACATION WE HAD TRAINING
CAMP. AT OUR SCHOOL, THE ENTIRE BASEBALL CLUB WENT
TO SHODO ISLAND, FAMOUS FOR ITS OLIVES AND ITS MONKEYS.
EVEN WHILE ON THE TRIP, EVERYONE WAS REQUIRED TO WEAR
OUR BLACK SCHOOL UNIFORM PANTS WITH WHITE SHIRTS.
THE NUMBER OF MEMBERS IN THE BASEBALL CLUB USUALLY
TOTALED ABOUT 45, AND WE WOULD RENT A BUS AND SET
OUT FOR CAMP WITH GREAT POMP AND SPLENDOR.
WE HAD GOOD TIMES -- AND MORE THAN A LITTLE PAIN --
DURING OUR STAYS ON SHODO ISLAND, AND IT WAS OUR
TRADITION TO END THE EXPERIENCE EACH SUMMER BY
CLIMBING THE LOCAL TOURIST RESORT'S "MONKEY MOUNTAIN"
RIGHT BEFORE WE LEFT.
...IF I REMEMBER CORRECTLY, IT WAS WHEN I WAS IN THE
EIGHTH GRADE THAT I WAS INVOLVED IN AN INCIDENT SO
TERRIBLE THAT ITS INFAMY IS UNPARALLELED IN THE ANNALS
OF THE TRAINING CAMP HISTORY -- A DISASTROUS EVENT THAT
COULD HAVE GOTTEN A LOT OF PEOPLE KILLED. WHENEVER
I RECALL WHAT I DID AND WHAT HAPPENED I WISH I COULD
FORGET... BUT I'M RUNNING OUT OF IDEAS FOR THIS FEATURE
NOW, SO I'M GOING TO FINALLY TELL THE TALE...

...NEXT TIME.

TO BE CONTINUED...

Number 76: Kiba Turns the Tables... ...and So Does Naruto?!

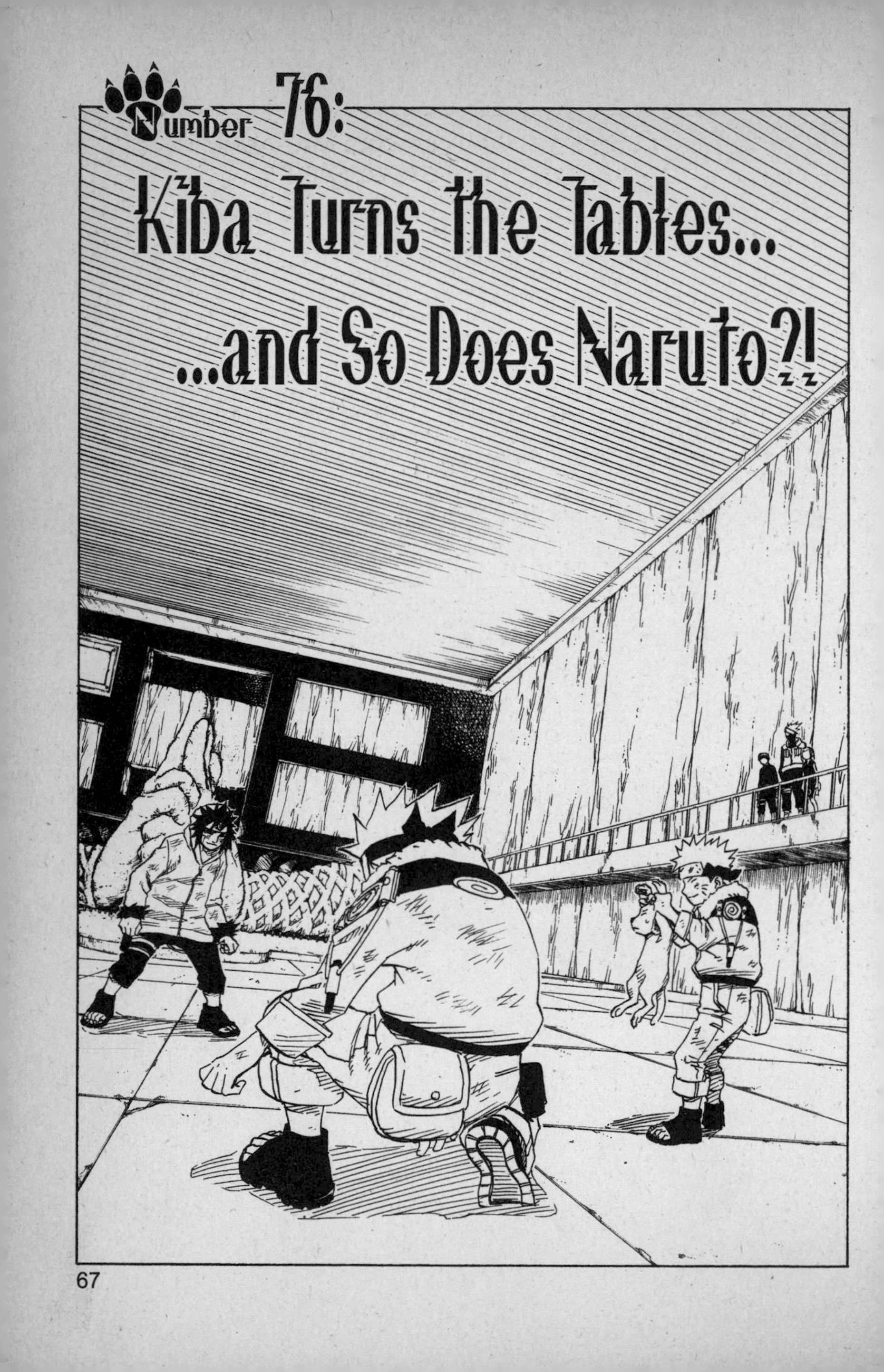

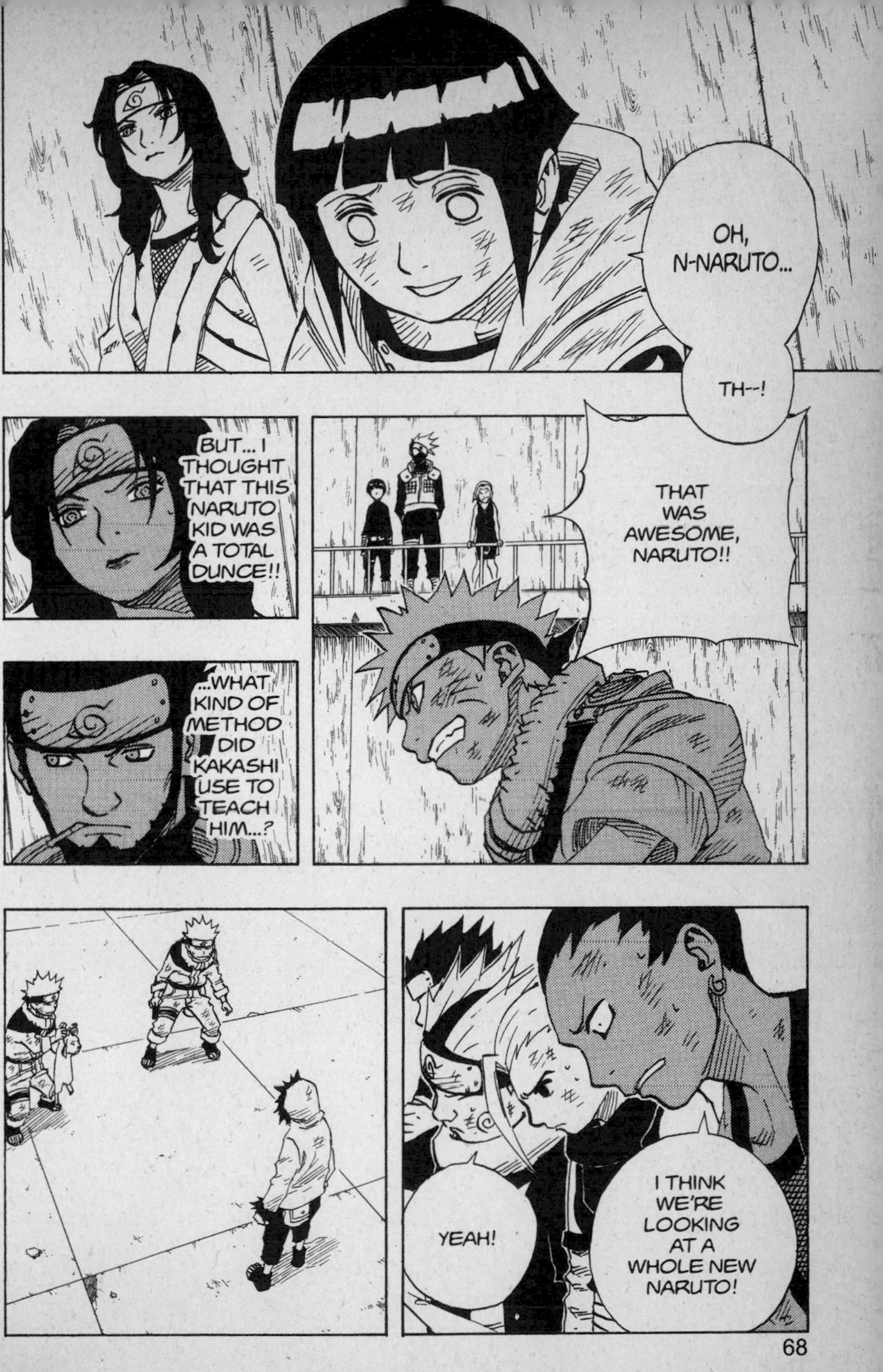
OH, N-NARUTO...
TH--!
THAT WAS AWESOME, NARUTO!!
BUT... I THOUGHT THAT THIS NARUTO KID WAS A TOTAL DUNCE!!
...WHAT KIND OF METHOD DID KAKASHI USE TO TEACH HIM...?
I THINK WE'RE LOOKING AT A WHOLE NEW NARUTO!
YEAH!

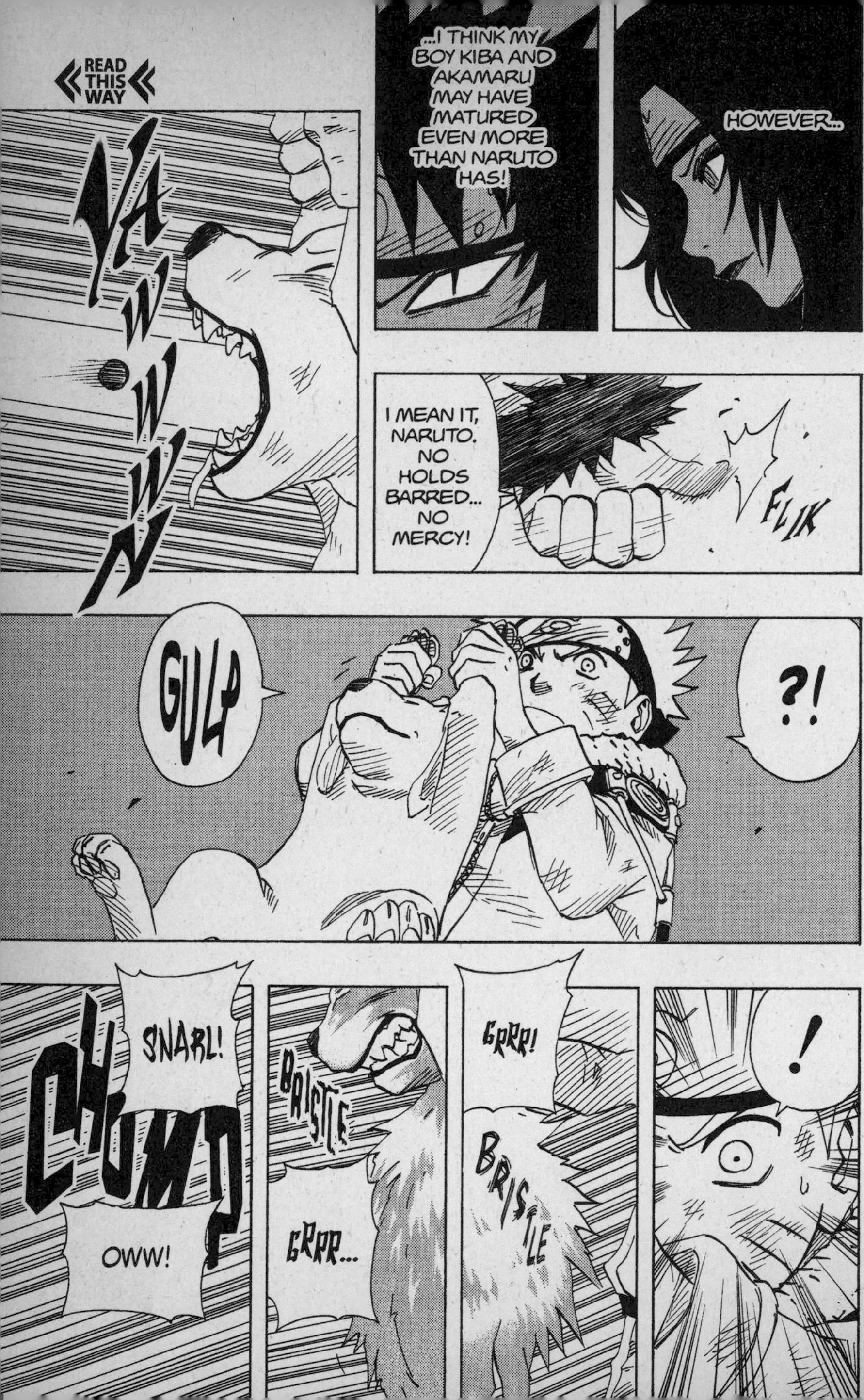

READ THIS WAY
HOWEVER...
...I THINK MY BOY KIBA AND AKAMARU MAY HAVE MATURED EVEN MORE THAN NARUTO HAS!
I MEAN IT, NARUTO. NO HOLDS BARRED... NO MERCY!
FLIK
YAWWWWWN
?!
GULP
!
GRRR!
BRISTLE
BRISTLE
GRRR...
SNARL!
CHOMP
OWW!

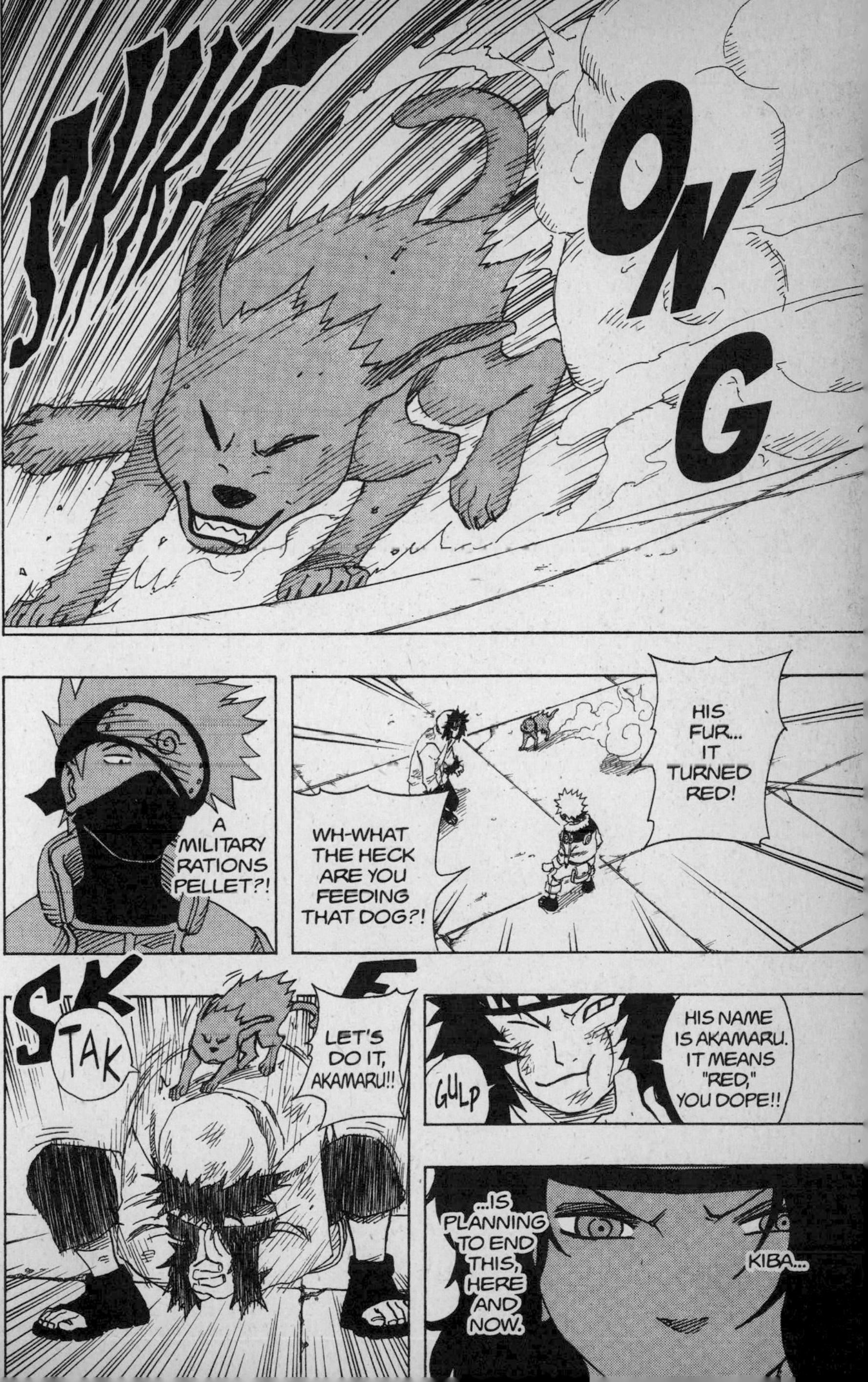
ONG
HIS FUR... IT TURNED RED!
WH-WHAT THE HECK ARE YOU FEEDING THAT DOG?!
A MILITARY RATIONS PELLET?!
HIS NAME IS AKAMARU. IT MEANS "RED," YOU DOPE!!
GULP
KIBA...
...IS PLANNING TO END THIS, HERE AND NOW.
LET'S DO IT, AKAMARU!!
TAK

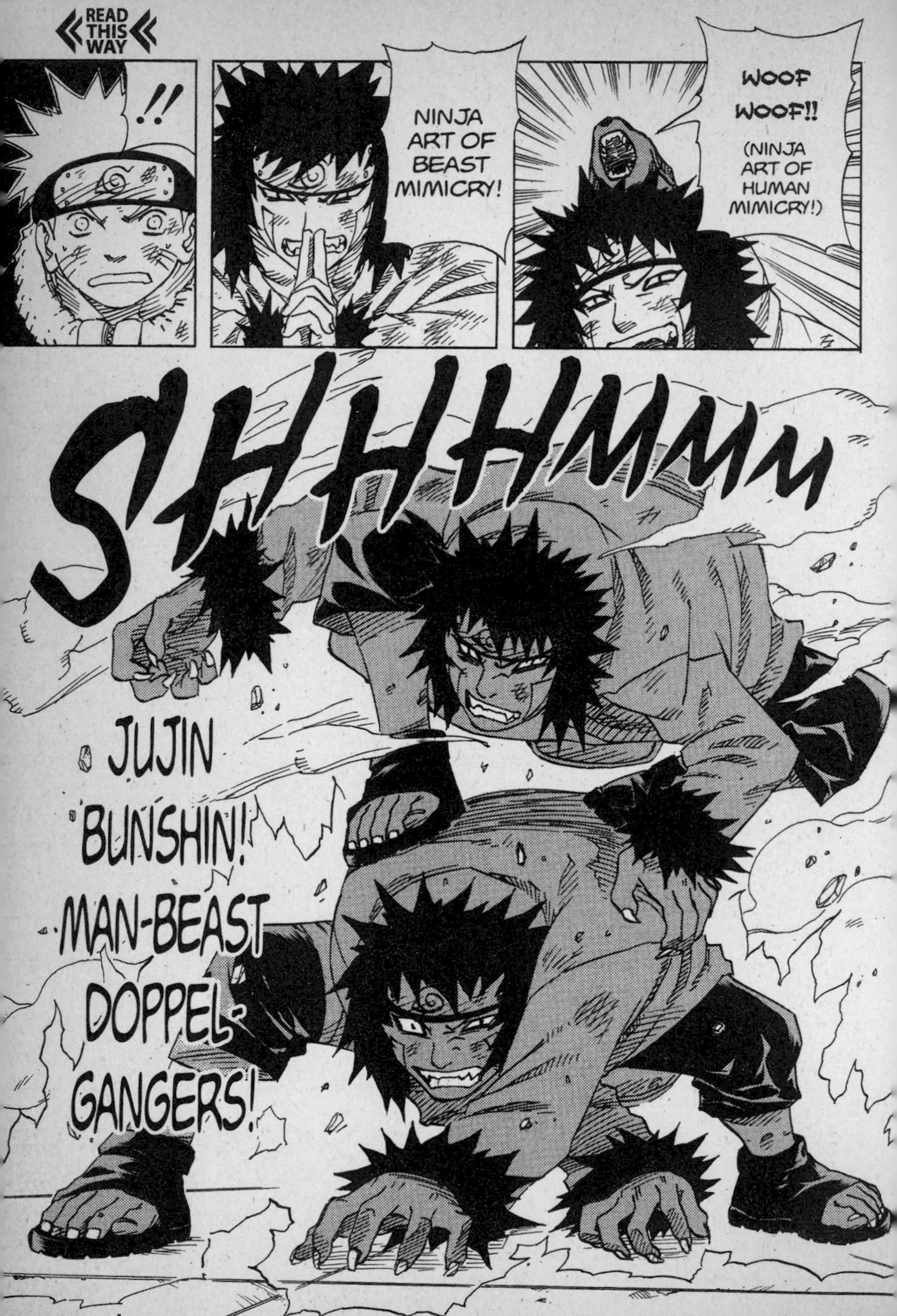
READ THIS WAY
WOOF WOOF!!
(NINJA ART OF HUMAN MIMICRY!)
NINJA ART OF BEAST MIMICRY!
!!
SHHHMMM
JUJIN BUNSHIN! MAN-BEAST DOPPEL-GANGERS!

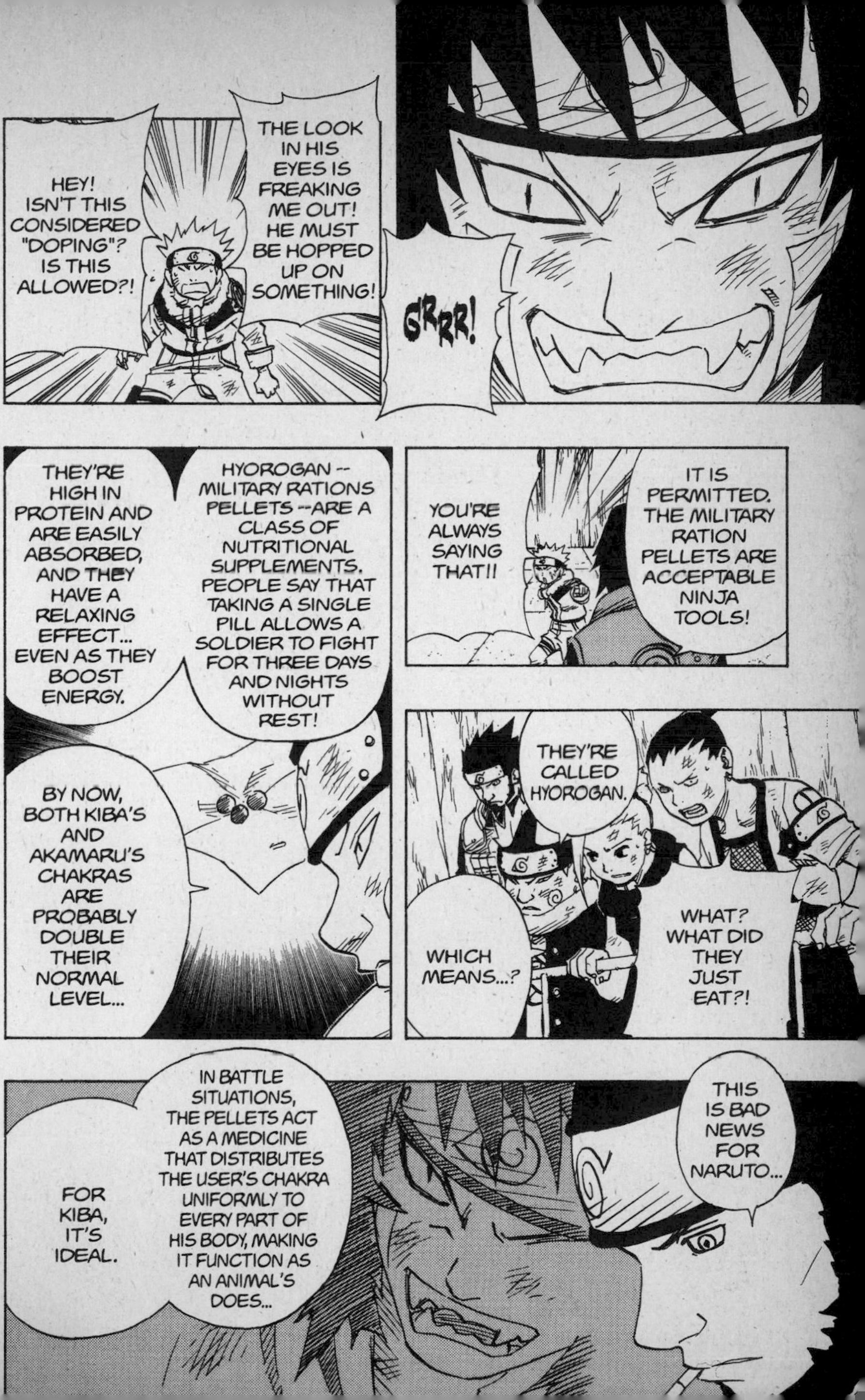
GRRR!
THE LOOK IN HIS EYES IS FREAKING ME OUT! HE MUST BE HOPPED UP ON SOMETHING!
HEY! ISN'T THIS CONSIDERED "DOPING"? IS THIS ALLOWED?!
IT IS PERMITTED. THE MILITARY RATION PELLETS ARE ACCEPTABLE NINJA TOOLS!
YOU'RE ALWAYS SAYING THAT!!
WHAT? WHAT DID THEY JUST EAT?!
THEY'RE CALLED HYOROGAN.
WHICH MEANS...?
HYOROGAN -- MILITARY RATIONS PELLETS -- ARE A CLASS OF NUTRITIONAL SUPPLEMENTS. PEOPLE SAY THAT TAKING A SINGLE PILL ALLOWS A SOLDIER TO FIGHT FOR THREE DAYS AND NIGHTS WITHOUT REST!
THEY'RE HIGH IN PROTEIN AND ARE EASILY ABSORBED, AND THEY HAVE A RELAXING EFFECT... EVEN AS THEY BOOST ENERGY.
BY NOW, BOTH KIBA'S AND AKAMARU'S CHAKRAS ARE PROBABLY DOUBLE THEIR NORMAL LEVEL...
THIS IS BAD NEWS FOR NARUTO...
IN BATTLE SITUATIONS, THE PELLETS ACT AS A MEDICINE THAT DISTRIBUTES THE USER'S CHAKRA UNIFORMLY TO EVERY PART OF HIS BODY, MAKING IT FUNCTION AS AN ANIMAL'S DOES...
FOR KIBA, IT'S IDEAL.

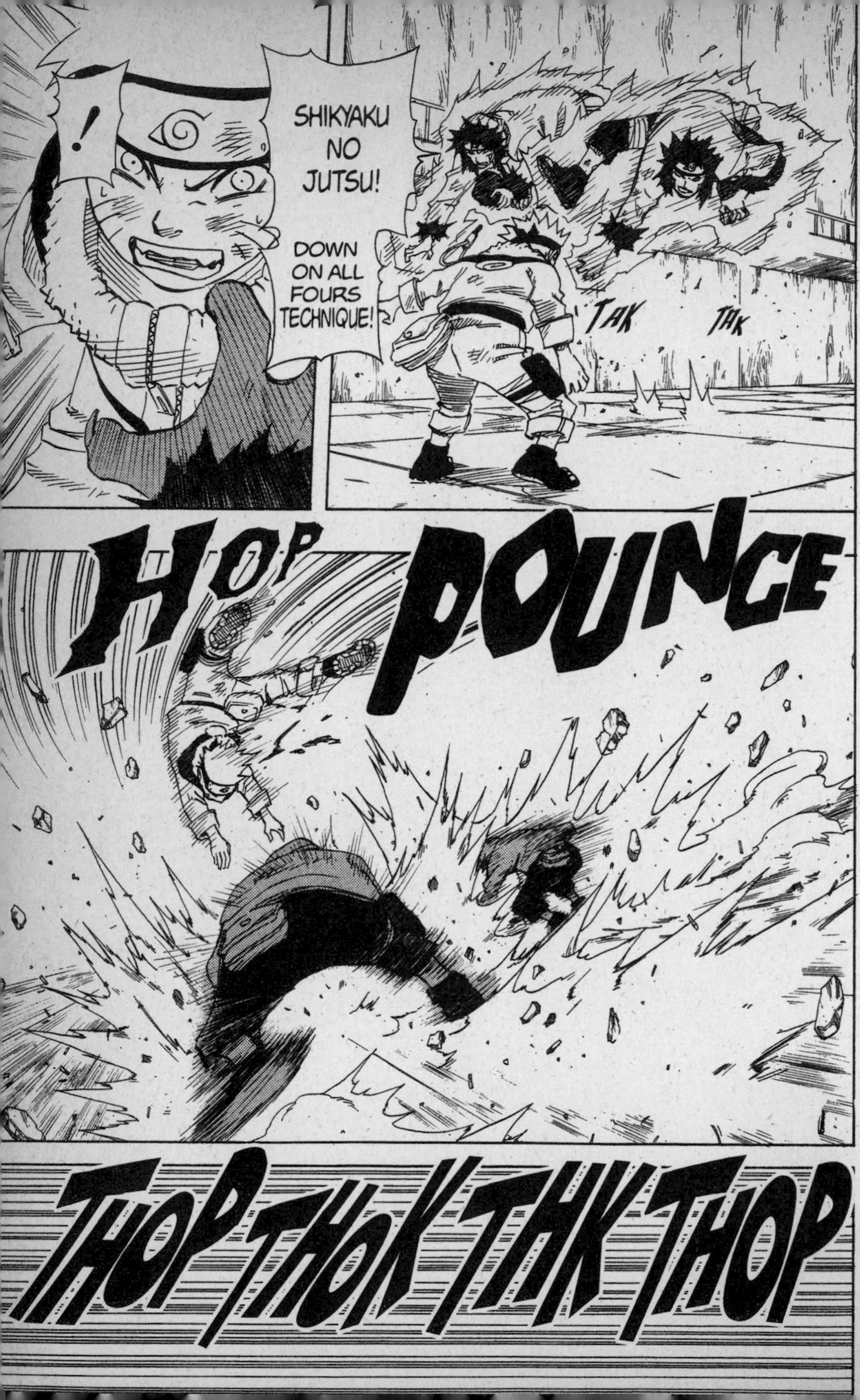
SHIKYAKU NO JUTSU!
DOWN ON ALL FOURS TECHNIQUE!
TAK
TAK
!
HOP
POUNCE
THOP THOK THK THOP

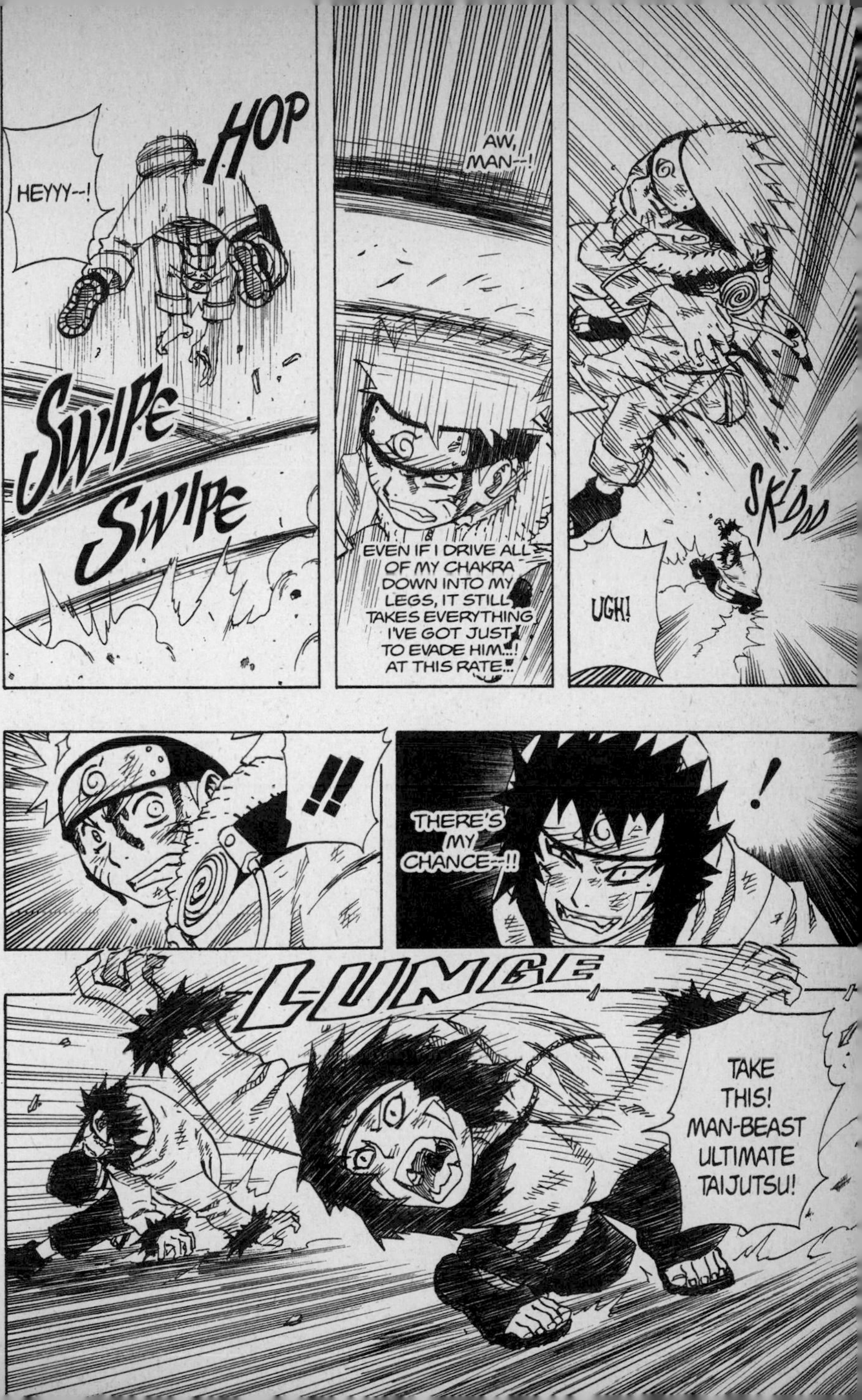
SKIDDD
UGH!
AW, MAN--!
EVEN IF I DRIVE ALL OF MY CHAKRA DOWN INTO MY LEGS, IT STILL TAKES EVERYTHING I'VE GOT JUST TO EVADE HIM...! AT THIS RATE...
HOP
HEYYY--!
SWIPE
SWIPE
!
THERE'S MY CHANCE--!!
!!
LUNGE
TAKE THIS! MAN-BEAST ULTIMATE TAIJUTSU!

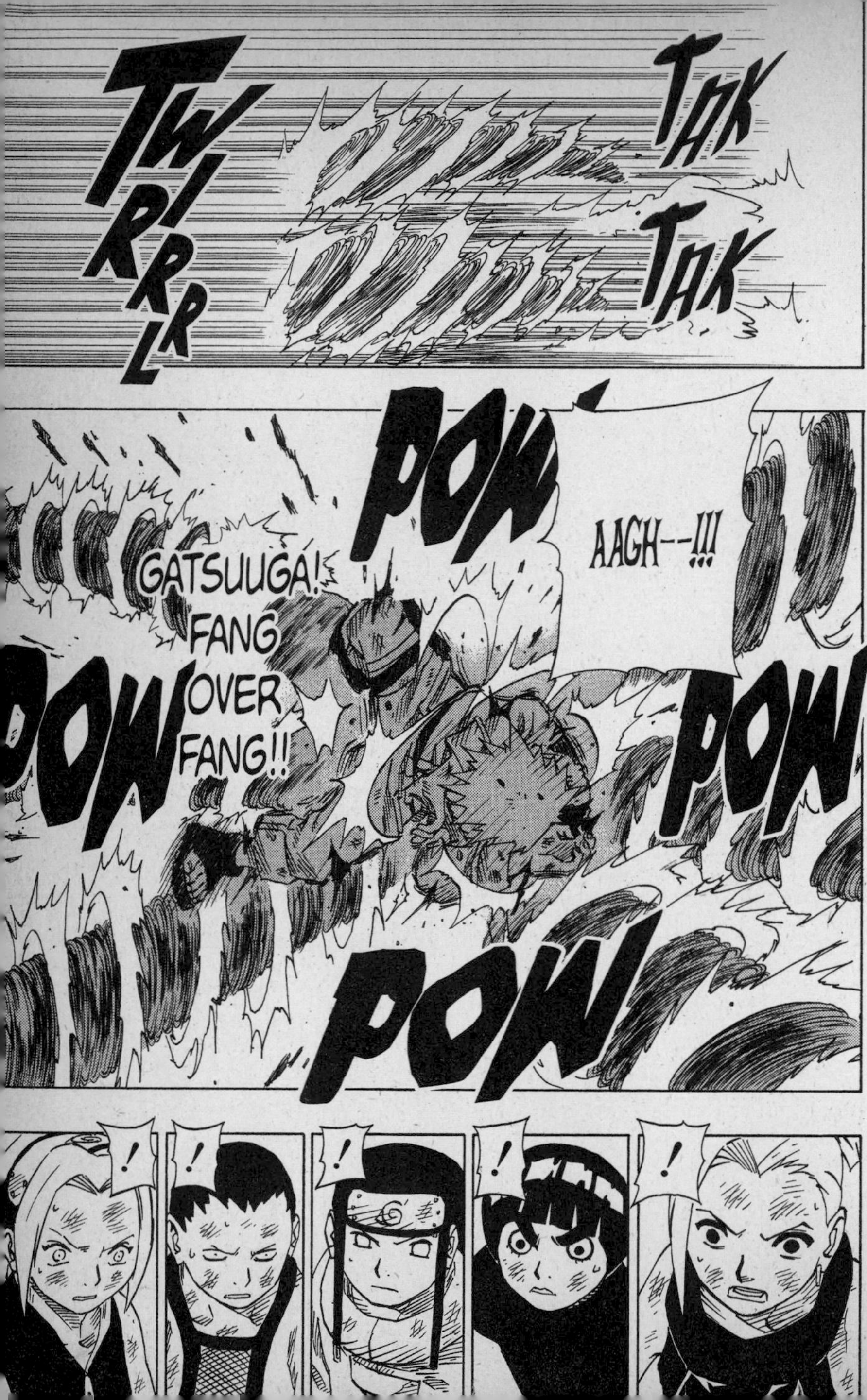
TAK
TAK
TWIRRRRL
AAGH--!!!
POW
POW
GATSUUGA! FANG OVER FANG!!
POW
POW
!
!
!
!
!

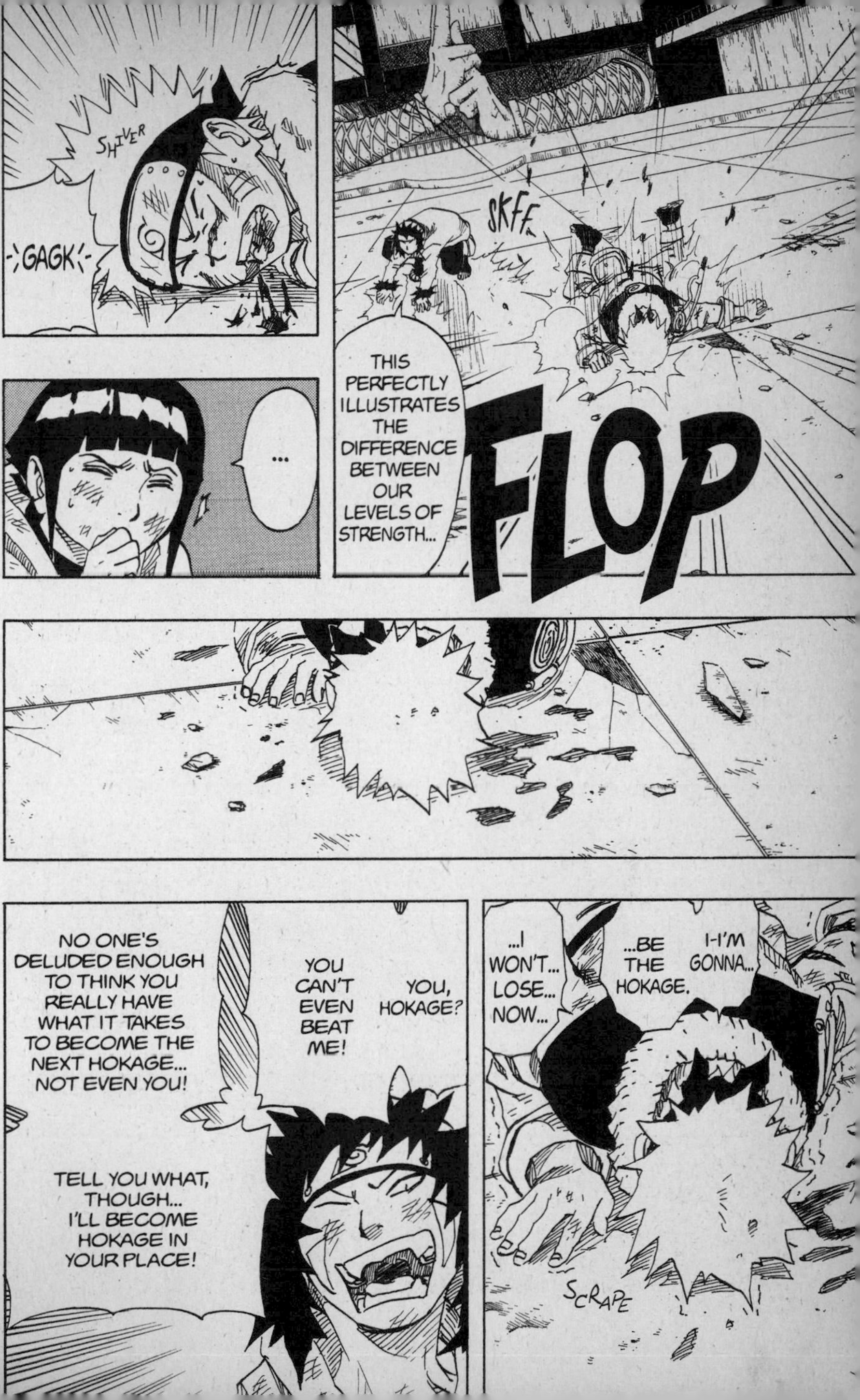
SKFF
THIS PERFECTLY ILLUSTRATES THE DIFFERENCE BETWEEN OUR LEVELS OF STRENGTH...
FLOP
SHIVER
GAGK
...
I-I'M GONNA...
...BE THE HOKAGE.
...I WON'T... LOSE... NOW...
SCRAPE
YOU, HOKAGE?
YOU CAN'T EVEN BEAT ME!
NO ONE'S DELUDED ENOUGH TO THINK YOU REALLY HAVE WHAT IT TAKES TO BECOME THE NEXT HOKAGE... NOT EVEN YOU!
TELL YOU WHAT, THOUGH... I'LL BECOME HOKAGE IN YOUR PLACE!

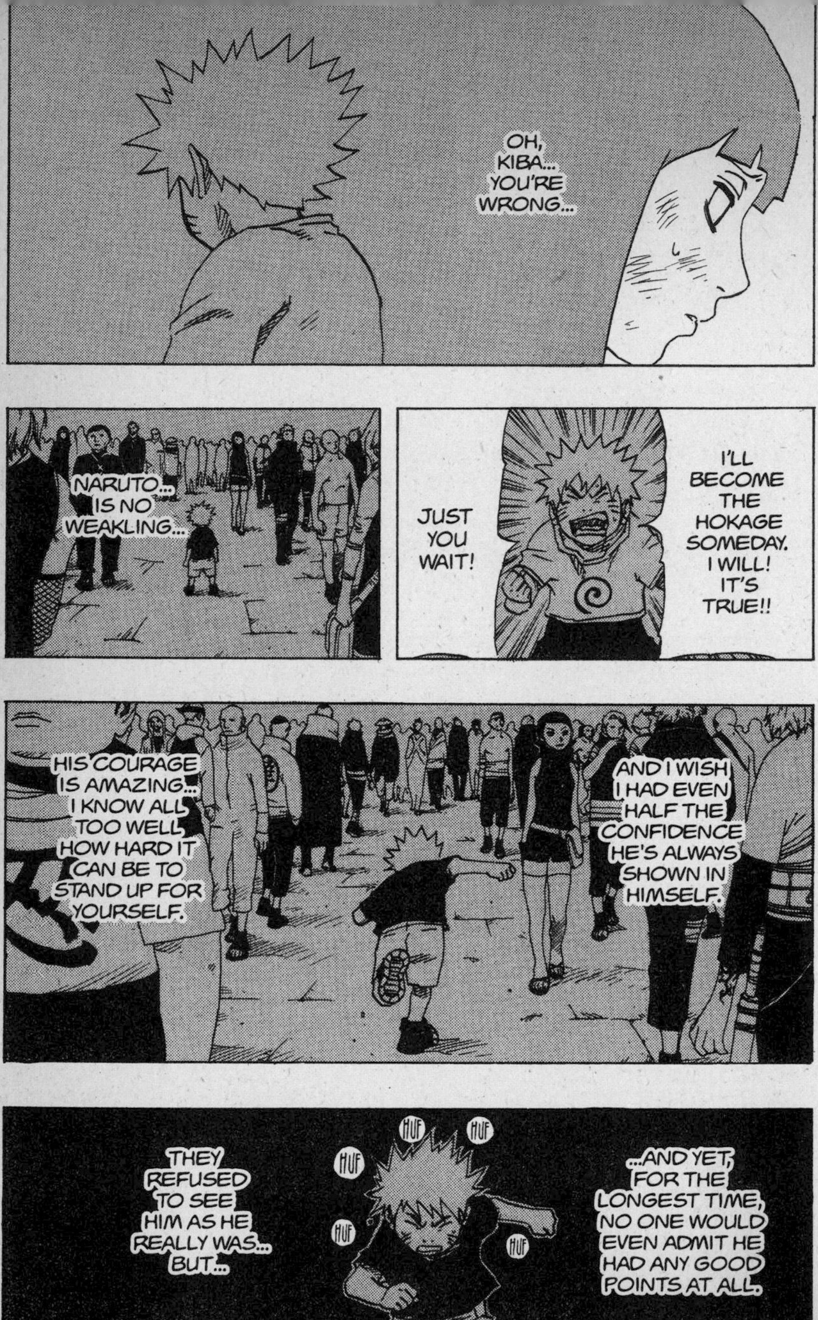
OH, KIBA... YOU'RE WRONG...
I'LL BECOME THE HOKAGE SOMEDAY. I WILL! IT'S TRUE!!
JUST YOU WAIT!
NARUTO... IS NO WEAKLING...
AND I WISH I HAD EVEN HALF THE CONFIDENCE HE'S ALWAYS SHOWN IN HIMSELF.
HIS COURAGE IS AMAZING... I KNOW ALL TOO WELL HOW HARD IT CAN BE TO STAND UP FOR YOURSELF.
...AND YET, FOR THE LONGEST TIME, NO ONE WOULD EVEN ADMIT HE HAD ANY GOOD POINTS AT ALL.
HUF
HUF
HUF
HUF
HUF
THEY REFUSED TO SEE HIM AS HE REALLY WAS... BUT...

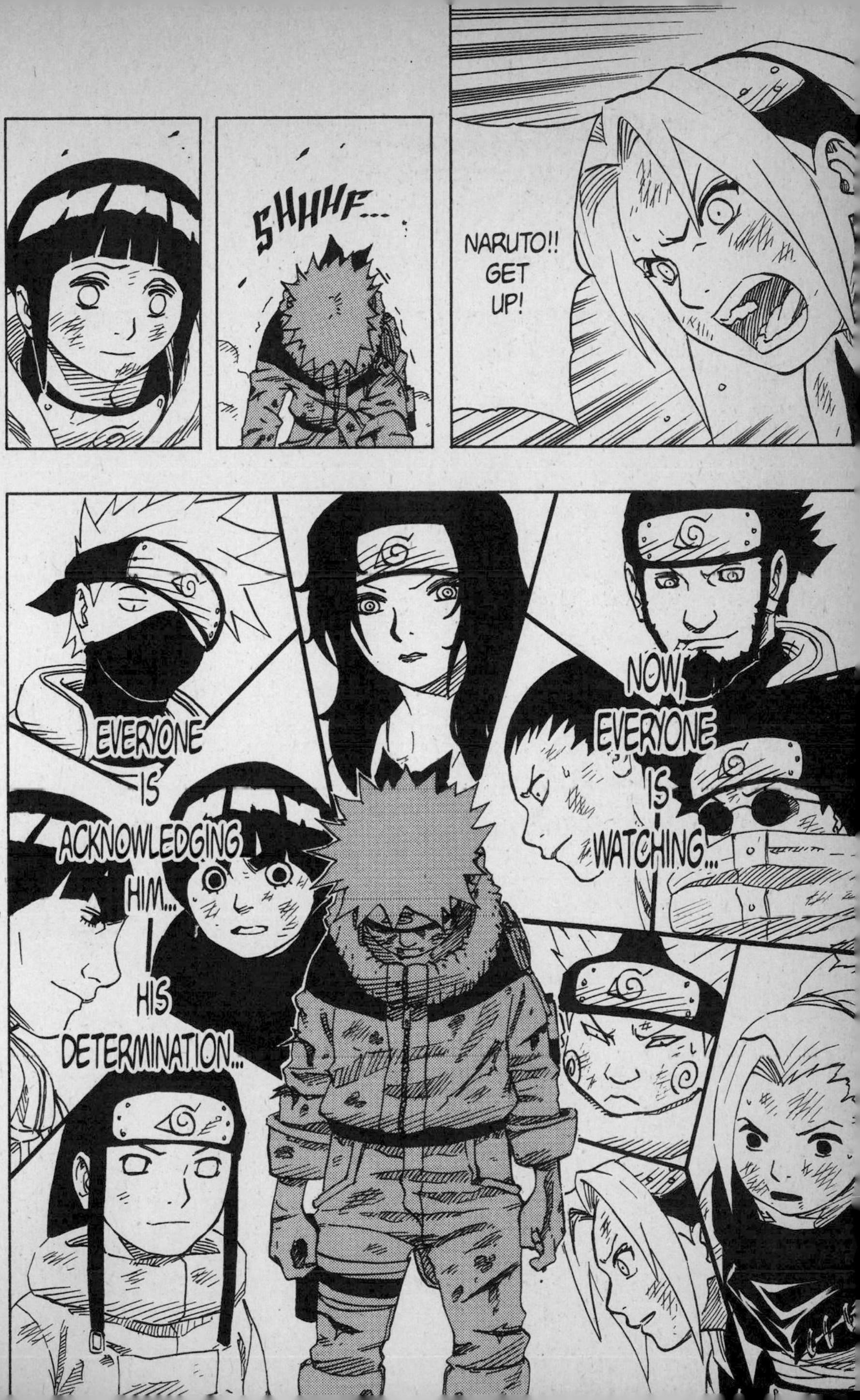
NARUTO!! GET UP!
SHHHF...
NOW, EVERYONE IS WATCHING...
EVERYONE IS ACKNOWLEDGING HIM... HIS DETERMINATION...

READ THIS WAY

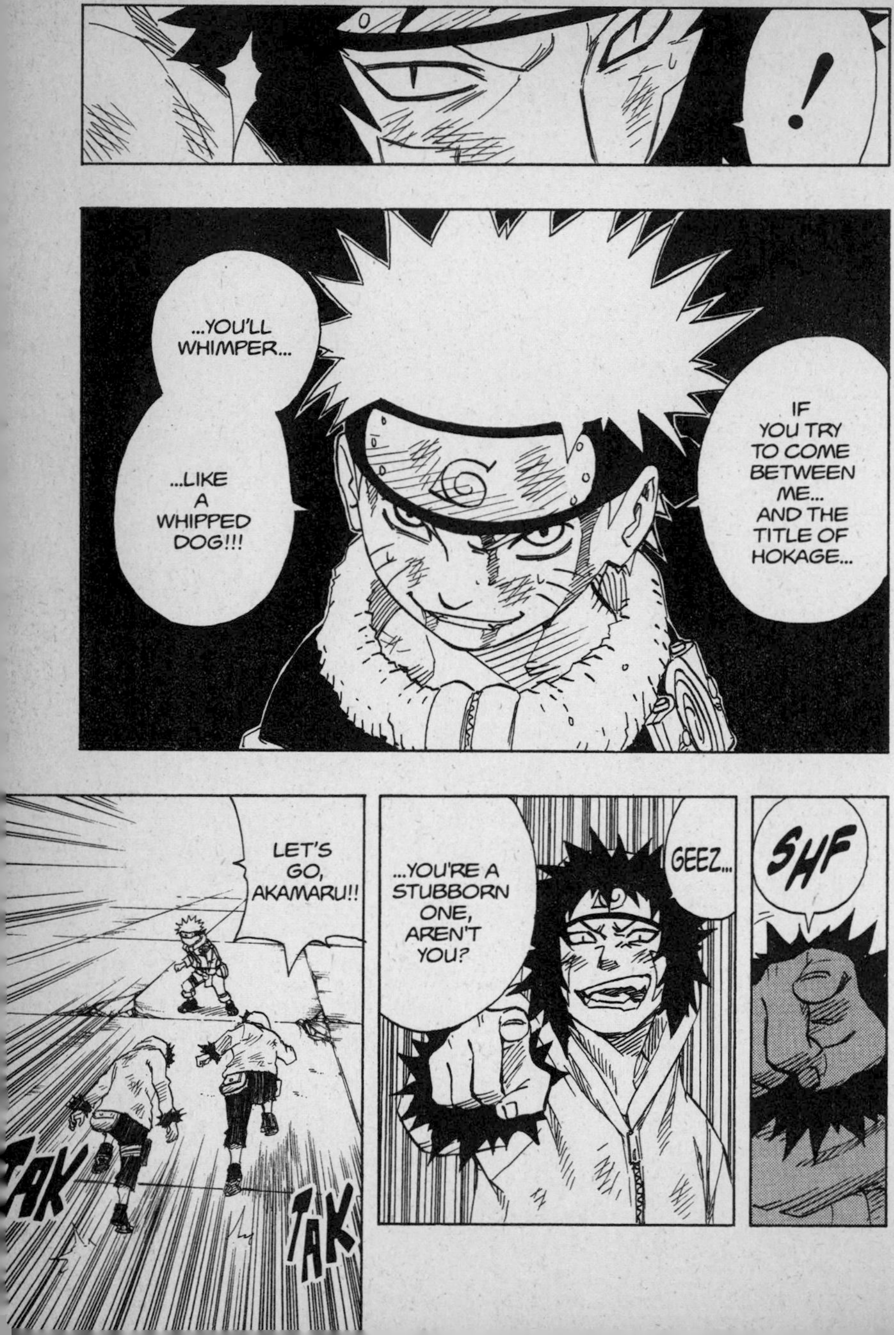
!
IF YOU TRY TO COME BETWEEN ME... AND THE TITLE OF HOKAGE...
...YOU'LL WHIMPER...
...LIKE A WHIPPED DOG!!!
SHF
GEEZ...
...YOU'RE A STUBBORN ONE, AREN'T YOU?
LET'S GO, AKAMARU!!
TAK
TAK

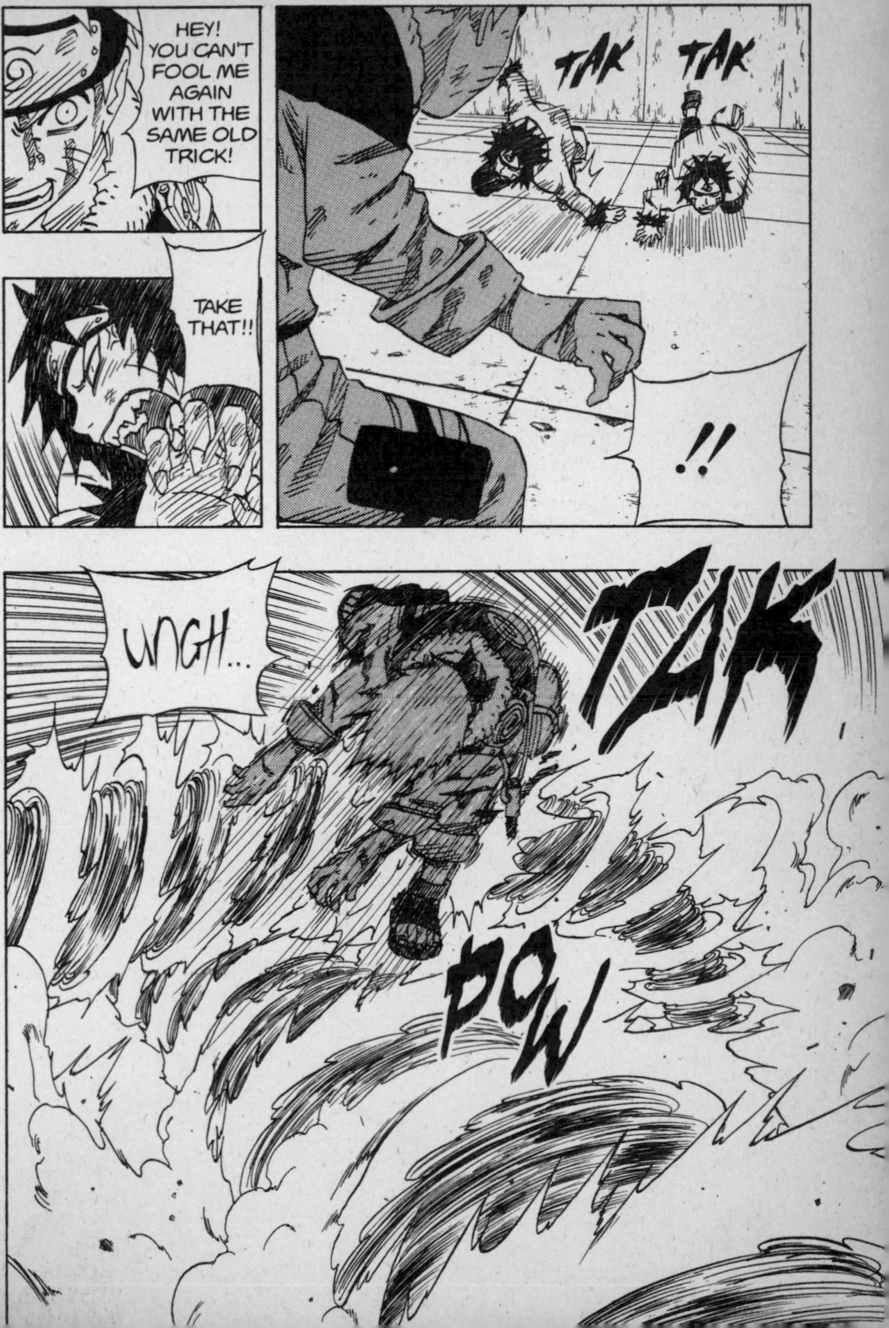
TAK TAK
!!
HEY! YOU CAN'T FOOL ME AGAIN WITH THE SAME OLD TRICK!
TAKE THAT!!
UNGH...
TAK
POW

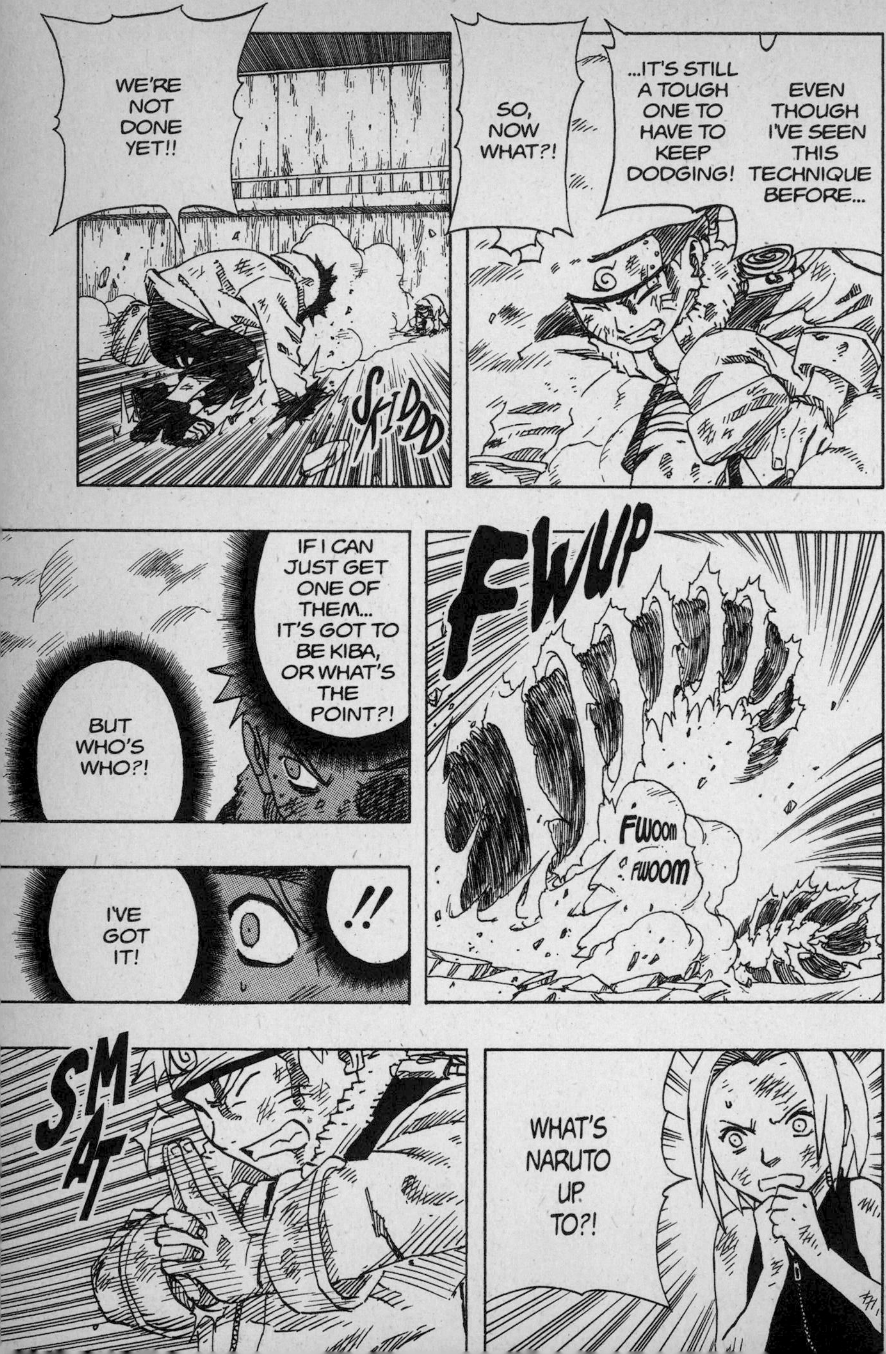
EVEN THOUGH I'VE SEEN THIS TECHNIQUE BEFORE...
...IT'S STILL A TOUGH ONE TO HAVE TO KEEP DODGING!
SO, NOW WHAT?!
WE'RE NOT DONE YET!!
SKIDDD
FWUP
FWOOM
FWOOM
IF I CAN JUST GET ONE OF THEM... IT'S GOT TO BE KIBA, OR WHAT'S THE POINT?!
BUT WHO'S WHO?!
!!
I'VE GOT IT!
WHAT'S NARUTO UP TO?!
SMAT

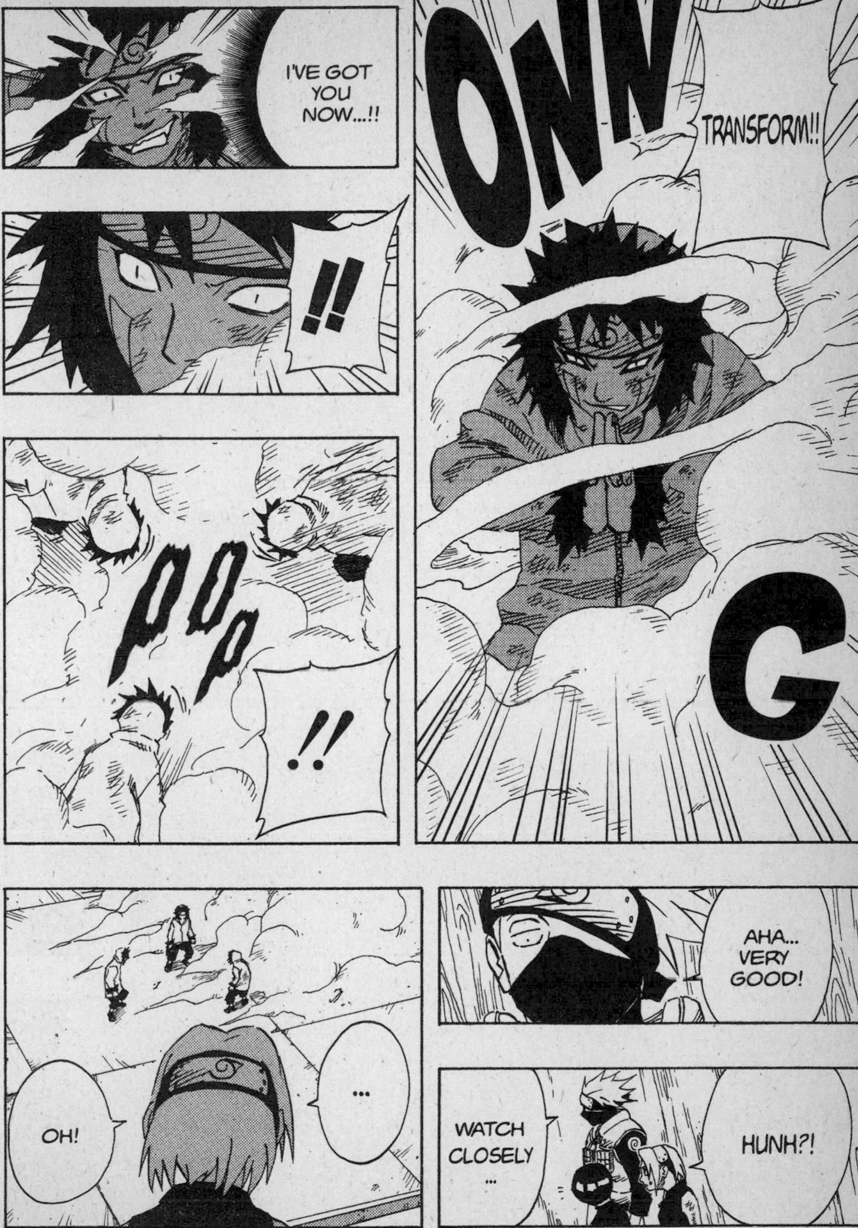
TRANSFORM!!
ONN
G
I'VE GOT YOU NOW...!!
!!
POP
!!
AHA... VERY GOOD!
HUNH?!
WATCH CLOSELY ...
...
OH!

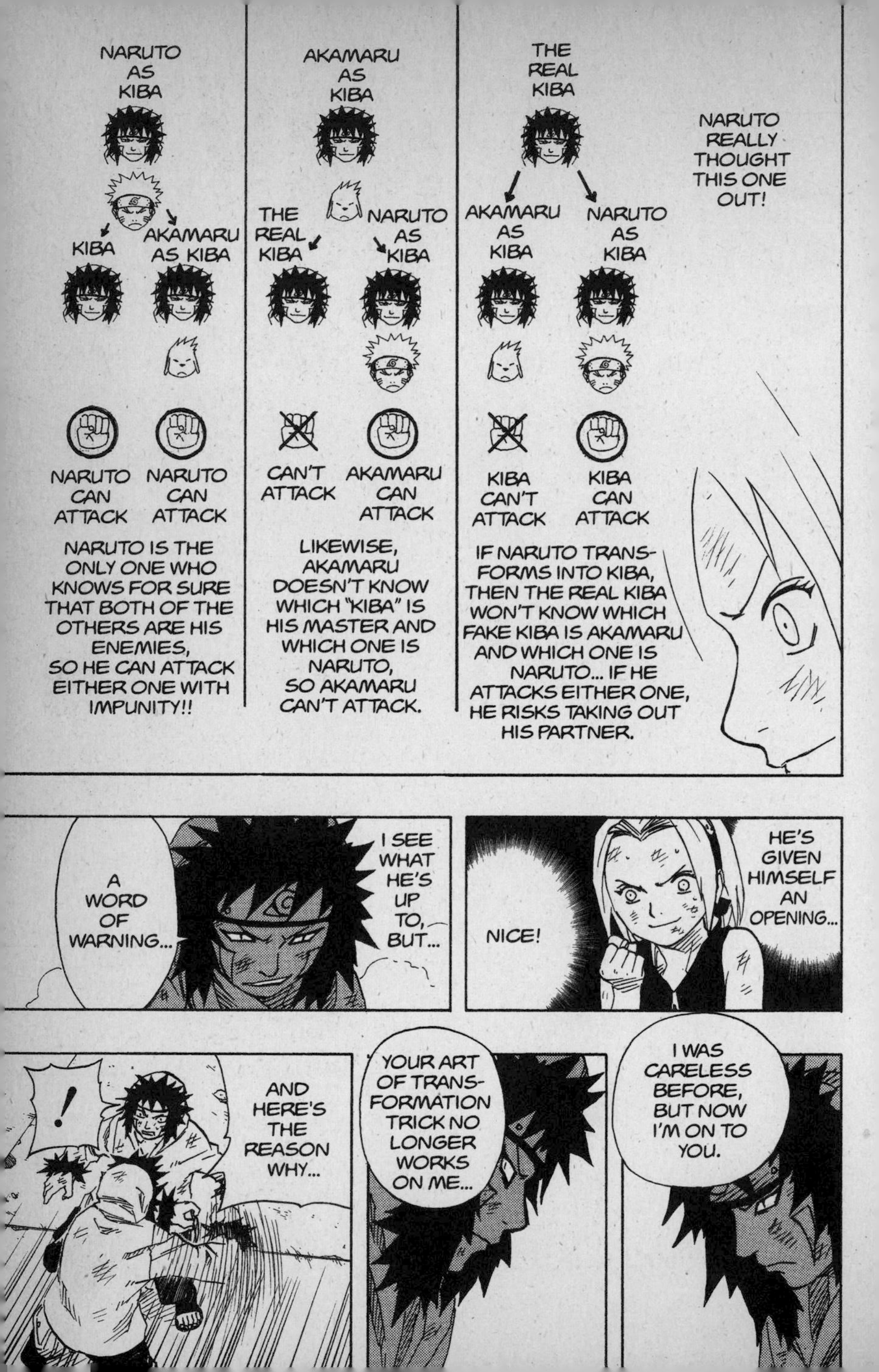
NARUTO REALLY THOUGHT THIS ONE OUT!
NARUTO AS KIBA
KIBA
AKAMARU AS KIBA
NARUTO CAN ATTACK
NARUTO CAN ATTACK
NARUTO IS THE ONLY ONE WHO KNOWS FOR SURE THAT BOTH OF THE OTHERS ARE HIS ENEMIES, SO HE CAN ATTACK EITHER ONE WITH IMPUNITY!!
AKAMARU AS KIBA
THE REAL KIBA
NARUTO AS KIBA
CAN'T ATTACK
AKAMARU CAN ATTACK
LIKEWISE, AKAMARU DOESN'T KNOW WHICH "KIBA" IS HIS MASTER AND WHICH ONE IS NARUTO, SO AKAMARU CAN'T ATTACK.
THE REAL KIBA
AKAMARU AS KIBA
NARUTO AS KIBA
KIBA CAN'T ATTACK
KIBA CAN ATTACK
IF NARUTO TRANSFORMS INTO KIBA, THEN THE REAL KIBA WON'T KNOW WHICH FAKE KIBA IS AKAMARU AND WHICH ONE IS NARUTO... IF HE ATTACKS EITHER ONE, HE RISKS TAKING OUT HIS PARTNER.
HE'S GIVEN HIMSELF AN OPENING...
NICE!
I SEE WHAT HE'S UP TO, BUT...
A WORD OF WARNING...
I WAS CARELESS BEFORE, BUT NOW I'M ON TO YOU.
YOUR ART OF TRANSFORMATION TRICK NO LONGER WORKS ON ME...
AND HERE'S THE REASON WHY...
!

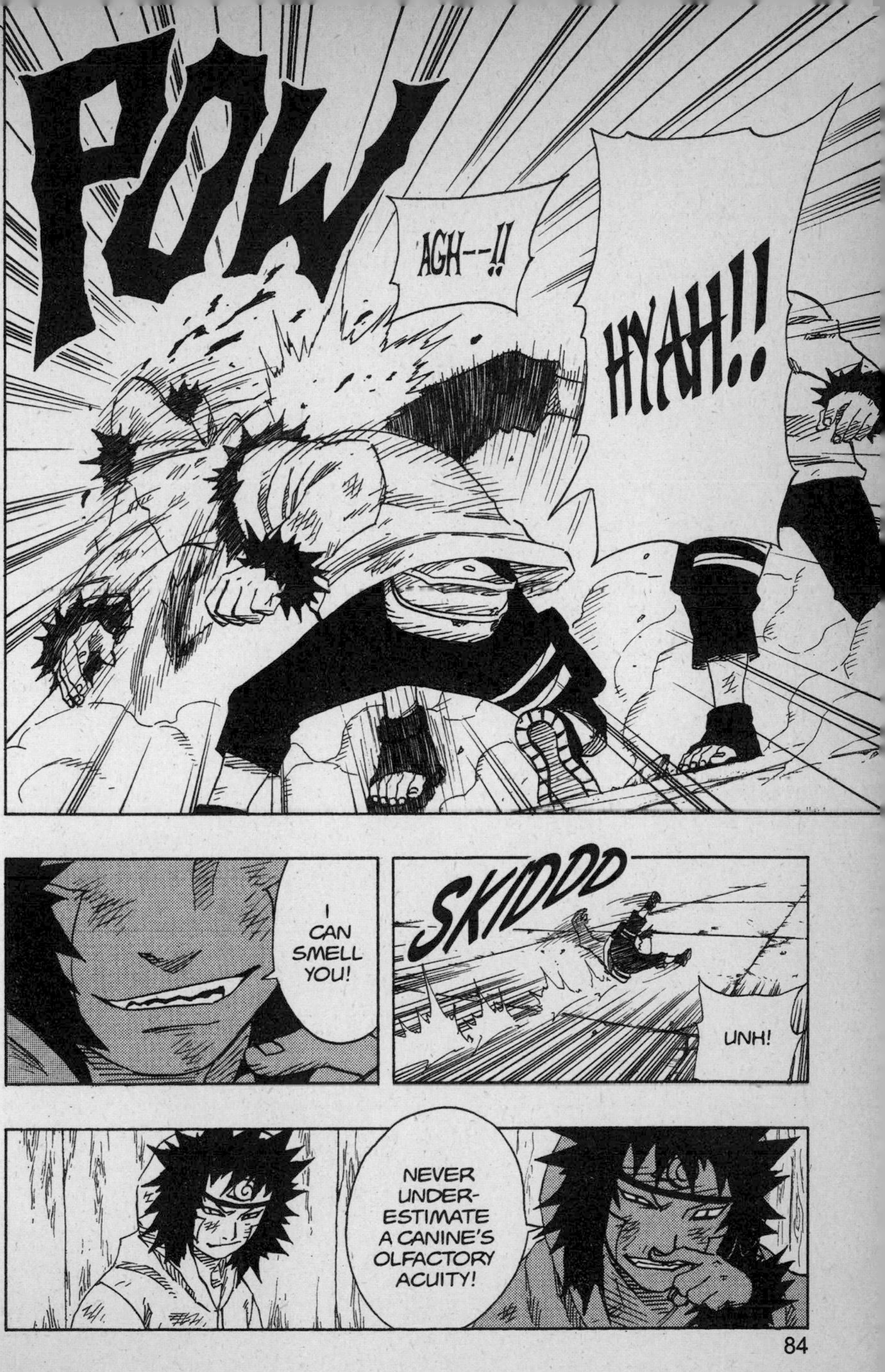
HYAH!!
AGH--!!
POW
SKIDDD
UNH!
I CAN SMELL YOU!
NEVER UNDER-ESTIMATE A CANINE'S OLFACTORY ACUITY!

READ THIS WAY

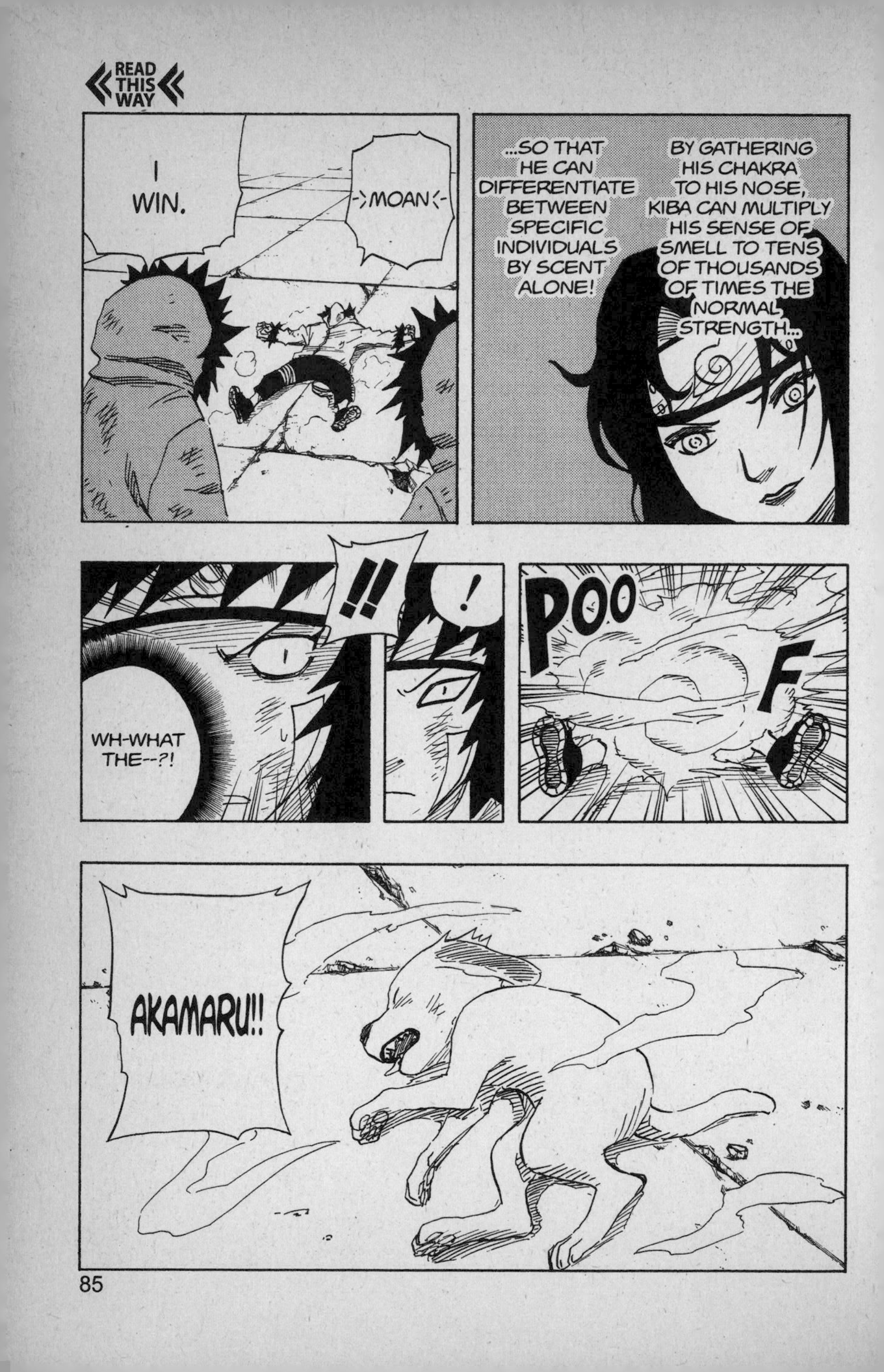

BY GATHERING HIS CHAKRA TO HIS NOSE, KIBA CAN MULTIPLY HIS SENSE OF SMELL TO TENS OF THOUSANDS OF TIMES THE NORMAL STRENGTH...
...SO THAT HE CAN DIFFERENTIATE BETWEEN SPECIFIC INDIVIDUALS BY SCENT ALONE!
I WIN.
MOAN
POOF
!
!!
WH-WHAT THE--?!
AKAMARU!!

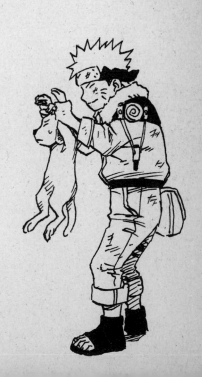

Number 77: Naruto's Clever Scheme!!

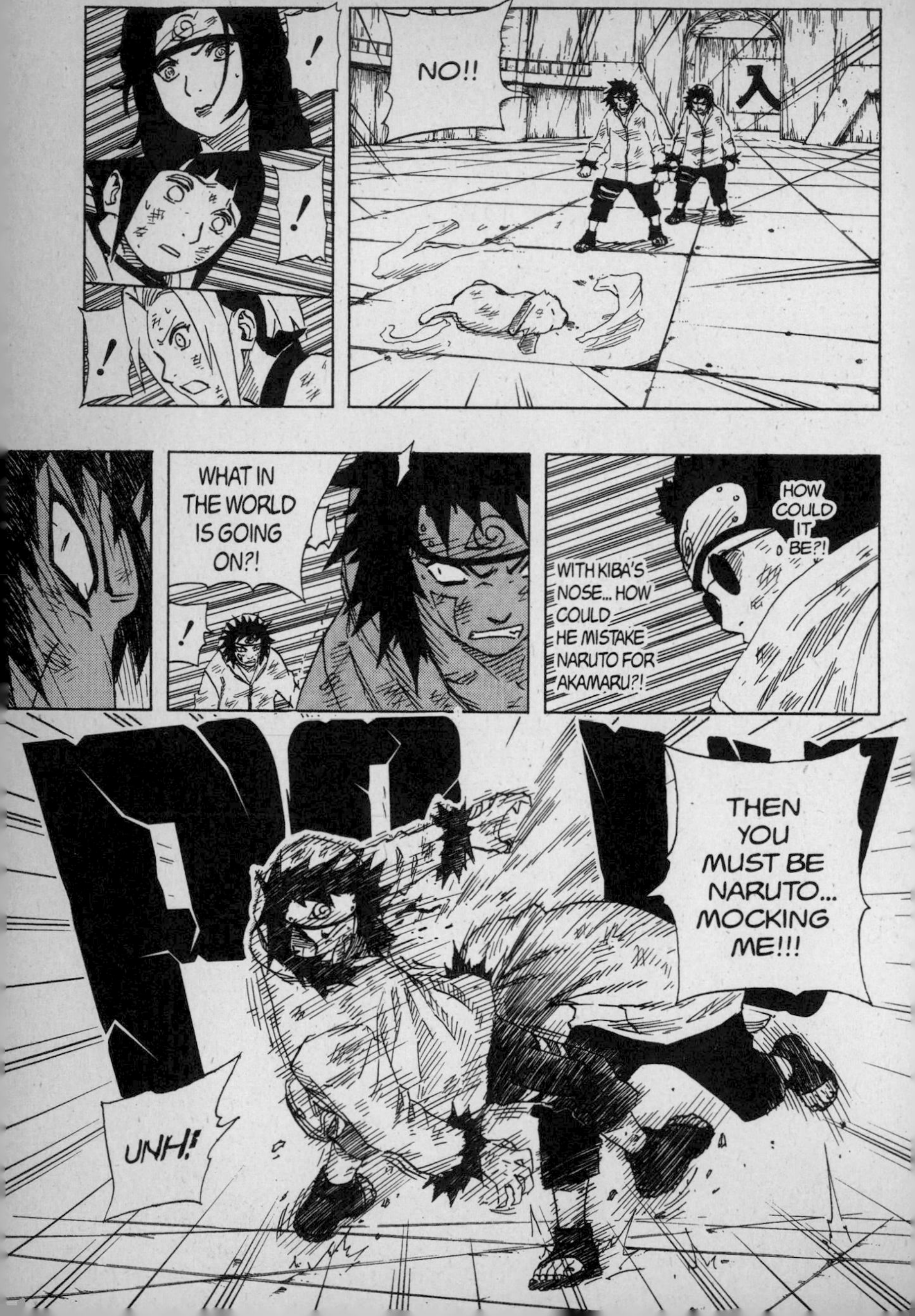
NO!!
!
!
!
HOW COULD IT BE?!
WITH KIBA'S NOSE... HOW COULD HE MISTAKE NARUTO FOR AKAMARU?!
WHAT IN THE WORLD IS GOING ON?!
!
THEN YOU MUST BE NARUTO... MOCKING ME!!!
UNH!

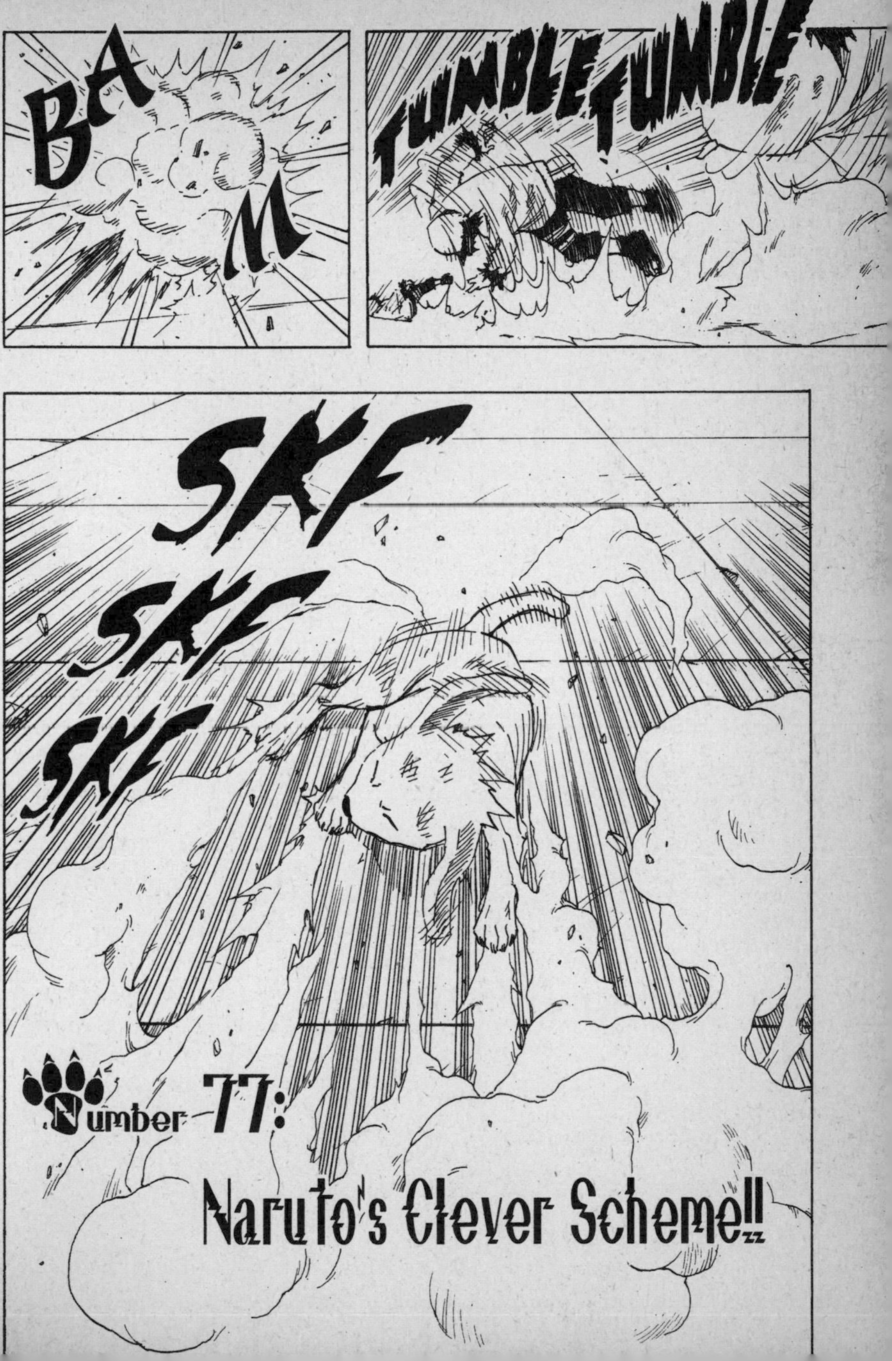
TUMBLE TUMBLE
BAM
SKF SKF SKF
Number 77:
Naruto's Clever Scheme!!

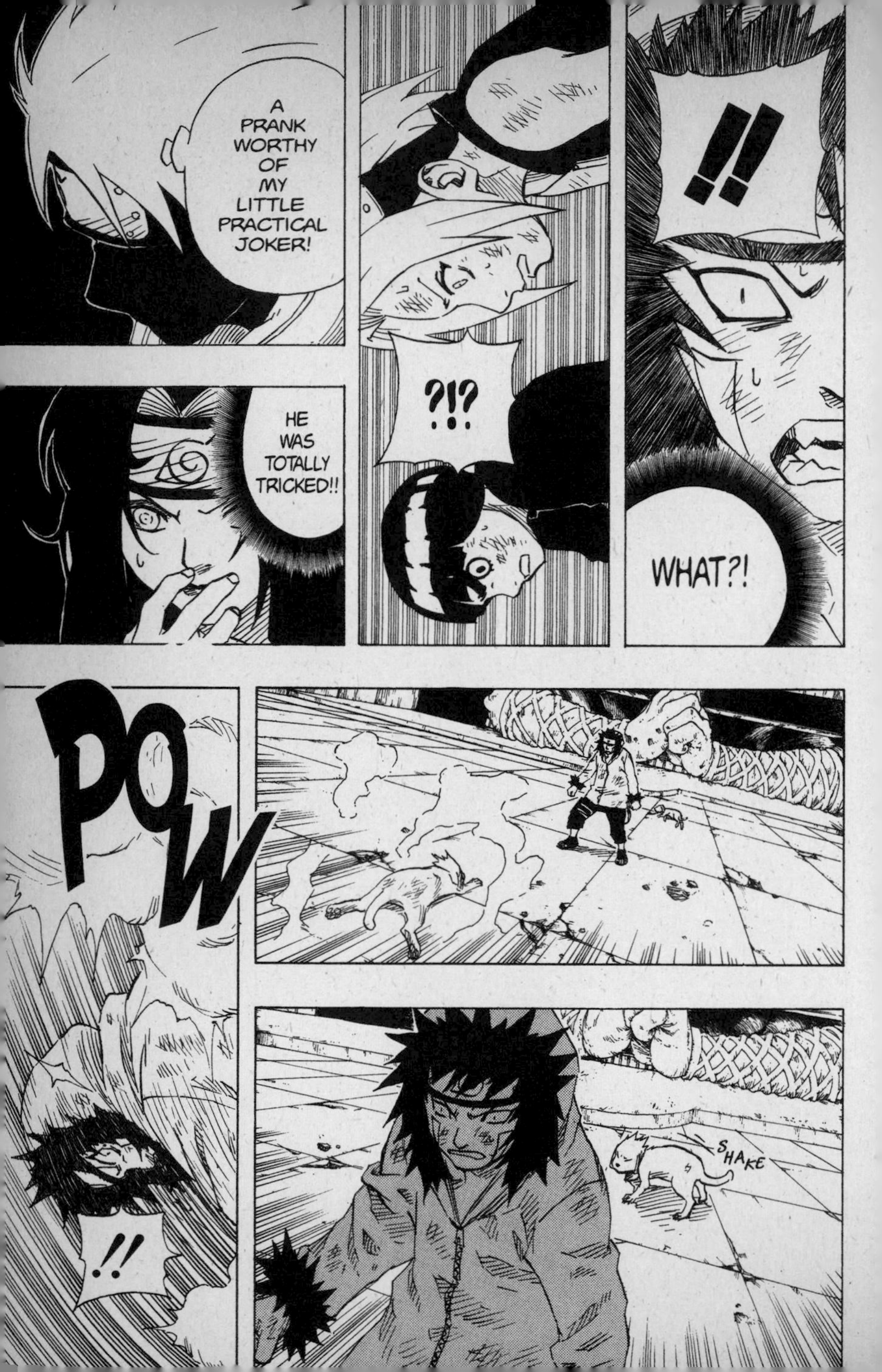
!!
WHAT?!
?!?
A PRANK WORTHY OF MY LITTLE PRACTICAL JOKER!
HE WAS TOTALLY TRICKED!!
SHAKE
POW
!!

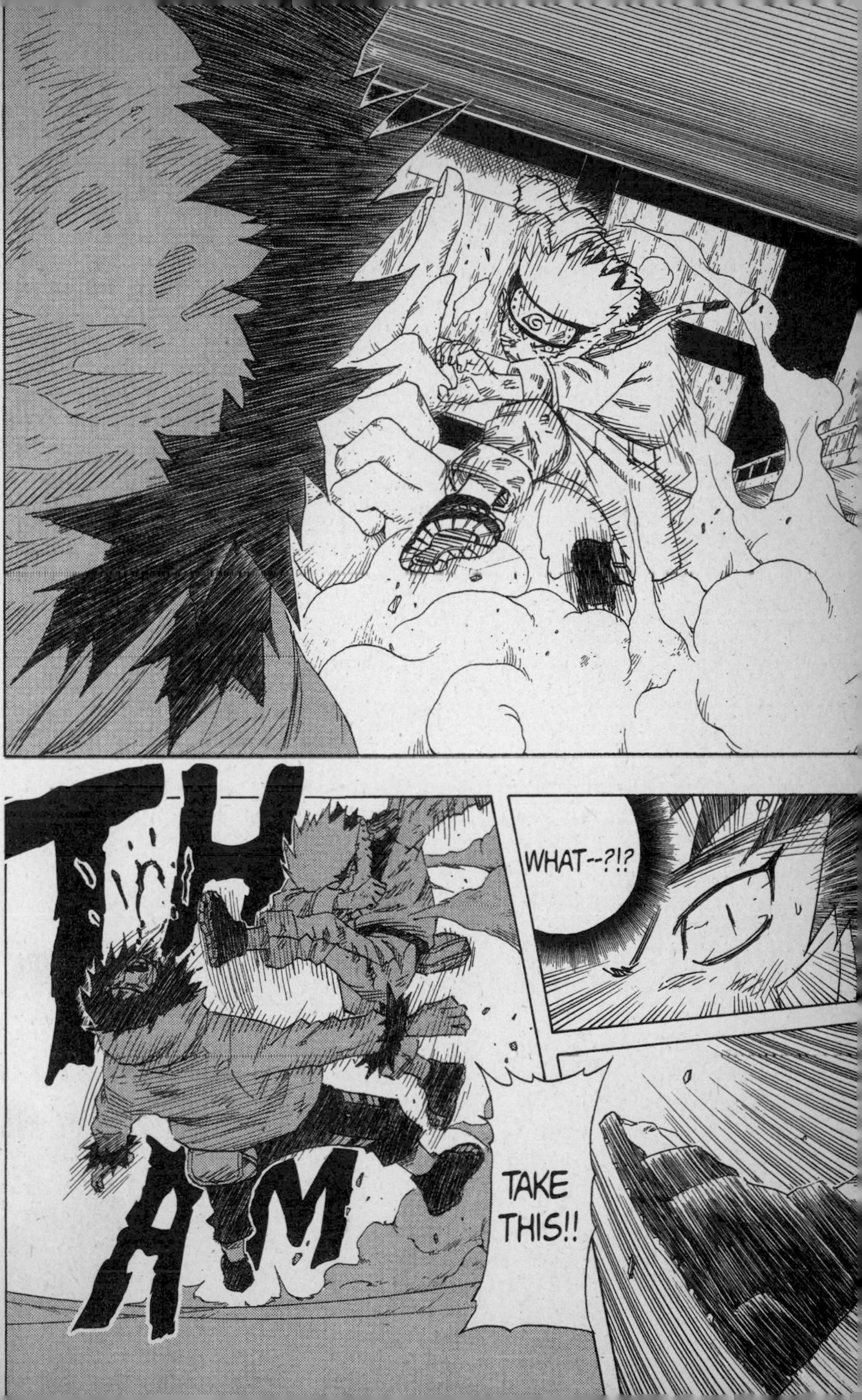
WHAT--?!?
TAKE THIS!!
THAM

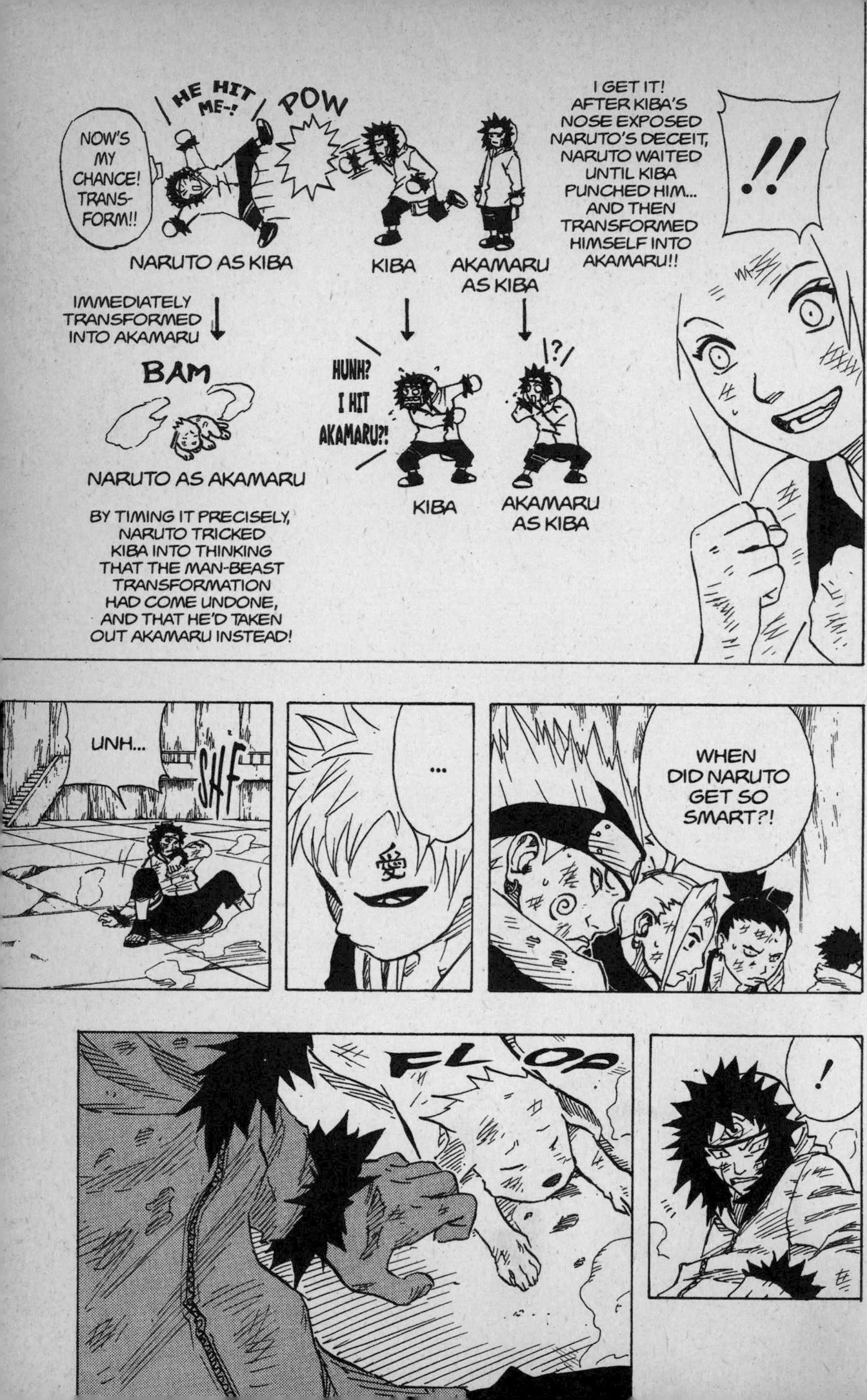
!!
I GET IT! AFTER KIBA'S NOSE EXPOSED NARUTO'S DECEIT, NARUTO WAITED UNTIL KIBA PUNCHED HIM... AND THEN TRANSFORMED HIMSELF INTO AKAMARU!!
NOW'S MY CHANCE! TRANS-FORM!!
HE HIT ME-!
POW
NARUTO AS KIBA
KIBA
AKAMARU AS KIBA
IMMEDIATELY TRANSFORMED INTO AKAMARU
BAM
NARUTO AS AKAMARU
HUNH? I HIT AKAMARU?!
?
KIBA
AKAMARU AS KIBA
BY TIMING IT PRECISELY, NARUTO TRICKED KIBA INTO THINKING THAT THE MAN-BEAST TRANSFORMATION HAD COME UNDONE, AND THAT HE'D TAKEN OUT AKAMARU INSTEAD!
WHEN DID NARUTO GET SO SMART?!
...
UNH...
SHF
!
FLOP

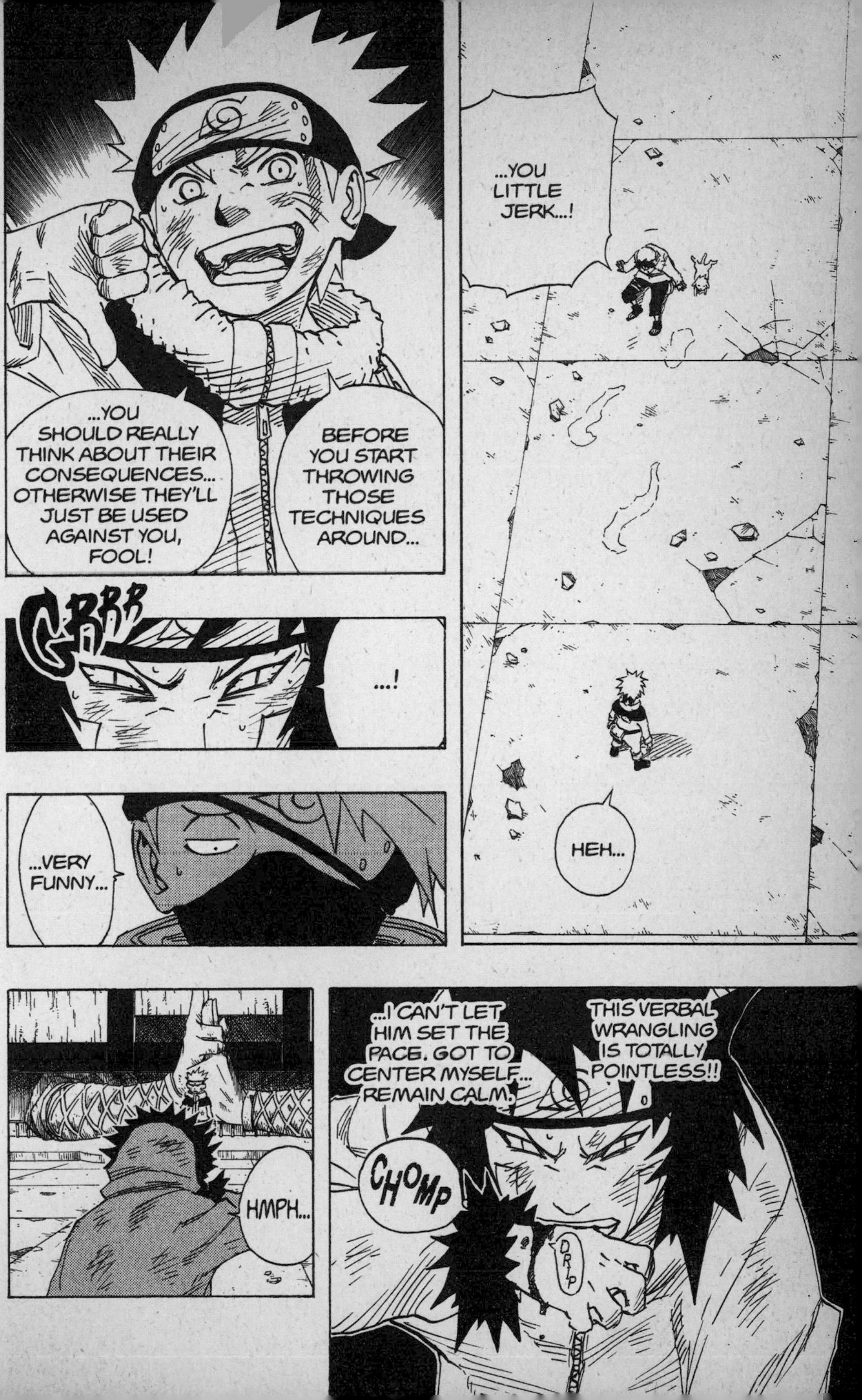
...YOU LITTLE JERK...!
HEH...
BEFORE YOU START THROWING THOSE TECHNIQUES AROUND...
...YOU SHOULD REALLY THINK ABOUT THEIR CONSEQUENCES... OTHERWISE THEY'LL JUST BE USED AGAINST YOU, FOOL!
GRRR
...!
...VERY FUNNY...
THIS VERBAL WRANGLING IS TOTALLY POINTLESS!!
...I CAN'T LET HIM SET THE PACE. GOT TO CENTER MYSELF... REMAIN CALM.
CHOMP
DRIP
HMPH...

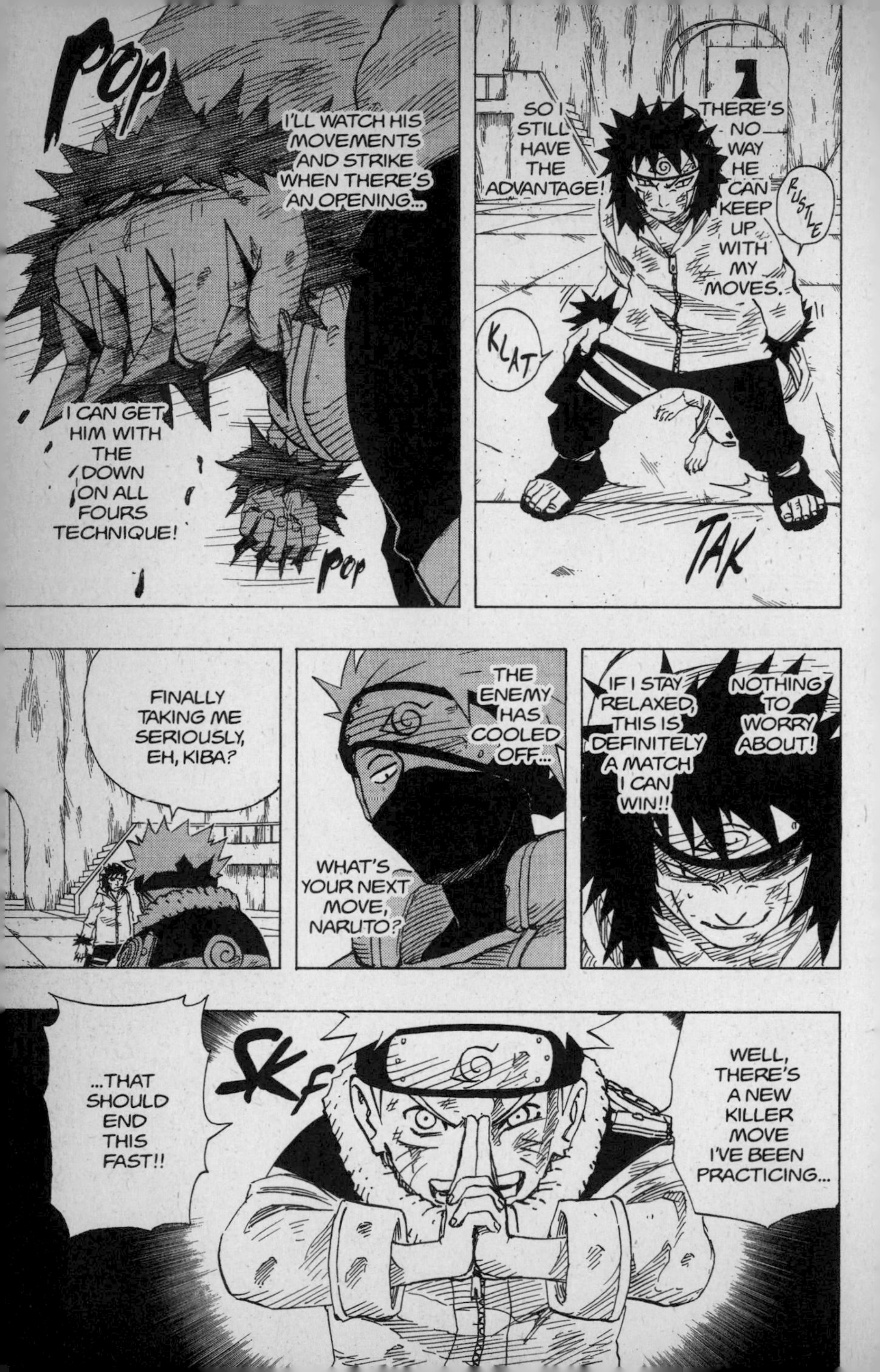
RUSTLE
THERE'S NO WAY HE CAN KEEP UP WITH MY MOVES.
SO I STILL HAVE THE ADVANTAGE!
KLAT
TAK
POP
I'LL WATCH HIS MOVEMENTS AND STRIKE WHEN THERE'S AN OPENING...
I CAN GET HIM WITH THE DOWN ON ALL FOURS TECHNIQUE!
POP
NOTHING TO WORRY ABOUT!
IF I STAY RELAXED, THIS IS DEFINITELY A MATCH I CAN WIN!!
THE ENEMY HAS COOLED OFF...
WHAT'S YOUR NEXT MOVE, NARUTO?
FINALLY TAKING ME SERIOUSLY, EH, KIBA?
WELL, THERE'S A NEW KILLER MOVE I'VE BEEN PRACTICING...
SKF
...THAT SHOULD END THIS FAST!!

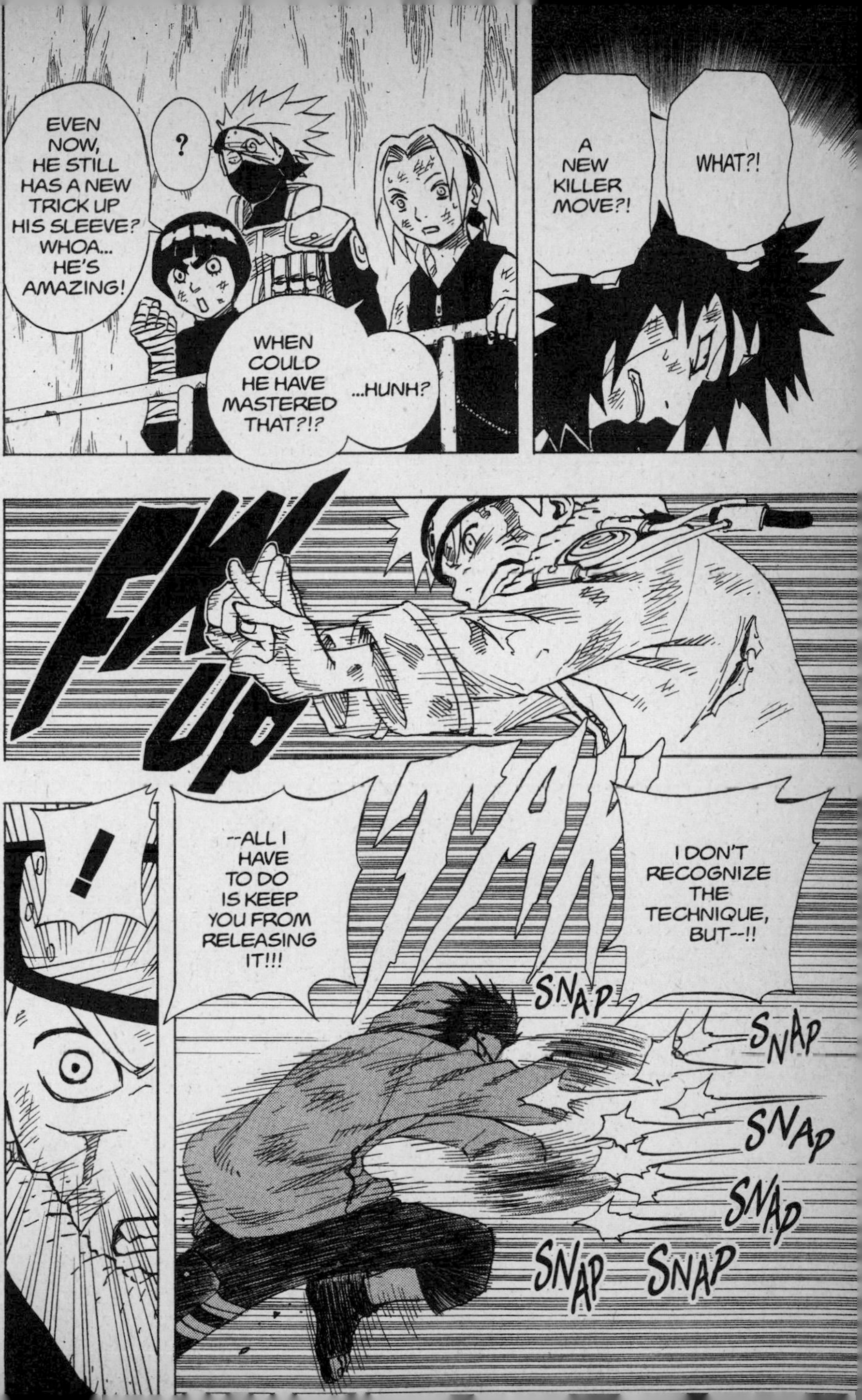
WHAT?!
A NEW KILLER MOVE?!
?
EVEN NOW, HE STILL HAS A NEW TRICK UP HIS SLEEVE? WHOA... HE'S AMAZING!
...HUNH?
WHEN COULD HE HAVE MASTERED THAT?!?
FWUP
I DON'T RECOGNIZE THE TECHNIQUE, BUT--!!
--ALL I HAVE TO DO IS KEEP YOU FROM RELEASING IT!!!
SNAP
SNAP
SNAP
SNAP
SNAP
SNAP
!

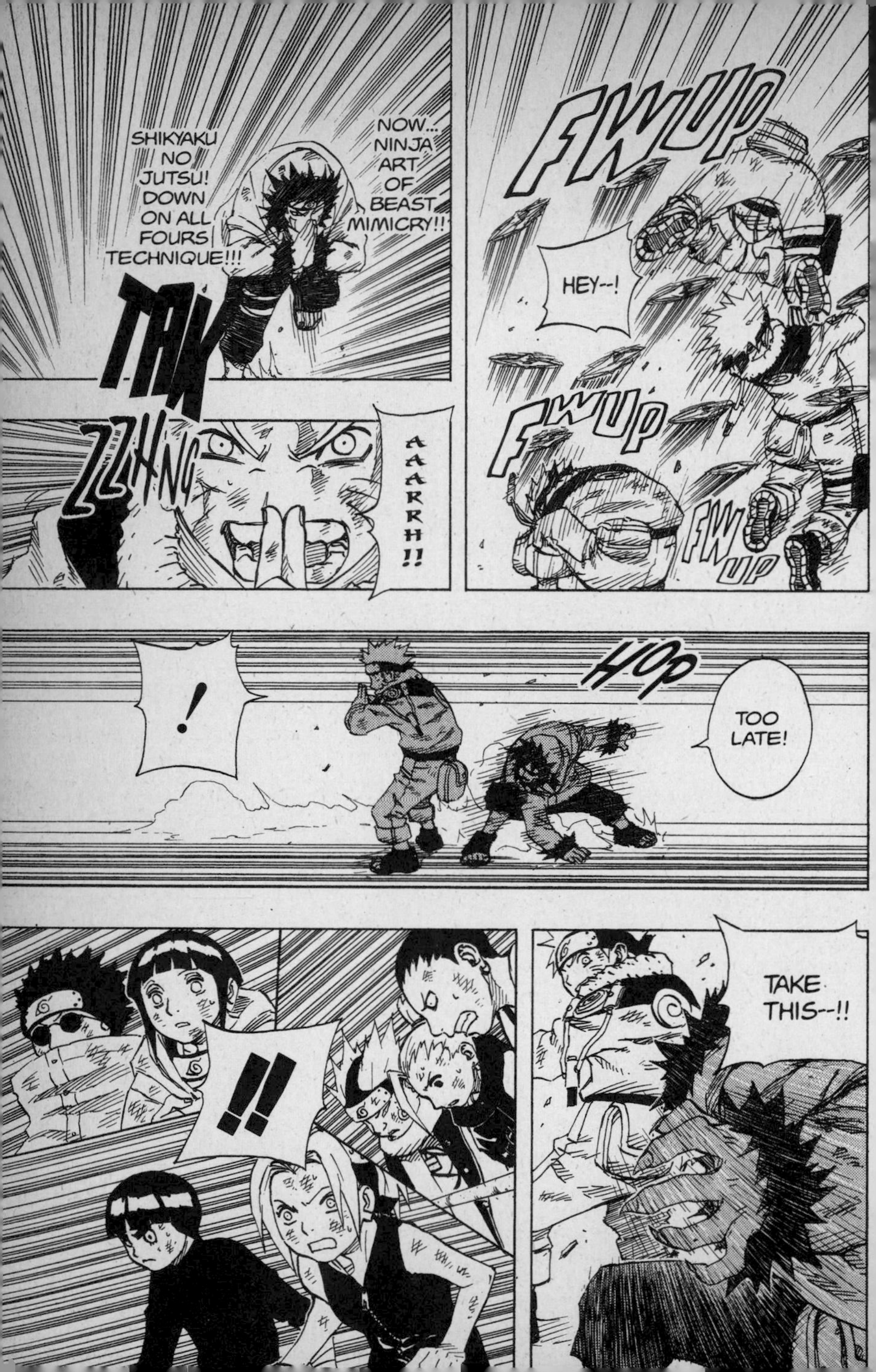
FWUP
HEY--!
FWUP
FWUP
NOW... NINJA ART OF BEAST MIMICRY!!
SHIKYAKU NO JUTSU! DOWN ON ALL FOURS TECHNIQUE!!!
TAK
AAAARRH!!
ZZHNG
TOO LATE!
HOP
!
TAKE THIS--!!
!!

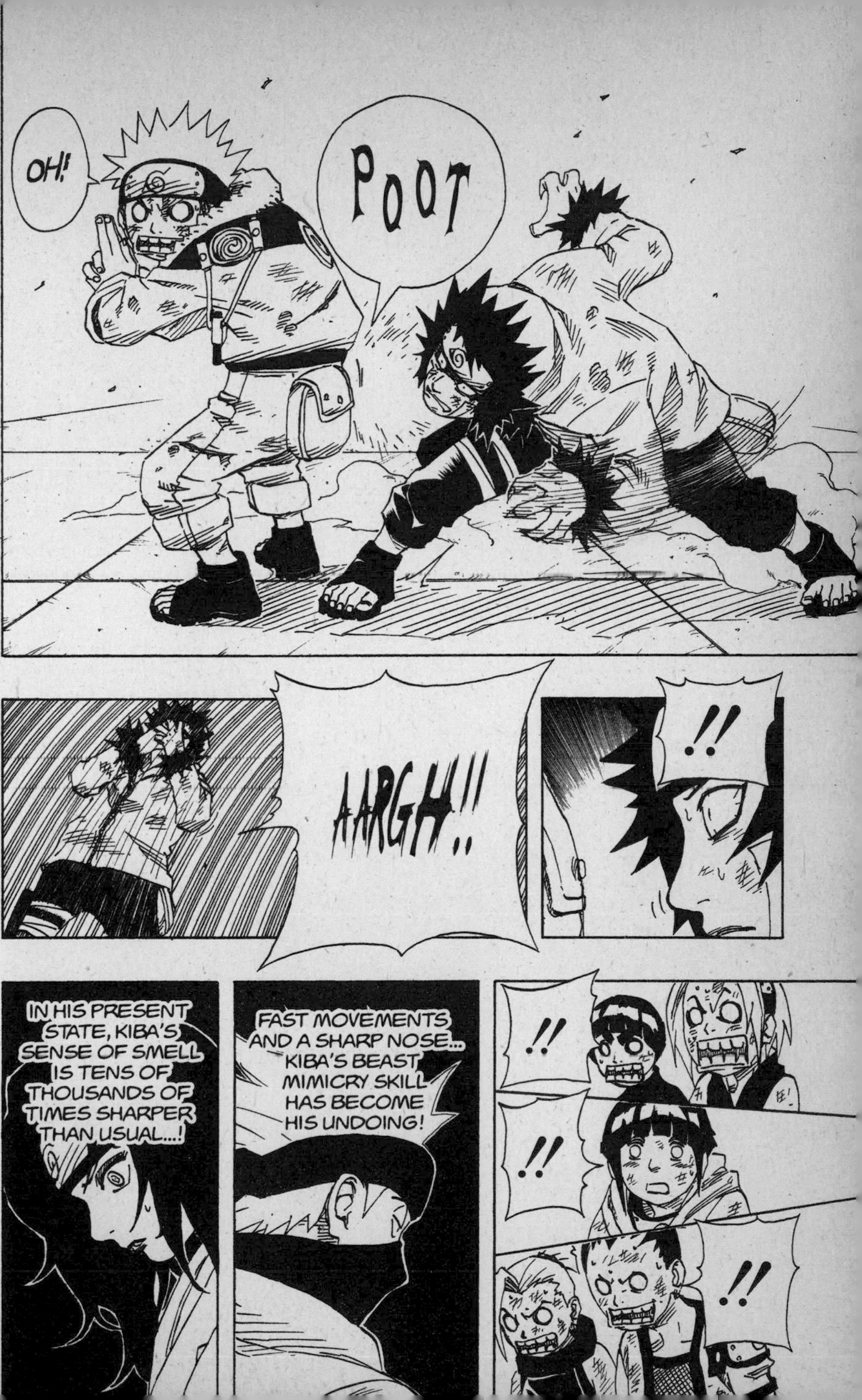
POOT
OH!
!!
AARGH!!
!!
!!
!!
FAST MOVEMENTS AND A SHARP NOSE... KIBA'S BEAST MIMICRY SKILL HAS BECOME HIS UNDOING!
IN HIS PRESENT STATE, KIBA'S SENSE OF SMELL IS TENS OF THOUSANDS OF TIMES SHARPER THAN USUAL...!

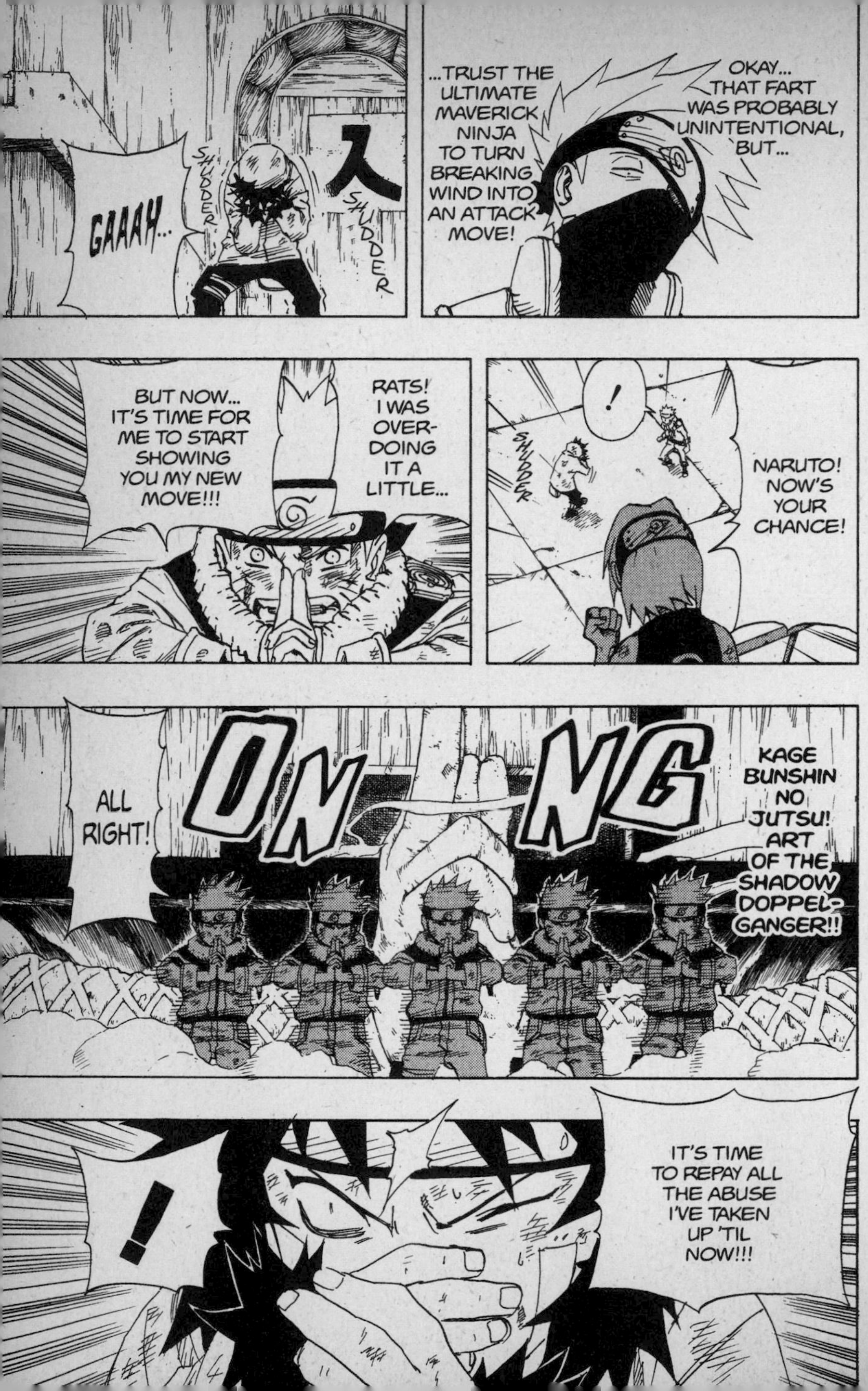

OKAY... THAT FART WAS PROBABLY UNINTENTIONAL, BUT...
...TRUST THE ULTIMATE MAVERICK NINJA TO TURN BREAKING WIND INTO AN ATTACK MOVE!
SHUDDER
SHUDDER
GAAAH...
!
SHUDDER
NARUTO! NOW'S YOUR CHANCE!
RATS! I WAS OVER-DOING IT A LITTLE...
BUT NOW... IT'S TIME FOR ME TO START SHOWING YOU MY NEW MOVE!!!
KAGE BUNSHIN NO JUTSU! ART OF THE SHADOW DOPPEL-GANGER!!
ALL RIGHT!
IT'S TIME TO REPAY ALL THE ABUSE I'VE TAKEN UP 'TIL NOW!!!
!

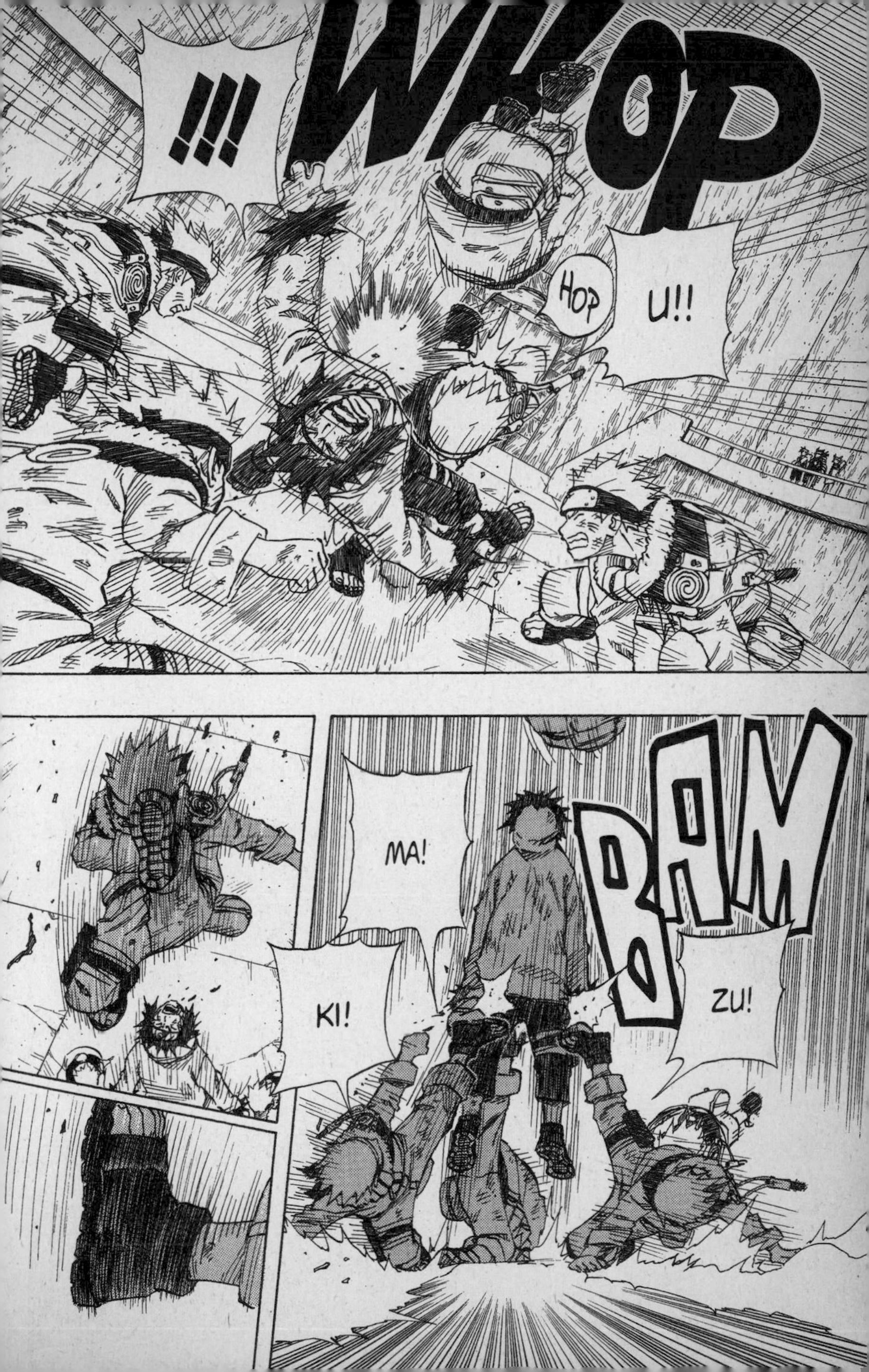
WHOP
!!!
U!!
HOP
BAM
ZU!
MA!
KI!

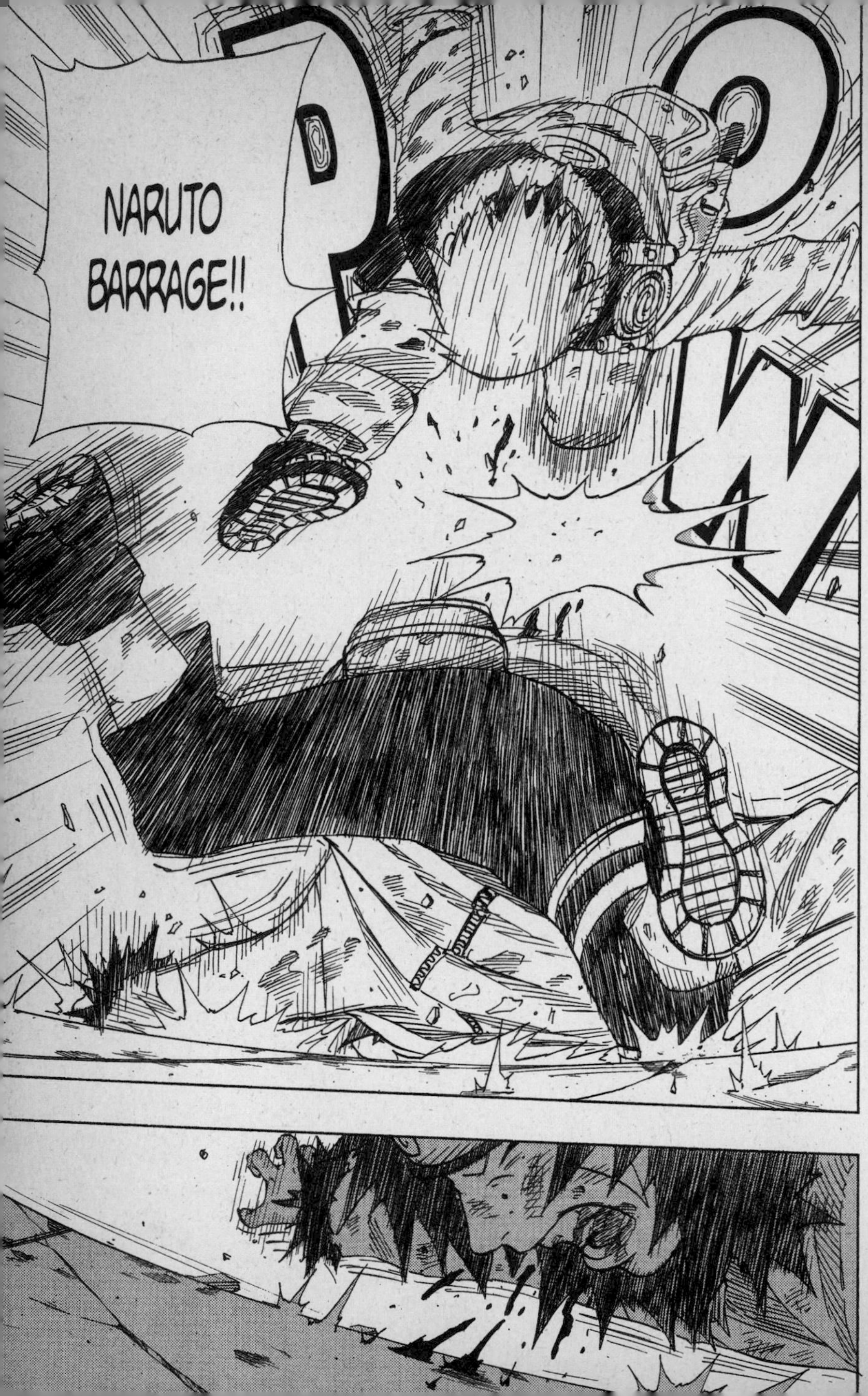
NARUTO BARRAGE!!
POW

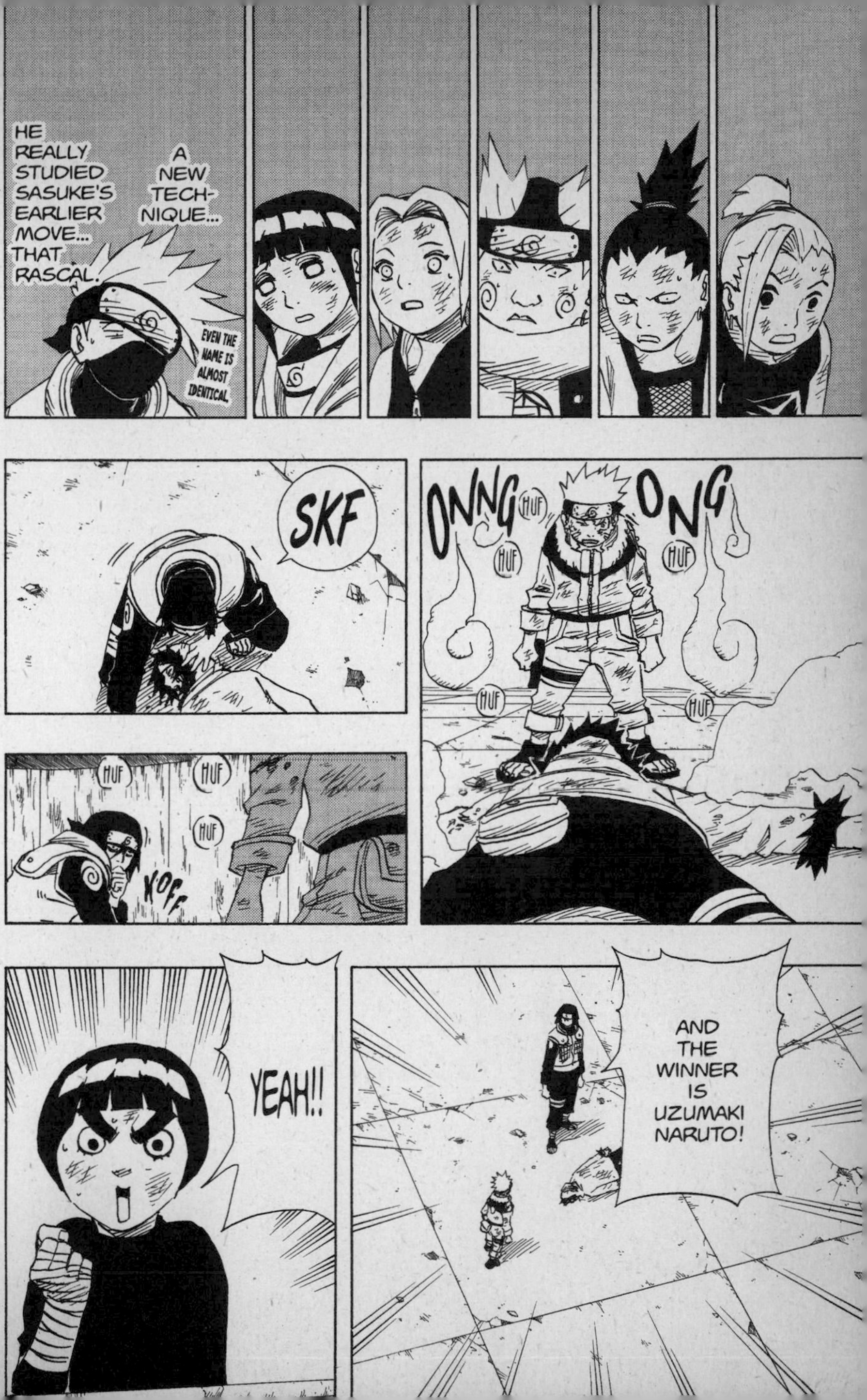
A NEW TECH-NIQUE...
HE REALLY STUDIED SASUKE'S EARLIER MOVE... THAT RASCAL.
EVEN THE NAME IS ALMOST IDENTICAL
ONG
HUF
HUF
ONNG
HUF
HUF
HUF
HUF
SKF
HUF
HUF
HUF
K'OFF
AND THE WINNER IS UZUMAKI NARUTO!
YEAH!!

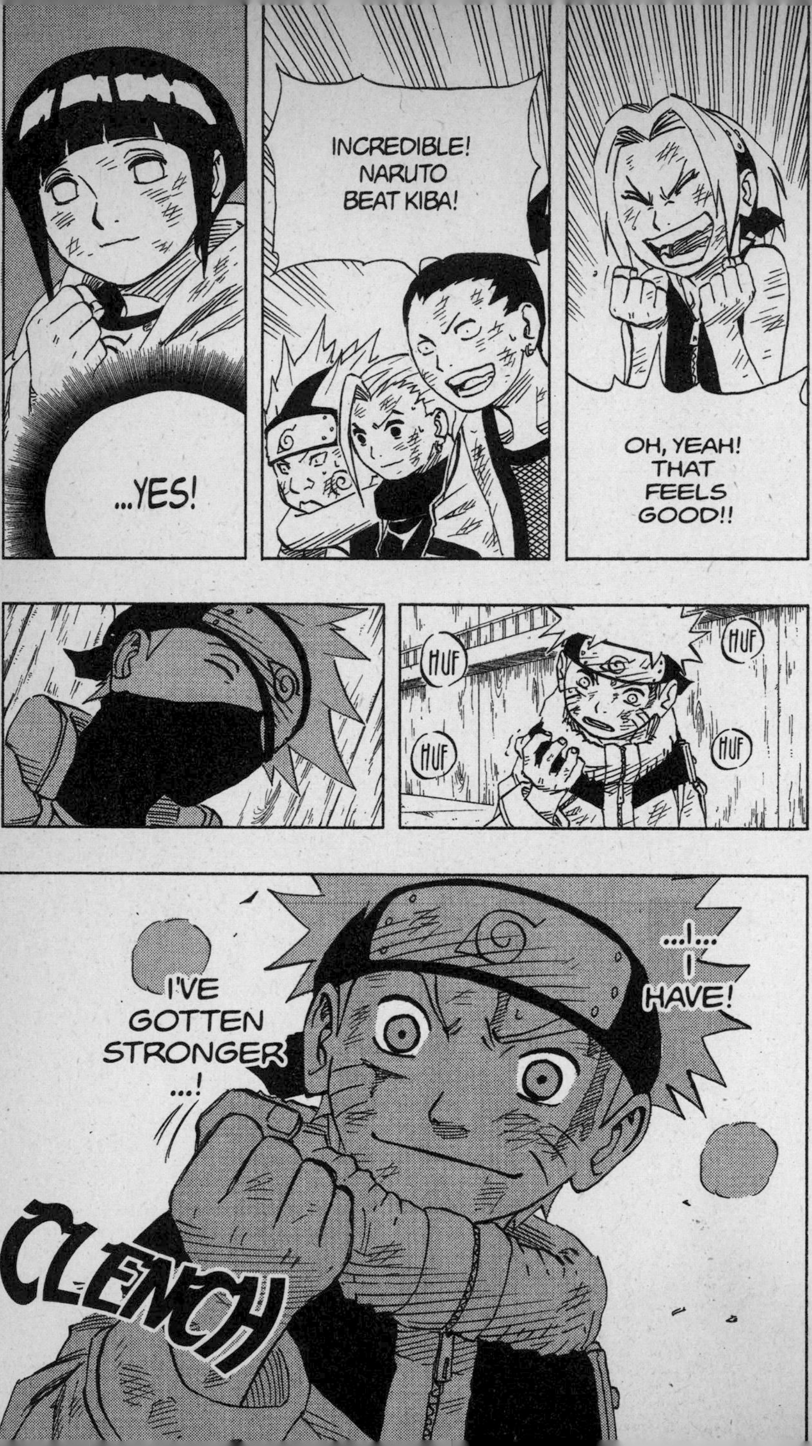
OH, YEAH! THAT FEELS GOOD!!
INCREDIBLE! NARUTO BEAT KIBA!
...YES!
HUF
HUF
HUF
HUF
...I... I HAVE!
I'VE GOTTEN STRONGER ...!
CLENCH

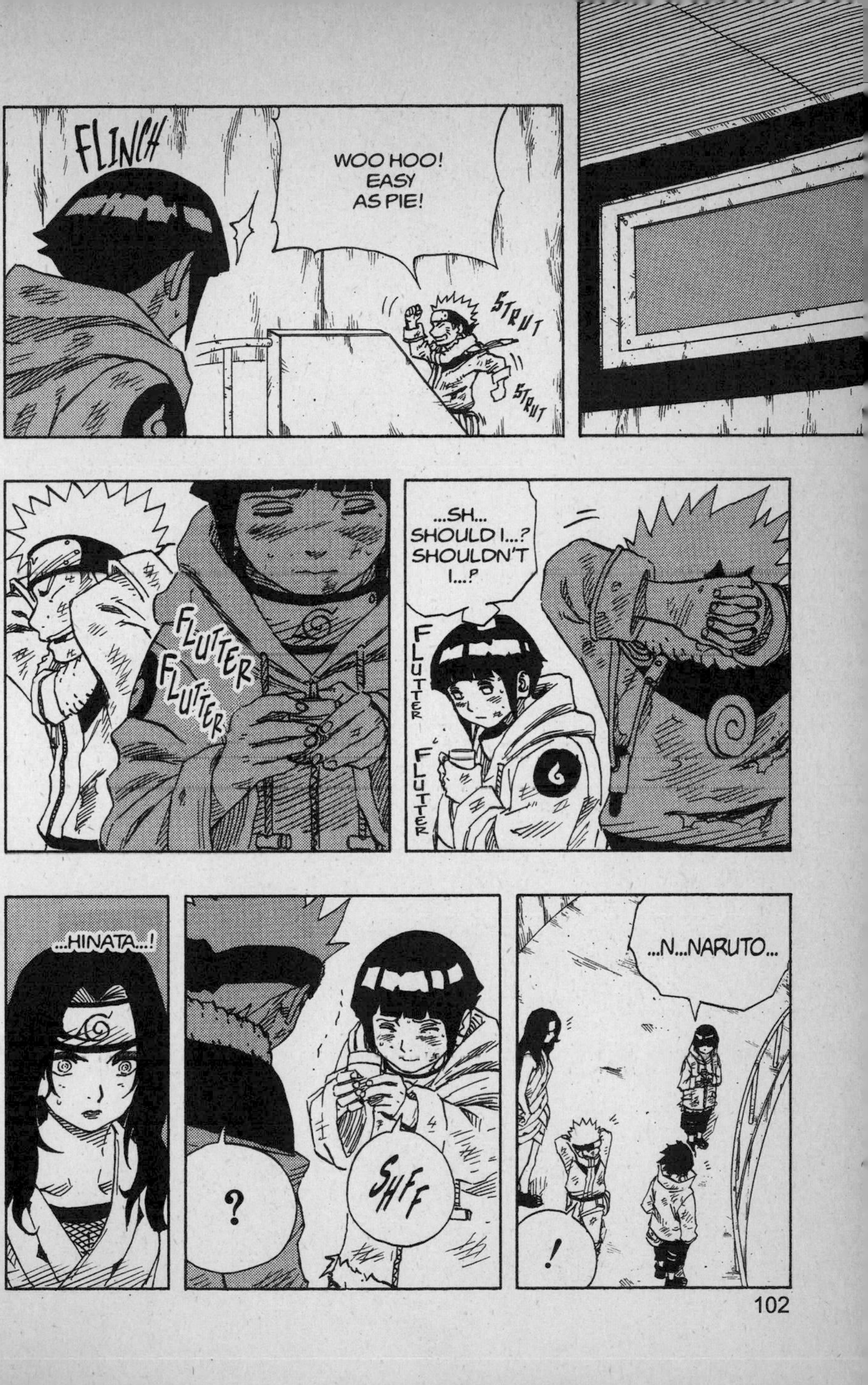
WOO HOO! EASY AS PIE!
STRUT
STRUT
FLINCH
...SH... SHOULD I...? SHOULDN'T I...?
FLUTTER
FLUTTER
FLUTTER
FLUTTER
...N...NARUTO...
!
SHFF
?
...HINATA...!

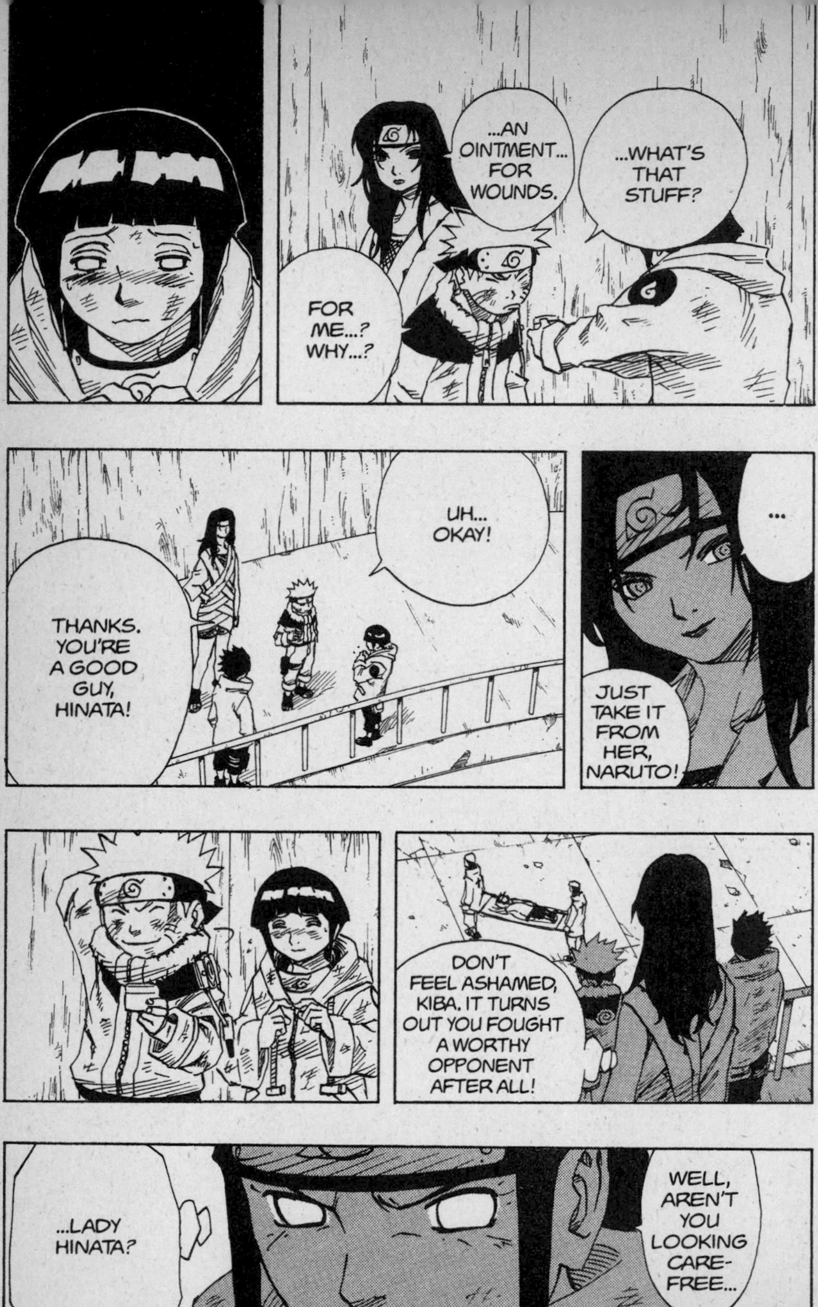
...WHAT'S THAT STUFF?
...AN OINTMENT... FOR WOUNDS.
FOR ME...? WHY...?
...
JUST TAKE IT FROM HER, NARUTO!
UH... OKAY!
THANKS. YOU'RE A GOOD GUY, HINATA!
DON'T FEEL ASHAMED, KIBA. IT TURNS OUT YOU FOUGHT A WORTHY OPPONENT AFTER ALL!
WELL, AREN'T YOU LOOKING CARE-FREE...
...LADY HINATA?

THE WORLD OF KISHIMOTO MASASHI
MY PERSONAL HISTORY, PART 10

...THE INFAMOUS INCIDENT... IT HAPPENED RIGHT AFTER THE END OF TRAINING CAMP, THE DAY THAT ALL 45 OF US IN THE BASEBALL CLUB CLIMBED THE RESORT'S MONKEY MOUNTAIN TOGETHER.

TO BEGIN AT THE BEGINNING, AS WE STARTED TO CLIMB THE MOUNTAIN, WE SAW A PLACARD THAT SAID, "DO NOT LOOK THE WILD MONKEYS IN THE EYE. IT IS EXTREMELY DANGEROUS." THE SIGN ALONE WAS ENOUGH TO GIVE US THE JITTERS, BUT AS WE CONTINUED UP THE 200-METER MOUNTAIN PATH WITH THE GLARING EYES OF VAST NUMBERS OF WILD MONKEYS UPON US, WE GOADED EACH OTHER FURTHER, SAYING STUFF LIKE, "WHOA! GETTING CLOSE TO MONKEYS IS SCARY! THEY'LL GET MAD IF YOU SO MUCH AS SPIT OUT YOUR GUM! AND THEY'VE GOT THESE HUGE FANGS, MAN. THEY ARE BAD NEWS!" AND SO ON AND SO FORTH... WE WERE GETTING THOROUGHLY FREAKED OUT. WHEN WE REACHED THE SUMMIT, THERE WERE ABOUT 100 TAME MONKEYS BEING MANAGED BY AN ANIMAL TRAINER, AND THEY CAME OVER TO GREET US. UNLIKE THEIR WILD COUNTERPARTS THAT WE'D BEEN WARNED AGAINST, THESE TAME ONES WERE GENTLE, PEOPLE-FRIENDLY, SWEET MONKEYS, ACCORDING TO THEIR HANDLER. HE TOLD US THAT THERE WAS ONE ALPHA MALE AMONG THE SUMMIT MONKEYS, AND THEY SEEMED TO BE CREATING AN INDEPENDENT COLONY. AND THEN HE POINTED THE BOSS MONKEY OUT TO US. NOT SURPRISINGLY, IT WAS HUGE... WE COULDN'T HELP NOTICING THE MANY SCARS THAT CRISS-CROSSED ITS BODY, EACH UNDOUBTEDLY REPRESENTING A VICTORY IN ONE OF THE HUNDREDS OF DIFFERENT BATTLES IT HAD ENDURED ON ITS ROAD TO BECOME THE HEAD OF THE COLONY. WHILE I LOOKED UP AT THE ALPHA MONKEY, WHICH WAS SITTING FIRMLY ATOP A PROMINENT BOULDER, I NERVOUSLY EDGED TOWARD IT, WANTING TO GET A CLOSER LOOK.

AND THAT WAS IT!
THE MOMENT WHEN IT HAPPENED!!

(TO BE CONTINUED...)

Number 78: Neji and Hinata

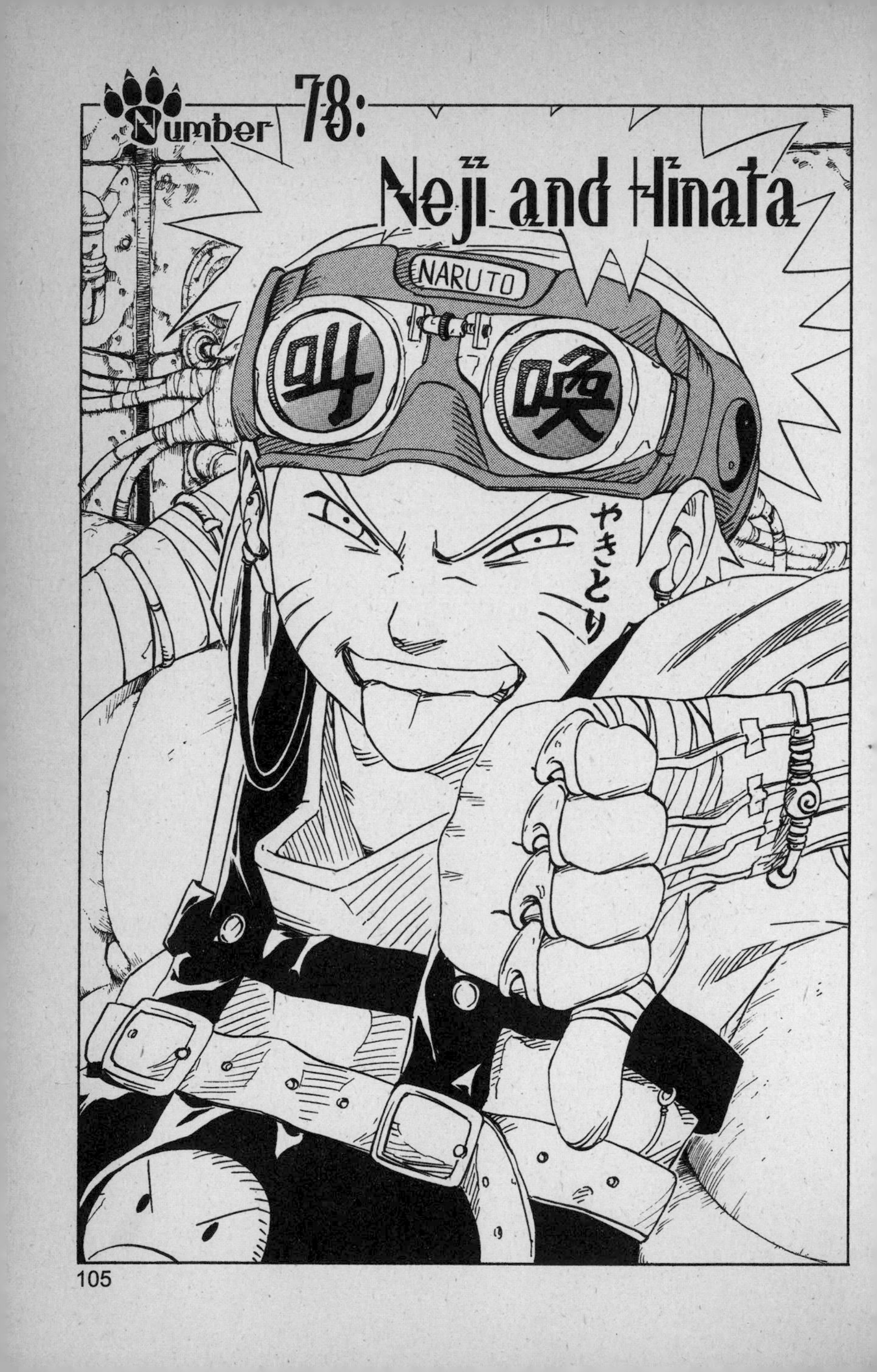
NARUTO
叫
喚
やきとり

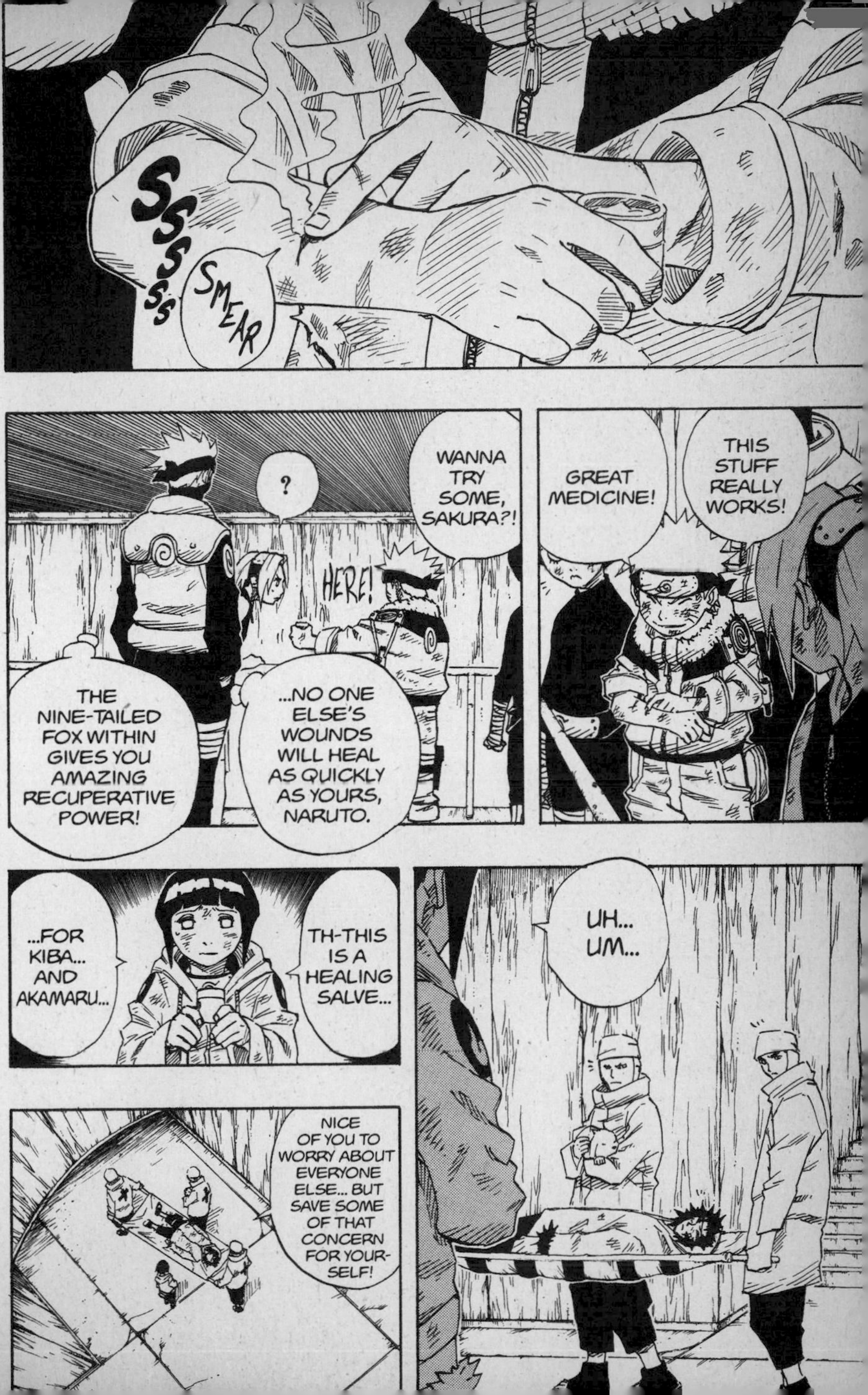
SSSSS
SMEAR
THIS STUFF REALLY WORKS!
GREAT MEDICINE!
WANNA TRY SOME, SAKURA?!
HERE!
?
...NO ONE ELSE'S WOUNDS WILL HEAL AS QUICKLY AS YOURS, NARUTO.
THE NINE-TAILED FOX WITHIN GIVES YOU AMAZING RECUPERATIVE POWER!
UH... UM...
TH-THIS IS A HEALING SALVE...
...FOR KIBA... AND AKAMARU...
NICE OF YOU TO WORRY ABOUT EVERYONE ELSE... BUT SAVE SOME OF THAT CONCERN FOR YOURSELF!

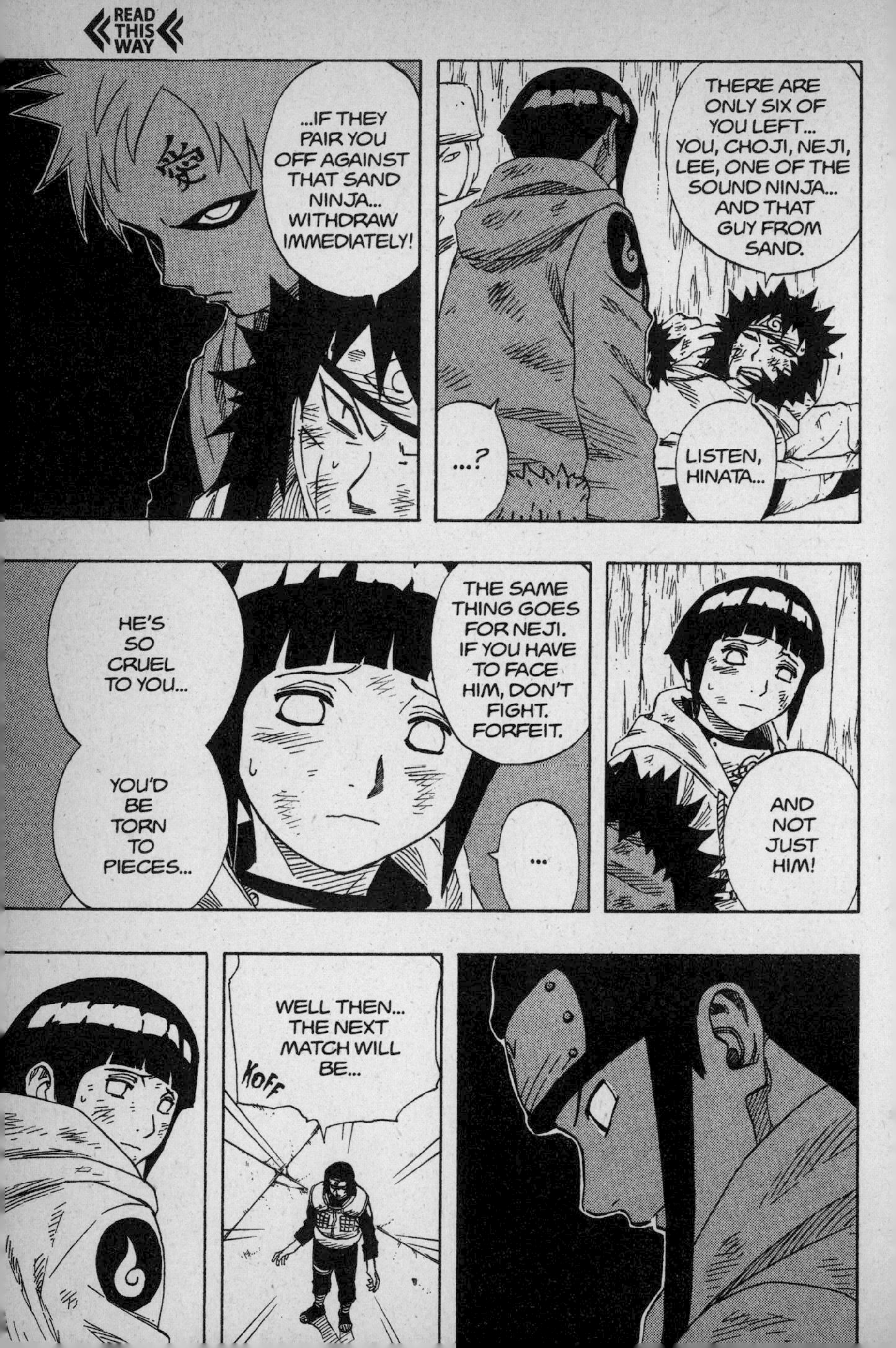
READ THIS WAY
THERE ARE ONLY SIX OF YOU LEFT... YOU, CHOJI, NEJI, LEE, ONE OF THE SOUND NINJA... AND THAT GUY FROM SAND.
LISTEN, HINATA...
...?
...IF THEY PAIR YOU OFF AGAINST THAT SAND NINJA... WITHDRAW IMMEDIATELY!
AND NOT JUST HIM!
THE SAME THING GOES FOR NEJI. IF YOU HAVE TO FACE HIM, DON'T FIGHT. FORFEIT.
...
HE'S SO CRUEL TO YOU...
YOU'D BE TORN TO PIECES...
WELL THEN... THE NEXT MATCH WILL BE...
KOFF

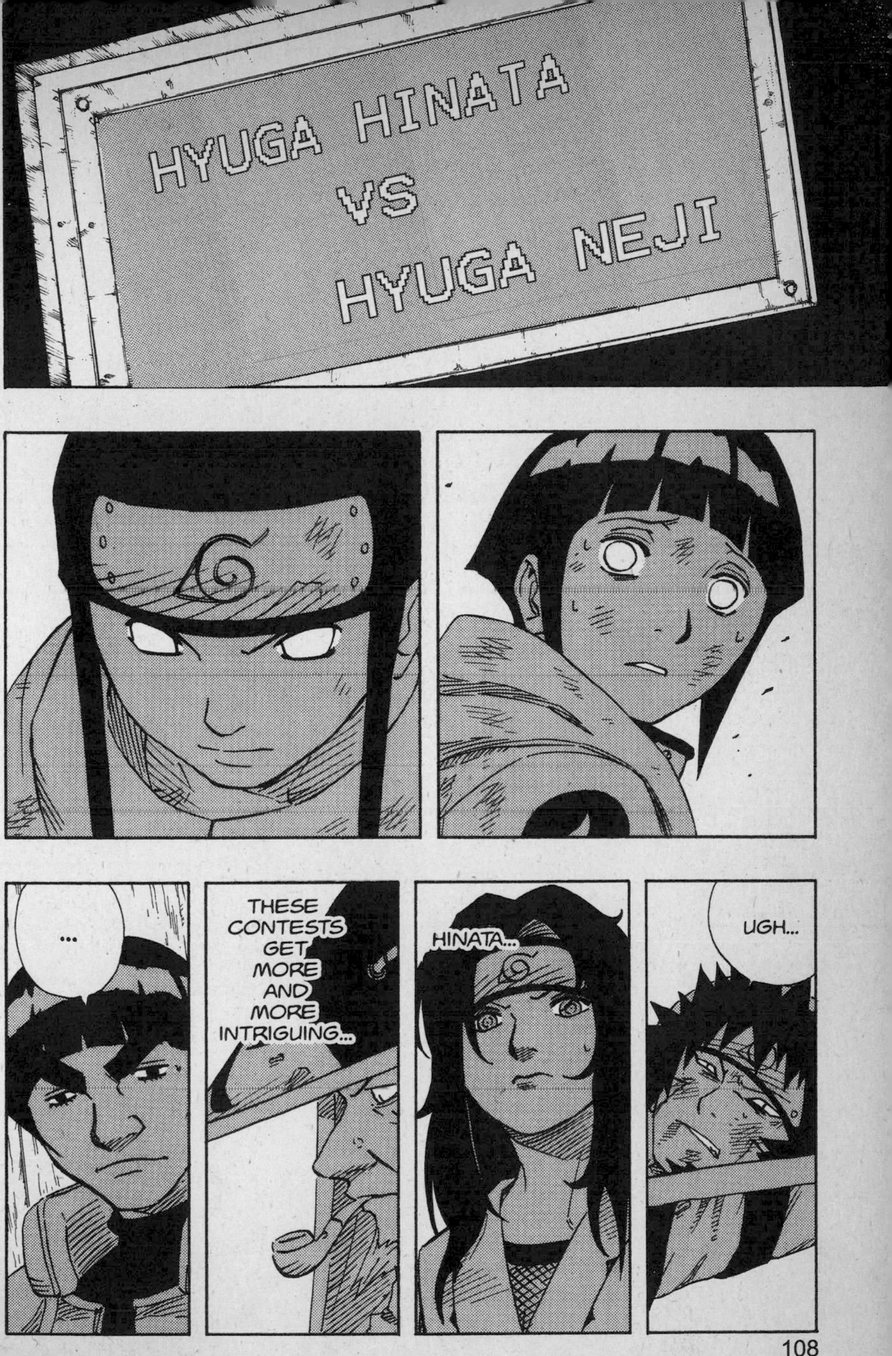
HYUGA HINATA VS HYUGA NEJI
UGH...
HINATA...
THESE CONTESTS GET MORE AND MORE INTRIGUING...
...

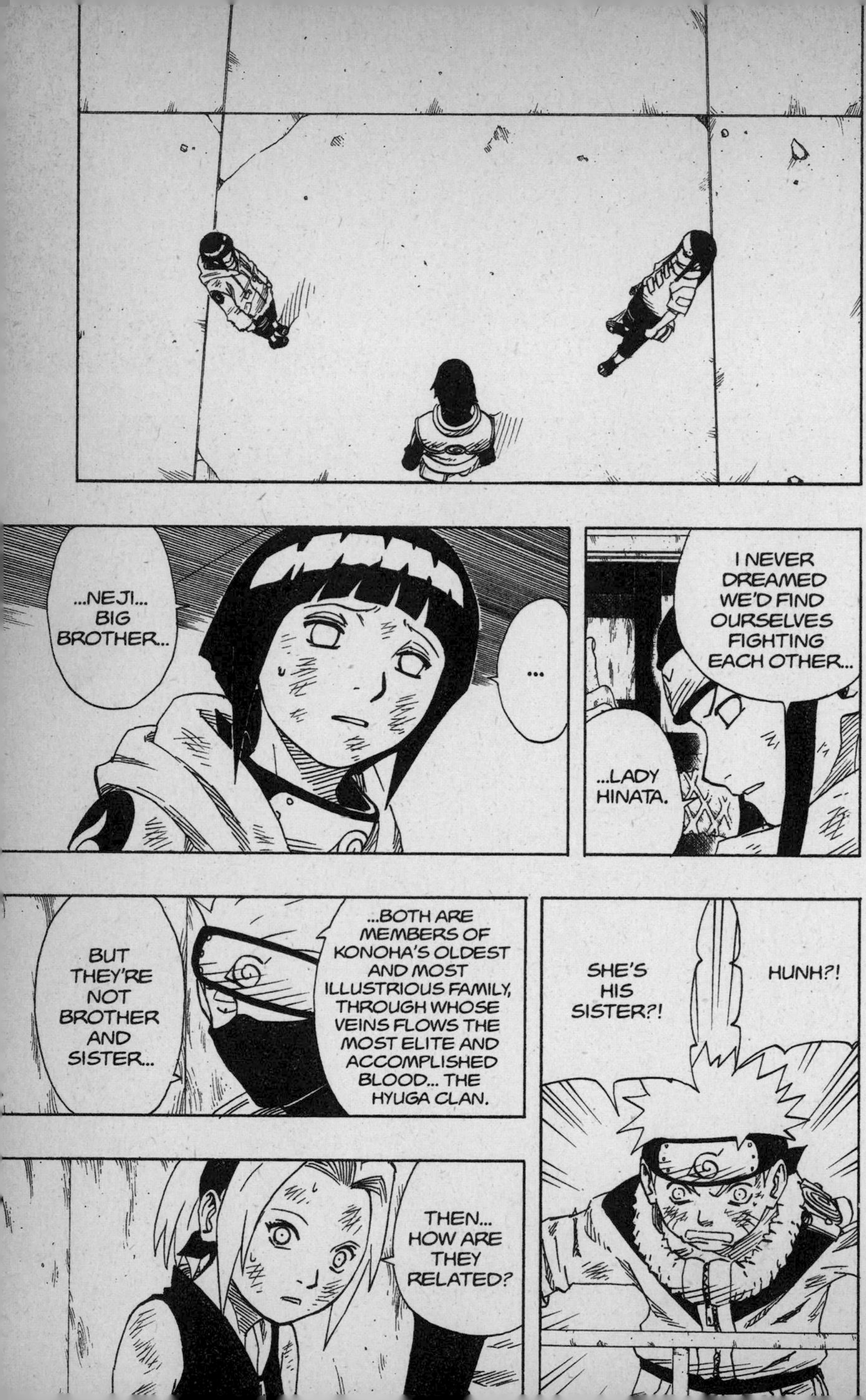

I NEVER DREAMED WE'D FIND OURSELVES FIGHTING EACH OTHER...
...LADY HINATA.
...
...NEJI... BIG BROTHER...
HUNH?!
SHE'S HIS SISTER?!
...BOTH ARE MEMBERS OF KONOHA'S OLDEST AND MOST ILLUSTRIOUS FAMILY, THROUGH WHOSE VEINS FLOWS THE MOST ELITE AND ACCOMPLISHED BLOOD... THE HYUGA CLAN.
BUT THEY'RE NOT BROTHER AND SISTER...
THEN... HOW ARE THEY RELATED?

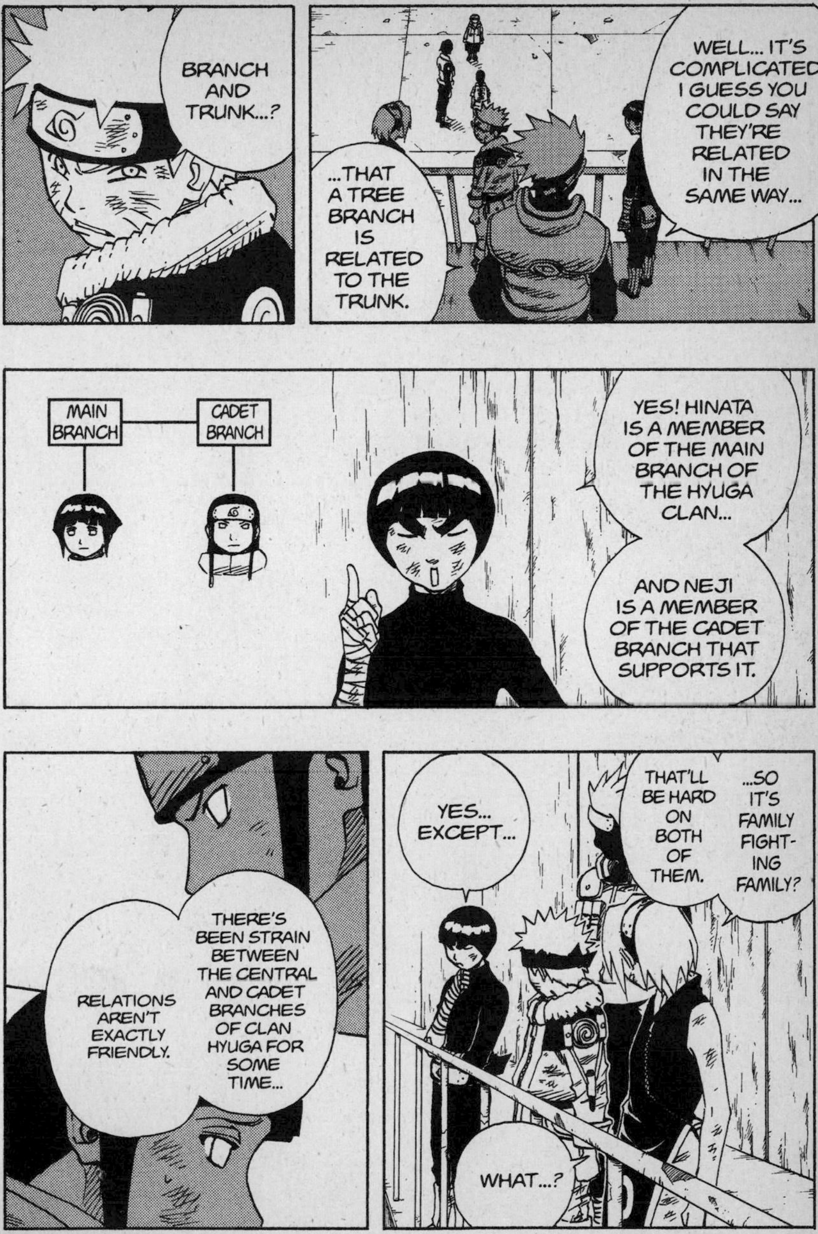
WELL... IT'S COMPLICATED... I GUESS YOU COULD SAY THEY'RE RELATED IN THE SAME WAY...
...THAT A TREE BRANCH IS RELATED TO THE TRUNK.
BRANCH AND TRUNK...?
YES! HINATA IS A MEMBER OF THE MAIN BRANCH OF THE HYUGA CLAN...
AND NEJI IS A MEMBER OF THE CADET BRANCH THAT SUPPORTS IT.
MAIN BRANCH
CADET BRANCH
...SO IT'S FAMILY FIGHT-ING FAMILY?
THAT'LL BE HARD ON BOTH OF THEM.
YES... EXCEPT...
WHAT...?
THERE'S BEEN STRAIN BETWEEN THE CENTRAL AND CADET BRANCHES OF CLAN HYUGA FOR SOME TIME...
RELATIONS AREN'T EXACTLY FRIENDLY.

READ THIS WAY

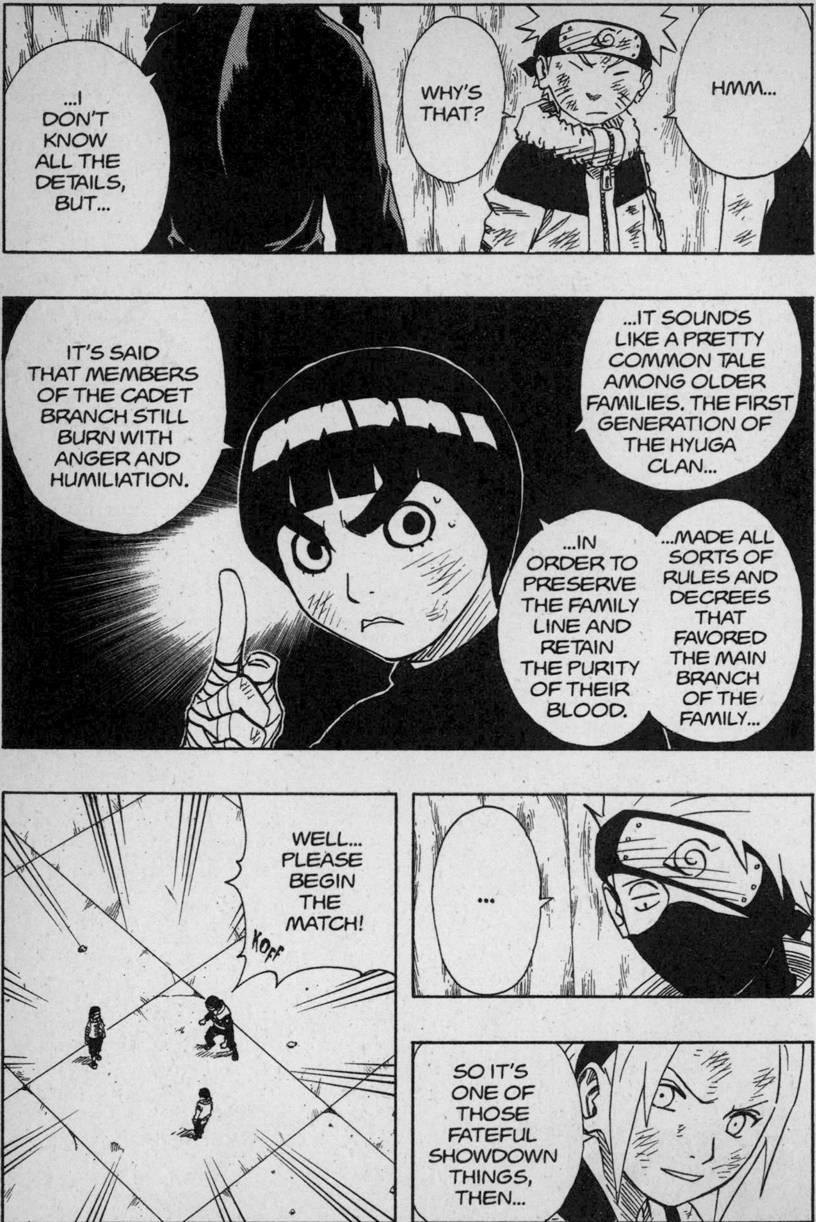
HMM...
WHY'S THAT?
...I DON'T KNOW ALL THE DETAILS, BUT...
...IT SOUNDS LIKE A PRETTY COMMON TALE AMONG OLDER FAMILIES. THE FIRST GENERATION OF THE HYUGA CLAN...
...MADE ALL SORTS OF RULES AND DECREES THAT FAVORED THE MAIN BRANCH OF THE FAMILY...
...IN ORDER TO PRESERVE THE FAMILY LINE AND RETAIN THE PURITY OF THEIR BLOOD.
IT'S SAID THAT MEMBERS OF THE CADET BRANCH STILL BURN WITH ANGER AND HUMILIATION.
...
SO IT'S ONE OF THOSE FATEFUL SHOWDOWN THINGS, THEN...
WELL... PLEASE BEGIN THE MATCH!
KOFF

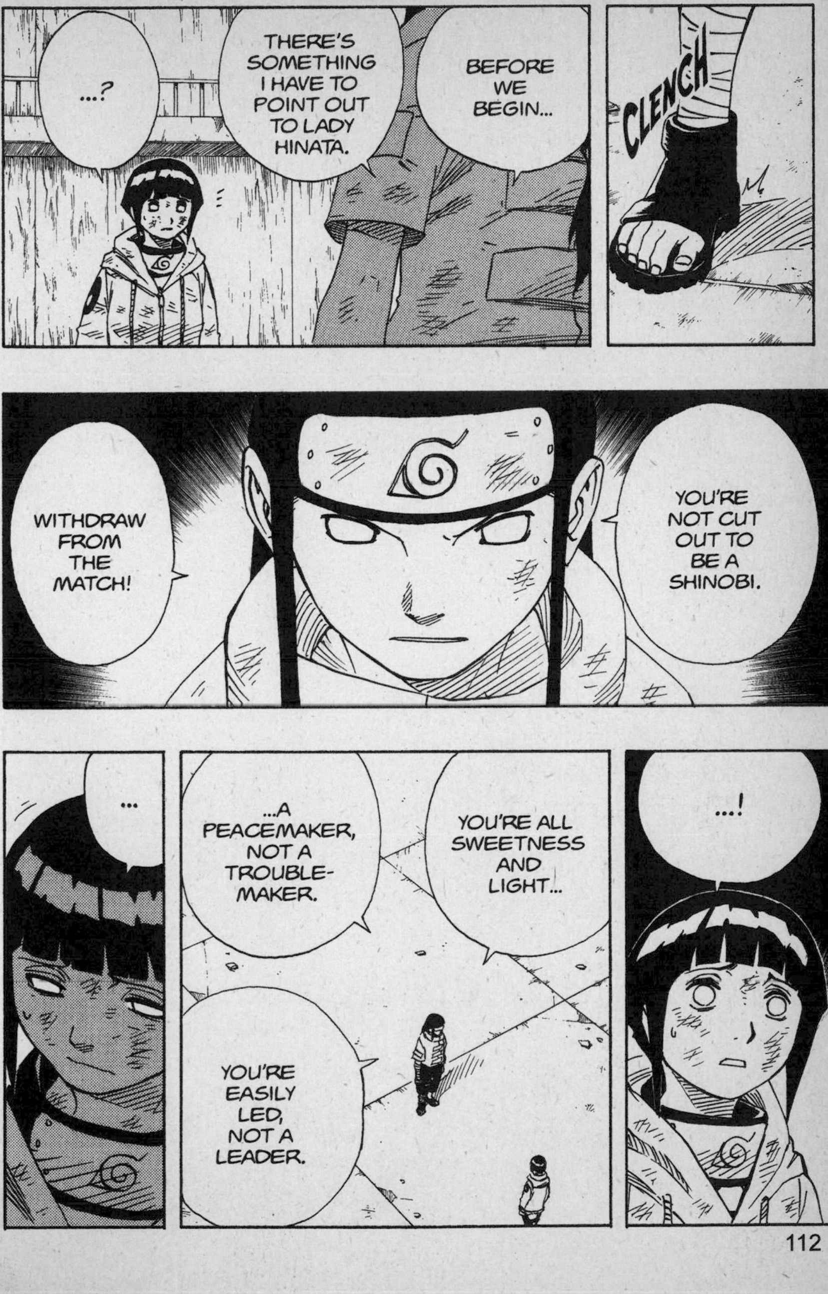
CLENCH
BEFORE WE BEGIN...
THERE'S SOMETHING I HAVE TO POINT OUT TO LADY HINATA.
...?
YOU'RE NOT CUT OUT TO BE A SHINOBI.
WITHDRAW FROM THE MATCH!
...!
YOU'RE ALL SWEETNESS AND LIGHT...
...A PEACEMAKER, NOT A TROUBLE-MAKER.
YOU'RE EASILY LED, NOT A LEADER.
...

READ THIS WAY

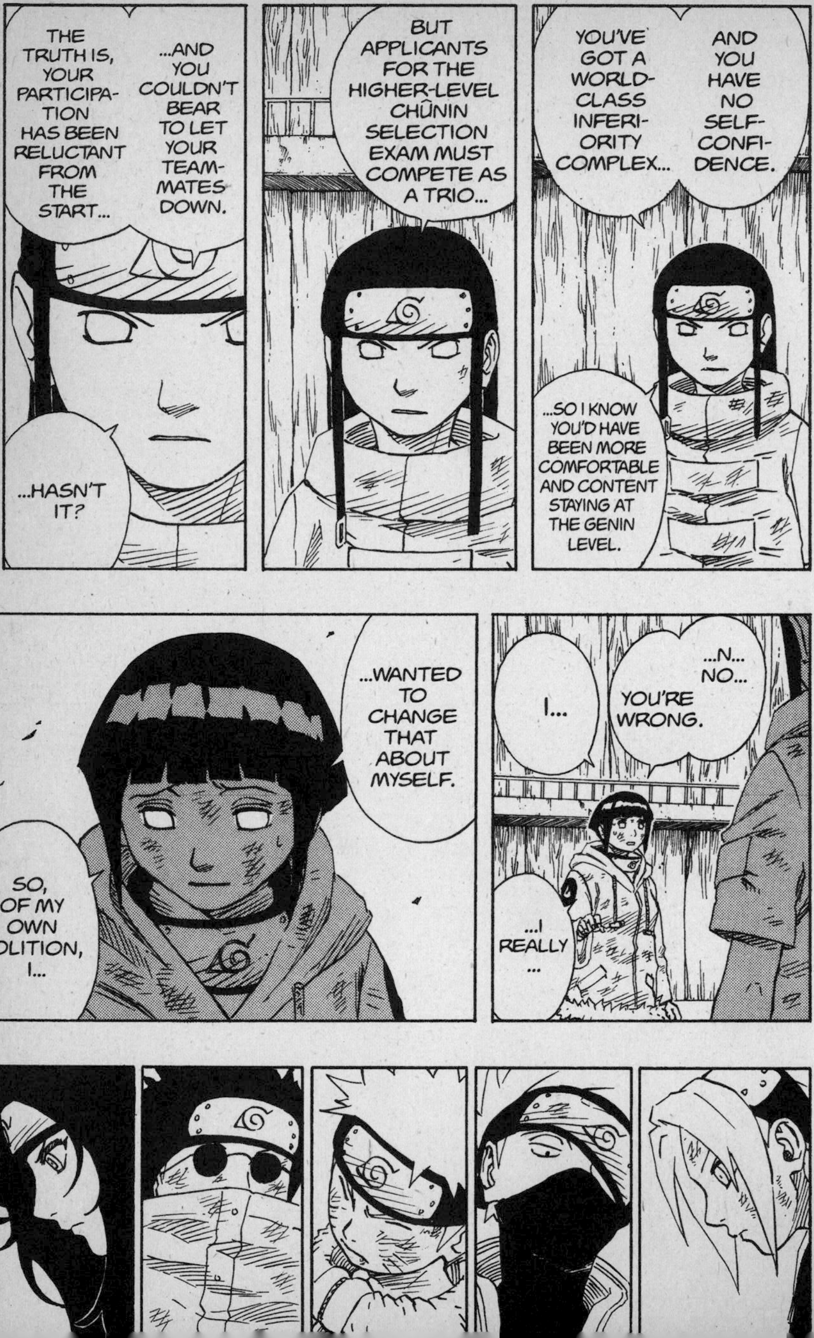
AND YOU HAVE NO SELF-CONFIDENCE.
YOU'VE GOT A WORLD-CLASS INFERIORITY COMPLEX...
...SO I KNOW YOU'D HAVE BEEN MORE COMFORTABLE AND CONTENT STAYING AT THE GENIN LEVEL.
BUT APPLICANTS FOR THE HIGHER-LEVEL CHÛNIN SELECTION EXAM MUST COMPETE AS A TRIO...
...AND YOU COULDN'T BEAR TO LET YOUR TEAM-MATES DOWN.
THE TRUTH IS, YOUR PARTICIPA-TION HAS BEEN RELUCTANT FROM THE START...
...HASN'T IT?
...N... NO... YOU'RE WRONG.
I...
...I REALLY ...
...WANTED TO CHANGE THAT ABOUT MYSELF.
SO, OF MY OWN VOLITION, I...

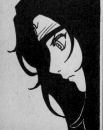

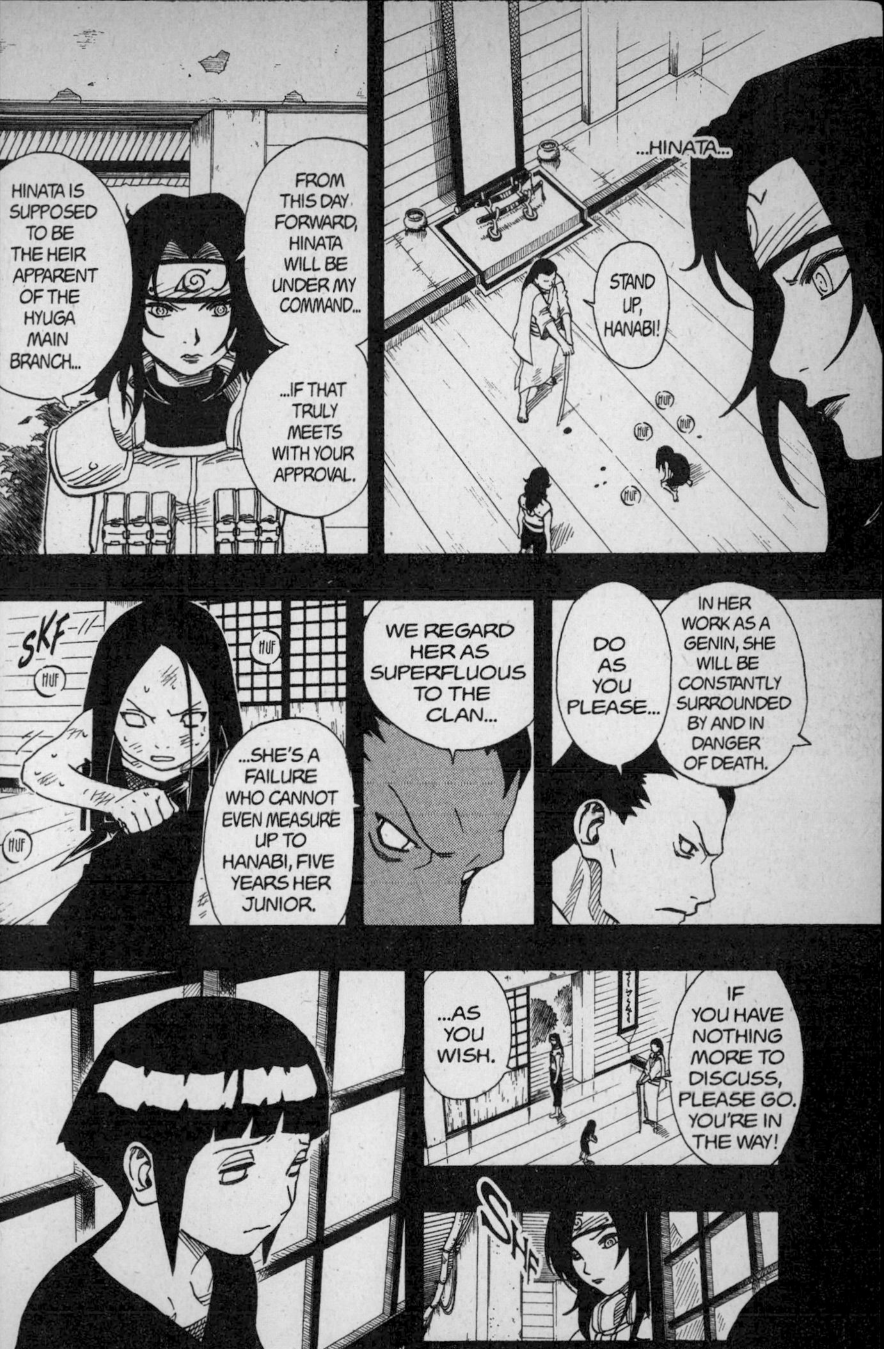
...HINATA...
STAND UP, HANABI!
HUF
HUF
HUF
HUF
FROM THIS DAY FORWARD, HINATA WILL BE UNDER MY COMMAND...
...IF THAT TRULY MEETS WITH YOUR APPROVAL.
HINATA IS SUPPOSED TO BE THE HEIR APPARENT OF THE HYUGA MAIN BRANCH...
IN HER WORK AS A GENIN, SHE WILL BE CONSTANTLY SURROUNDED BY AND IN DANGER OF DEATH.
DO AS YOU PLEASE...
WE REGARD HER AS SUPERFLUOUS TO THE CLAN...
...SHE'S A FAILURE WHO CANNOT EVEN MEASURE UP TO HANABI, FIVE YEARS HER JUNIOR.
HUF
SKF
HUF
HUF
IF YOU HAVE NOTHING MORE TO DISCUSS, PLEASE GO. YOU'RE IN THE WAY!
...AS YOU WISH.
SHF

READ THIS WAY

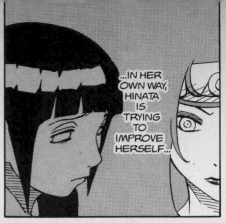

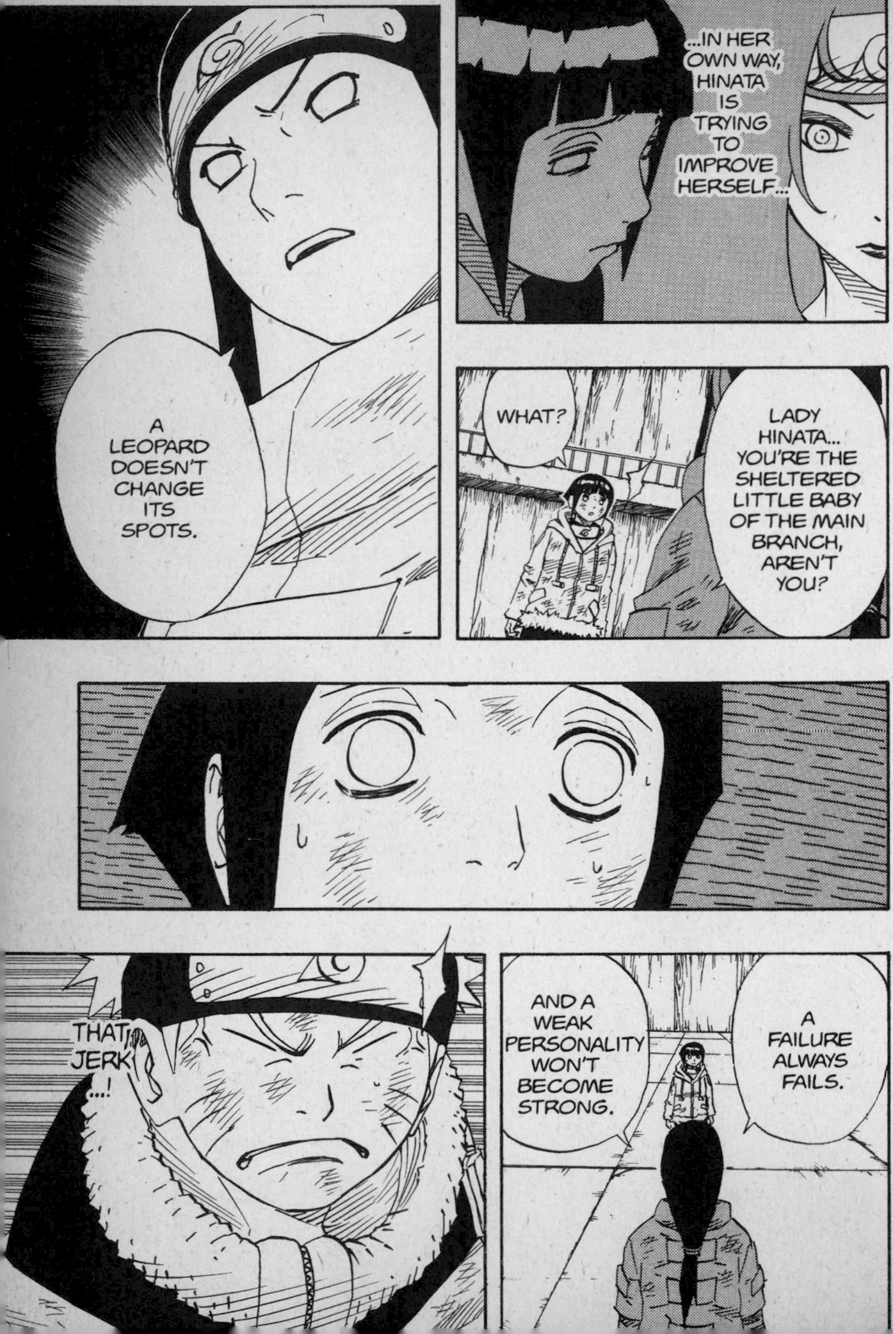
...IN HER OWN WAY, HINATA IS TRYING TO IMPROVE HERSELF...
LADY HINATA... YOU'RE THE SHELTERED LITTLE BABY OF THE MAIN BRANCH, AREN'T YOU?
WHAT?
A LEOPARD DOESN'T CHANGE ITS SPOTS.
A FAILURE ALWAYS FAILS.
AND A WEAK PERSONALITY WON'T BECOME STRONG.
THAT JERK...!

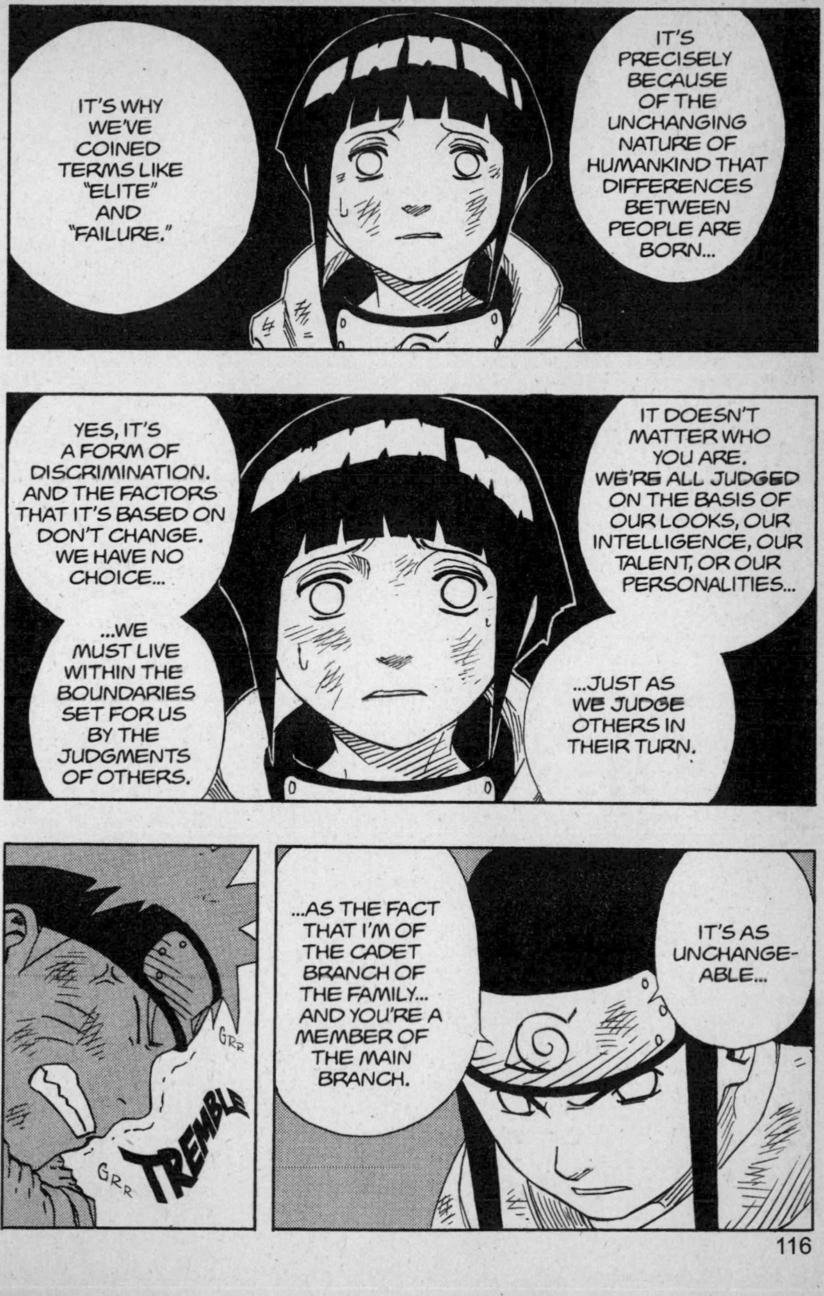
IT'S PRECISELY BECAUSE OF THE UNCHANGING NATURE OF HUMANKIND THAT DIFFERENCES BETWEEN PEOPLE ARE BORN...
IT'S WHY WE'VE COINED TERMS LIKE "ELITE" AND "FAILURE."
IT DOESN'T MATTER WHO YOU ARE. WE'RE ALL JUDGED ON THE BASIS OF OUR LOOKS, OUR INTELLIGENCE, OUR TALENT, OR OUR PERSONALITIES...
...JUST AS WE JUDGE OTHERS IN THEIR TURN.
YES, IT'S A FORM OF DISCRIMINATION. AND THE FACTORS THAT IT'S BASED ON DON'T CHANGE. WE HAVE NO CHOICE...
...WE MUST LIVE WITHIN THE BOUNDARIES SET FOR US BY THE JUDGMENTS OF OTHERS.
IT'S AS UNCHANGE-ABLE...
...AS THE FACT THAT I'M OF THE CADET BRANCH OF THE FAMILY... AND YOU'RE A MEMBER OF THE MAIN BRANCH.
GRR
TREMBLE
GRR

READ THIS WAY

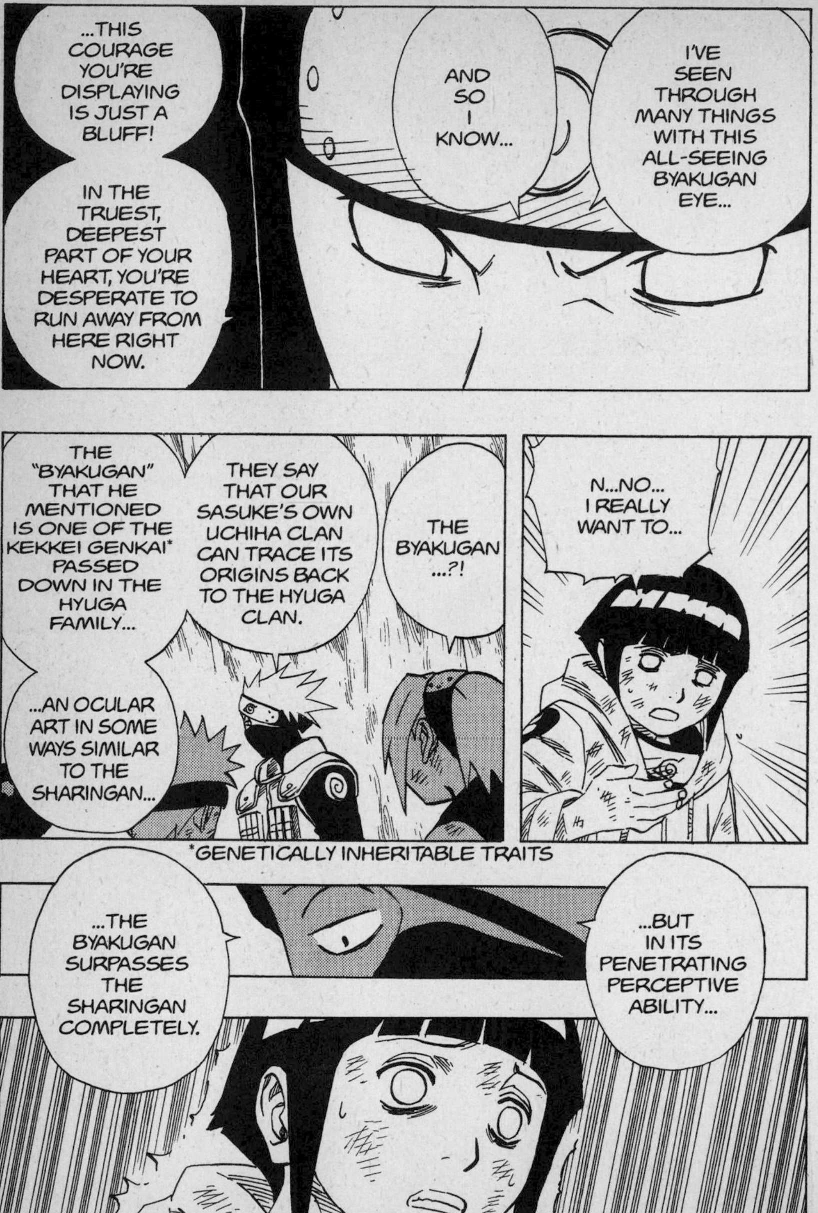
I'VE SEEN THROUGH MANY THINGS WITH THIS ALL-SEEING BYAKUGAN EYE...
AND SO I KNOW...
...THIS COURAGE YOU'RE DISPLAYING IS JUST A BLUFF!
IN THE TRUEST, DEEPEST PART OF YOUR HEART, YOU'RE DESPERATE TO RUN AWAY FROM HERE RIGHT NOW.
N...NO... I REALLY WANT TO...
THE BYAKUGAN ...?!
THEY SAY THAT OUR SASUKE'S OWN UCHIHA CLAN CAN TRACE ITS ORIGINS BACK TO THE HYUGA CLAN.
THE "BYAKUGAN" THAT HE MENTIONED IS ONE OF THE KEKKEI GENKAI* PASSED DOWN IN THE HYUGA FAMILY...
...AN OCULAR ART IN SOME WAYS SIMILAR TO THE SHARINGAN...
*GENETICALLY INHERITABLE TRAITS
...BUT IN ITS PENETRATING PERCEPTIVE ABILITY...
...THE BYAKUGAN SURPASSES THE SHARINGAN COMPLETELY.

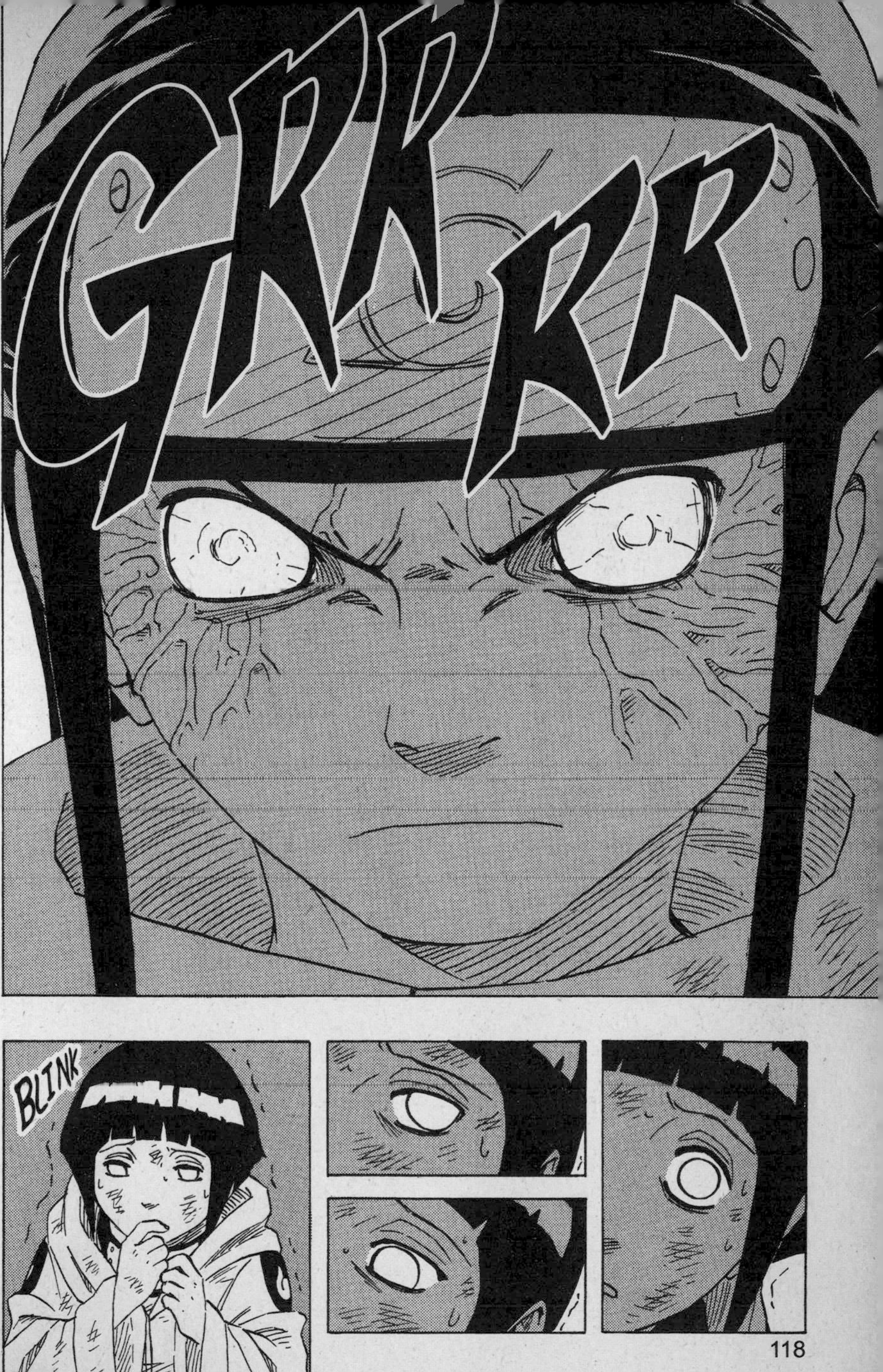
GRRRRR
BLINK

READ THIS WAY

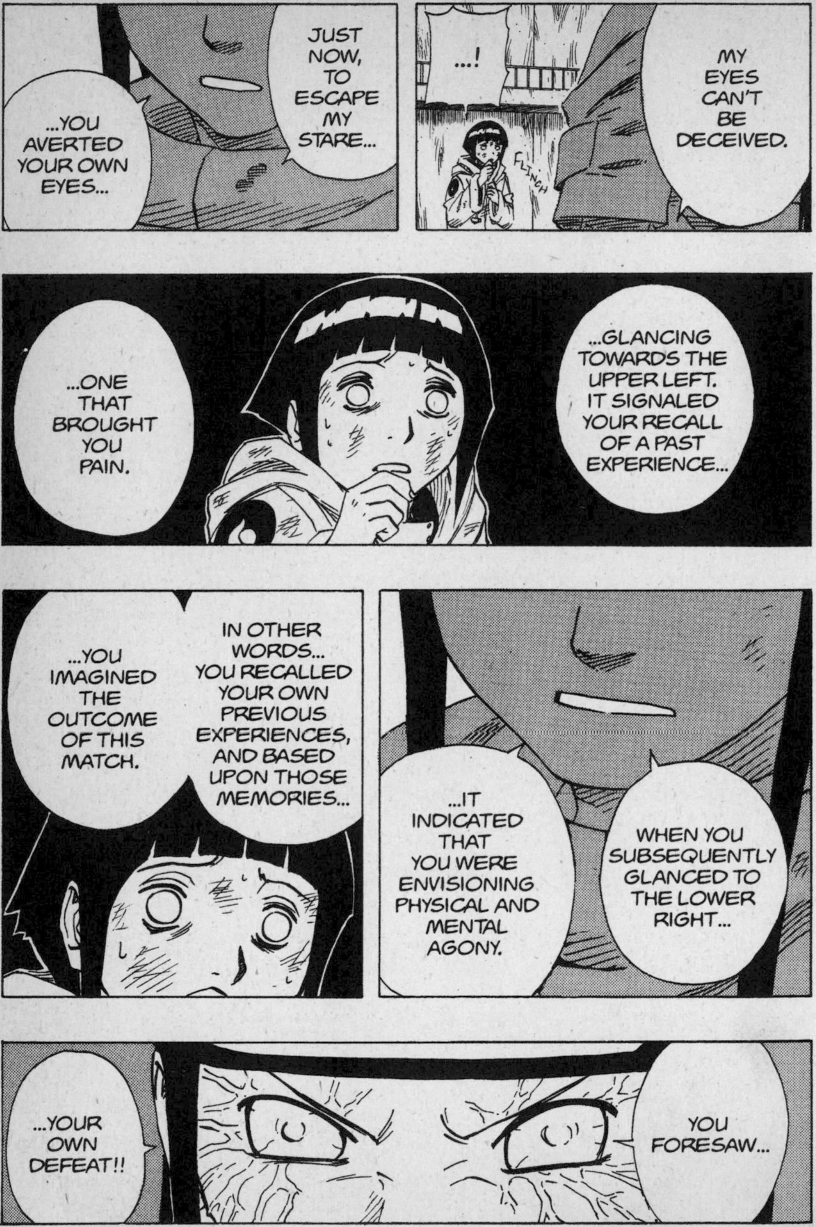
MY EYES CAN'T BE DECEIVED.
...!
FLINCH
JUST NOW, TO ESCAPE MY STARE...
...YOU AVERTED YOUR OWN EYES...
...GLANCING TOWARDS THE UPPER LEFT. IT SIGNALED YOUR RECALL OF A PAST EXPERIENCE...
...ONE THAT BROUGHT YOU PAIN.
WHEN YOU SUBSEQUENTLY GLANCED TO THE LOWER RIGHT...
...IT INDICATED THAT YOU WERE ENVISIONING PHYSICAL AND MENTAL AGONY.
IN OTHER WORDS... YOU RECALLED YOUR OWN PREVIOUS EXPERIENCES, AND BASED UPON THOSE MEMORIES...
...YOU IMAGINED THE OUTCOME OF THIS MATCH.
YOU FORESAW...
...YOUR OWN DEFEAT!!

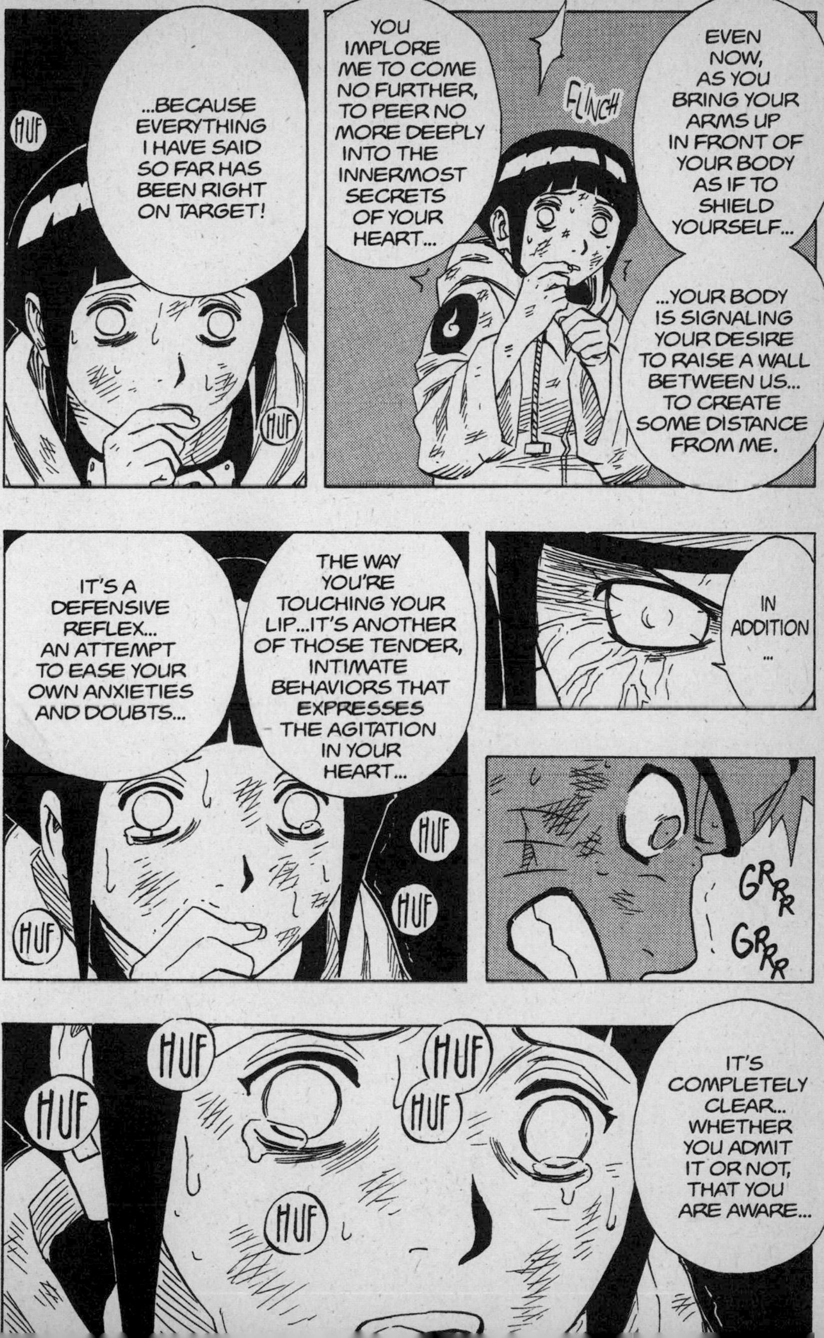
EVEN NOW, AS YOU BRING YOUR ARMS UP IN FRONT OF YOUR BODY AS IF TO SHIELD YOURSELF...
FLINCH
...YOUR BODY IS SIGNALING YOUR DESIRE TO RAISE A WALL BETWEEN US... TO CREATE SOME DISTANCE FROM ME.
YOU IMPLORE ME TO COME NO FURTHER, TO PEER NO MORE DEEPLY INTO THE INNERMOST SECRETS OF YOUR HEART...
...BECAUSE EVERYTHING I HAVE SAID SO FAR HAS BEEN RIGHT ON TARGET!
HUF
HUF
IN ADDITION...
GRRR
GRRR
THE WAY YOU'RE TOUCHING YOUR LIP...IT'S ANOTHER OF THOSE TENDER, INTIMATE BEHAVIORS THAT EXPRESSES THE AGITATION IN YOUR HEART...
IT'S A DEFENSIVE REFLEX... AN ATTEMPT TO EASE YOUR OWN ANXIETIES AND DOUBTS...
HUF
HUF
HUF
IT'S COMPLETELY CLEAR... WHETHER YOU ADMIT IT OR NOT, THAT YOU ARE AWARE...
HUF
HUF
HUF
HUF
HUF

READ THIS WAY

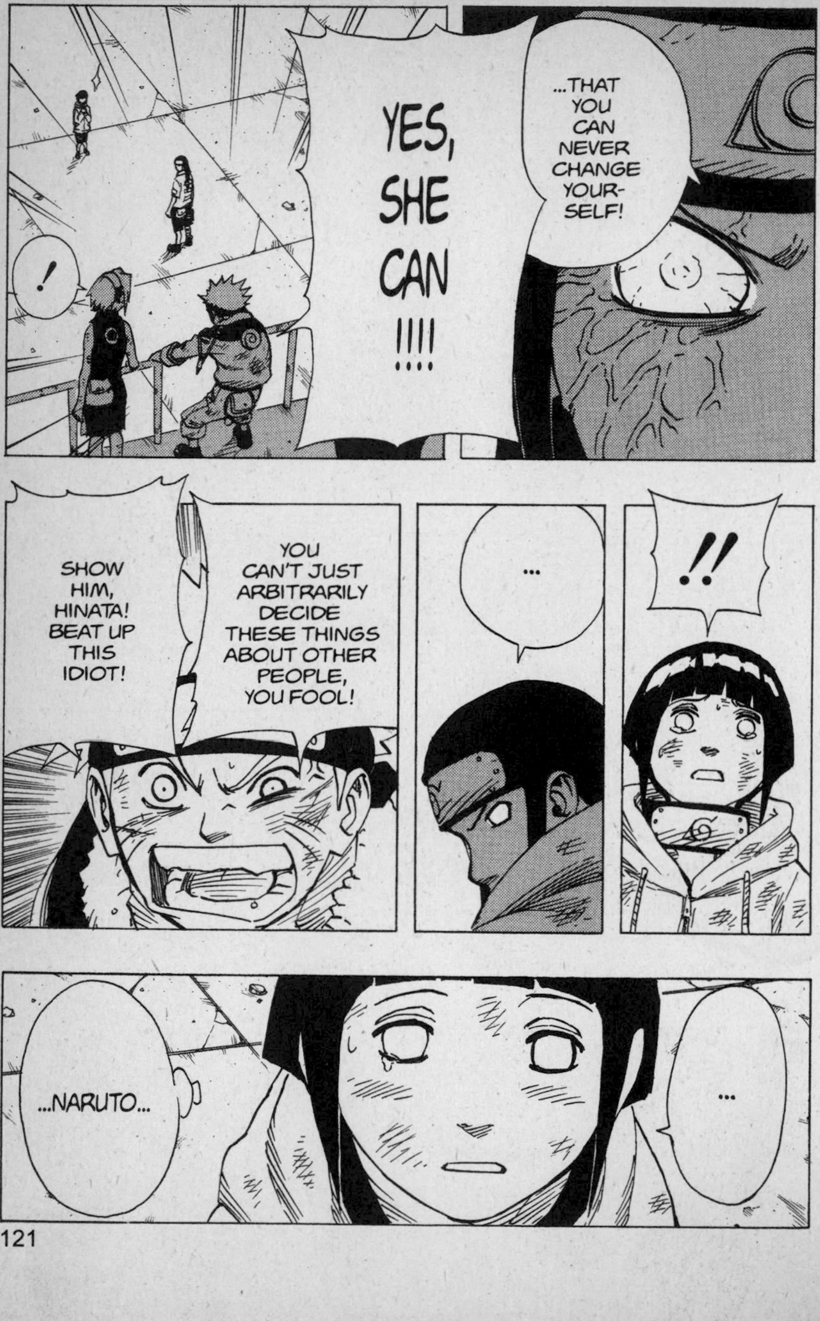
...THAT YOU CAN NEVER CHANGE YOUR-SELF!
YES, SHE CAN!!!!
!
!!
...
YOU CAN'T JUST ARBITRARILY DECIDE THESE THINGS ABOUT OTHER PEOPLE, YOU FOOL!
SHOW HIM, HINATA! BEAT UP THIS IDIOT!
...
...NARUTO...

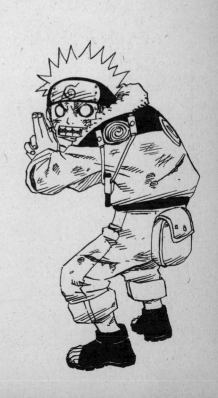

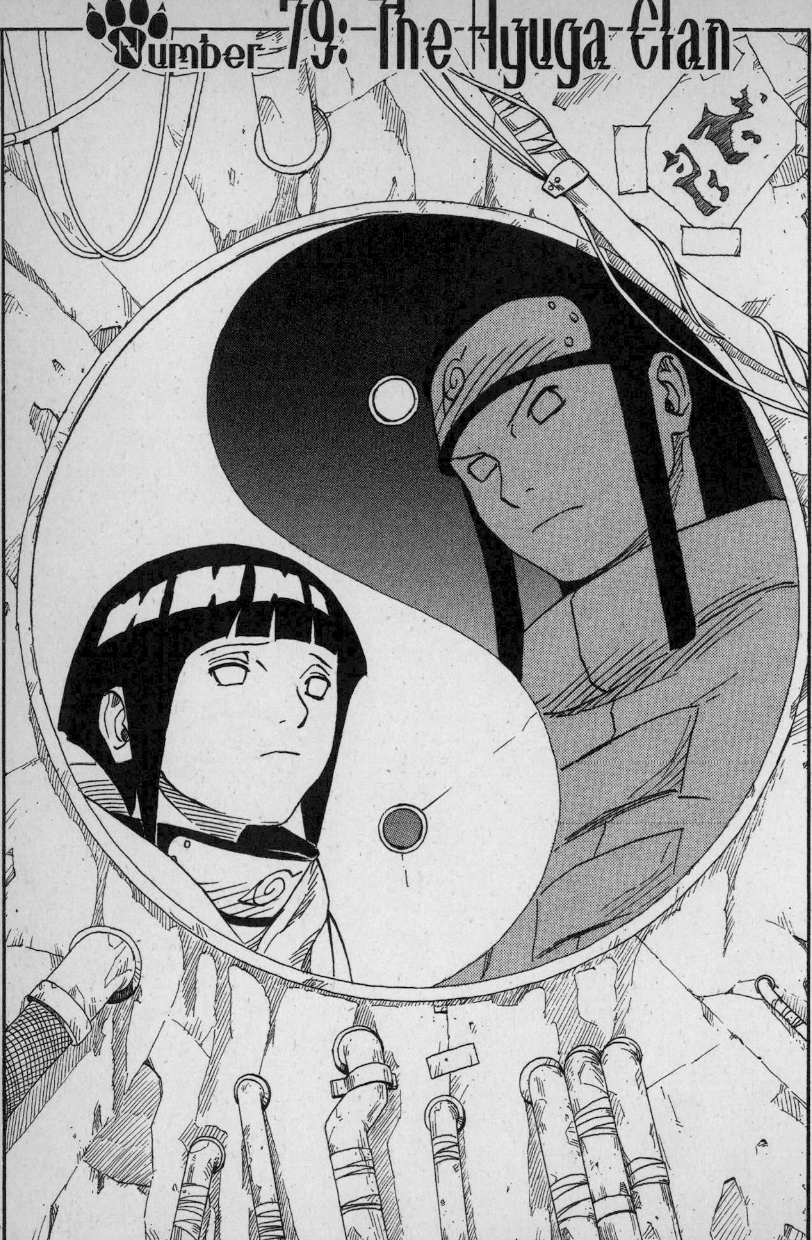
Number 79: The Hyuga Clan

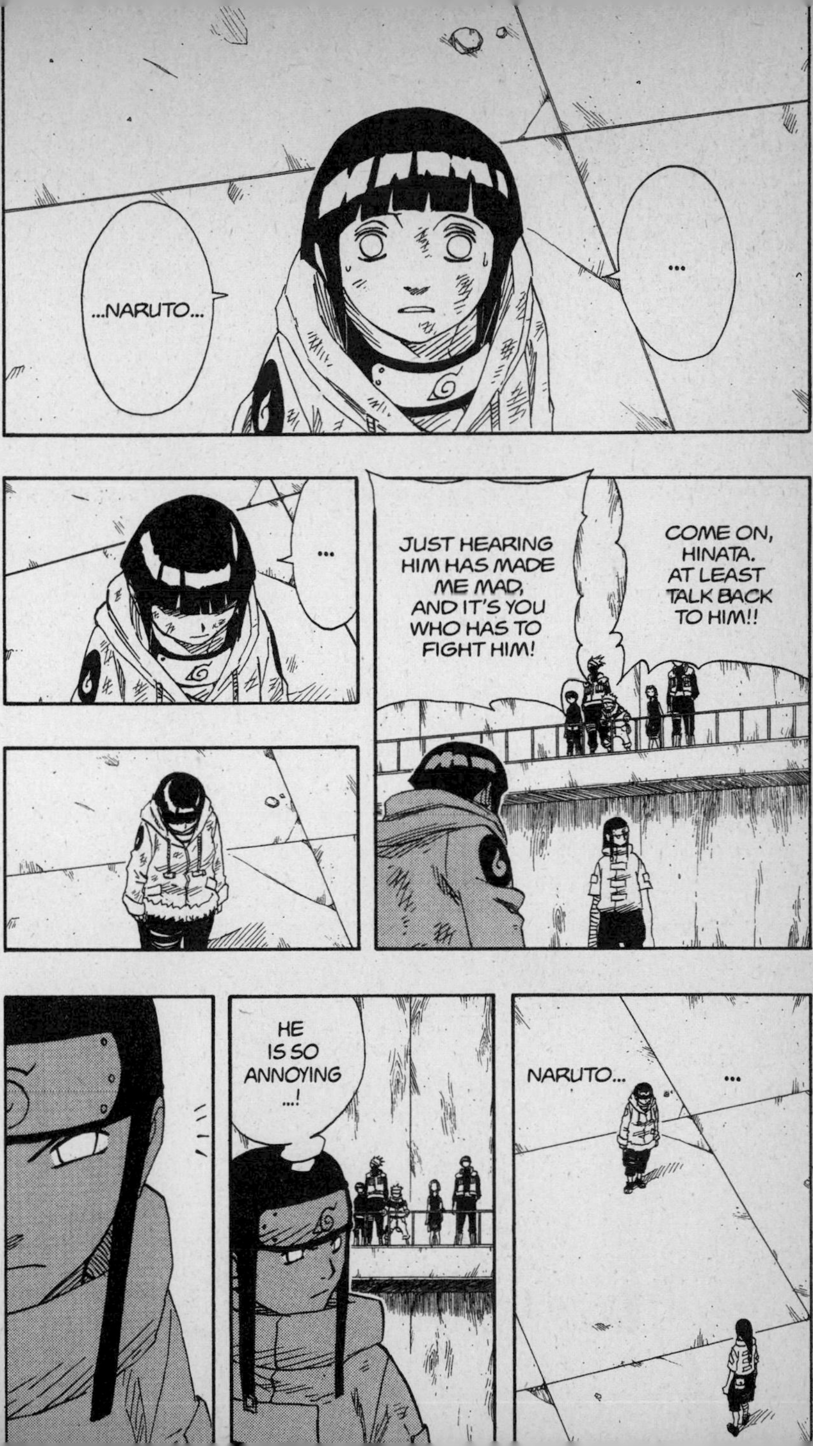
...
...NARUTO...
COME ON, HINATA. AT LEAST TALK BACK TO HIM!!
JUST HEARING HIM HAS MADE ME MAD, AND IT'S YOU WHO HAS TO FIGHT HIM!
...
...
NARUTO...
HE IS SO ANNOYING ...!

READ THIS WAY

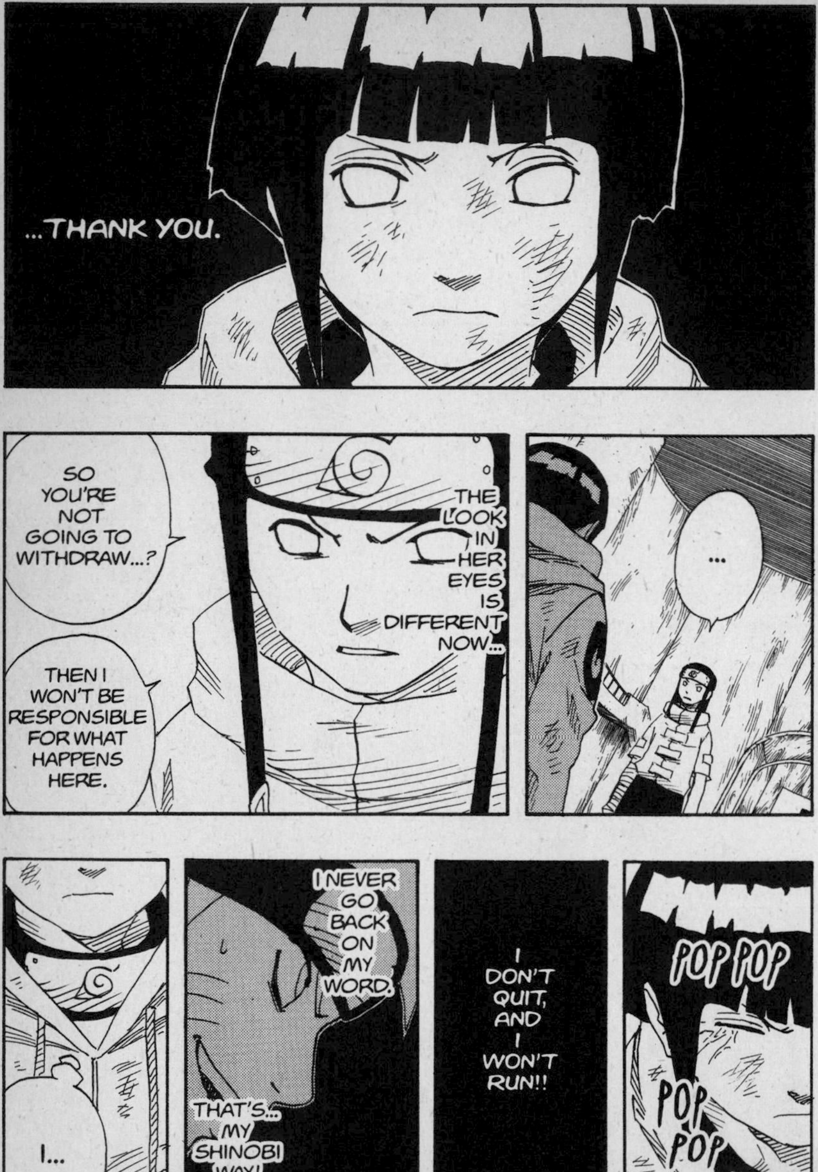
...THANK YOU.
...
THE LOOK IN HER EYES IS DIFFERENT NOW...
SO YOU'RE NOT GOING TO WITHDRAW...?
THEN I WON'T BE RESPONSIBLE FOR WHAT HAPPENS HERE.
POP POP
POP POP
I DON'T QUIT, AND I WON'T RUN!!
I NEVER GO BACK ON MY WORD.
THAT'S... MY SHINOBI WAY!
I...

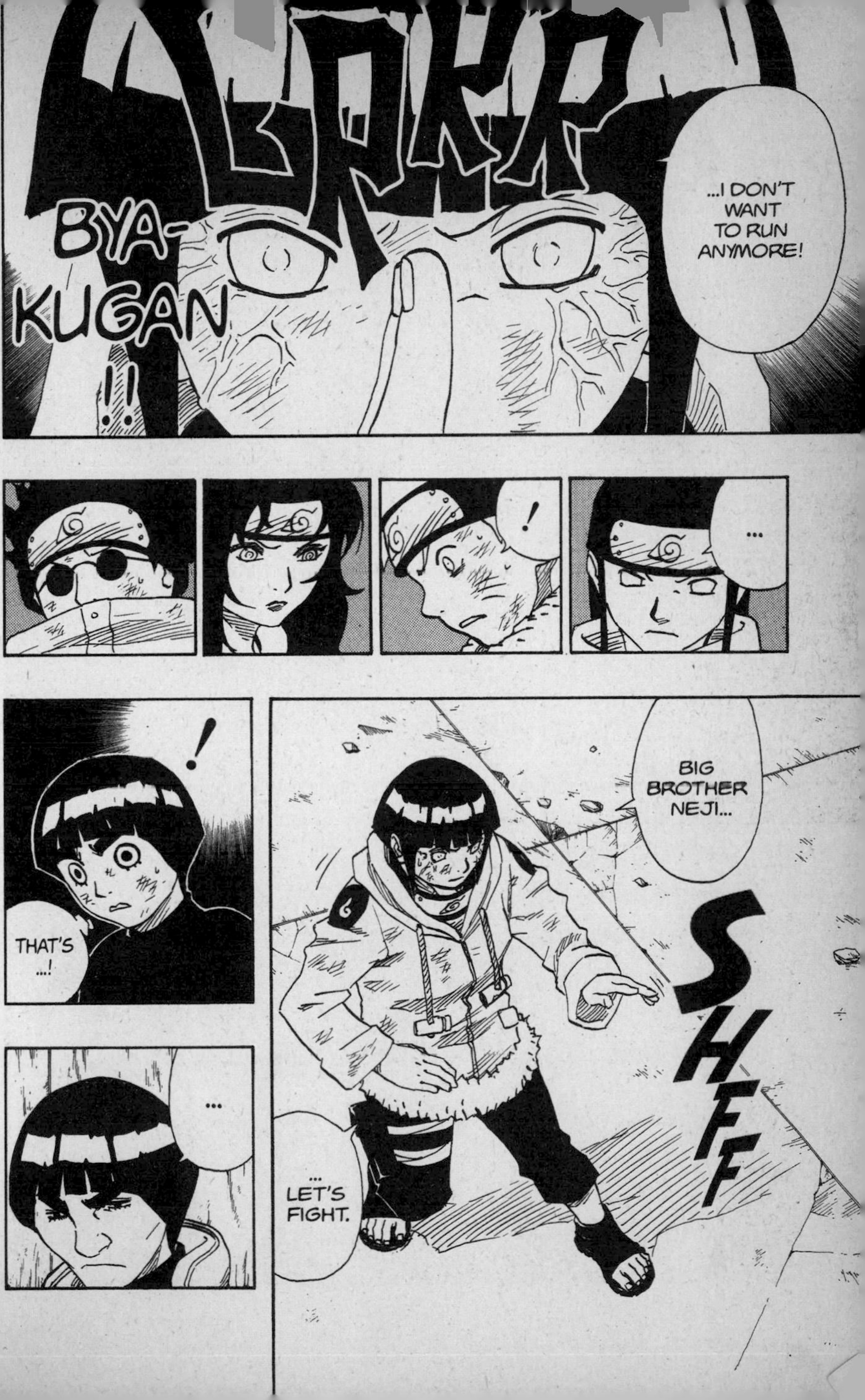
...I DON'T WANT TO RUN ANYMORE!
BYA-KUGAN!!
...
!
BIG BROTHER NEJI...
SHFFF
... LET'S FIGHT.
!
THAT'S ...!
...

READ THIS WAY

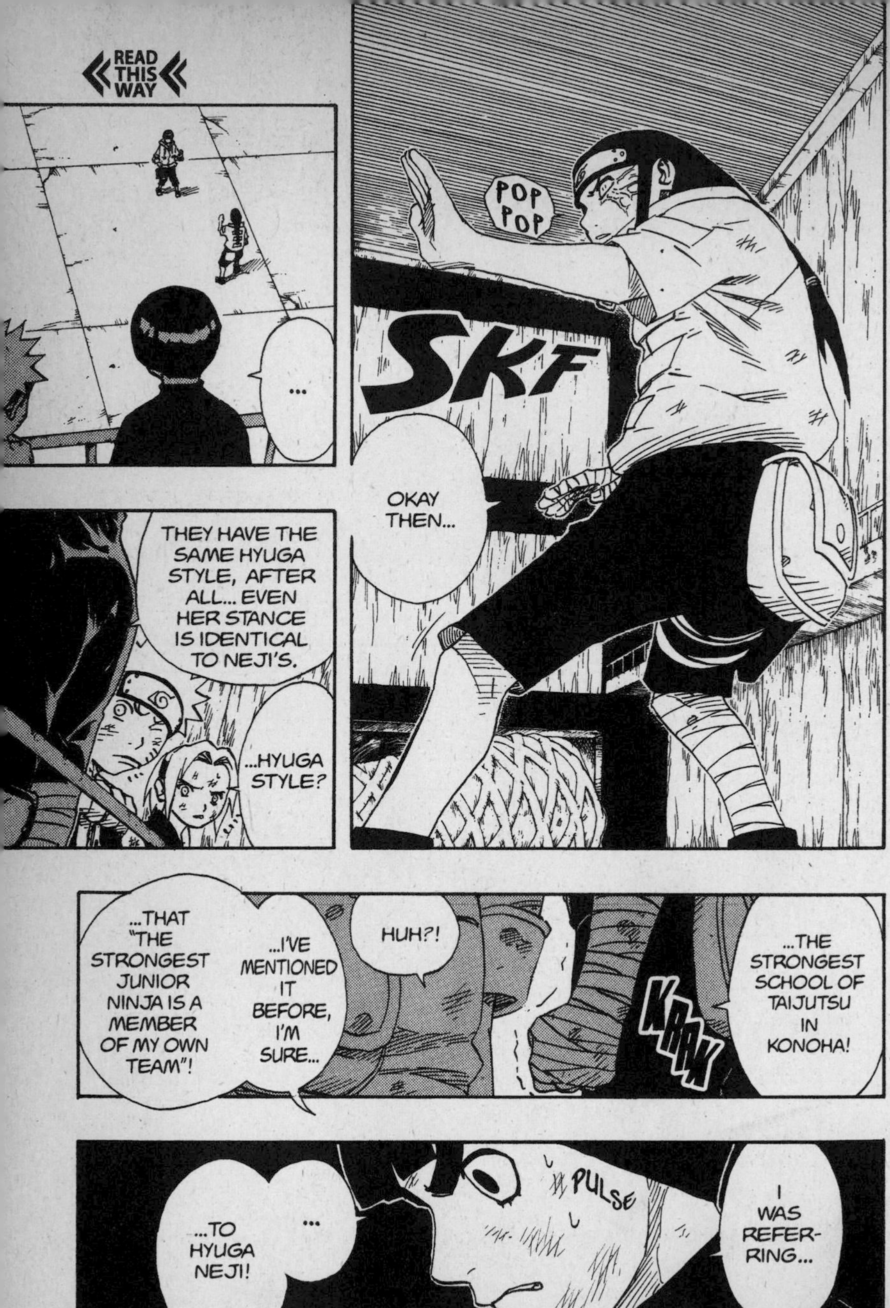
POP POP
SKF
OKAY THEN...
...
THEY HAVE THE SAME HYUGA STYLE, AFTER ALL... EVEN HER STANCE IS IDENTICAL TO NEJI'S.
...HYUGA STYLE?
...THE STRONGEST SCHOOL OF TAIJUTSU IN KONOHA!
KRAK
HUH?!
...I'VE MENTIONED IT BEFORE, I'M SURE...
...THAT "THE STRONGEST JUNIOR NINJA IS A MEMBER OF MY OWN TEAM"!
I WAS REFER-RING...
PULSE
...
...TO HYUGA NEJI!

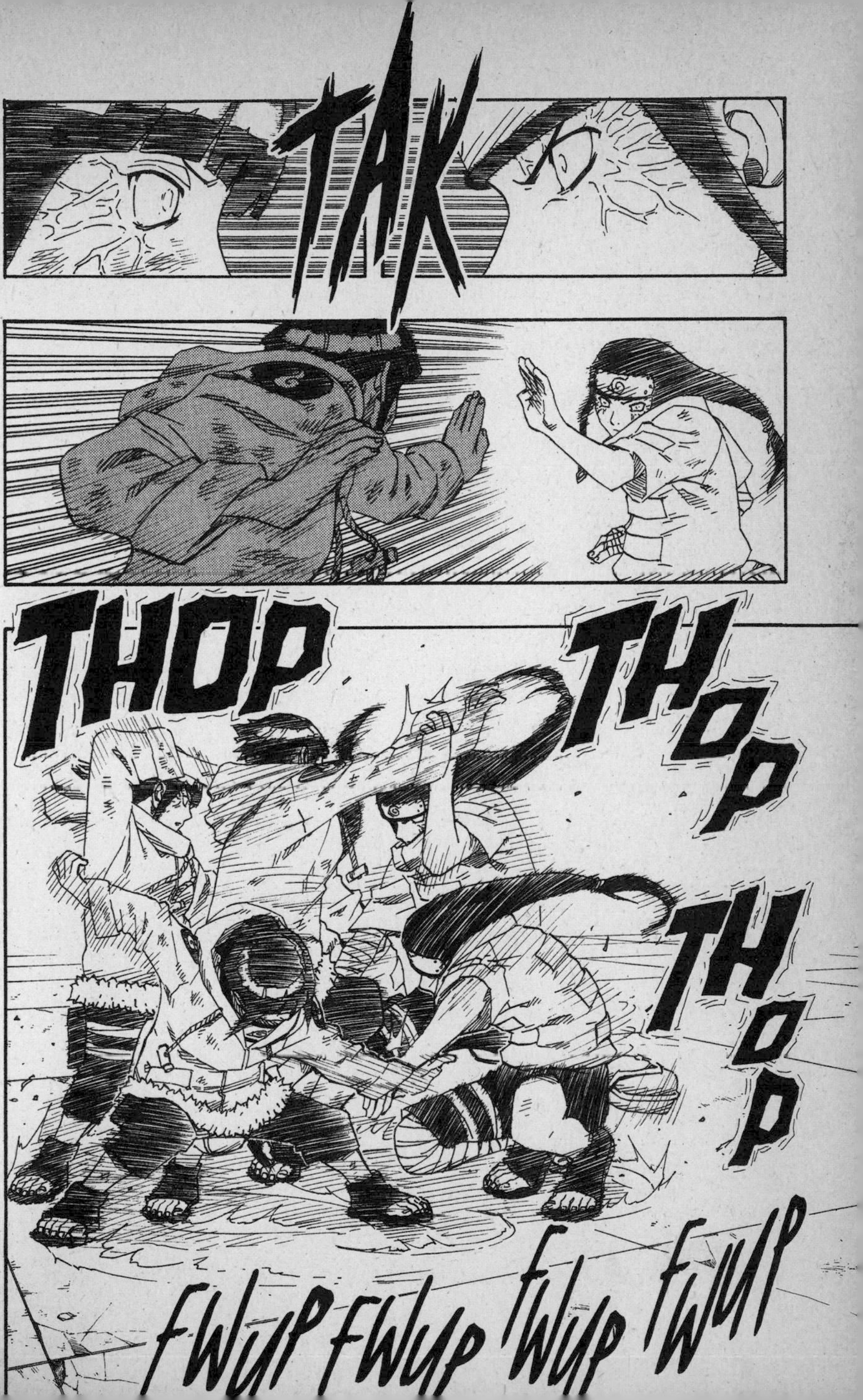
TAK
THOP
THOP
THOP
THOP
FWUP FWUP FWUP FWUP

READ THIS WAY

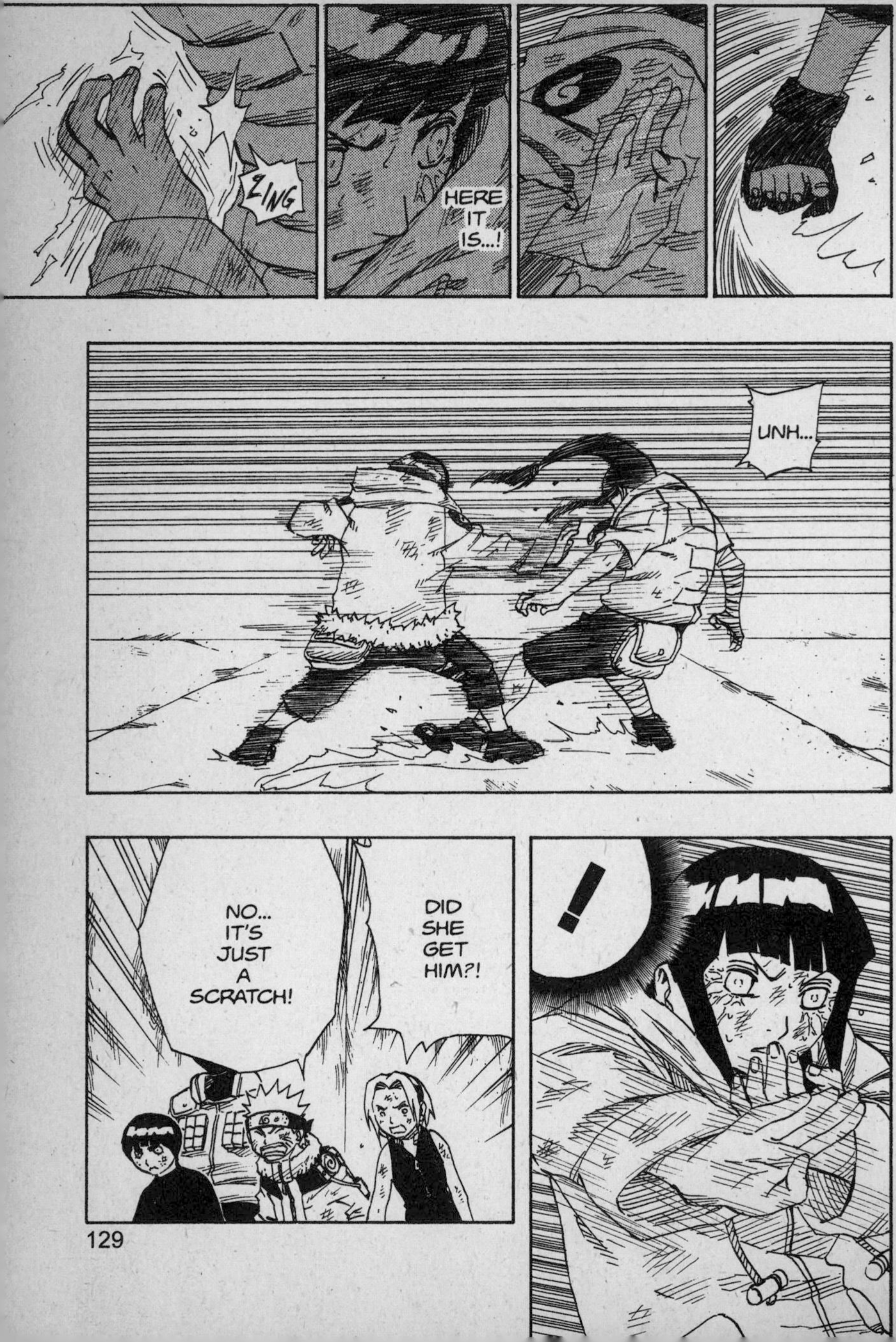

HERE IT IS...!
ZING
UNH...
!
DID SHE GET HIM?!
NO... IT'S JUST A SCRATCH!

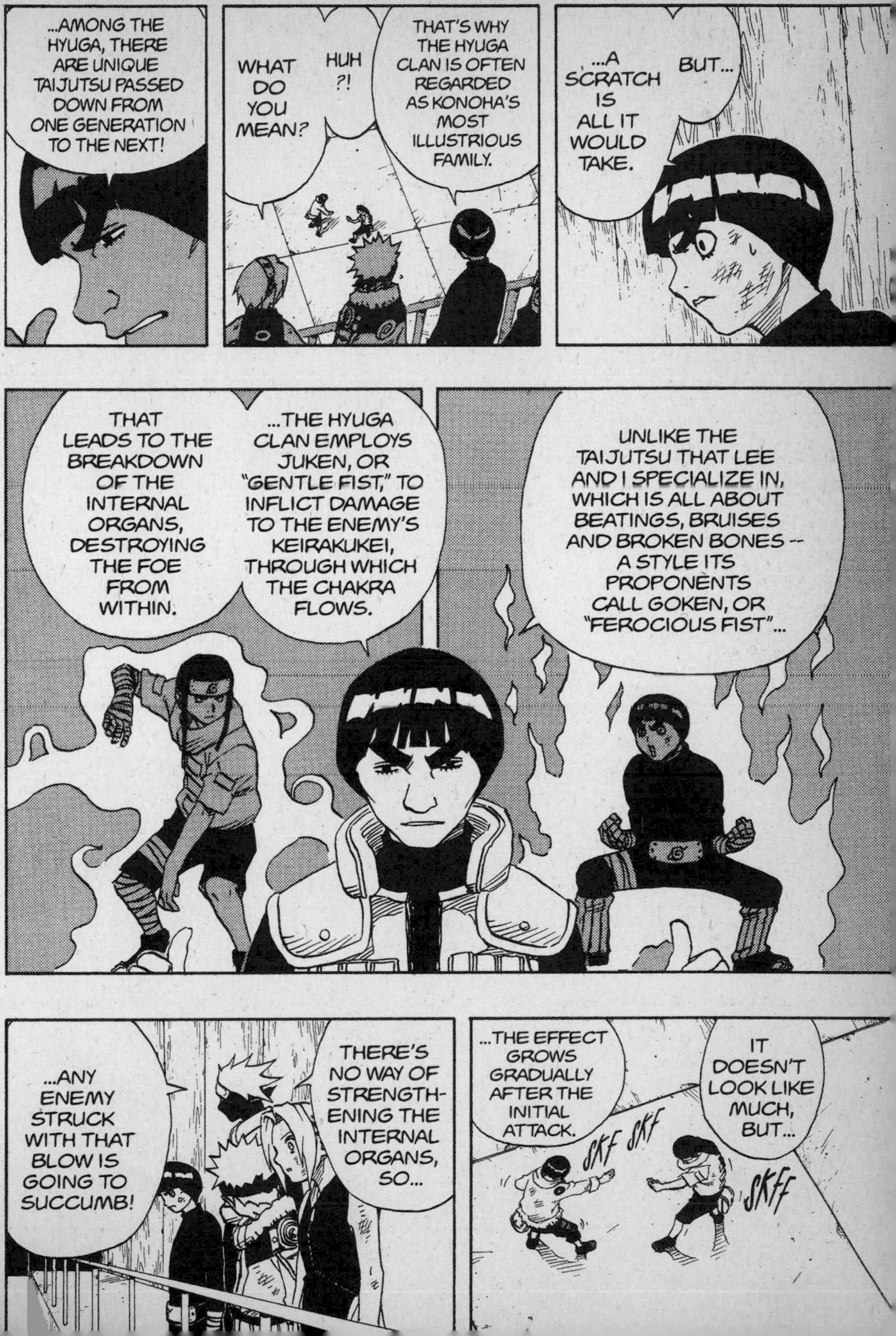
BUT...
...A SCRATCH IS ALL IT WOULD TAKE.
THAT'S WHY THE HYUGA CLAN IS OFTEN REGARDED AS KONOHA'S MOST ILLUSTRIOUS FAMILY.
HUH ?!
WHAT DO YOU MEAN?
...AMONG THE HYUGA, THERE ARE UNIQUE TAIJUTSU PASSED DOWN FROM ONE GENERATION TO THE NEXT!
UNLIKE THE TAIJUTSU THAT LEE AND I SPECIALIZE IN, WHICH IS ALL ABOUT BEATINGS, BRUISES AND BROKEN BONES -- A STYLE ITS PROPONENTS CALL GOKEN, OR "FEROCIOUS FIST"...
...THE HYUGA CLAN EMPLOYS JUKEN, OR "GENTLE FIST," TO INFLICT DAMAGE TO THE ENEMY'S KEIRAKUKEI, THROUGH WHICH THE CHAKRA FLOWS.
THAT LEADS TO THE BREAKDOWN OF THE INTERNAL ORGANS, DESTROYING THE FOE FROM WITHIN.
IT DOESN'T LOOK LIKE MUCH, BUT...
...THE EFFECT GROWS GRADUALLY AFTER THE INITIAL ATTACK.
SKFF
SKF SKF
THERE'S NO WAY OF STRENGTHENING THE INTERNAL ORGANS, SO...
...ANY ENEMY STRUCK WITH THAT BLOW IS GOING TO SUCCUMB!

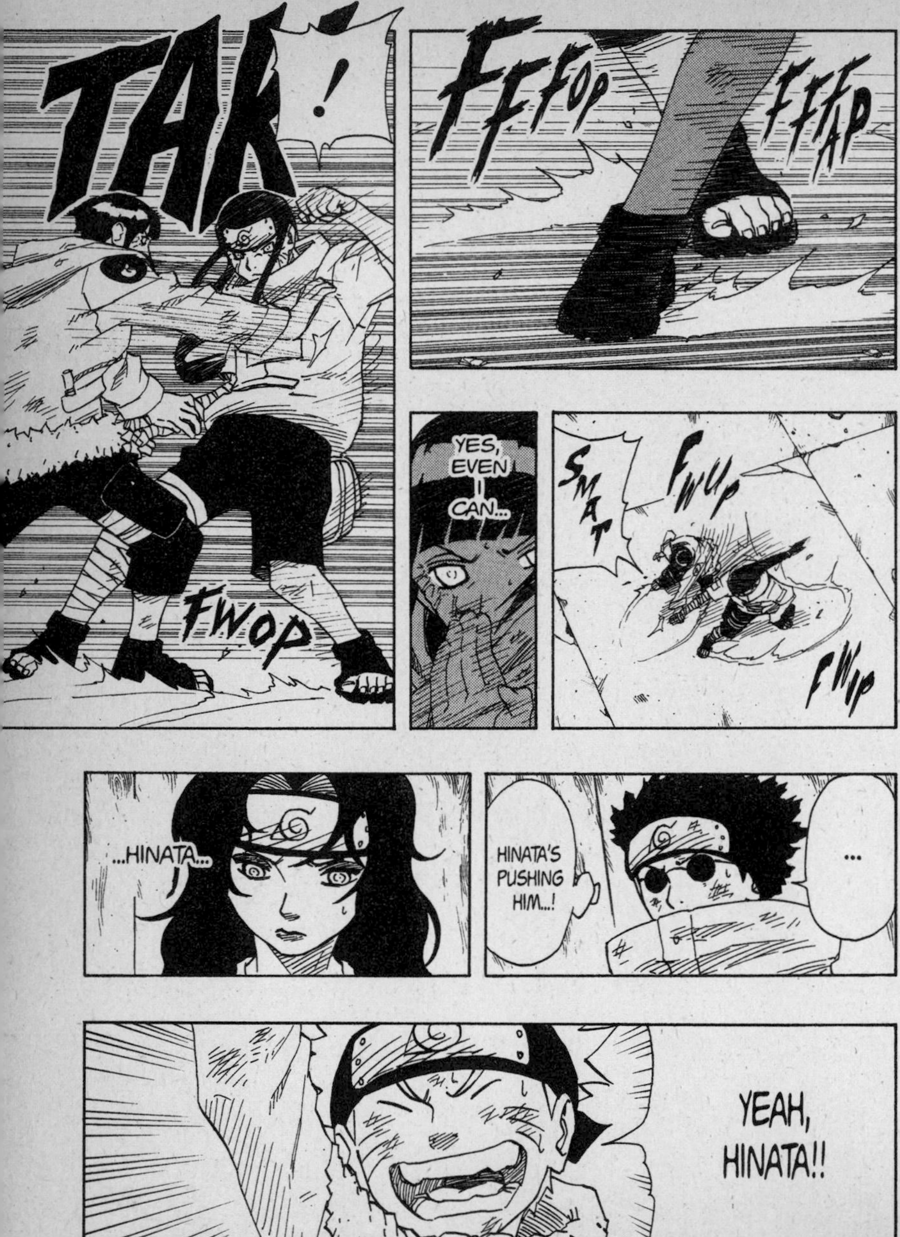
FFFAP
FFFOP
FWUP
SMAT
FWUP
YES, EVEN I CAN...
TAK!
FWOP
...
HINATA'S PUSHING HIM...!
...HINATA...
YEAH, HINATA!!

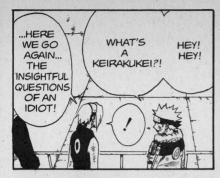

WHAT KIND OF PEOPLE ARE THEY...
...TO ATTACK THE KEIRAKUKEI?!
HEY! HEY!
WHAT'S A KEIRAKUKEI?!
!
...HERE WE GO AGAIN... THE INSIGHTFUL QUESTIONS OF AN IDIOT!
ALLOW ME, SAKURA.
THE KEIRAKUKEI IS A KIND OF NETWORK OF ENERGY LINES, SPREAD THROUGHOUT OUR BODIES IN MUCH THE SAME WAY AS THE HUMAN CIRCULATORY SYSTEM.
IT'S LIKE A SYSTEM OF VESSELS THAT CARRY CHAKRA THROUGHOUT OUR BODIES!!
OH... LIKE PASSAGEWAYS FOR CHAKRA, EH?
YES... AND IT'S DELICATELY INTERTWINED WITH THE ORGANS THAT MANIPULATE CHAKRA.
ATTACK THE KEIRAKUKEI...
...AND THE ORGANS WILL SUFFER AS WELL!

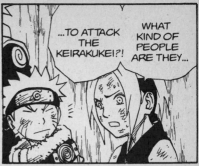

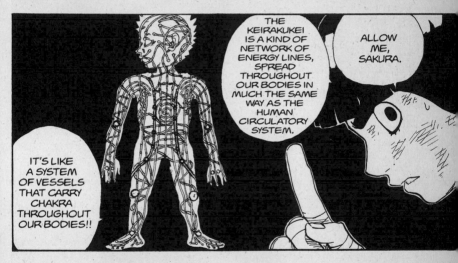

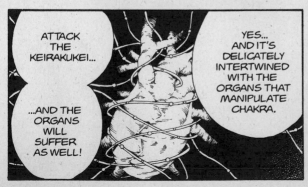

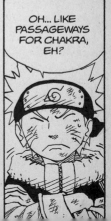

READ THIS WAY

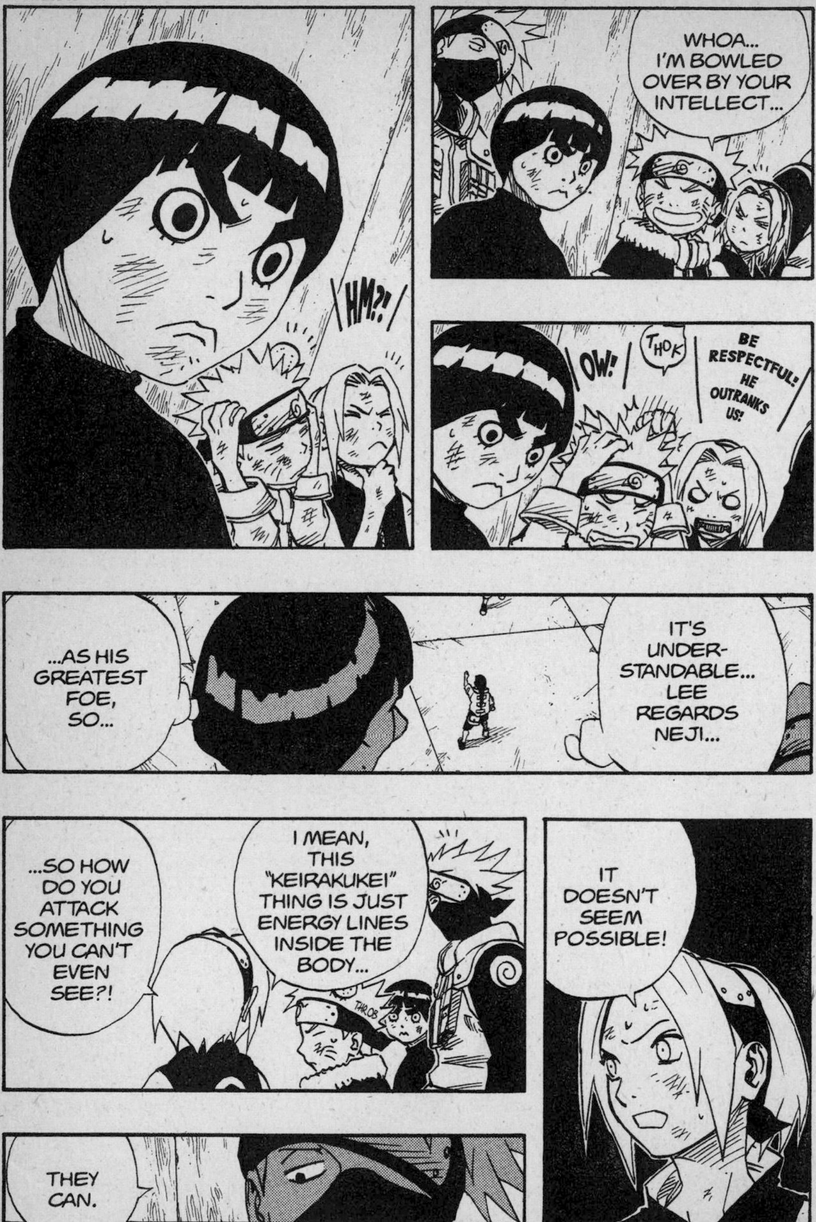
WHOA... I'M BOWLED OVER BY YOUR INTELLECT...
BE RESPECTFUL! HE OUTRANKS US!
THOK
OW!
HM?!
IT'S UNDER-STANDABLE... LEE REGARDS NEJI...
...AS HIS GREATEST FOE, SO...
IT DOESN'T SEEM POSSIBLE!
I MEAN, THIS "KEIRAKUKEI" THING IS JUST ENERGY LINES INSIDE THE BODY...
THROB
...SO HOW DO YOU ATTACK SOMETHING YOU CAN'T EVEN SEE?!
THEY CAN.

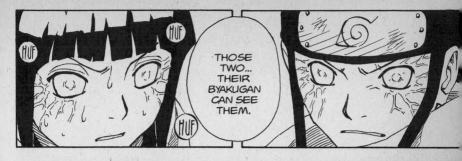

THOSE TWO... THEIR BYAKUGAN CAN SEE THEM.
HUF
HUF
HUF
AND GENTLE FIST ATTACKS ARE DIFFERENT FROM THE PURELY BRUTE-FORCE, PHYSICAL KIND...
YOU TAKE YOUR OWN CHAKRA AND RELEASE IT THROUGH THE ENERGY PORTALS IN YOUR HANDS, FORCING IT INTO THE BODY OF YOUR FOE....
...WHERE IT CAN INFLICT MASSIVE DAMAGE ON THE ENEMY'S KEIRAKUKEI.
TAK

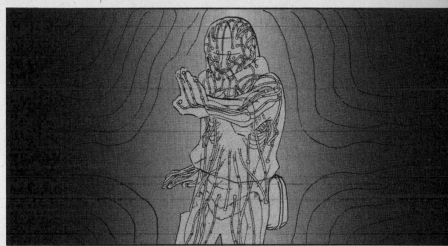

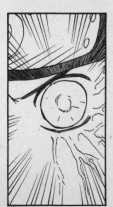

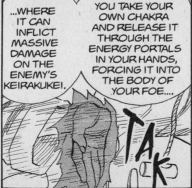

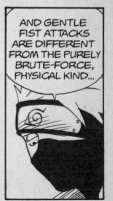

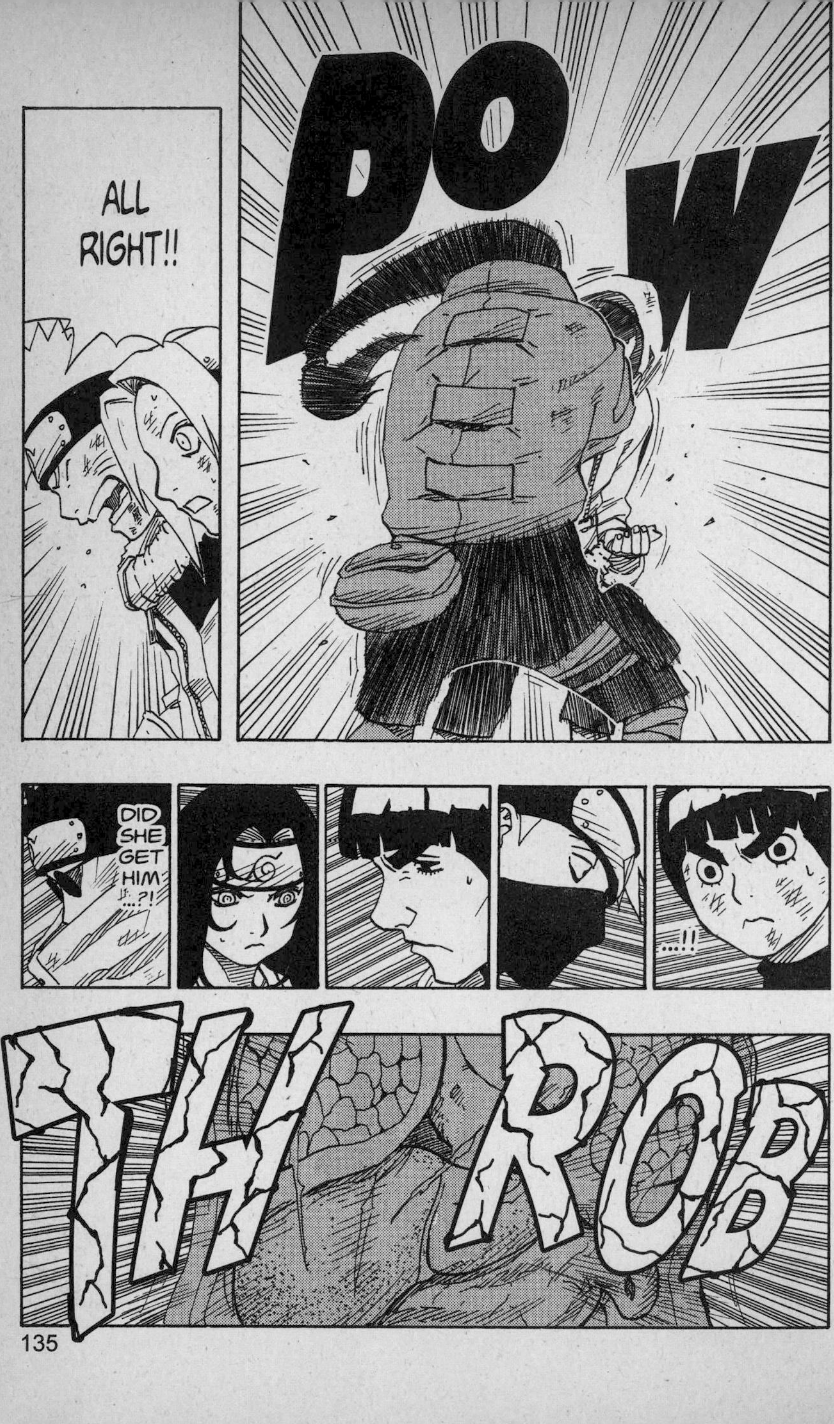
POW
ALL RIGHT!!
...!!
DID SHE GET HIM ...?!
THROB

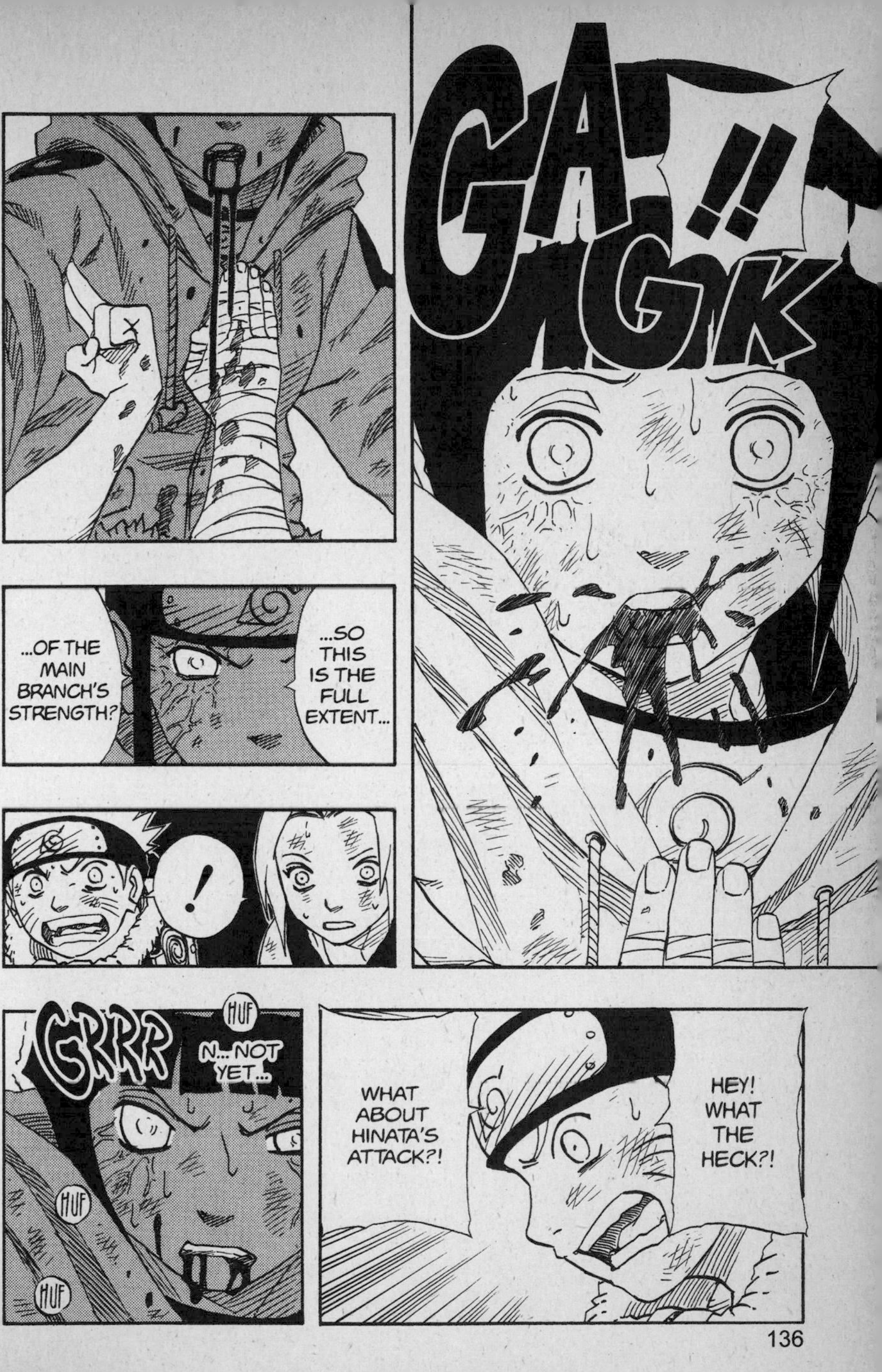
GAGK!!
...SO THIS IS THE FULL EXTENT...
...OF THE MAIN BRANCH'S STRENGTH?
!
HEY! WHAT THE HECK?!
WHAT ABOUT HINATA'S ATTACK?!
HUF
N...NOT YET...
GRRR
HUF
HUF

READ THIS WAY

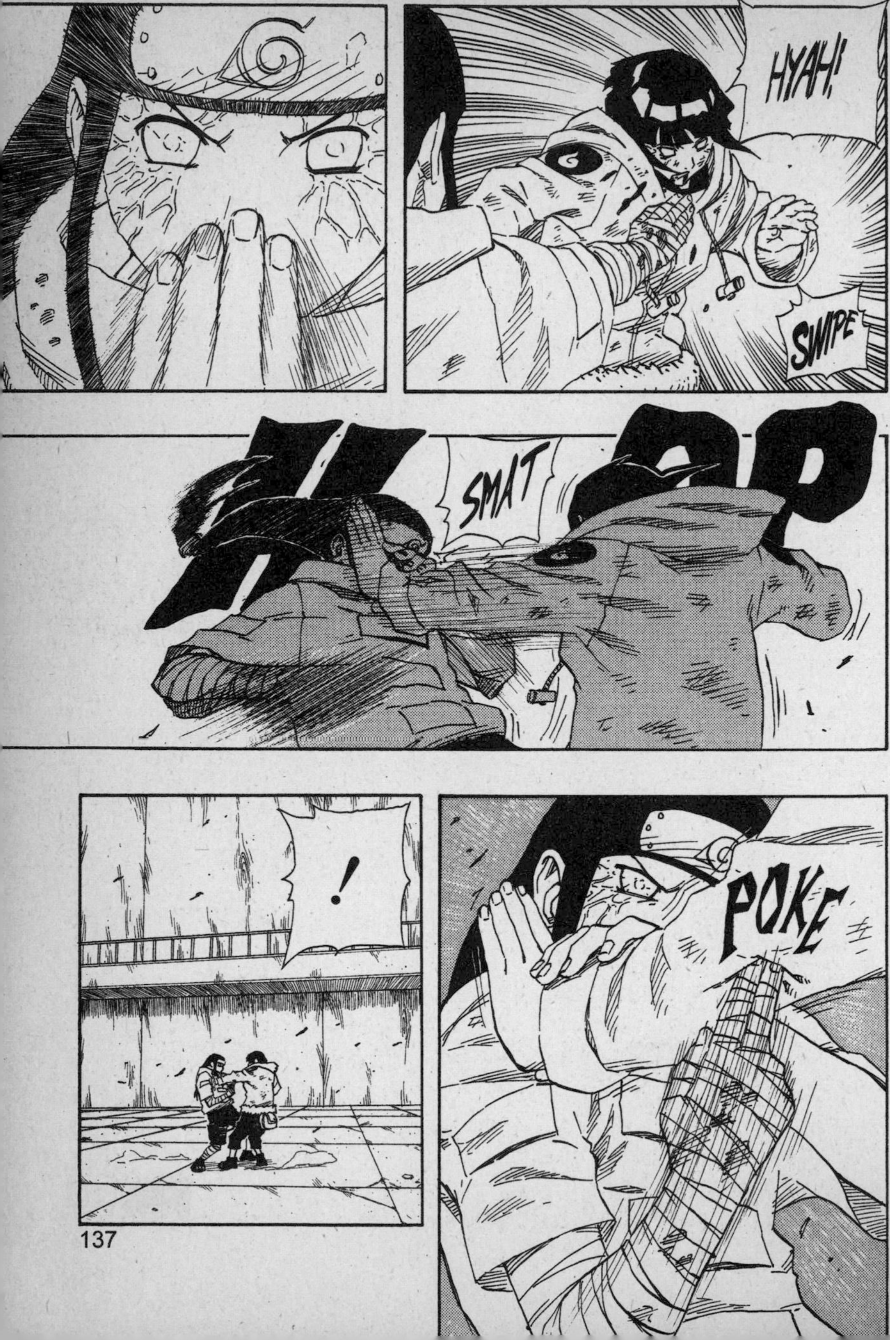
HYAH!
SWIPE
SMAT
POKE
!

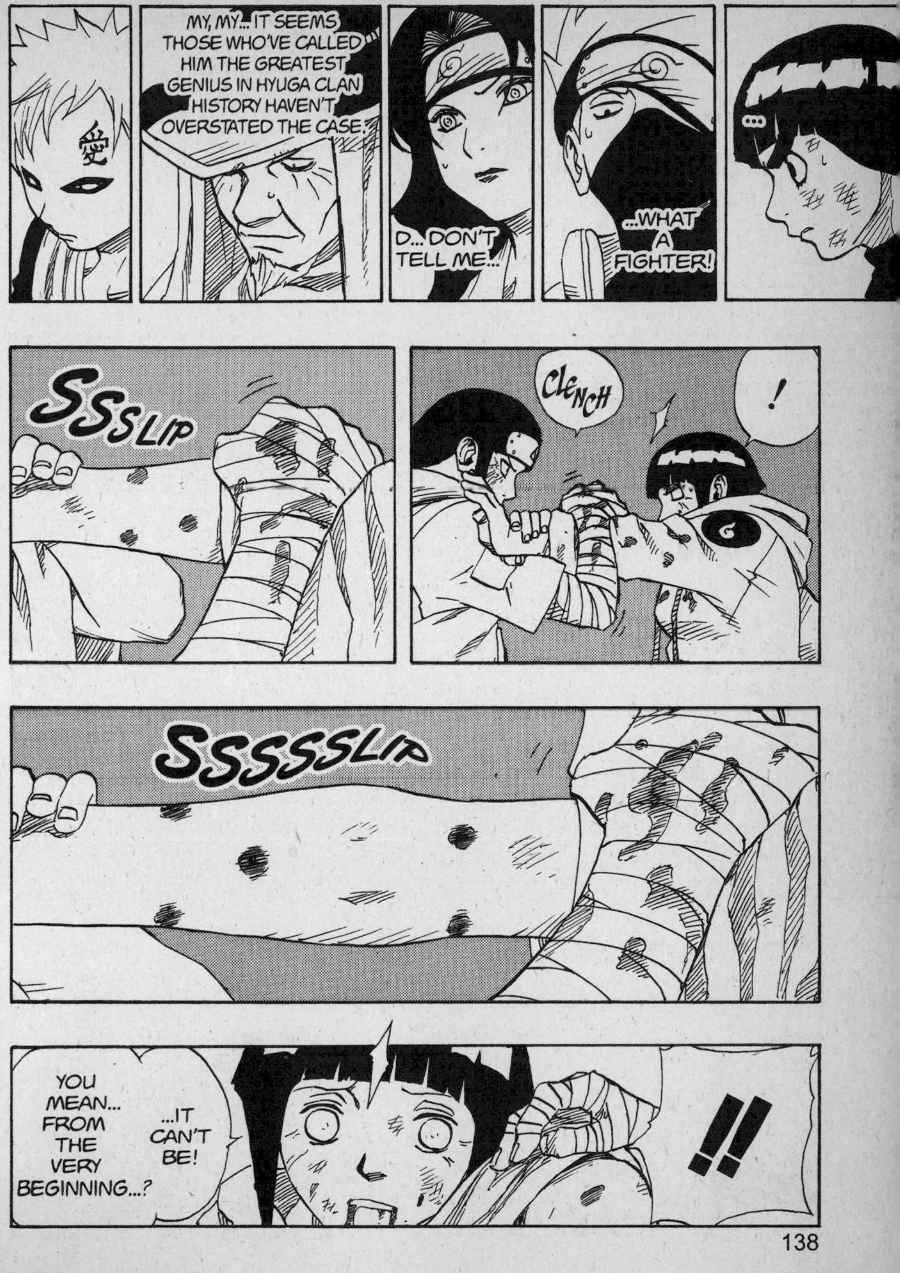
...
...WHAT A FIGHTER!
D... DON'T TELL ME...
MY, MY... IT SEEMS THOSE WHO'VE CALLED HIM THE GREATEST GENIUS IN HYUGA CLAN HISTORY HAVEN'T OVERSTATED THE CASE.
!
CLENCH
SSSLIP
SSSSSLIP
!!
...IT CAN'T BE!
YOU MEAN... FROM THE VERY BEGINNING...?

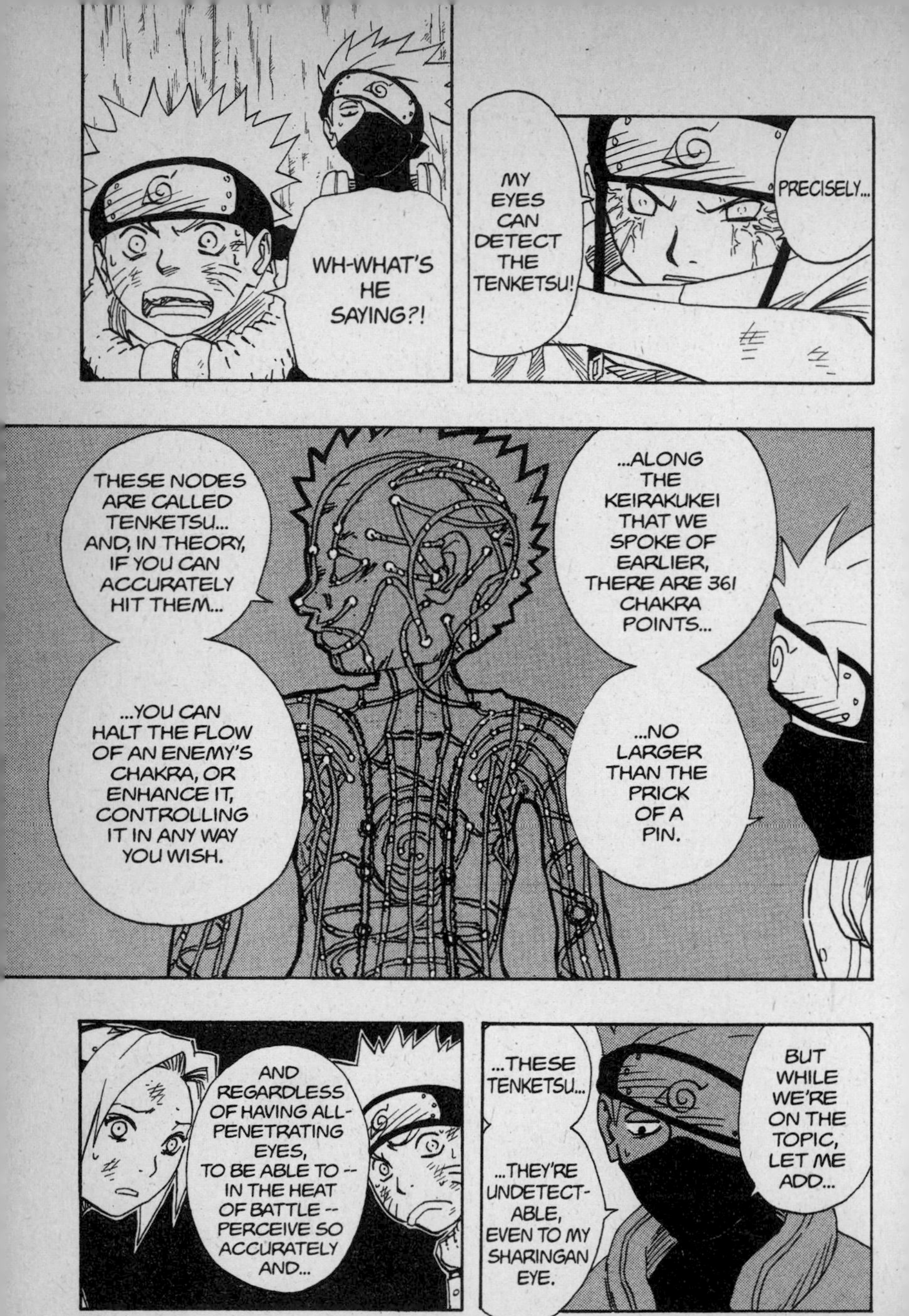
MY EYES CAN DETECT THE TENKETSU!
PRECISELY...
WH-WHAT'S HE SAYING?!
...ALONG THE KEIRAKUKEI THAT WE SPOKE OF EARLIER, THERE ARE 361 CHAKRA POINTS...
...NO LARGER THAN THE PRICK OF A PIN.
THESE NODES ARE CALLED TENKETSU... AND, IN THEORY, IF YOU CAN ACCURATELY HIT THEM...
...YOU CAN HALT THE FLOW OF AN ENEMY'S CHAKRA, OR ENHANCE IT, CONTROLLING IT IN ANY WAY YOU WISH.
BUT WHILE WE'RE ON THE TOPIC, LET ME ADD...
...THESE TENKETSU...
...THEY'RE UNDETECT-ABLE, EVEN TO MY SHARINGAN EYE.
AND REGARDLESS OF HAVING ALL-PENETRATING EYES, TO BE ABLE TO -- IN THE HEAT OF BATTLE -- PERCEIVE SO ACCURATELY AND...

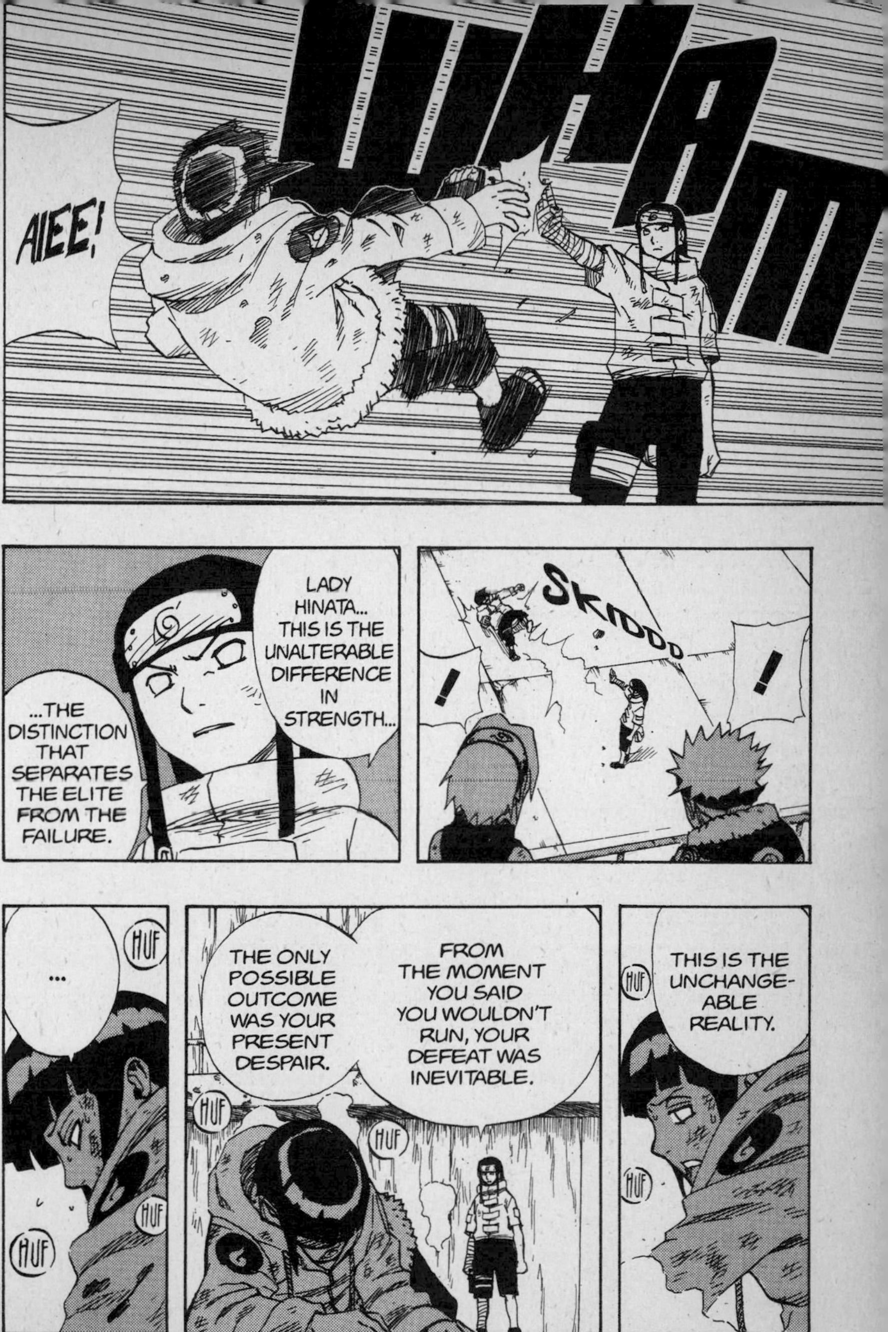
WHAM
AIEE!
SKIDDD
!
!
LADY HINATA... THIS IS THE UNALTERABLE DIFFERENCE IN STRENGTH...
...THE DISTINCTION THAT SEPARATES THE ELITE FROM THE FAILURE.
THIS IS THE UNCHANGE-ABLE REALITY.
HUF
HUF
FROM THE MOMENT YOU SAID YOU WOULDN'T RUN, YOUR DEFEAT WAS INEVITABLE.
THE ONLY POSSIBLE OUTCOME WAS YOUR PRESENT DESPAIR.
HUF
HUF
...
HUF
HUF
HUF

READ THIS WAY

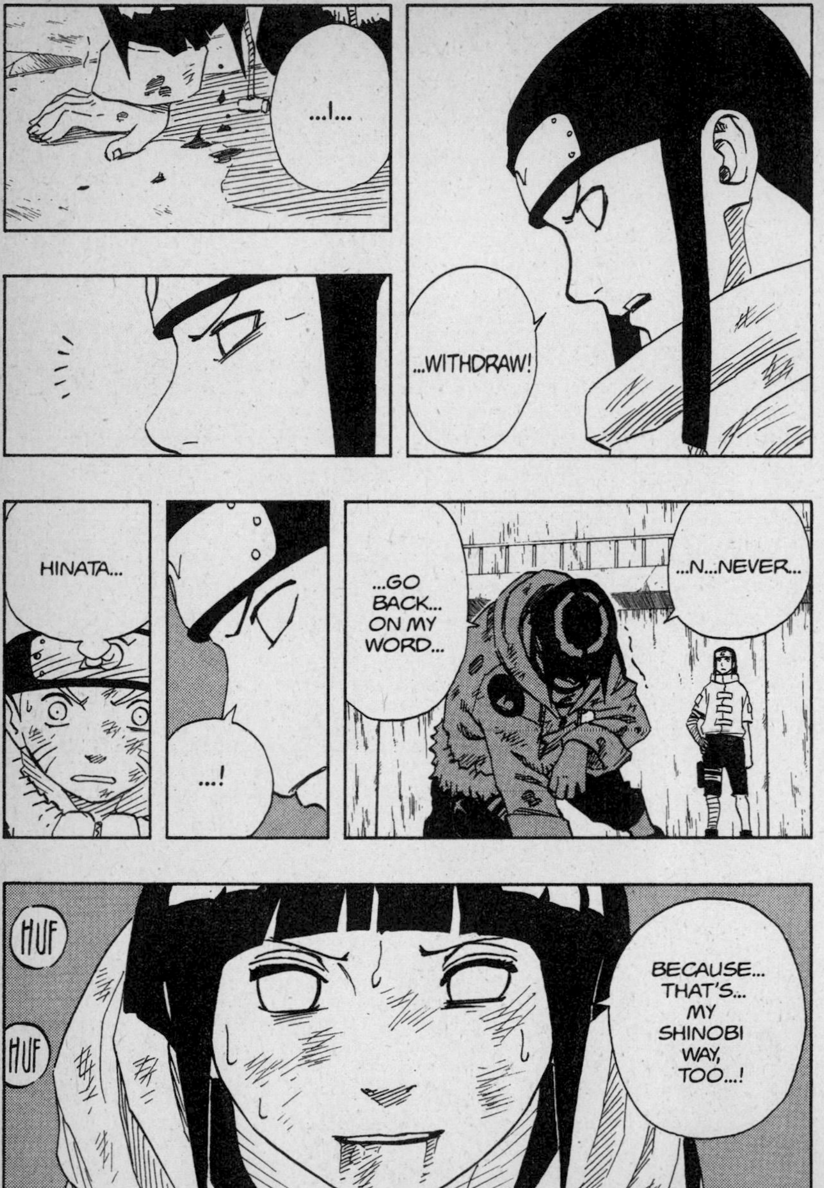
...WITHDRAW!
...I...
...N...NEVER...
...GO BACK... ON MY WORD...
...!
HINATA...
BECAUSE... THAT'S... MY SHINOBI WAY, TOO...!
HUF
HUF

THE WORLD OF KISHIMOTO MASASHI
MY PERSONAL HISTORY, PART II

I COULDN'T BELIEVE IT. I WAS SO FIXATED ON THE ALPHA MALE, I HADN'T BEEN LOOKING WHERE I WAS GOING, AND I STEPPED RIGHT ON ONE OF THE YOUNG MONKEYS!

THE POOR LITTLE MONKEY RAN OFF SCREAMING...AND IN ALMOST THE SAME INSTANT, I FELT SOMETHING CLAMP ONTO MY BACK! I LOOKED OVER MY SHOULDER, AND TO MY HORROR, IT WAS THE LITTLE MONKEY'S MOTHER, BARING HER TEETH AND LOOKING DETERMINED TO TAKE A BITE OUT OF ME! ALL I COULD THINK WAS "I'M GOING TO BE EATEN!!" I DESPERATELY TRIED TO SHAKE OFF THAT MOTHER MONKEY AND RUN AWAY, BUT I LOST MY BALANCE AND FELL OVER. AS I SCRAMBLED TO GET BACK UP, I LOOKED UP AND SAW THAT THE ENORMOUS BOSS MONKEY HAD LEAPT FROM HIS BOULDER TO ATTACK ME! IT WAS LIKE HE HAD TRANSFORMED INTO A *DRAGONBALL*-STYLE SAIYAN MONSTER MONKEY, SO I TRULY THOUGHT I WAS GOING TO DIE. I TRIED AGAIN TO STAND AND RUN AWAY... BUT MY KNEES WERE LIKE RUBBER AND I COULD BARELY STAND! I THOUGHT THAT WOULD BE THE END FOR ME, BUT RIGHT THEN THE MONKEYS' HANDLER TACKLED THE ALPHA MONKEY AND TRAPPED HIM. BEFORE THE RELIEF COULD EVEN FULLY REGISTER IN MY BRAIN, THE HANDLER GLARED AT ME WITH AN EXPRESSION THAT SCARED ME ALMOST AS MUCH AS THE HEAD MONKEY'S HAD AND YELLED, "**RUN!!**"

AS MY SENSES BEGAN TO RETURN TO ME, I LOOKED AROUND AND SAW A RIDICULOUS NUMBER OF MONKEYS CHARGING AT ME! "THERE'S NO SUCH THING AS TAME, FRIENDLY MONKEYS," I THOUGHT, CRYING MY EYES OUT AS I RAN!! AND ON TOP OF ALL THAT, I SAW THE MOST UNBELIEVABLE THING: THE ENTIRE BASEBALL CLUB WAS UNDER ASSAULT BY THE MONKEYS!! AAAUGH !

IT WAS AN AMAZING SIGHT. THERE WERE PLENTY OF OTHER, ORDINARY TOURISTS AROUND, AND THEY WERE BEING LEFT ALONE. WHY WERE THE MONKEYS ATTACKING ONLY THE BASEBALL CLUB?! THEN, THE OBVIOUS ANSWER CAME TO ME! WE ALL HAD THE SAME *GORINGARI* BUZZ-CUT HAIR AND WERE WEARING WHITE SHIRTS AND OUR BLACK SCHOOL UNIFORM PANTS. TO THE MONKEYS, WE PROBABLY LOOKED LIKE SOME WEIRD, SHAVED-HEADED, WHITE-AND-BLACK GANG OF INVADERS. IN ANY CASE, WE LEFT THE MONKEY MOUNTAIN JUST AS FAST AS WE COULD. ONCE WE WERE ALL SAFELY INSIDE THE BUS, EVERYONE WAS TRYING TO CATCH THEIR BREATH AND EXCITEDLY DISCUSSING THE INCIDENT, WONDERING WHY IT HAPPENED. IT OCCURRED TO ME THAT MY HAVING ACCIDENTALLY STEPPED ON THE LITTLE MONKEY WAS A PRETTY JUICY TIDBIT... SO I CONFESSED, EXPECTING THE REST OF THE CLUB TO LAUGH. BUT NO ONE FOUND IT THE LEAST BIT FUNNY.
(THIS IS A TRUE STORY!)

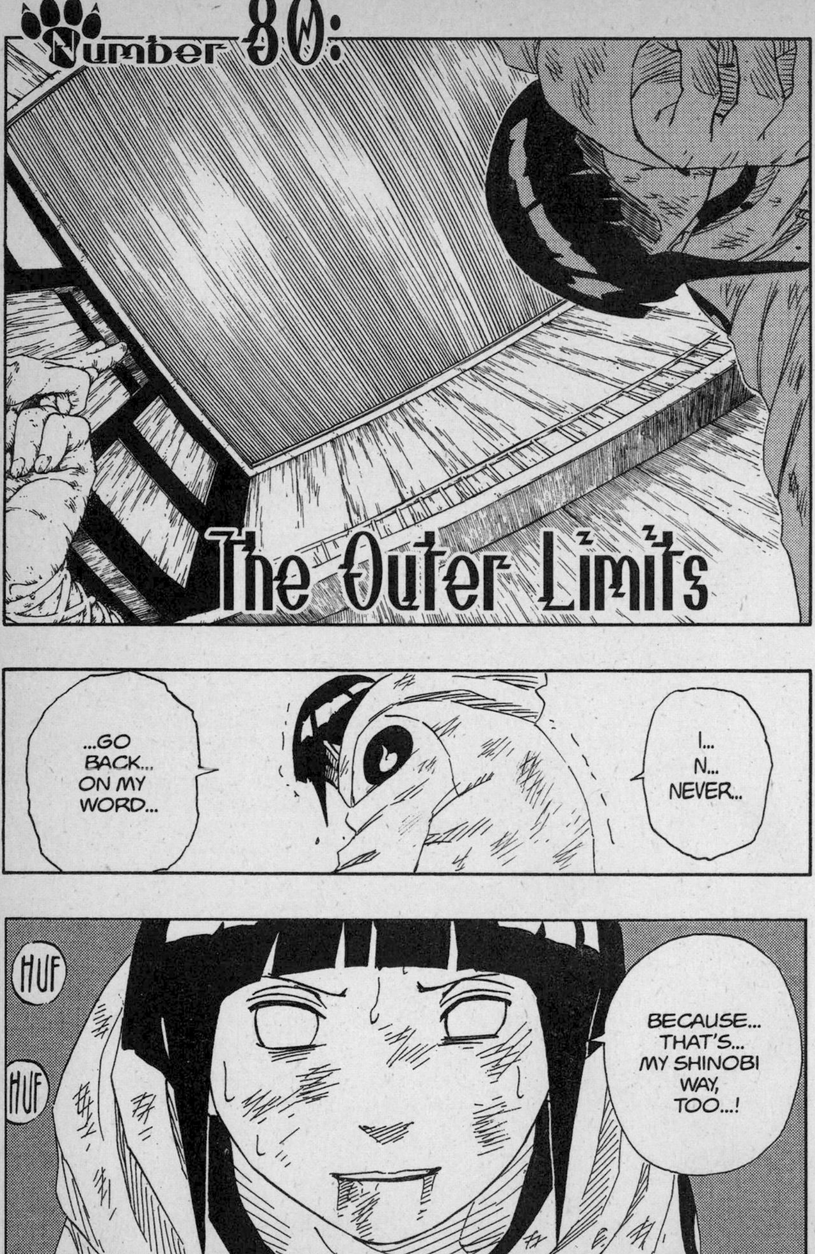
Number 80:
The Outer Limits
I... N... NEVER..
...GO BACK... ON MY WORD...
BECAUSE... THAT'S... MY SHINOBI WAY, TOO...!
HUF
HUF

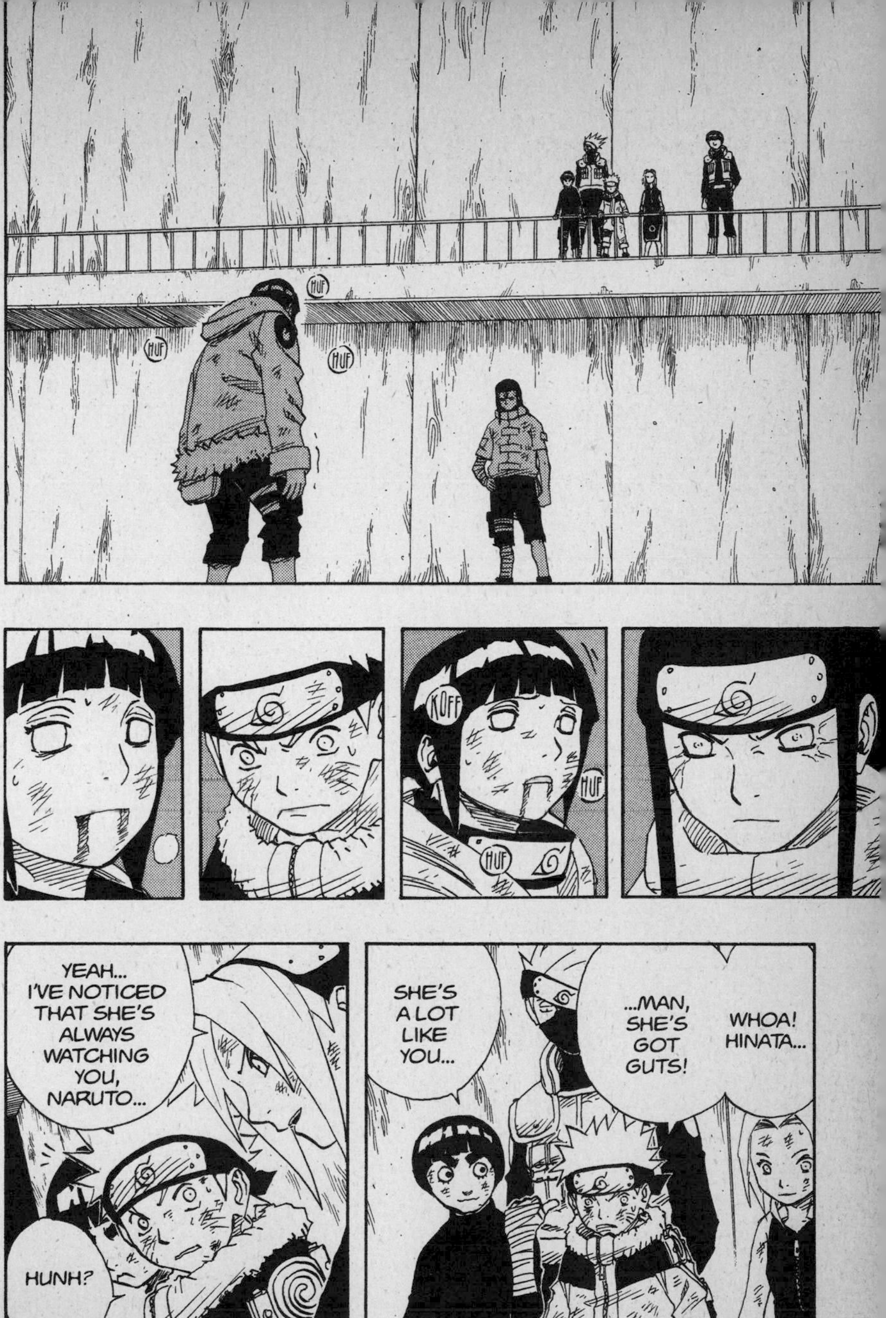
HUF
HUF
HUF
KOFF
HUF
HUF
WHOA! HINATA...
...MAN, SHE'S GOT GUTS!
SHE'S A LOT LIKE YOU...
YEAH... I'VE NOTICED THAT SHE'S ALWAYS WATCHING YOU, NARUTO...
HUNH?

READ THIS WAY

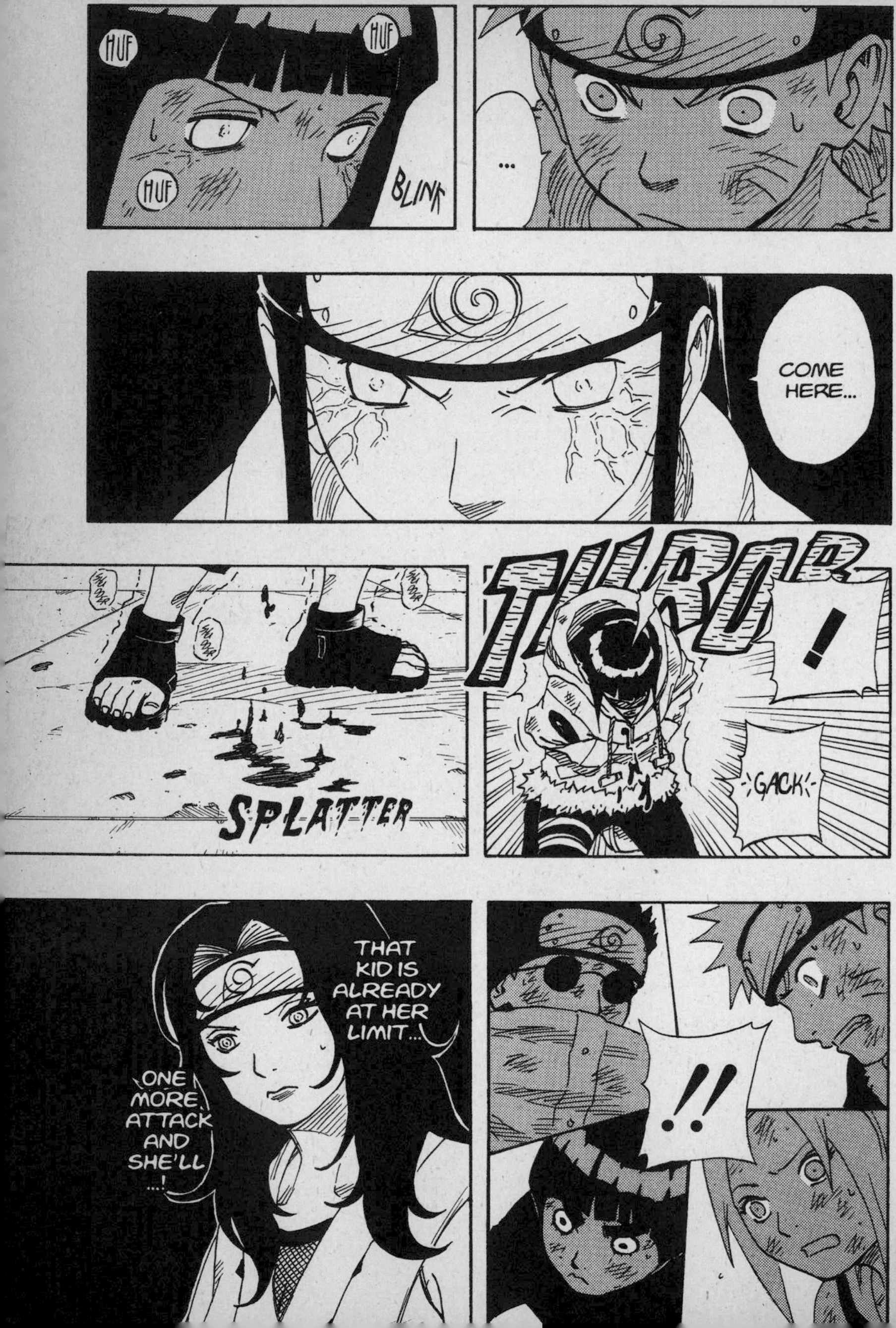
...
HUF
HUF
HUF
BLINK
COME HERE...
THROB
!
GACK
SPLATTER
!!
THAT KID IS ALREADY AT HER LIMIT...
ONE MORE ATTACK AND SHE'LL ...!

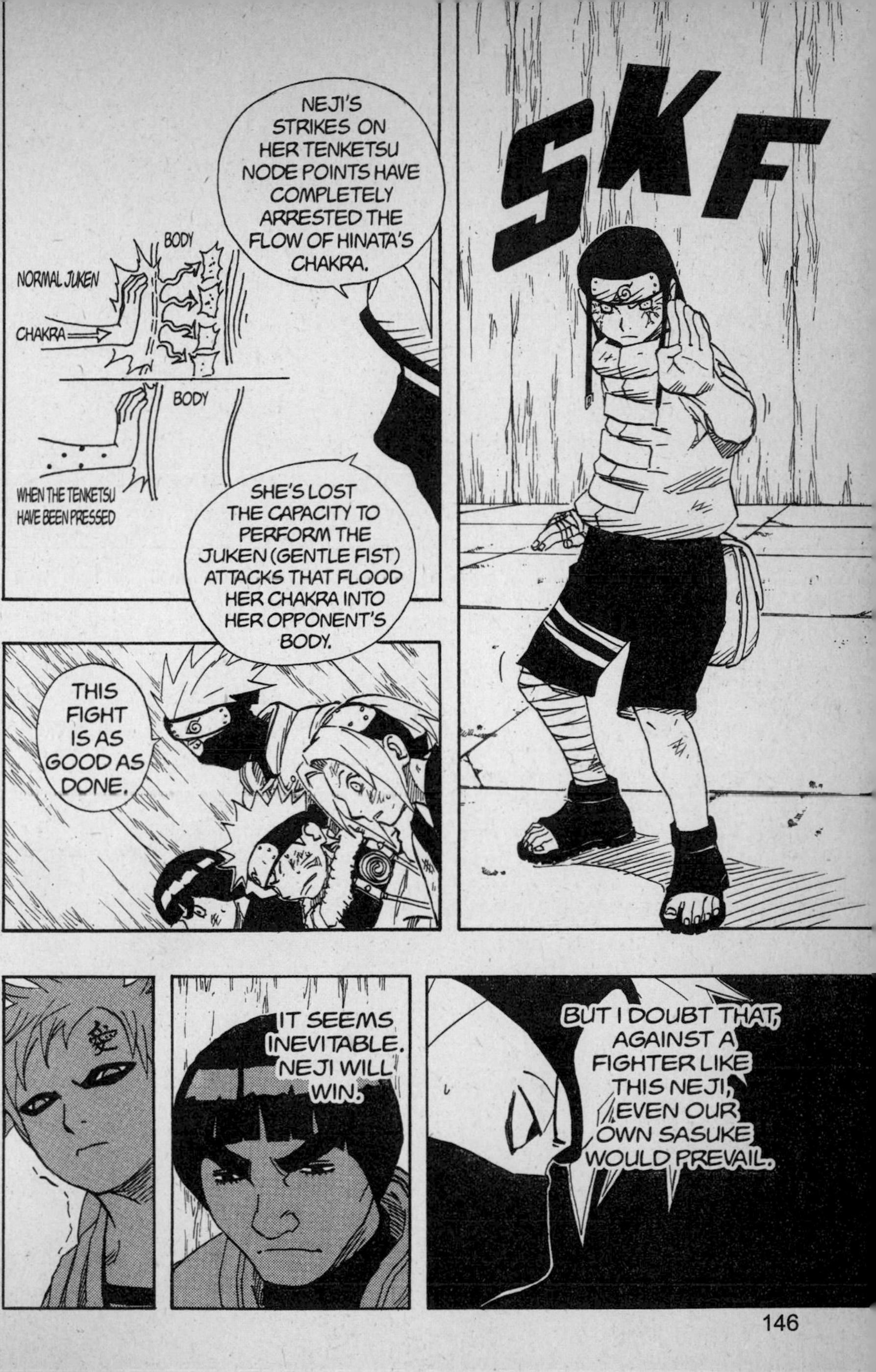
SKF
NEJI'S STRIKES ON HER TENKETSU NODE POINTS HAVE COMPLETELY ARRESTED THE FLOW OF HINATA'S CHAKRA.
BODY
NORMAL JUKEN
CHAKRA
BODY
WHEN THE TENKETSU HAVE BEEN PRESSED
SHE'S LOST THE CAPACITY TO PERFORM THE JUKEN (GENTLE FIST) ATTACKS THAT FLOOD HER CHAKRA INTO HER OPPONENT'S BODY.
THIS FIGHT IS AS GOOD AS DONE.
BUT I DOUBT THAT, AGAINST A FIGHTER LIKE THIS NEJI, EVEN OUR OWN SASUKE WOULD PREVAIL.
IT SEEMS INEVITABLE. NEJI WILL WIN.

READ THIS WAY

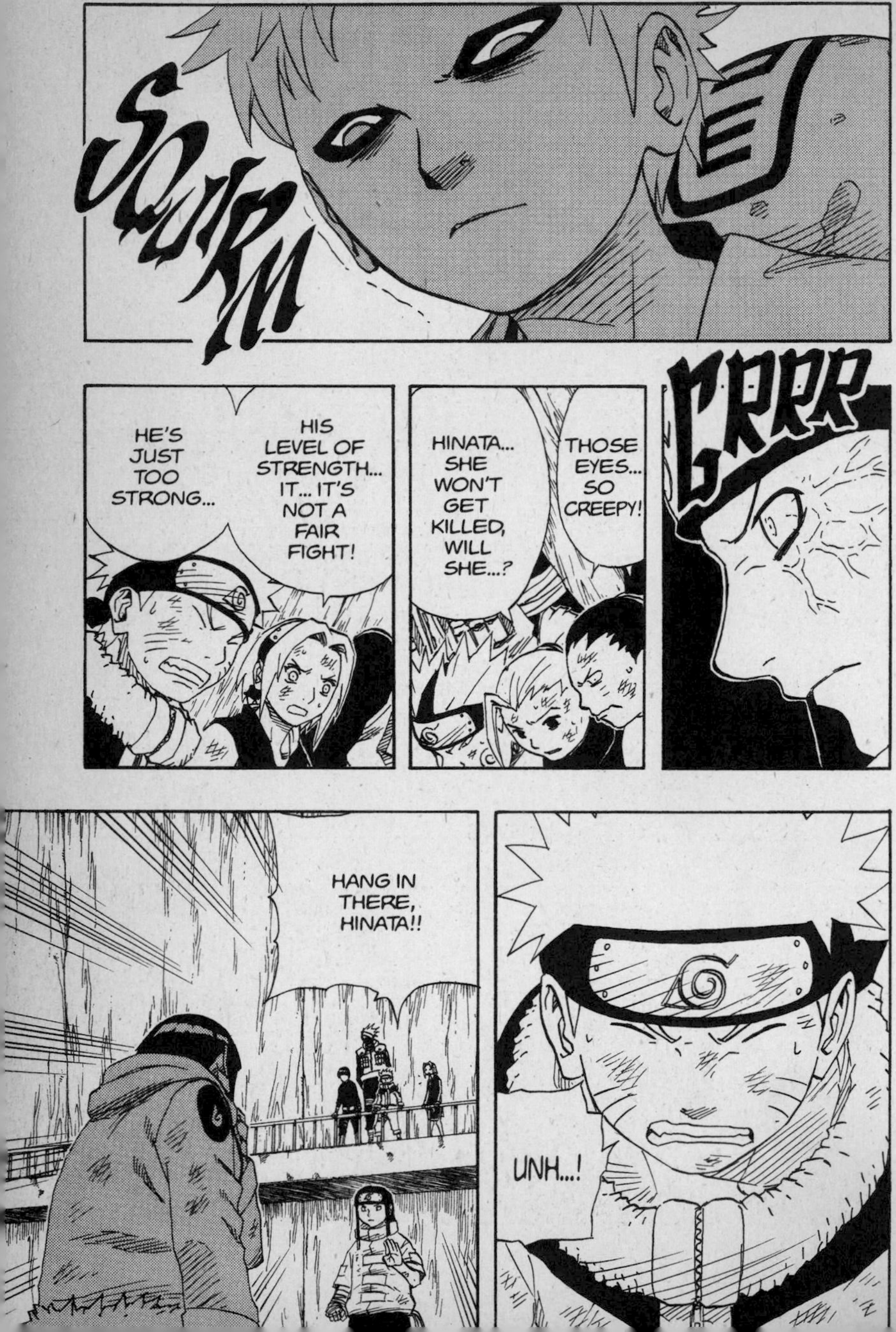
SQUIRM
GRRR
THOSE EYES... SO CREEPY!
HINATA... SHE WON'T GET KILLED, WILL SHE...?
HIS LEVEL OF STRENGTH... IT... IT'S NOT A FAIR FIGHT!
HE'S JUST TOO STRONG...
UNH...!
HANG IN THERE, HINATA!!

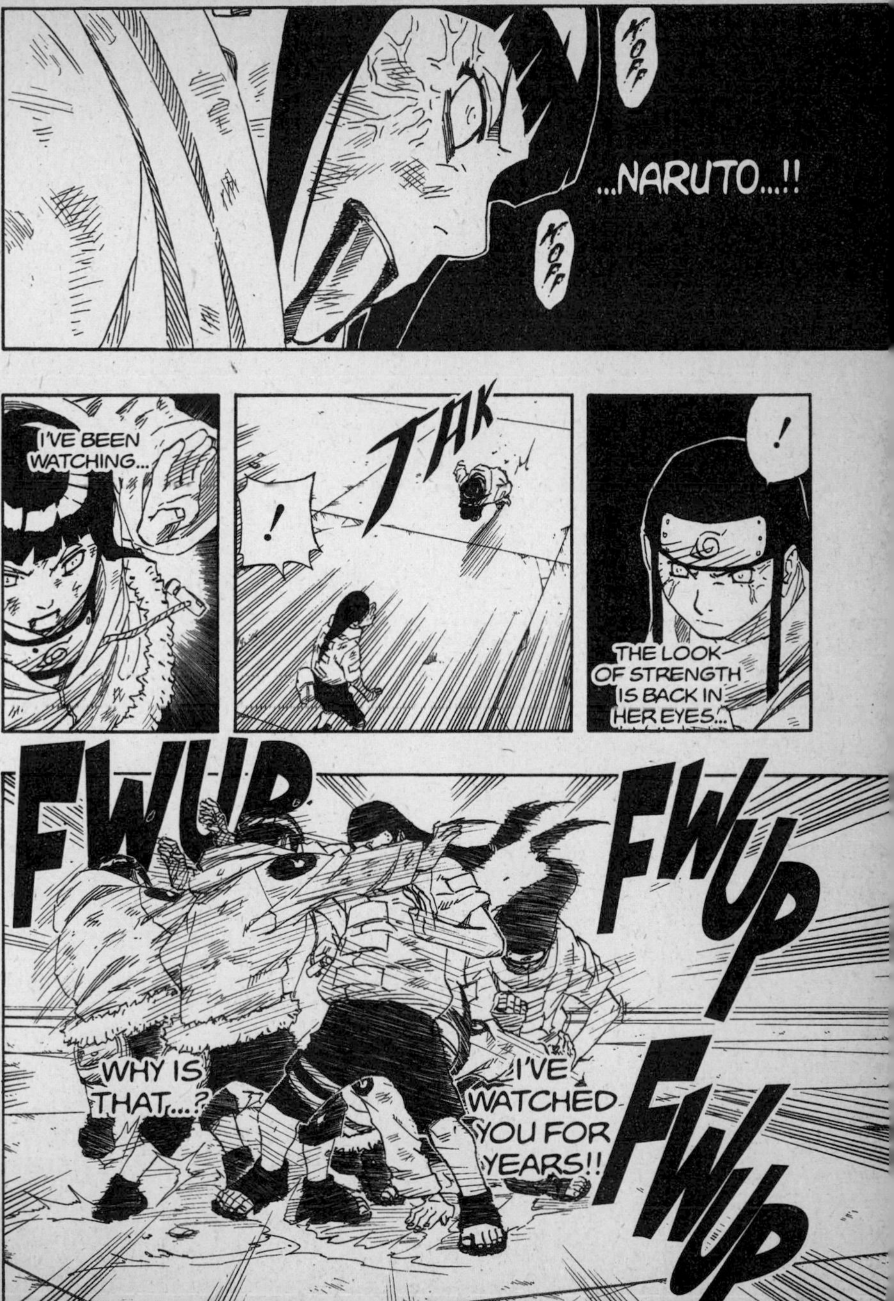
KOFF
...NARUTO...!!
KOFF
!
THE LOOK OF STRENGTH IS BACK IN HER EYES...
TAK
!
I'VE BEEN WATCHING...
FWUP
FWUP
FWUP
I'VE WATCHED YOU FOR YEARS!!
WHY IS THAT...?

READ THIS WAY

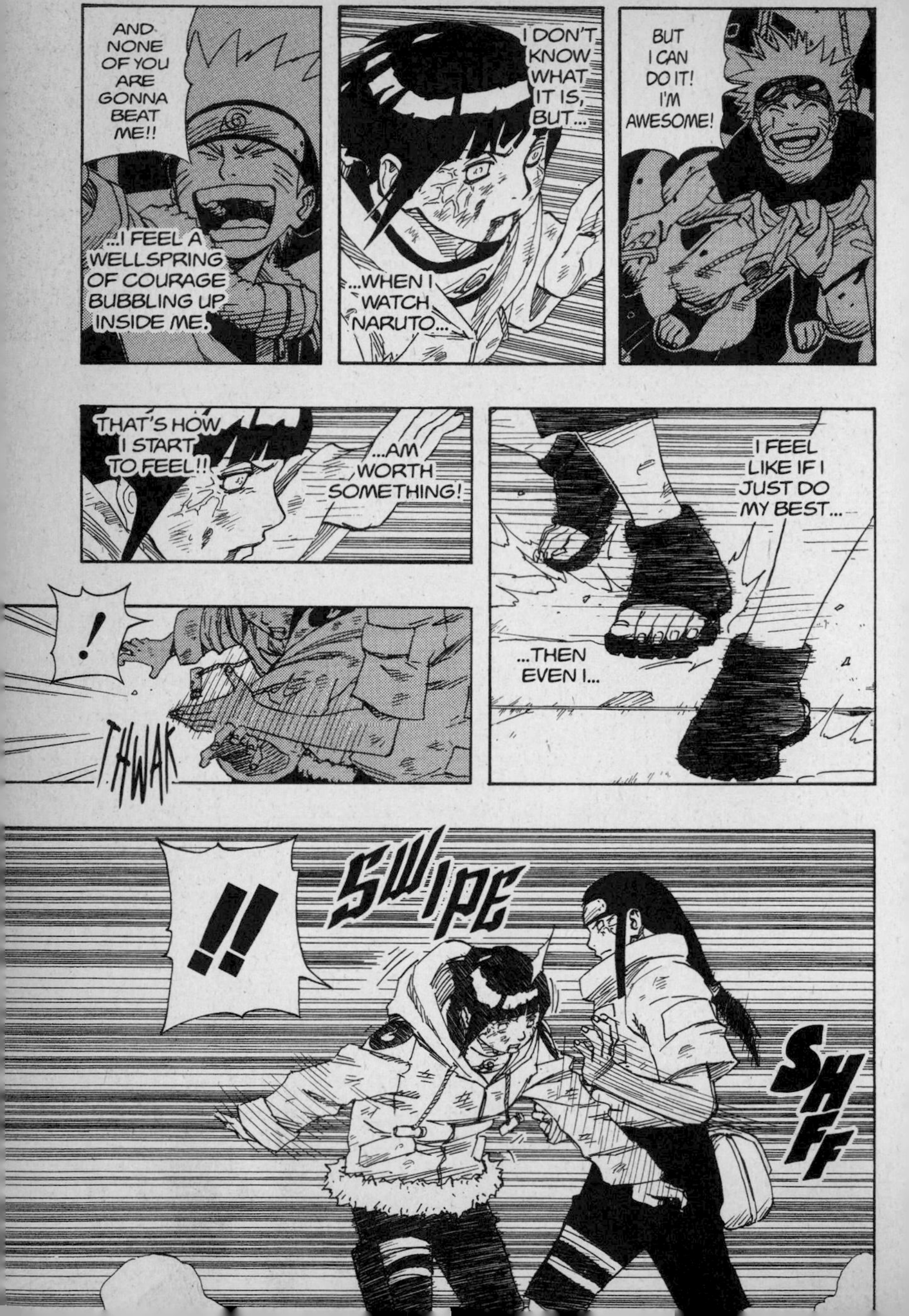
BUT I CAN DO IT! I'M AWESOME!
I DON'T KNOW WHAT IT IS, BUT...
...WHEN I WATCH NARUTO...
AND NONE OF YOU ARE GONNA BEAT ME!!
...I FEEL A WELLSPRING OF COURAGE BUBBLING UP INSIDE ME.
I FEEL LIKE IF I JUST DO MY BEST...
...THEN EVEN I...
...AM WORTH SOMETHING!
THAT'S HOW I START TO FEEL!!
!
THWAK
SHFF
SWIPE
!!

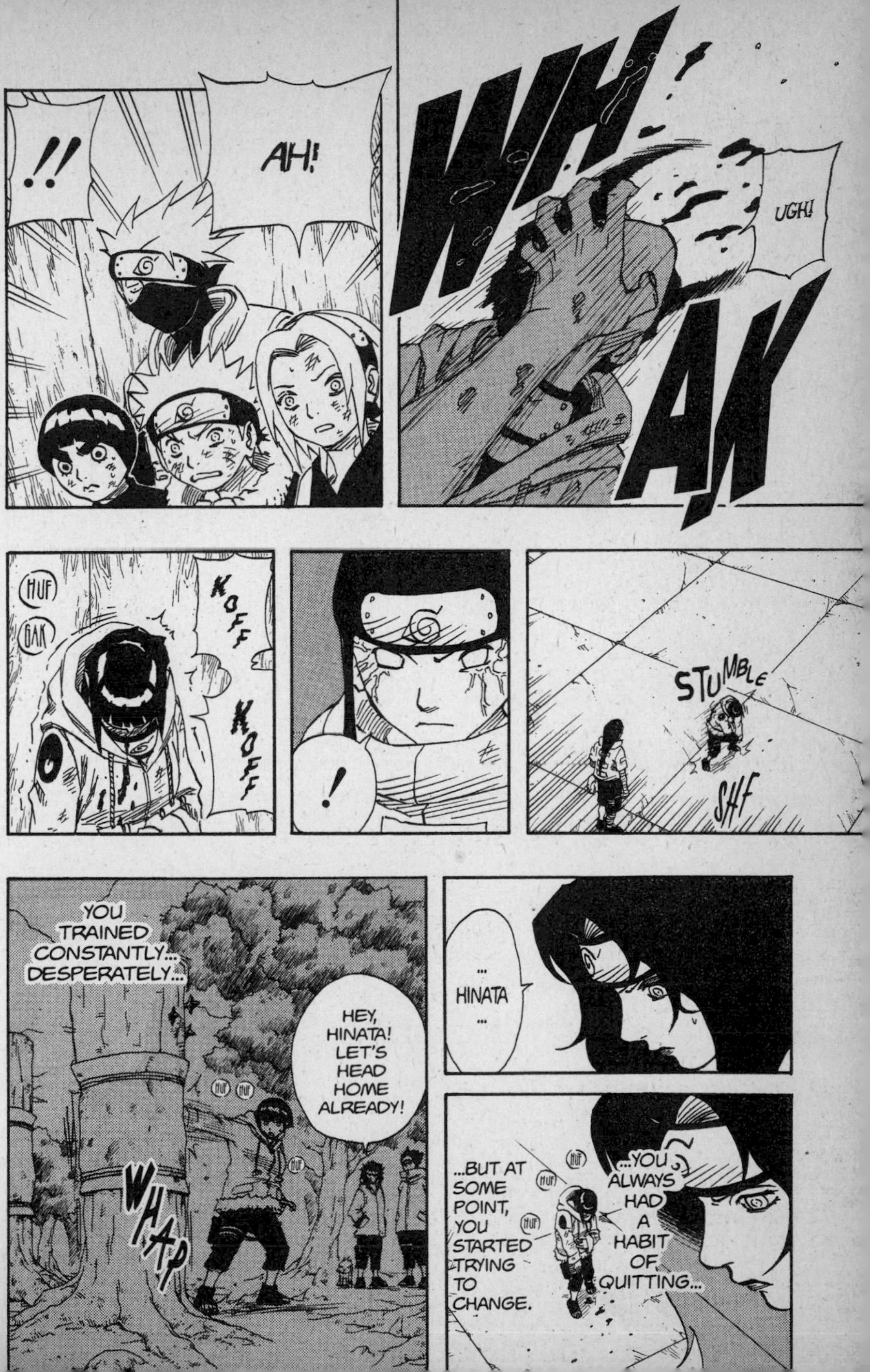
WHAK
UGH!
AH!
!!
STUMBLE
SHF
!
KOFF
KOFF
HUF
GAK
... HINATA ...
...YOU ALWAYS HAD A HABIT OF QUITTING...
...BUT AT SOME POINT, YOU STARTED TRYING TO CHANGE.
HUF
HUF
HUF
YOU TRAINED CONSTANTLY... DESPERATELY...
HEY, HINATA! LET'S HEAD HOME ALREADY!
HUF
HUF
HUF
WHAP

READ THIS WAY

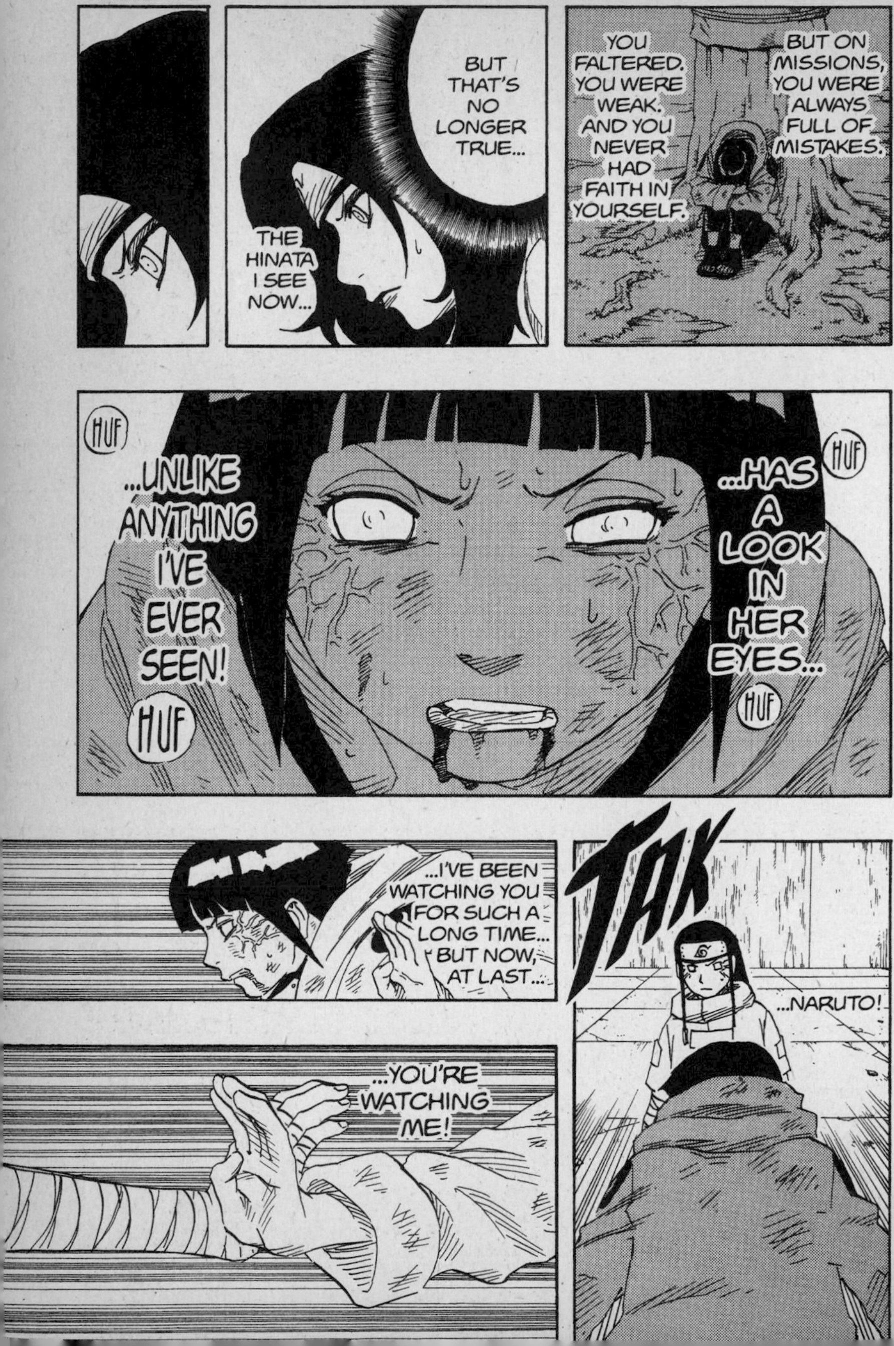
BUT ON MISSIONS, YOU WERE ALWAYS FULL OF MISTAKES.
YOU FALTERED. YOU WERE WEAK. AND YOU NEVER HAD FAITH IN YOURSELF.
BUT THAT'S NO LONGER TRUE...
THE HINATA I SEE NOW...
HUF
...HAS A LOOK IN HER EYES...
HUF
HUF
...UNLIKE ANYTHING I'VE EVER SEEN!
HUF
TAK
...NARUTO!
...I'VE BEEN WATCHING YOU FOR SUCH A LONG TIME... BUT NOW, AT LAST...
...YOU'RE WATCHING ME!

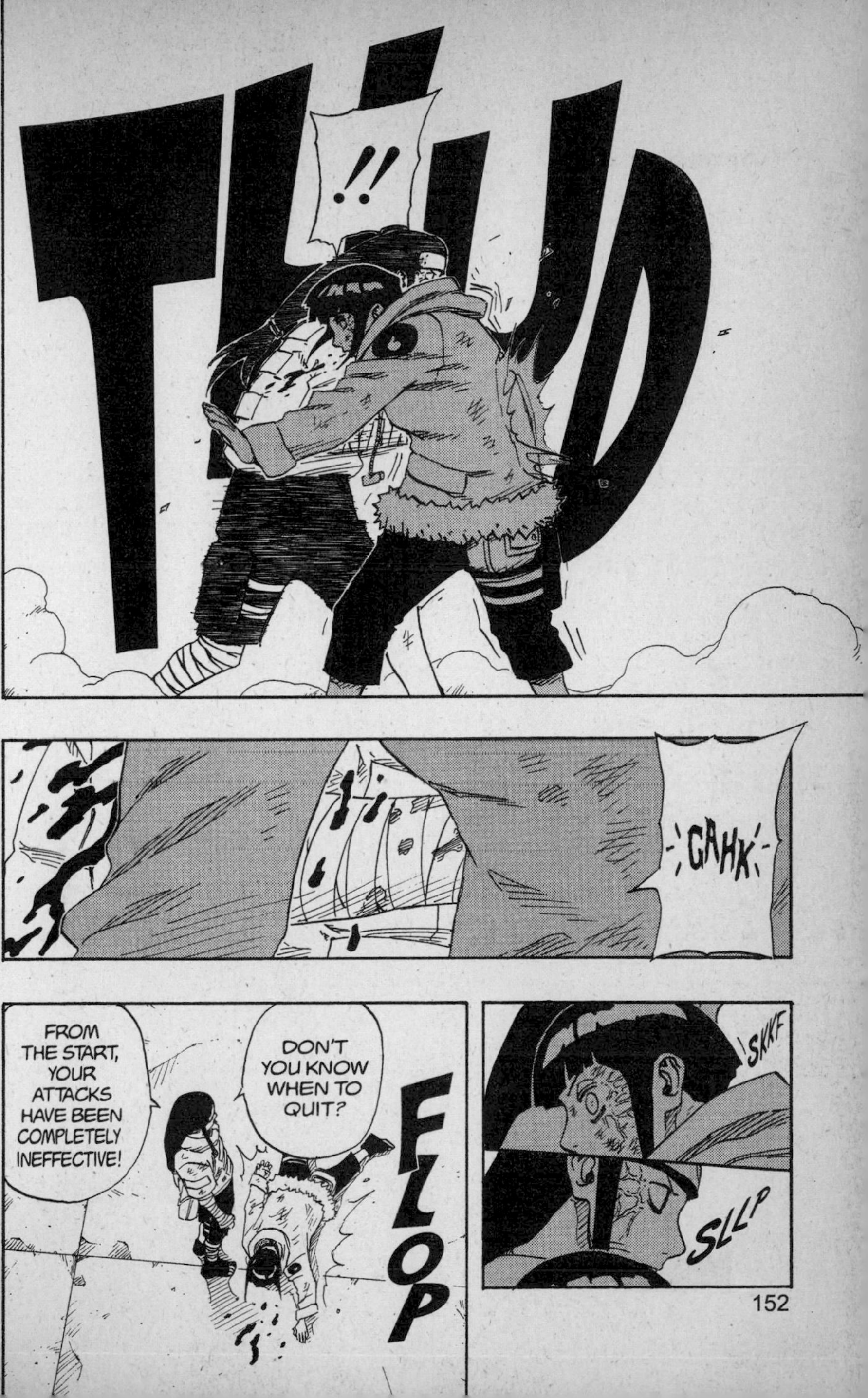
THUD
!!
GAHK
SKKF
SLLP
DON'T YOU KNOW WHEN TO QUIT?
FROM THE START, YOUR ATTACKS HAVE BEEN COMPLETELY INEFFECTIVE!
FLOP

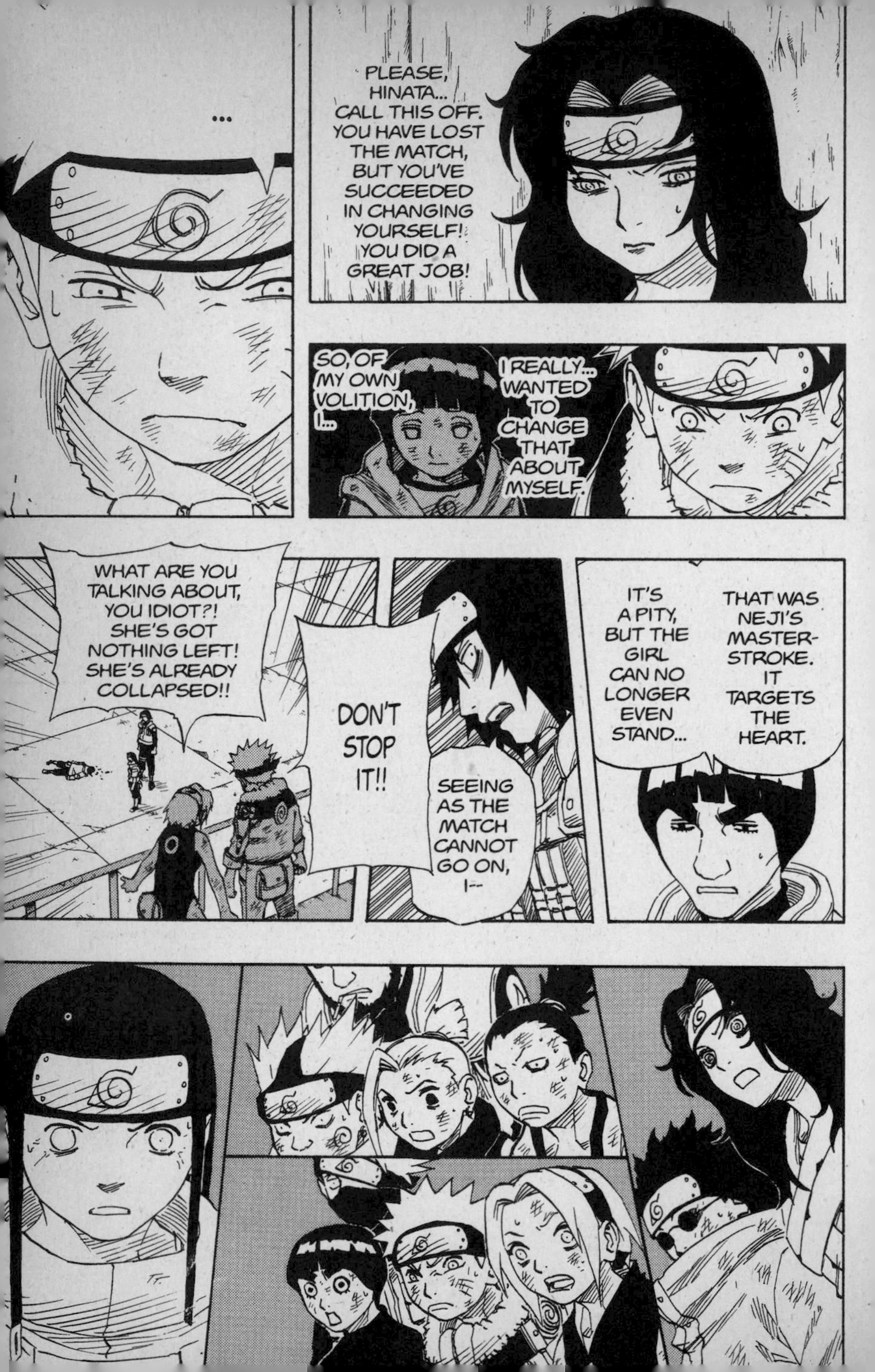
PLEASE, HINATA... CALL THIS OFF. YOU HAVE LOST THE MATCH, BUT YOU'VE SUCCEEDED IN CHANGING YOURSELF! YOU DID A GREAT JOB!
I REALLY... WANTED TO CHANGE THAT ABOUT MYSELF.
SO, OF MY OWN VOLITION, I...
...
THAT WAS NEJI'S MASTER-STROKE. IT TARGETS THE HEART.
IT'S A PITY, BUT THE GIRL CAN NO LONGER EVEN STAND...
SEEING AS THE MATCH CANNOT GO ON, I--
DON'T STOP IT!!
WHAT ARE YOU TALKING ABOUT, YOU IDIOT?! SHE'S GOT NOTHING LEFT! SHE'S ALREADY COLLAPSED!!

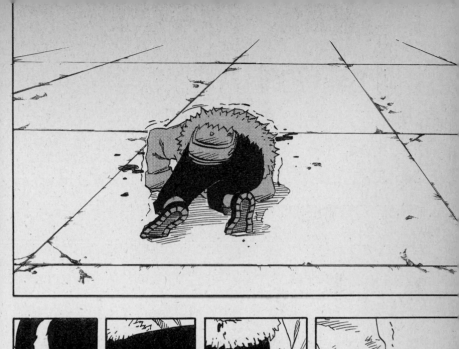

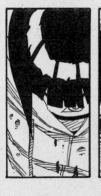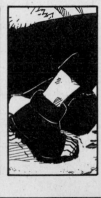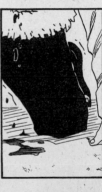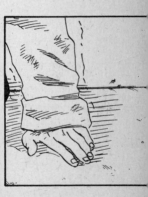

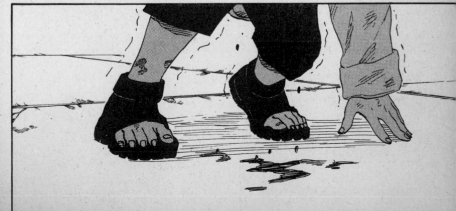

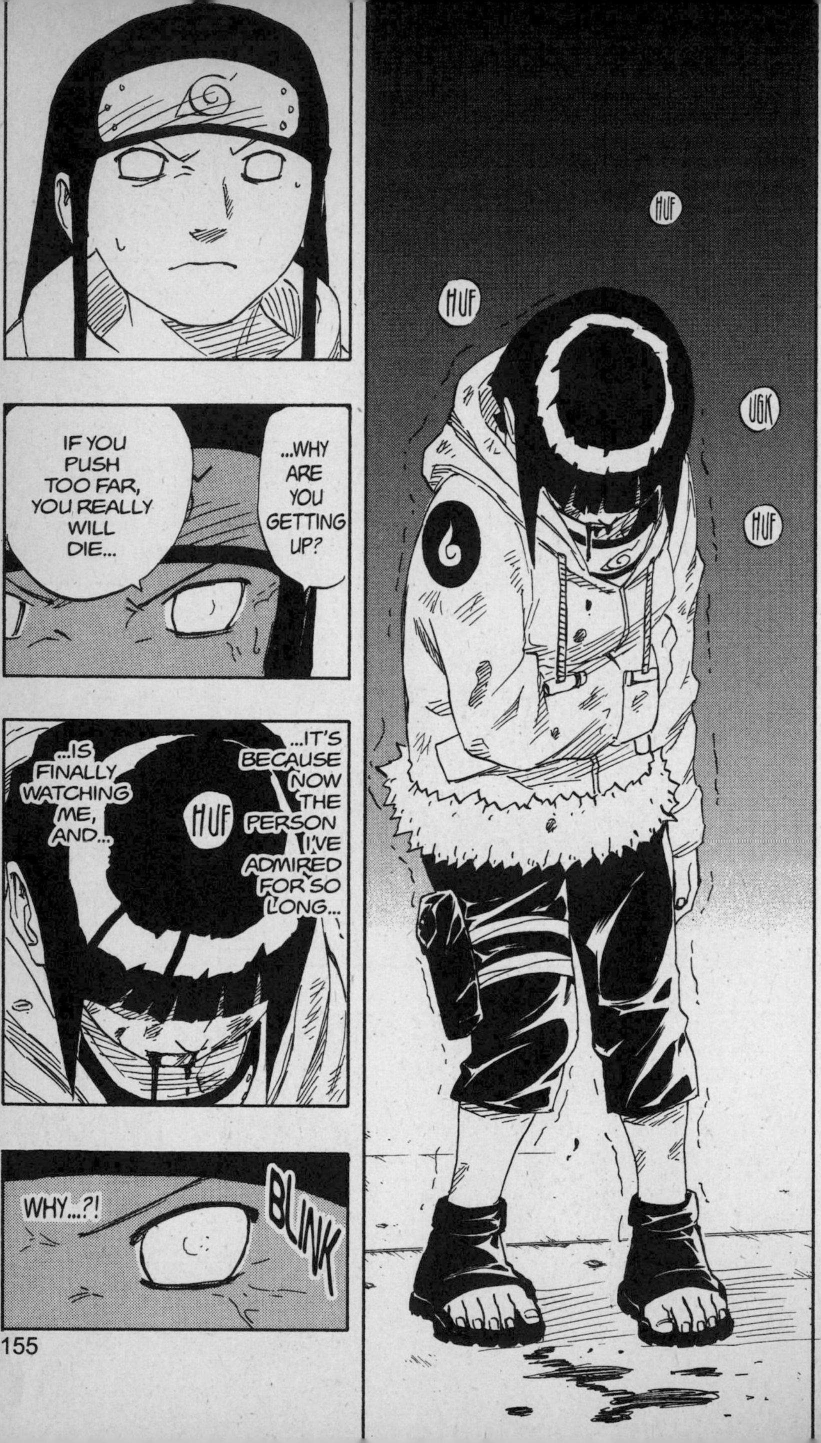
HUF
HUF
UGK
HUF
...WHY ARE YOU GETTING UP?
IF YOU PUSH TOO FAR, YOU REALLY WILL DIE...
...IT'S BECAUSE NOW THE PERSON I'VE ADMIRED FOR SO LONG...
HUF
...IS FINALLY WATCHING ME, AND...
BLINK
WHY...?!

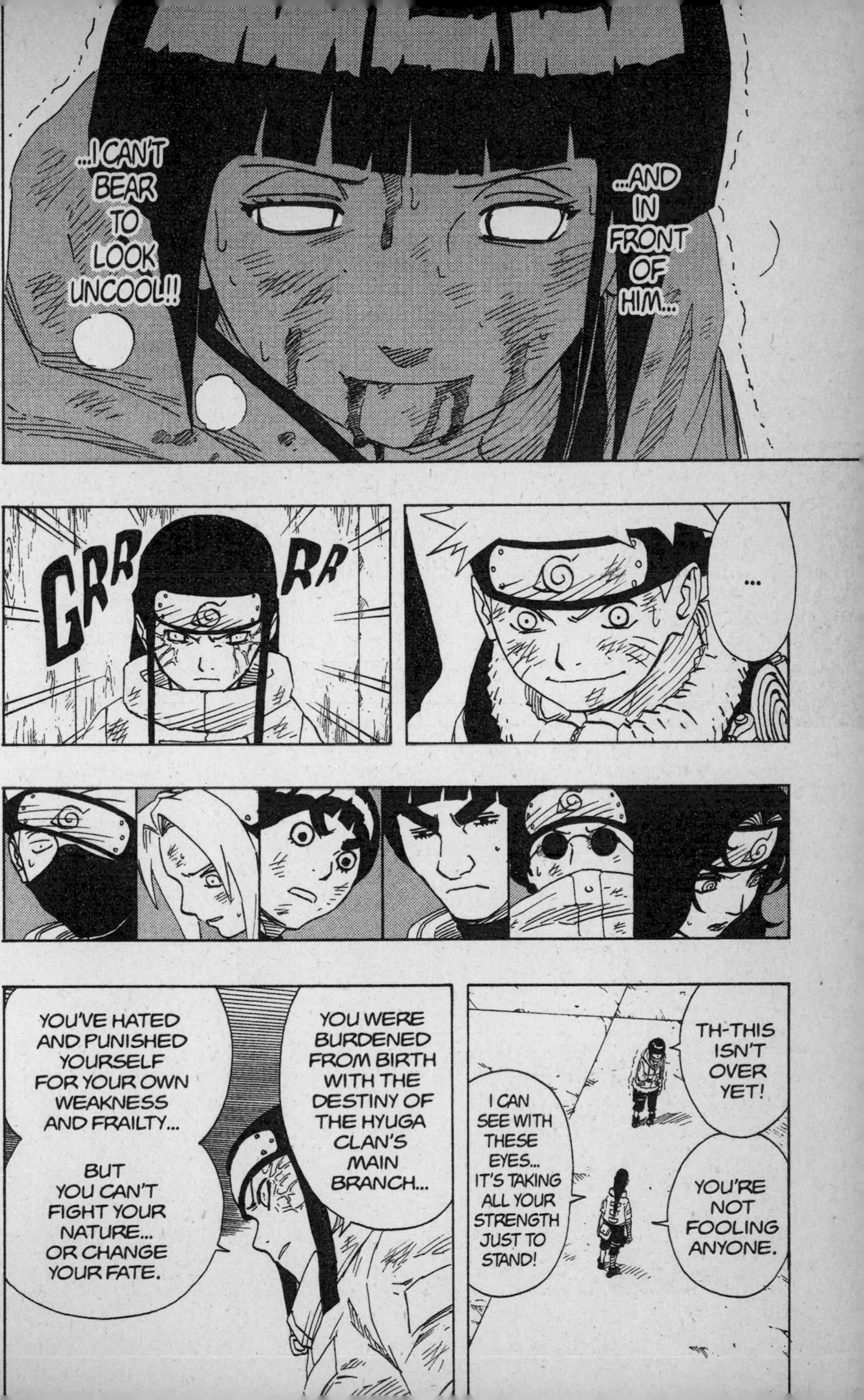
...AND IN FRONT OF HIM...
...I CAN'T BEAR TO LOOK UNCOOL!!
...
GRRRR
TH-THIS ISN'T OVER YET!
YOU'RE NOT FOOLING ANYONE.
I CAN SEE WITH THESE EYES... IT'S TAKING ALL YOUR STRENGTH JUST TO STAND!
YOU WERE BURDENED FROM BIRTH WITH THE DESTINY OF THE HYUGA CLAN'S MAIN BRANCH...
YOU'VE HATED AND PUNISHED YOURSELF FOR YOUR OWN WEAKNESS AND FRAILTY...
BUT YOU CAN'T FIGHT YOUR NATURE... OR CHANGE YOUR FATE.

READ THIS WAY

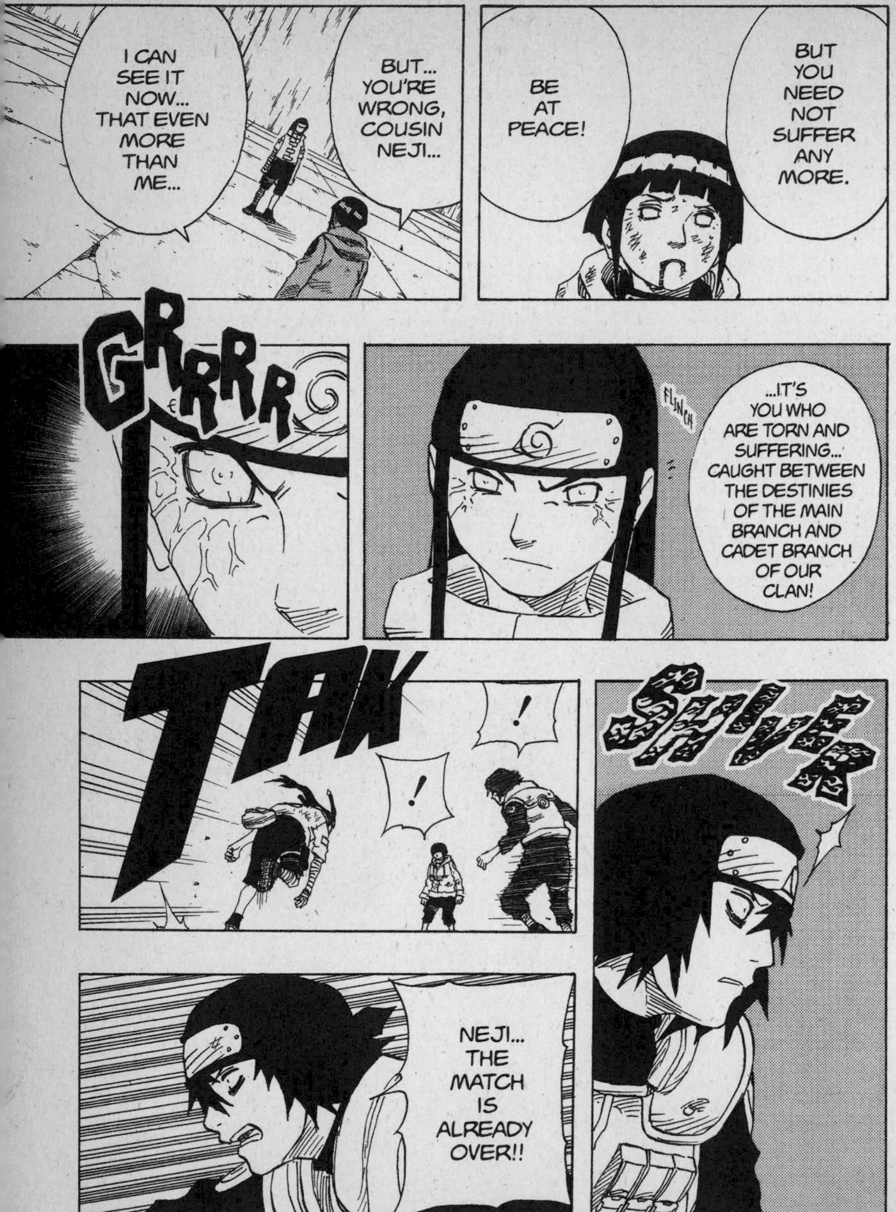
BUT YOU NEED NOT SUFFER ANY MORE.
BE AT PEACE!
BUT... YOU'RE WRONG, COUSIN NEJI...
I CAN SEE IT NOW... THAT EVEN MORE THAN ME...
FLINCH
...IT'S YOU WHO ARE TORN AND SUFFERING... CAUGHT BETWEEN THE DESTINIES OF THE MAIN BRANCH AND CADET BRANCH OF OUR CLAN!
GRRRR
SHVK
TAK
!
!
NEJI... THE MATCH IS ALREADY OVER!!

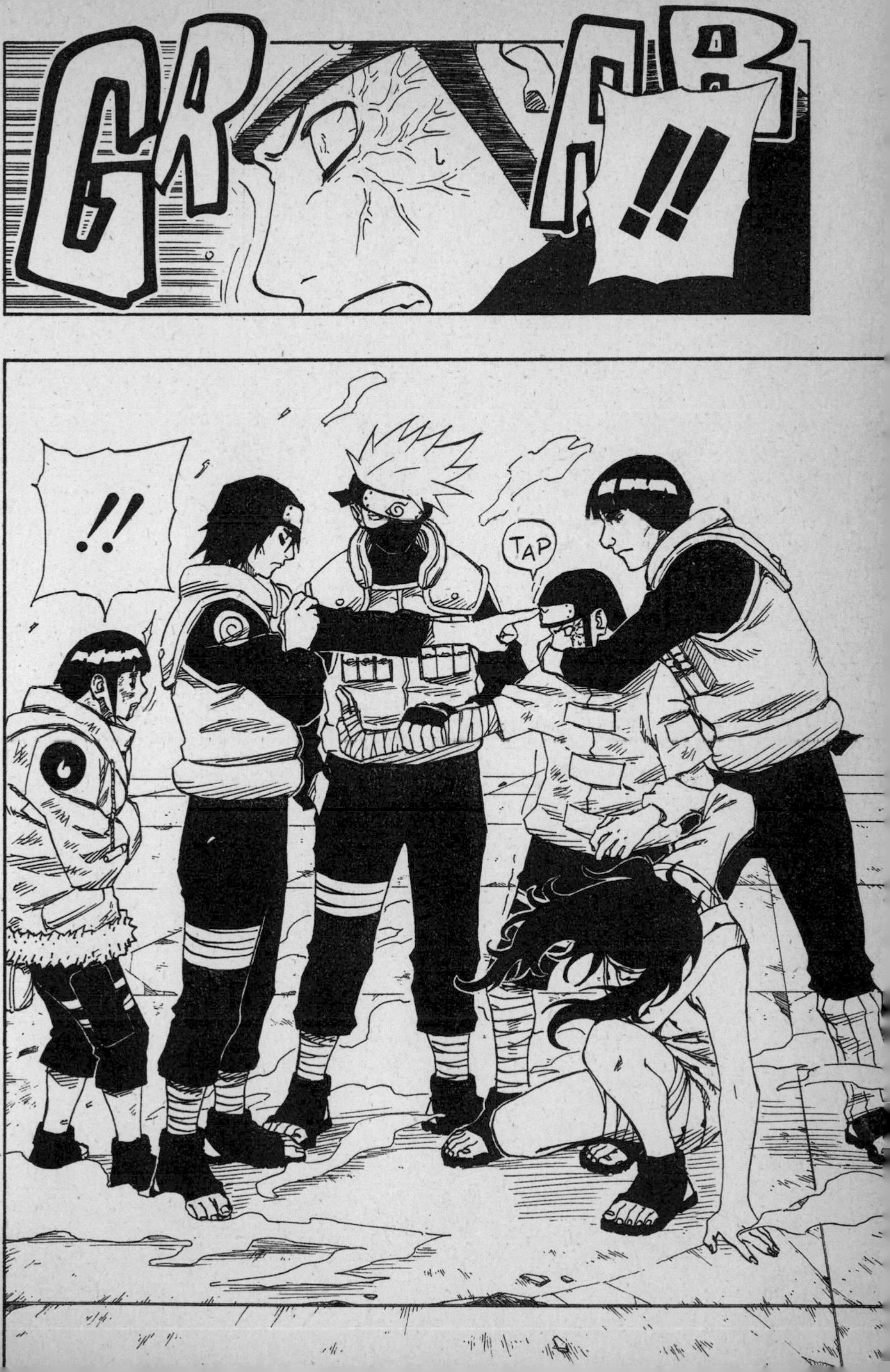
GRAR!!
TAP
!!

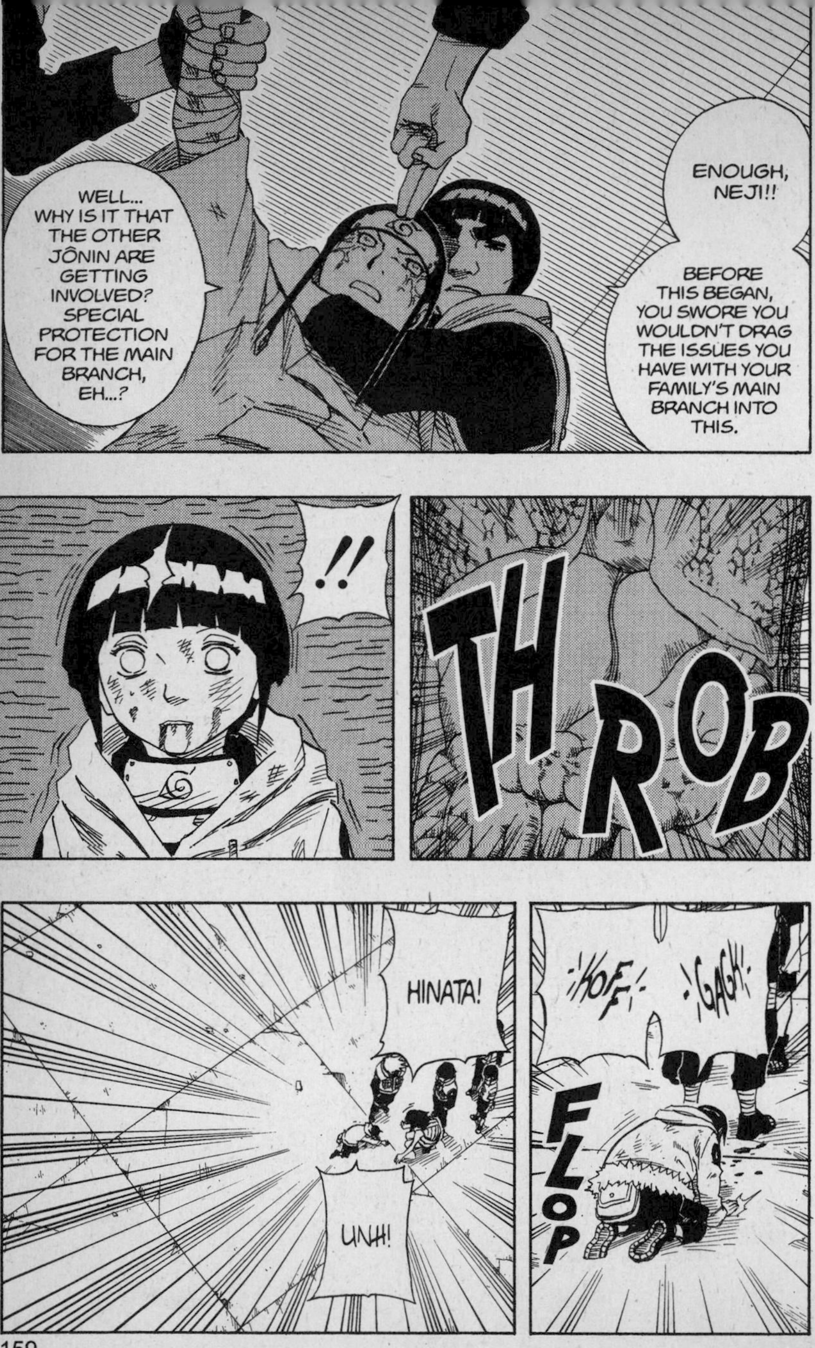
ENOUGH, NEJI!!
BEFORE THIS BEGAN, YOU SWORE YOU WOULDN'T DRAG THE ISSUES YOU HAVE WITH YOUR FAMILY'S MAIN BRANCH INTO THIS.
WELL... WHY IS IT THAT THE OTHER JÔNIN ARE GETTING INVOLVED? SPECIAL PROTECTION FOR THE MAIN BRANCH, EH...?
THROB
!!
KOFF
GAGH
FLOP
HINATA!
UNH!

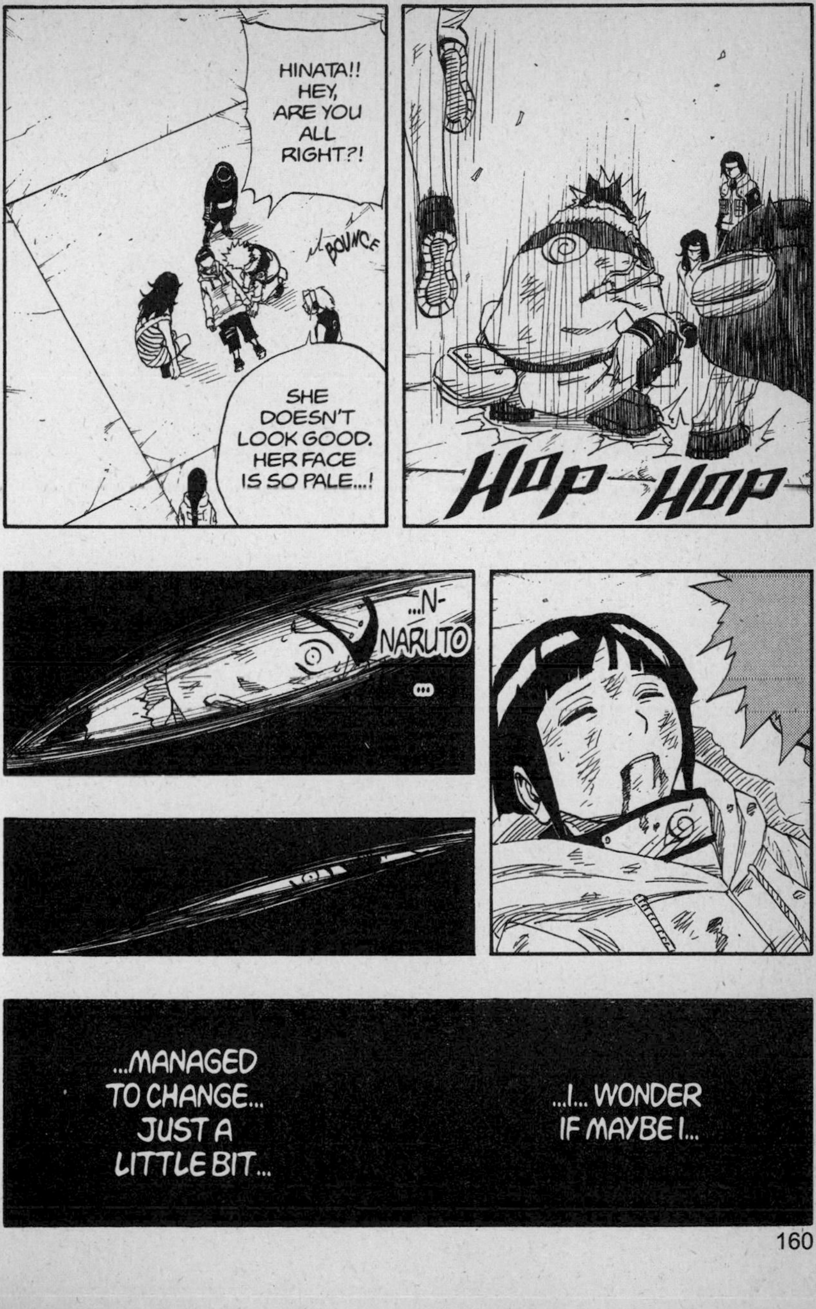
HOP HOP
HINATA!! HEY, ARE YOU ALL RIGHT?!
BOUNCE
SHE DOESN'T LOOK GOOD. HER FACE IS SO PALE...!
...N- NARUTO ...
...I... WONDER IF MAYBE I...
...MANAGED TO CHANGE... JUST A LITTLE BIT...

READ THIS WAY

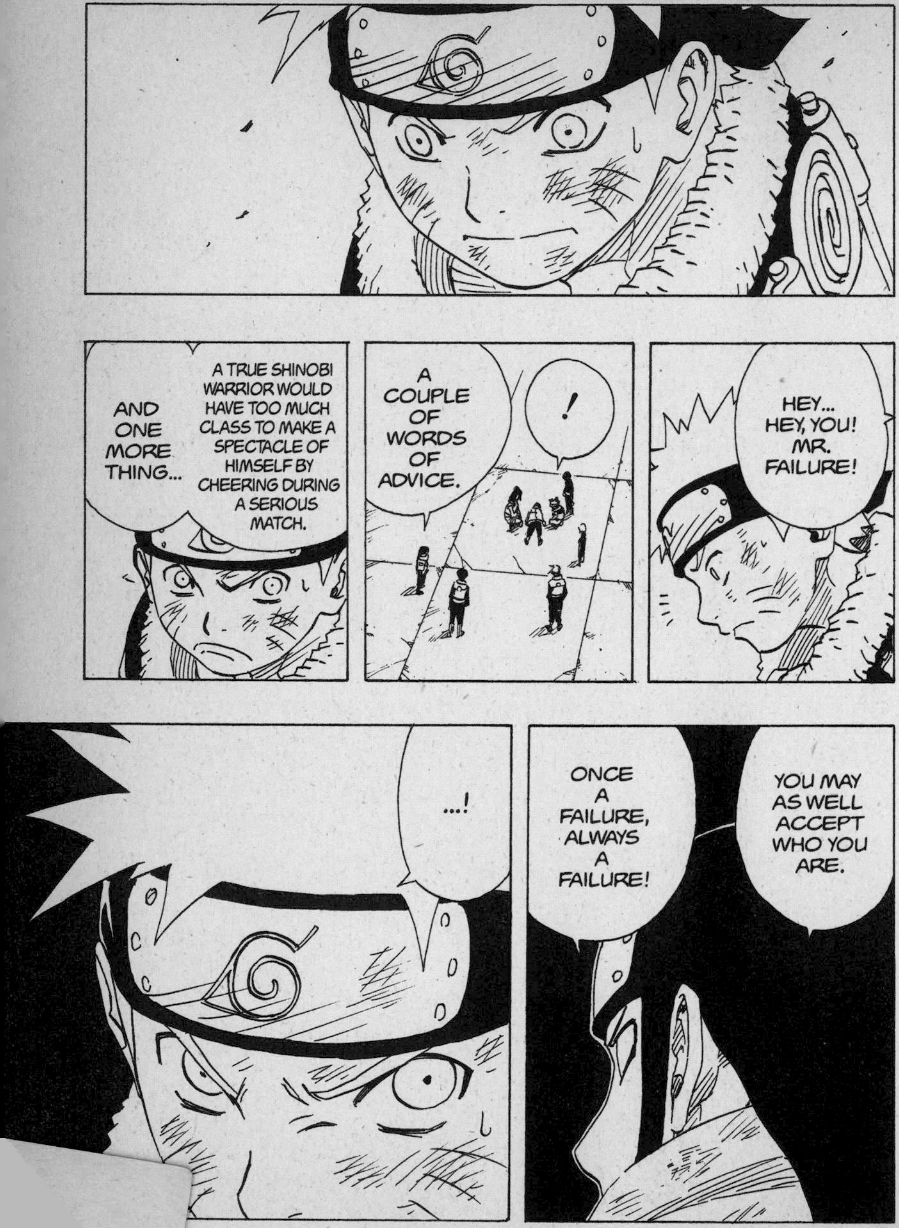
HEY... HEY, YOU! MR. FAILURE!
!
A COUPLE OF WORDS OF ADVICE.
A TRUE SHINOBI WARRIOR WOULD HAVE TOO MUCH CLASS TO MAKE A SPECTACLE OF HIMSELF BY CHEERING DURING A SERIOUS MATCH.
AND ONE MORE THING...
YOU MAY AS WELL ACCEPT WHO YOU ARE.
ONCE A FAILURE, ALWAYS A FAILURE!
...!

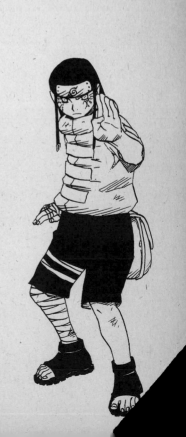

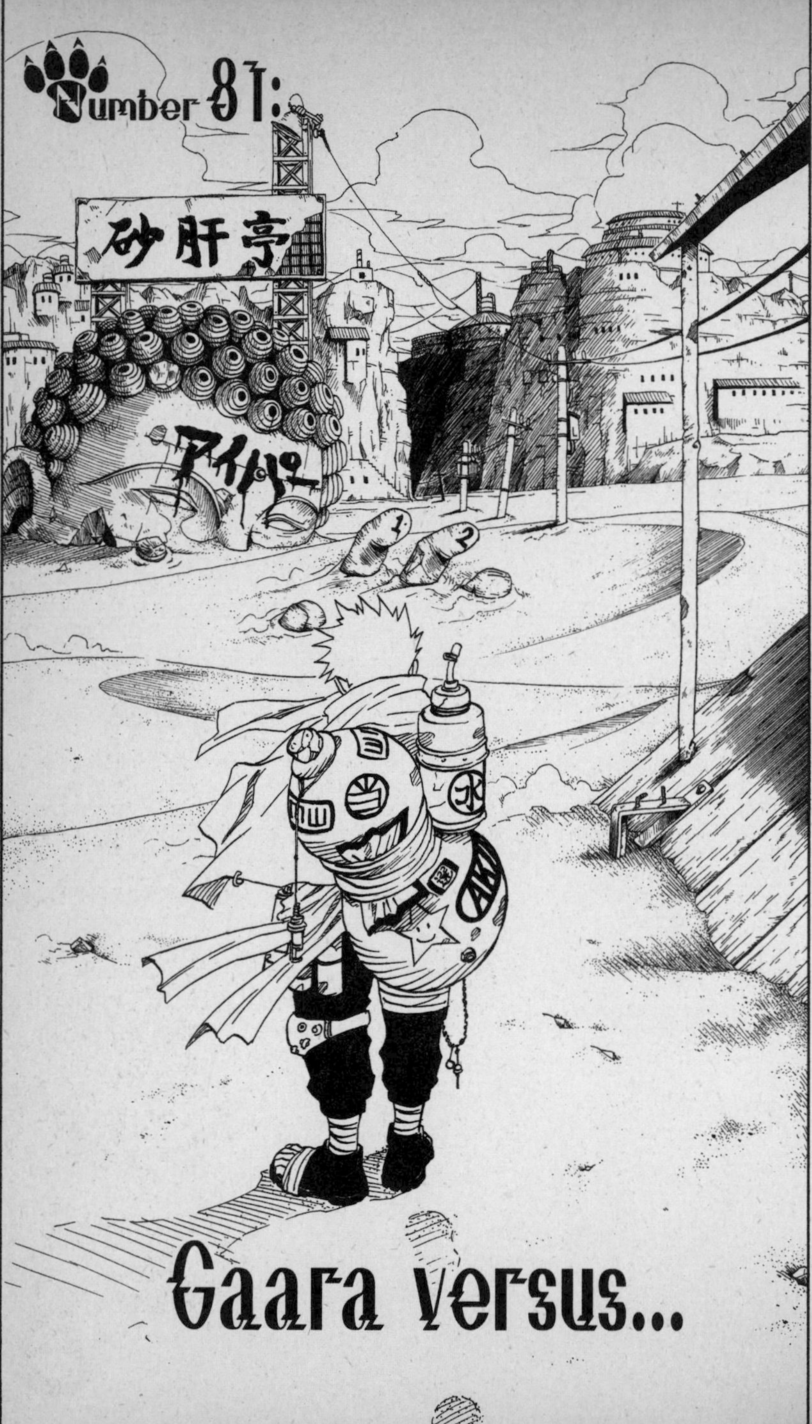
Number 81:
砂肝亭
Gaara versus...

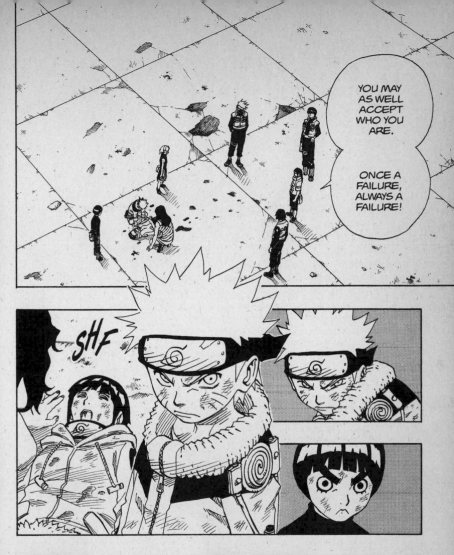

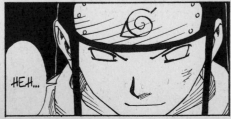

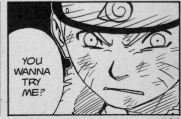

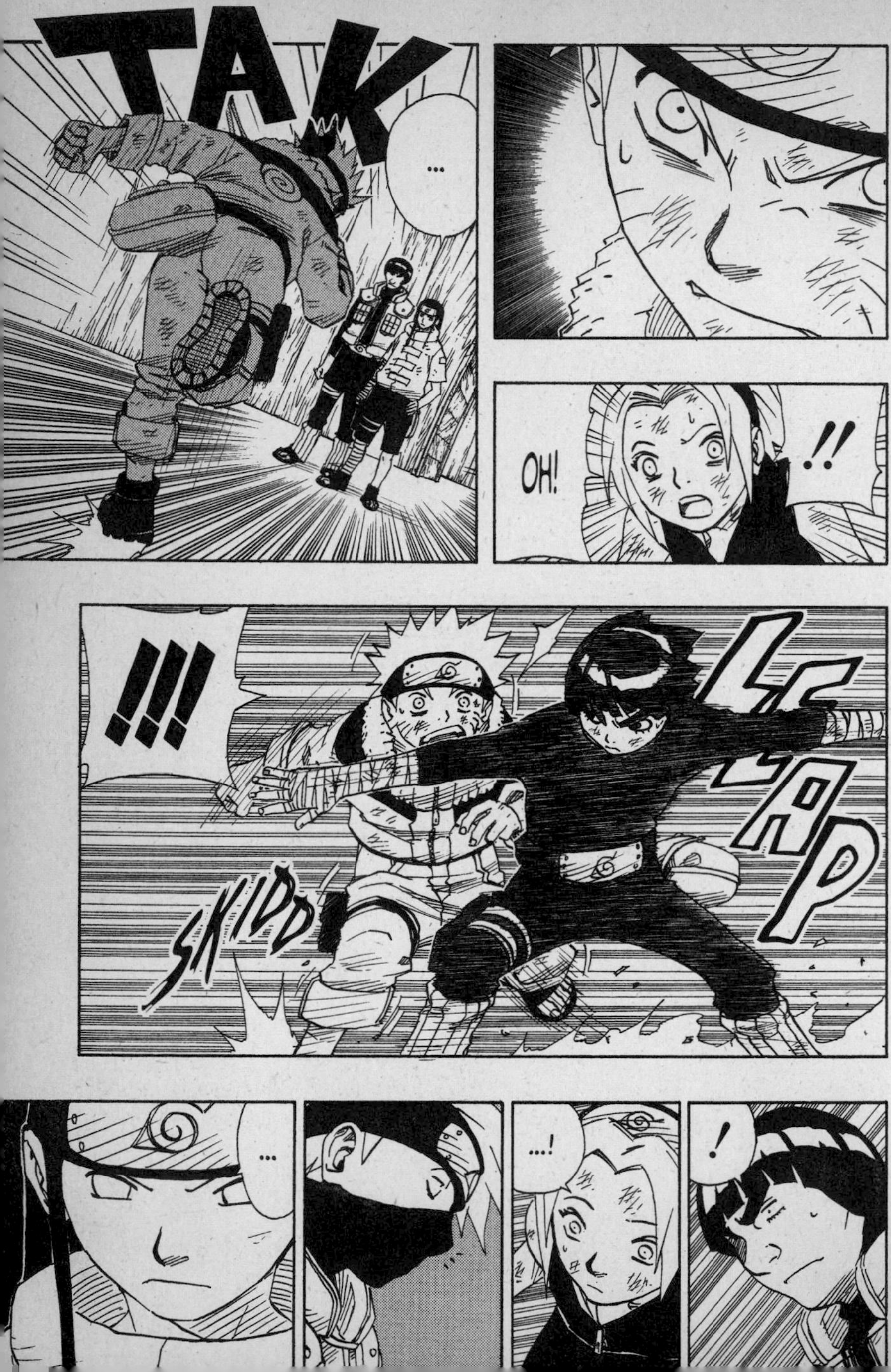
!!
OH!
TAK
...
LEAP
!!!
SKIDD
!
...!
...

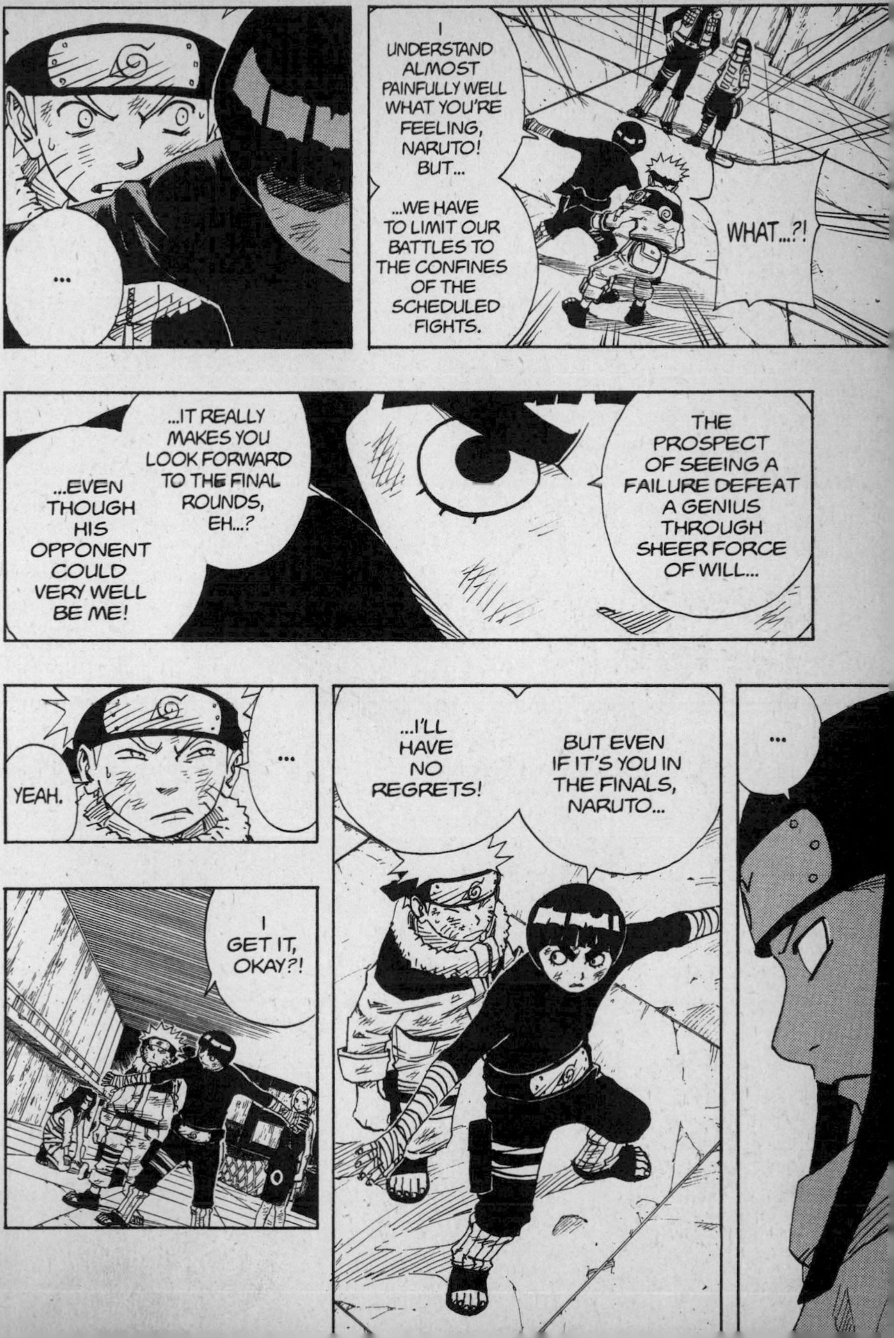
WHAT...?!
I UNDERSTAND ALMOST PAINFULLY WELL WHAT YOU'RE FEELING, NARUTO! BUT...
...WE HAVE TO LIMIT OUR BATTLES TO THE CONFINES OF THE SCHEDULED FIGHTS.
...
THE PROSPECT OF SEEING A FAILURE DEFEAT A GENIUS THROUGH SHEER FORCE OF WILL...
...IT REALLY MAKES YOU LOOK FORWARD TO THE FINAL ROUNDS, EH...?
...EVEN THOUGH HIS OPPONENT COULD VERY WELL BE ME!
...
BUT EVEN IF IT'S YOU IN THE FINALS, NARUTO...
...I'LL HAVE NO REGRETS!
...
YEAH.
I GET IT, OKAY?!

READ THIS WAY

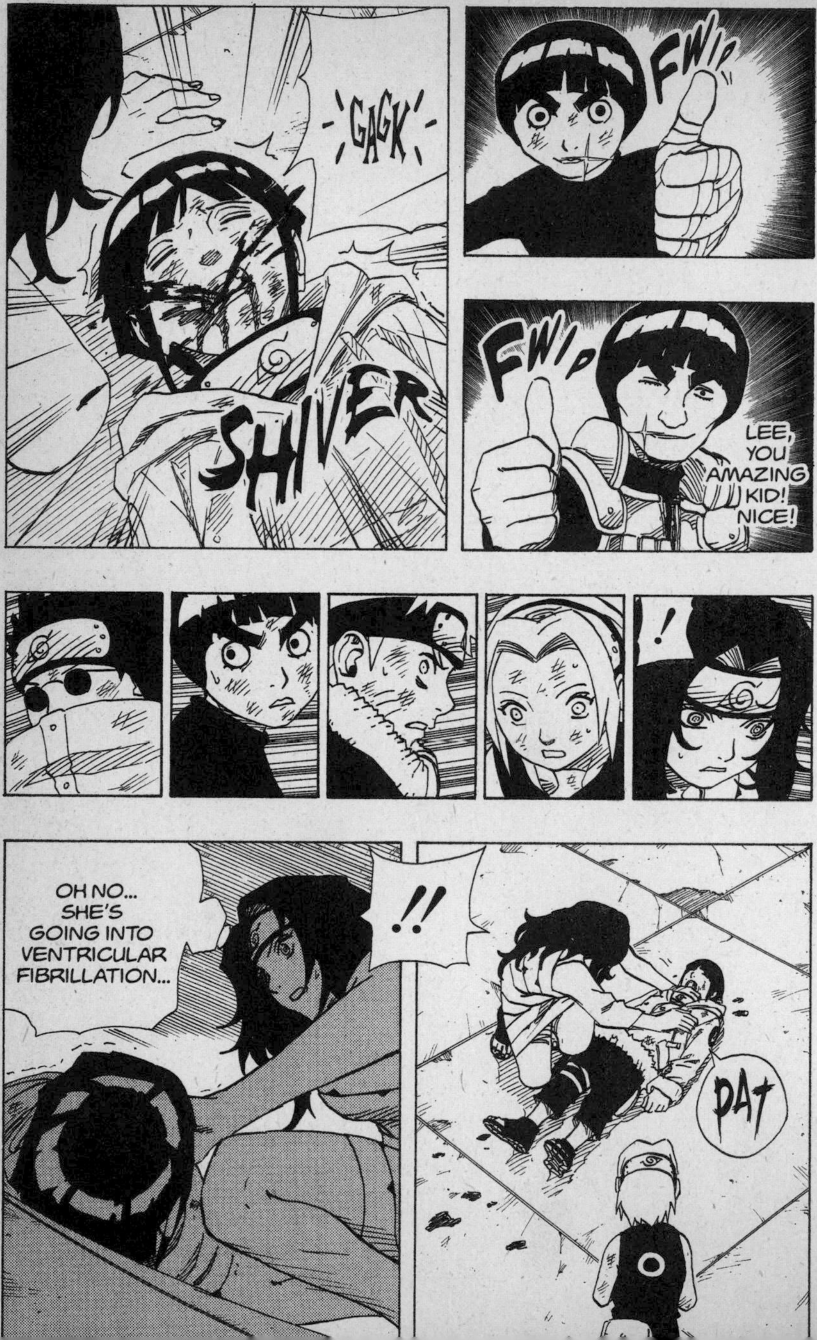
FWIP
FWIP
LEE, YOU AMAZING KID! NICE!
GAGK
SHIVER
!
PAT
!!
OH NO... SHE'S GOING INTO VENTRICULAR FIBRILLATION...

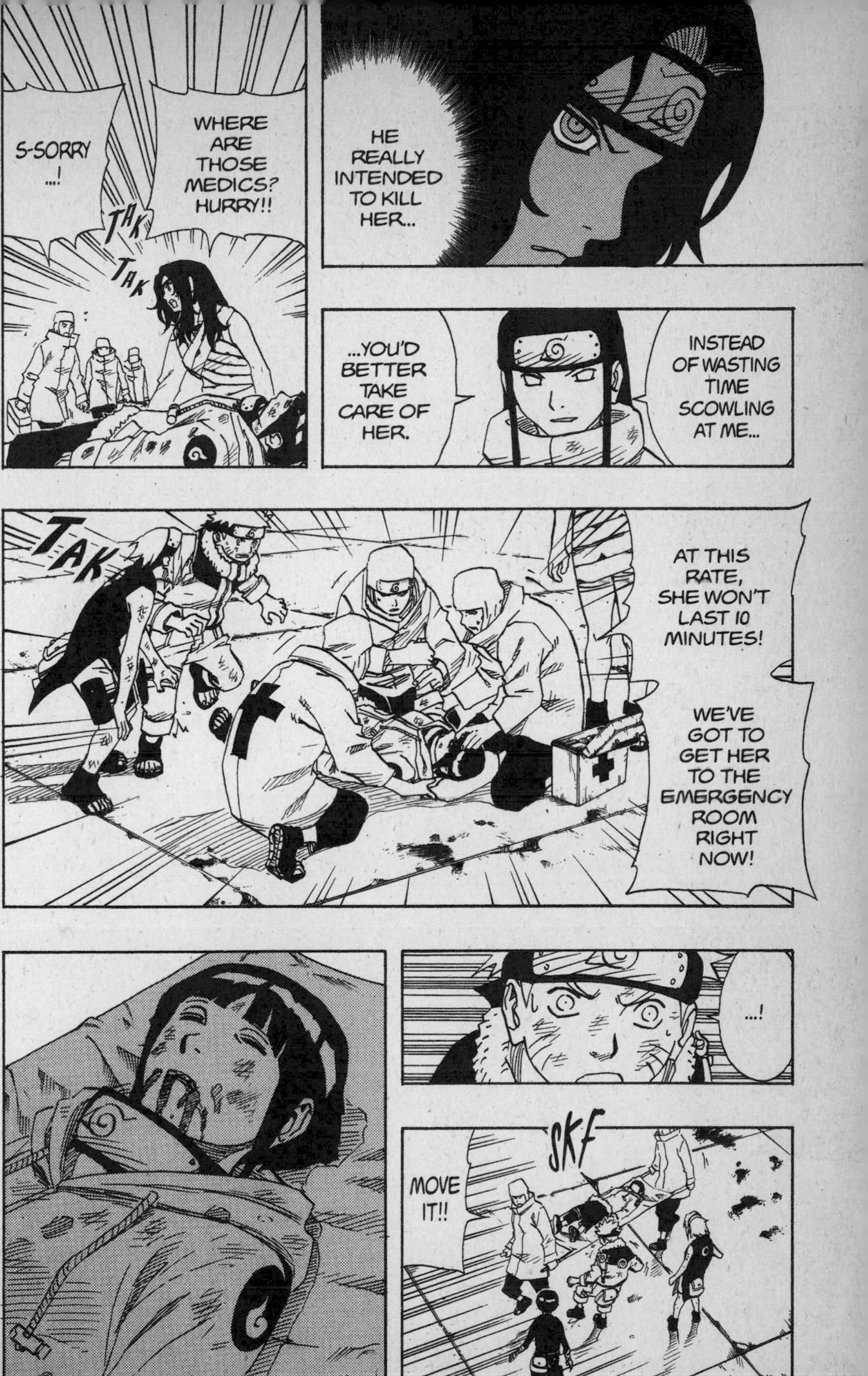
HE REALLY INTENDED TO KILL HER...
INSTEAD OF WASTING TIME SCOWLING AT ME...
...YOU'D BETTER TAKE CARE OF HER.
WHERE ARE THOSE MEDICS? HURRY!!
S-SORRY ...!
TAK
TAK
AT THIS RATE, SHE WON'T LAST 10 MINUTES!
WE'VE GOT TO GET HER TO THE EMERGENCY ROOM RIGHT NOW!
TAK
...!
SKF
MOVE IT!!

READ THIS WAY

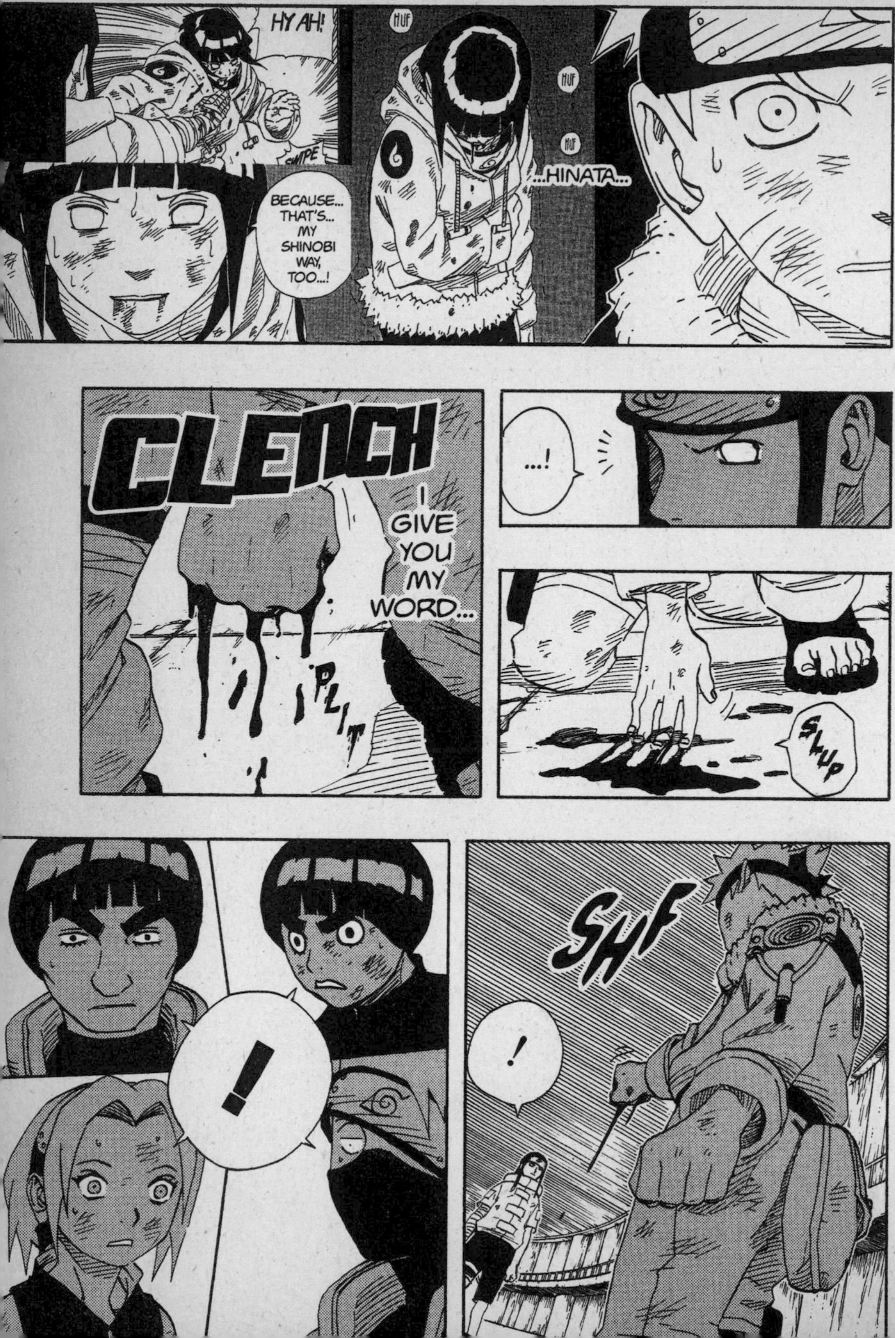
...HINATA...
HUF
HUF
HUF
HYAH!
SWIPE
BECAUSE... THAT'S... MY SHINOBI WAY, TOO...!
...!
SLUP
CLENCH
I GIVE YOU MY WORD...
PLIT
SHF
!
!

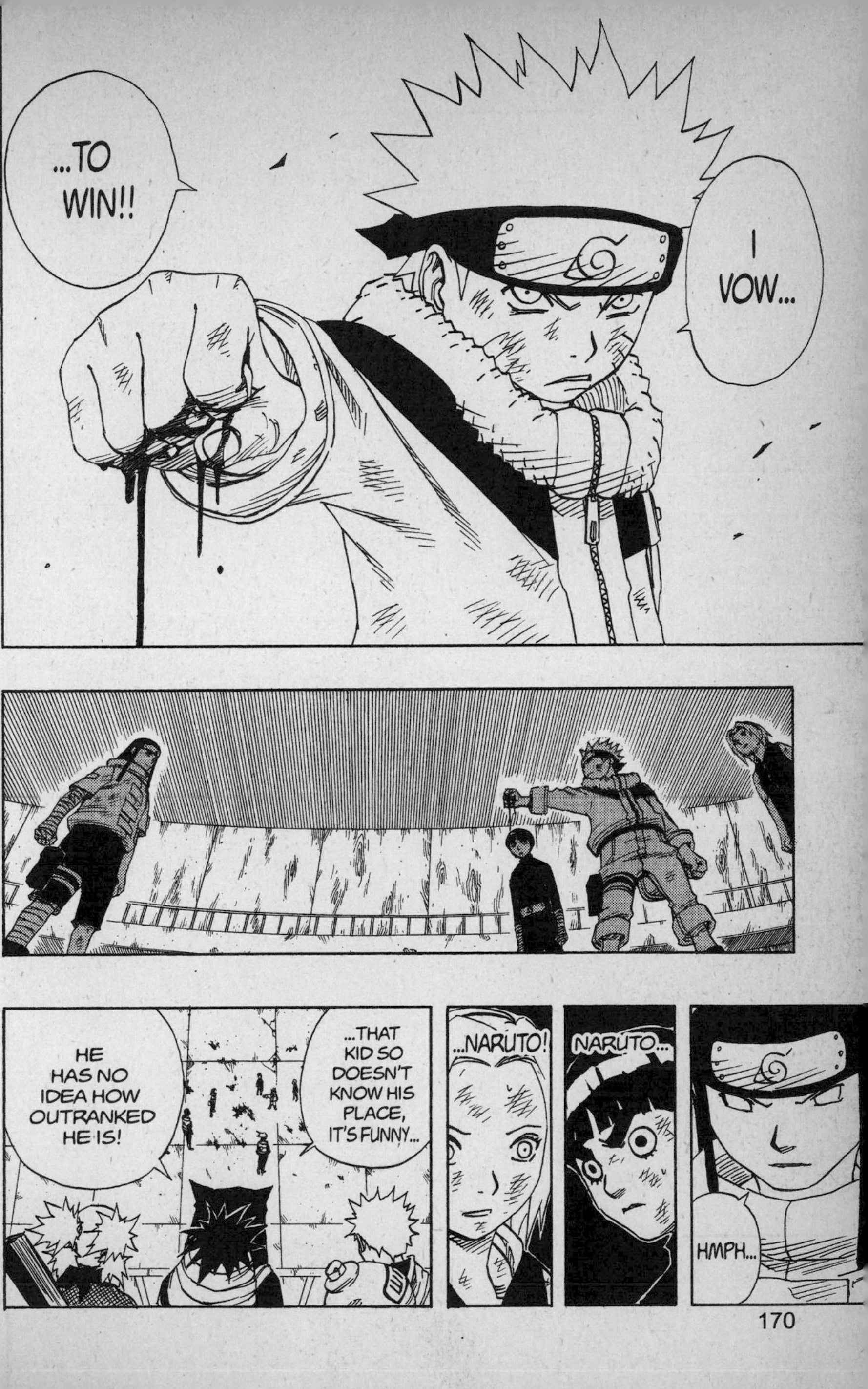
I VOW...
...TO WIN!!
HMPH...
NARUTO...
...NARUTO!
...THAT KID SO DOESN'T KNOW HIS PLACE, IT'S FUNNY...
HE HAS NO IDEA HOW OUTRANKED HE IS!

READ THIS WAY

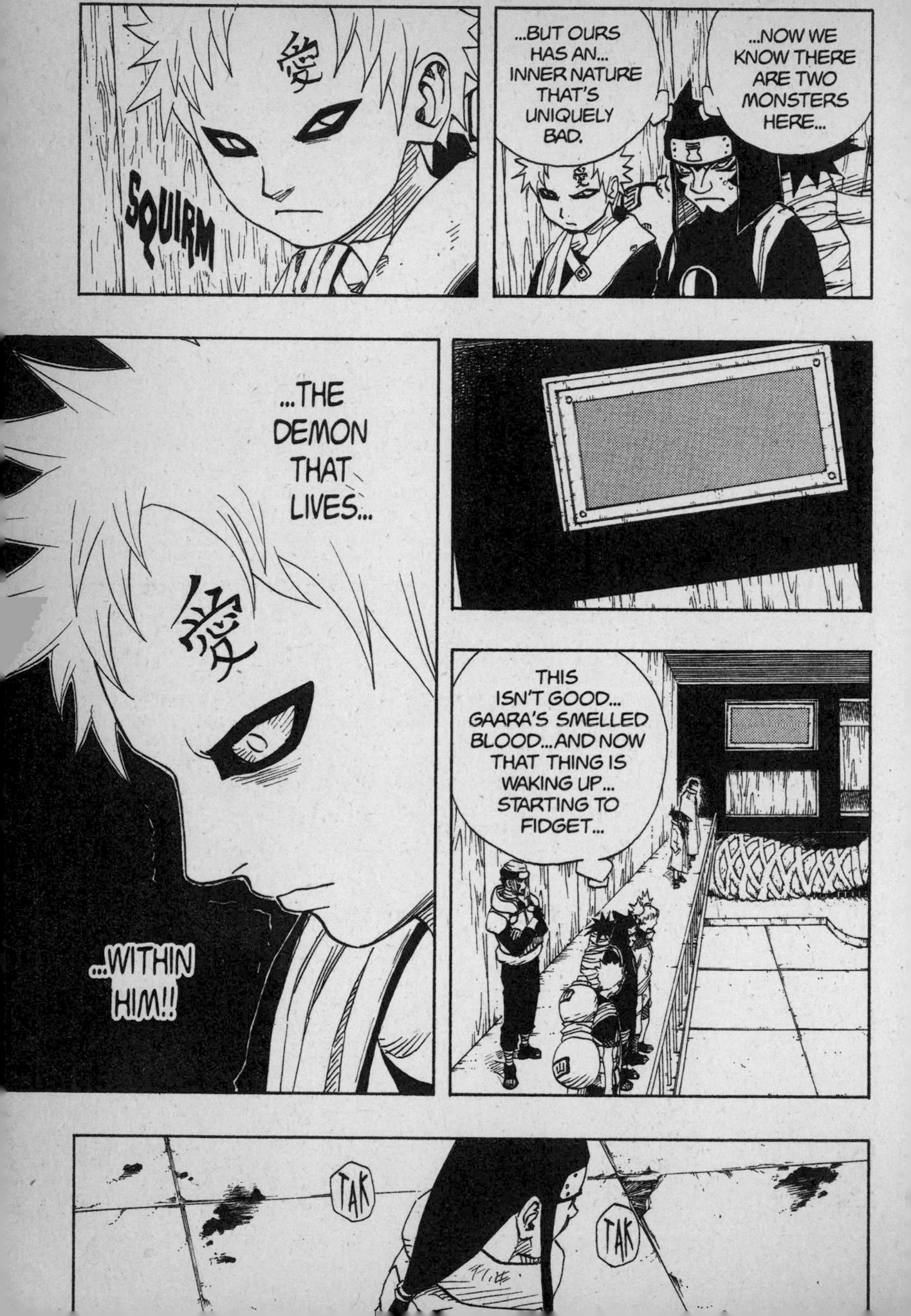

...NOW WE KNOW THERE ARE TWO MONSTERS HERE...
...BUT OURS HAS AN... INNER NATURE THAT'S UNIQUELY BAD.
SQUIRM
THIS ISN'T GOOD... GAARA'S SMELLED BLOOD...AND NOW THAT THING IS WAKING UP... STARTING TO FIDGET...
...THE DEMON THAT LIVES...
...WITHIN HIM!!
TAK
TAK

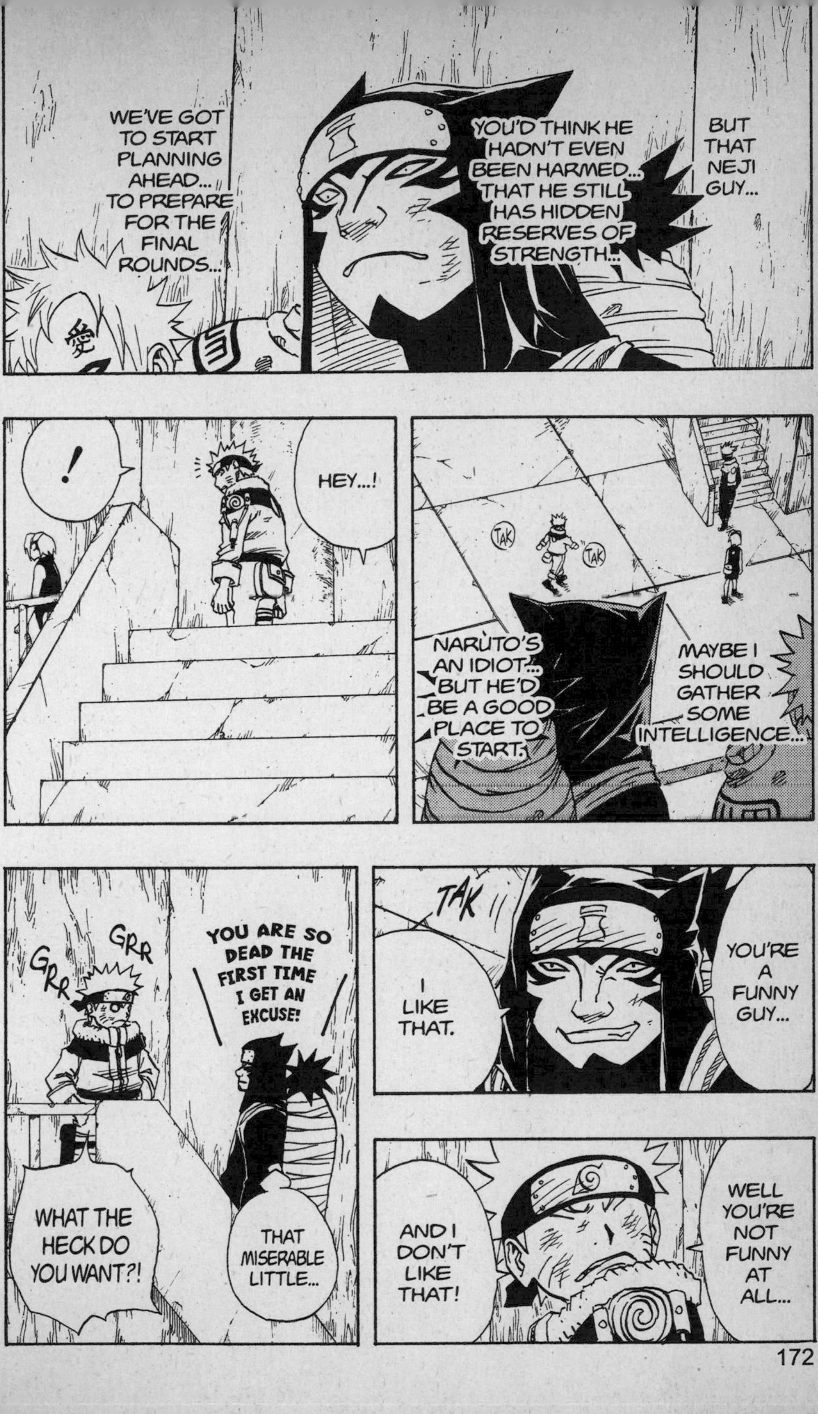
BUT THAT NEJI GUY...
YOU'D THINK HE HADN'T EVEN BEEN HARMED... THAT HE STILL HAS HIDDEN RESERVES OF STRENGTH...
WE'VE GOT TO START PLANNING AHEAD... TO PREPARE FOR THE FINAL ROUNDS...
TAK
TAK
MAYBE I SHOULD GATHER SOME INTELLIGENCE...
NARUTO'S AN IDIOT... BUT HE'D BE A GOOD PLACE TO START.
HEY...!
!
YOU'RE A FUNNY GUY...
TAK
I LIKE THAT.
WELL YOU'RE NOT FUNNY AT ALL...
AND I DON'T LIKE THAT!
YOU ARE SO DEAD THE FIRST TIME I GET AN EXCUSE!
GRR
GRR
THAT MISERABLE LITTLE...
WHAT THE HECK DO YOU WANT?!

READ THIS WAY

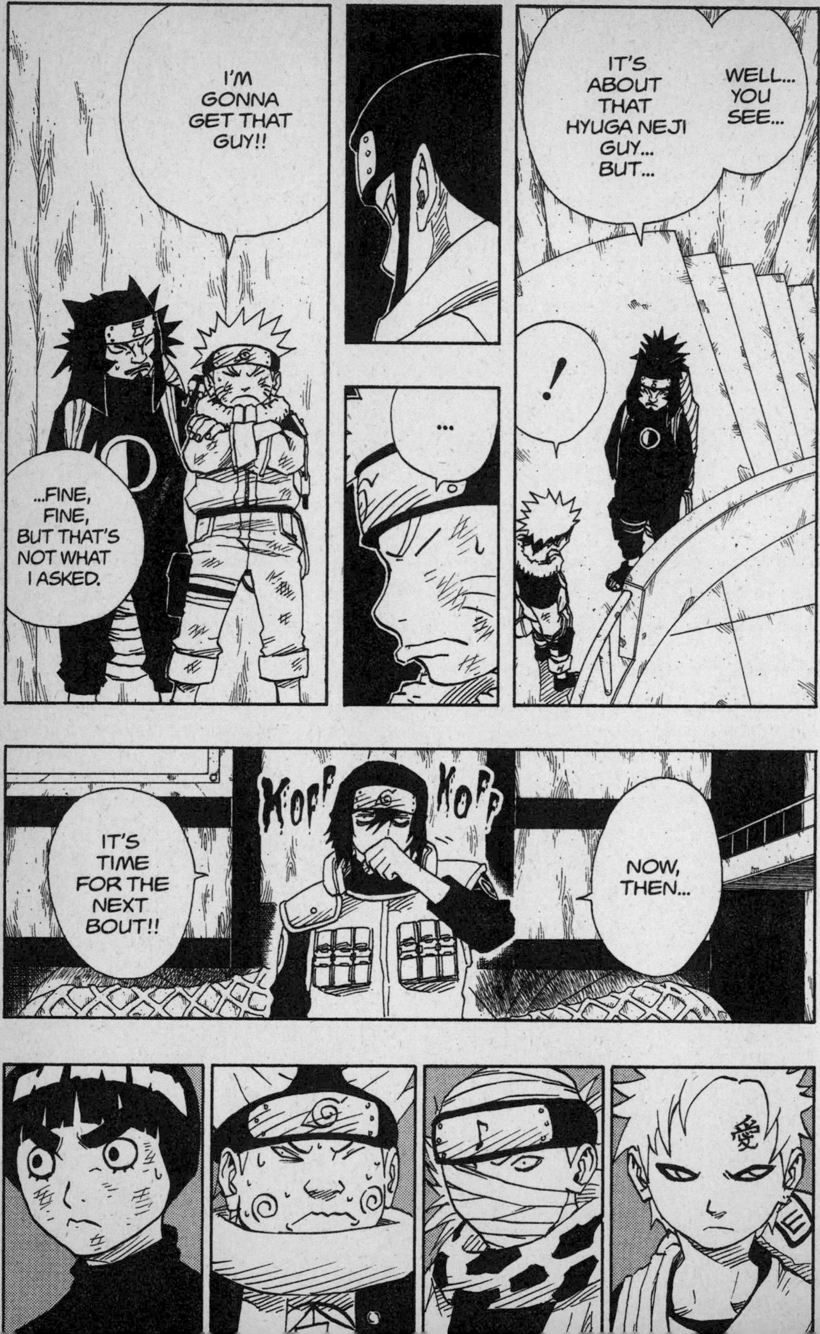
WELL... YOU SEE...
IT'S ABOUT THAT HYUGA NEJI GUY... BUT...
!
...
I'M GONNA GET THAT GUY!!
...FINE, FINE, BUT THAT'S NOT WHAT I ASKED.
NOW, THEN...
KOFF
KOFF
IT'S TIME FOR THE NEXT BOUT!!

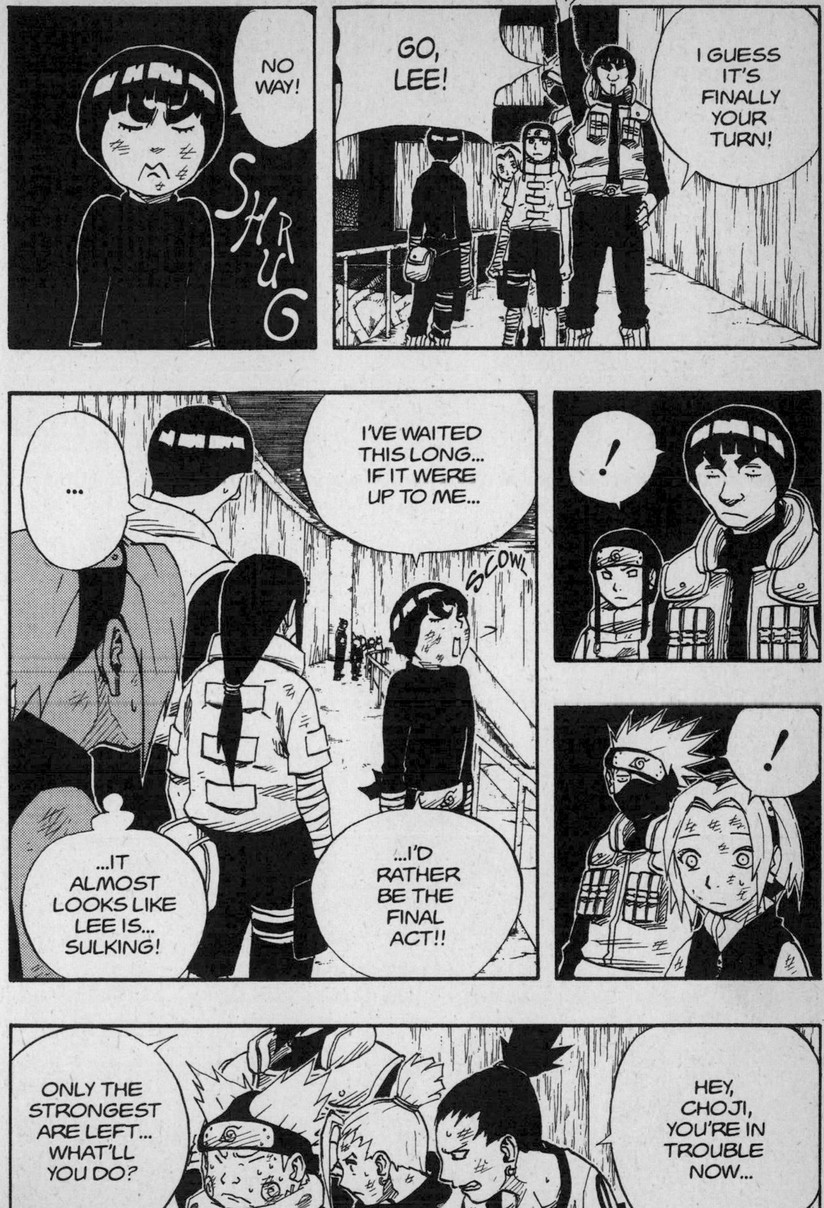
I GUESS IT'S FINALLY YOUR TURN!
GO, LEE!
NO WAY!
SHRUG
!
!
I'VE WAITED THIS LONG... IF IT WERE UP TO ME...
SCOWL
...
...I'D RATHER BE THE FINAL ACT!!
...IT ALMOST LOOKS LIKE LEE IS... SULKING!
HEY, CHOJI, YOU'RE IN TROUBLE NOW...
ONLY THE STRONGEST ARE LEFT... WHAT'LL YOU DO?

READ THIS WAY

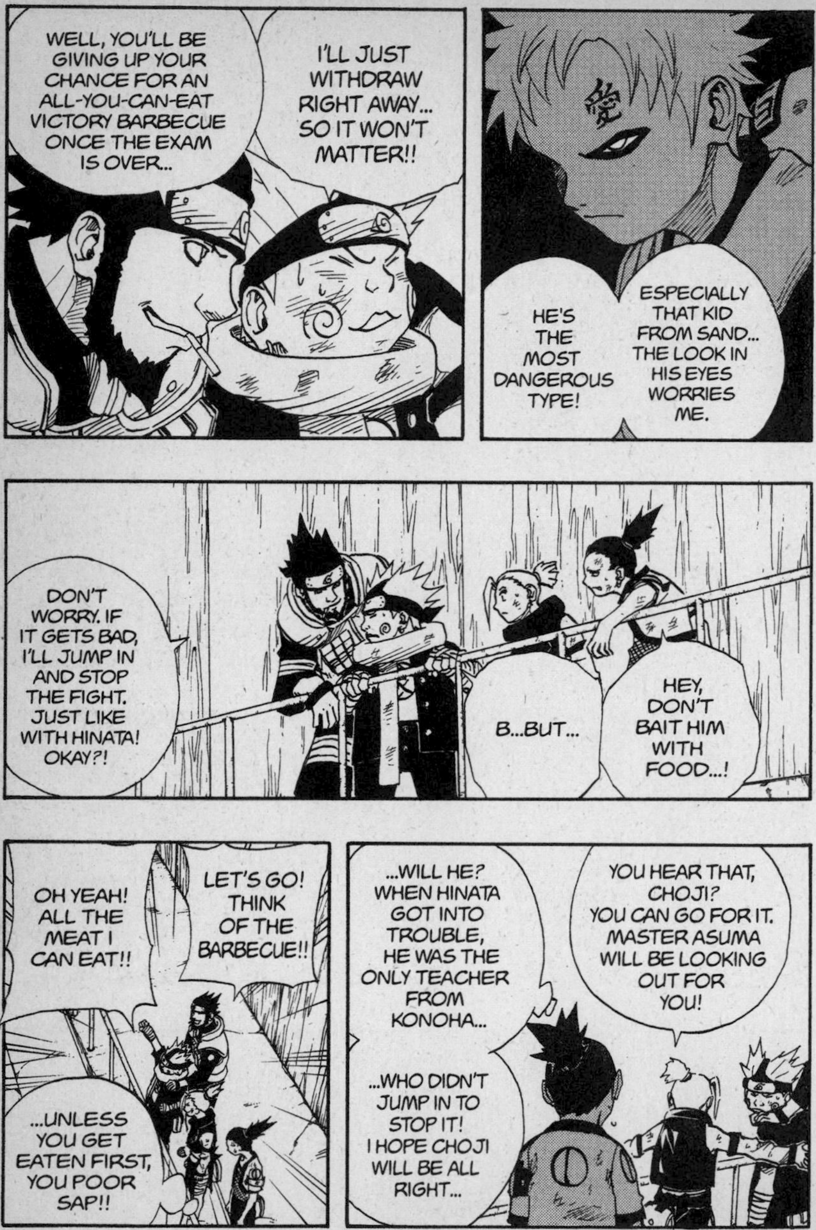
ESPECIALLY THAT KID FROM SAND... THE LOOK IN HIS EYES WORRIES ME.
HE'S THE MOST DANGEROUS TYPE!
I'LL JUST WITHDRAW RIGHT AWAY... SO IT WON'T MATTER!!
WELL, YOU'LL BE GIVING UP YOUR CHANCE FOR AN ALL-YOU-CAN-EAT VICTORY BARBECUE ONCE THE EXAM IS OVER...
HEY, DON'T BAIT HIM WITH FOOD...!
B...BUT...
DON'T WORRY. IF IT GETS BAD, I'LL JUMP IN AND STOP THE FIGHT. JUST LIKE WITH HINATA! OKAY?!
YOU HEAR THAT, CHOJI? YOU CAN GO FOR IT. MASTER ASUMA WILL BE LOOKING OUT FOR YOU!
...WILL HE? WHEN HINATA GOT INTO TROUBLE, HE WAS THE ONLY TEACHER FROM KONOHA...
...WHO DIDN'T JUMP IN TO STOP IT! I HOPE CHOJI WILL BE ALL RIGHT...
LET'S GO! THINK OF THE BARBECUE!!
OH YEAH! ALL THE MEAT I CAN EAT!!
...UNLESS YOU GET EATEN FIRST, YOU POOR SAP!!

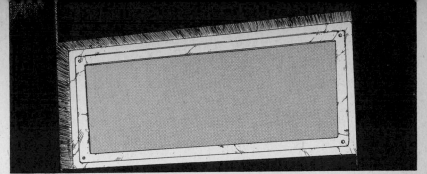

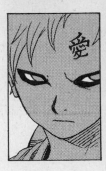
LUB
DUB
NOW...
GULP

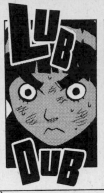
SHF

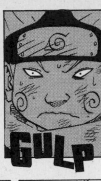

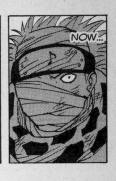

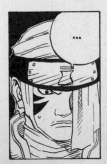
...

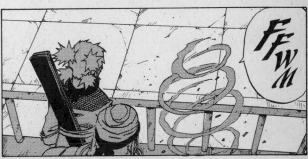
FFWM

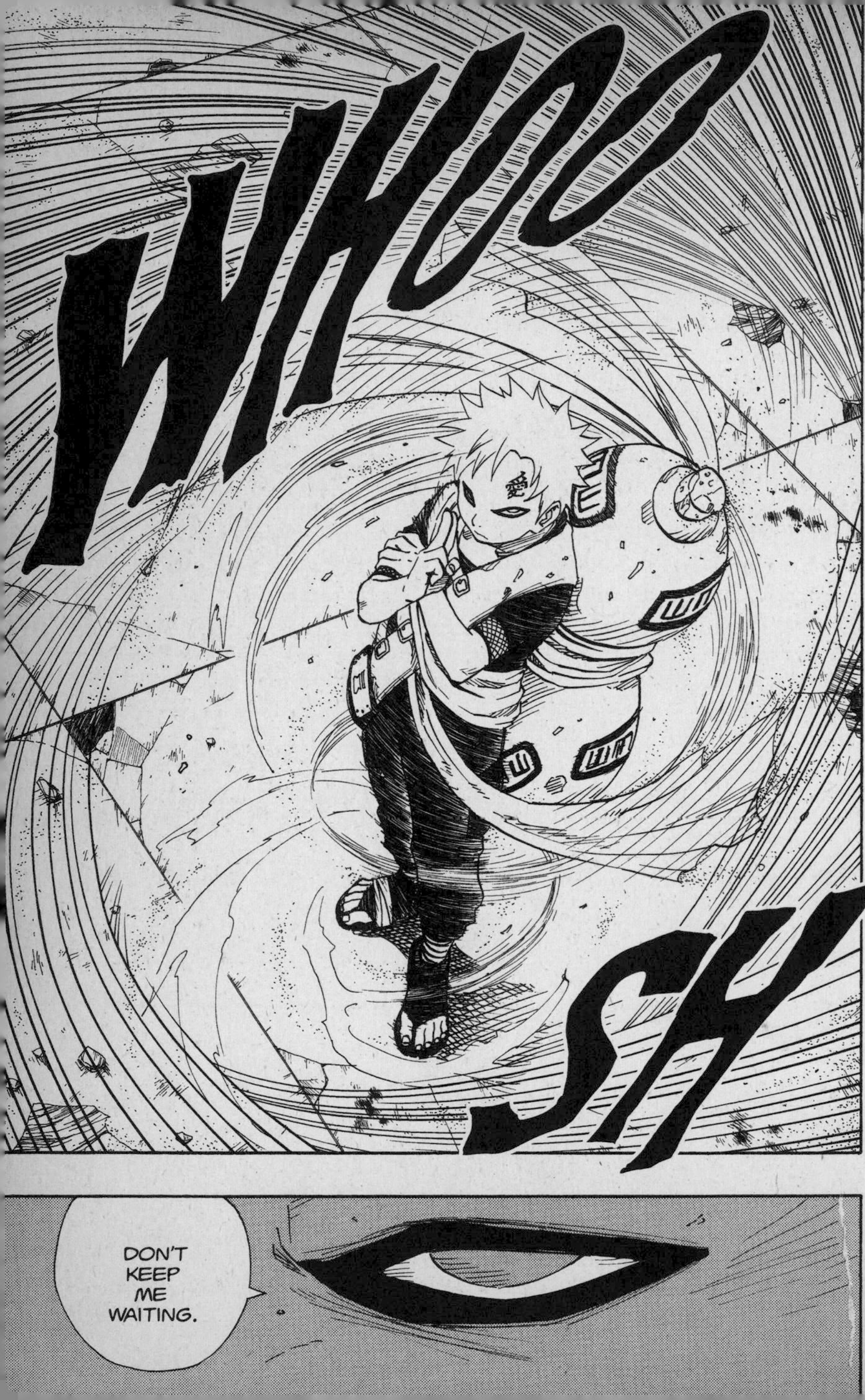
WHOOOSH
DON'T KEEP ME WAITING.

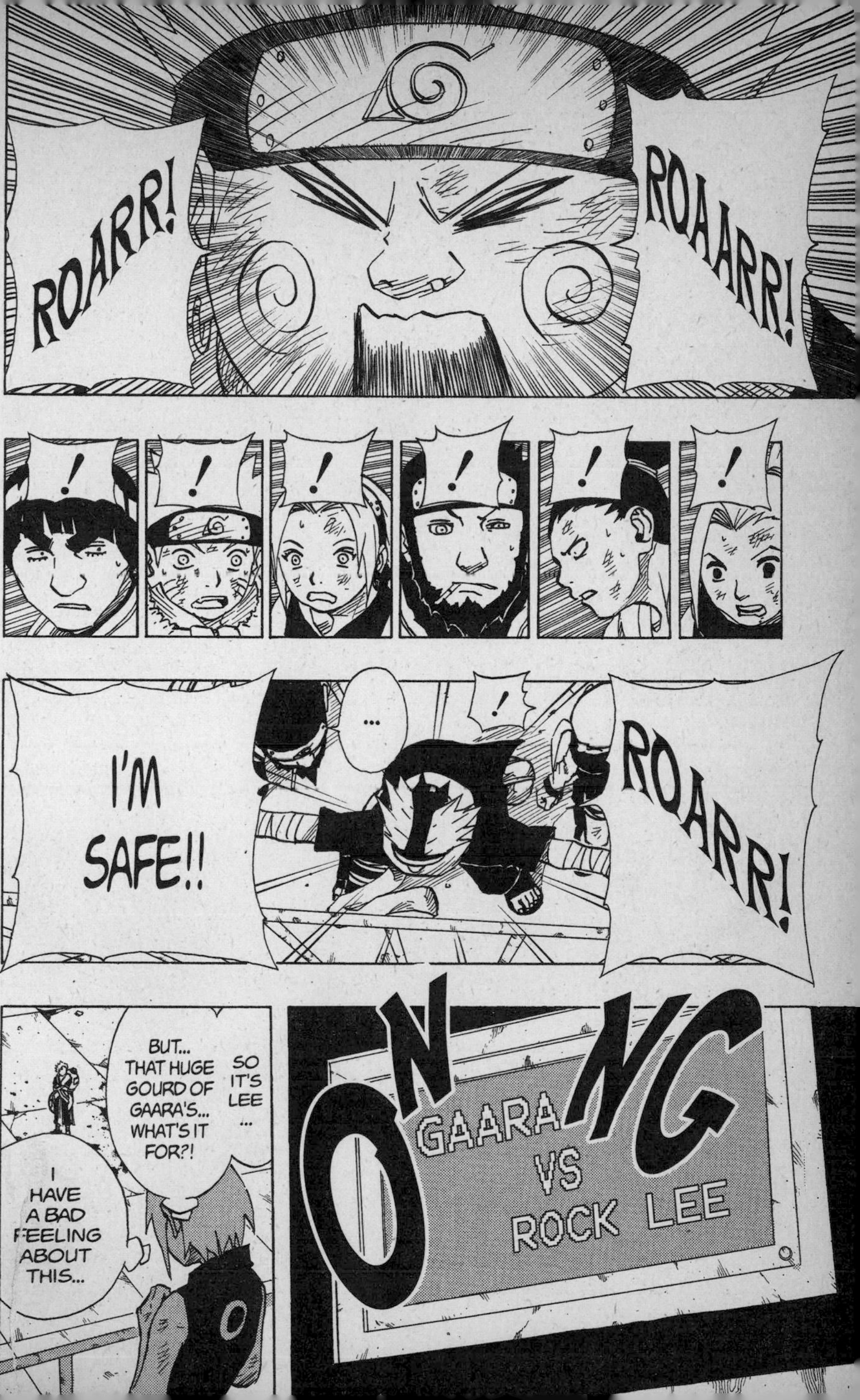
ROAARR!
ROARR!
!
!
!
!
!
!
ROARR!
!
...
I'M SAFE!!
ONNG
GAARA VS ROCK LEE
SO IT'S LEE...
BUT... THAT HUGE GOURD OF GAARA'S... WHAT'S IT FOR?!
I HAVE A BAD FEELING ABOUT THIS...

READ THIS WAY

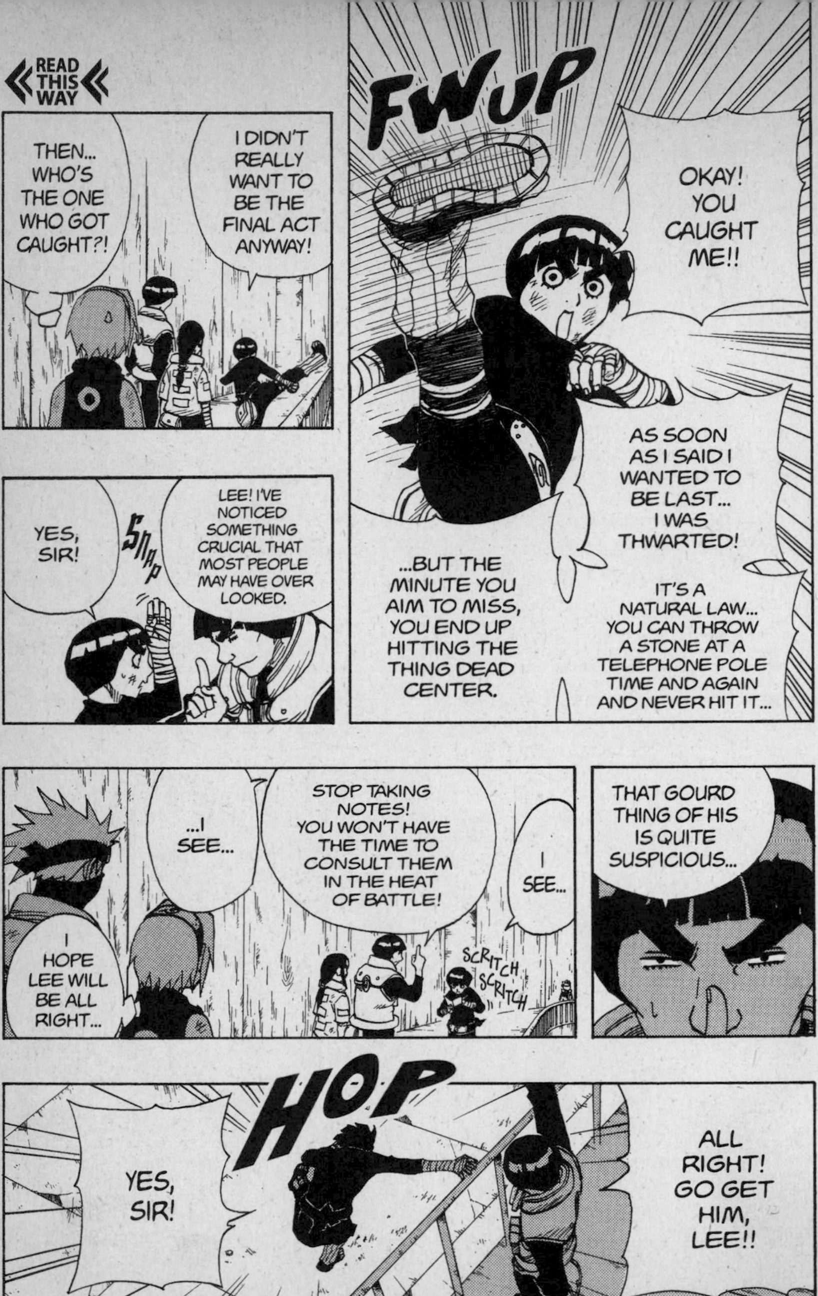
FWUP
OKAY! YOU CAUGHT ME!!
AS SOON AS I SAID I WANTED TO BE LAST... I WAS THWARTED!
IT'S A NATURAL LAW... YOU CAN THROW A STONE AT A TELEPHONE POLE TIME AND AGAIN AND NEVER HIT IT...
...BUT THE MINUTE YOU AIM TO MISS, YOU END UP HITTING THE THING DEAD CENTER.
I DIDN'T REALLY WANT TO BE THE FINAL ACT ANYWAY!
THEN... WHO'S THE ONE WHO GOT CAUGHT?!
LEE! I'VE NOTICED SOMETHING CRUCIAL THAT MOST PEOPLE MAY HAVE OVER LOOKED.
SNAP
YES, SIR!
THAT GOURD THING OF HIS IS QUITE SUSPICIOUS...
I SEE...
SCRITCH SCRITCH
STOP TAKING NOTES! YOU WON'T HAVE THE TIME TO CONSULT THEM IN THE HEAT OF BATTLE!
...I SEE...
I HOPE LEE WILL BE ALL RIGHT...
ALL RIGHT! GO GET HIM, LEE!!
HOP
YES, SIR!

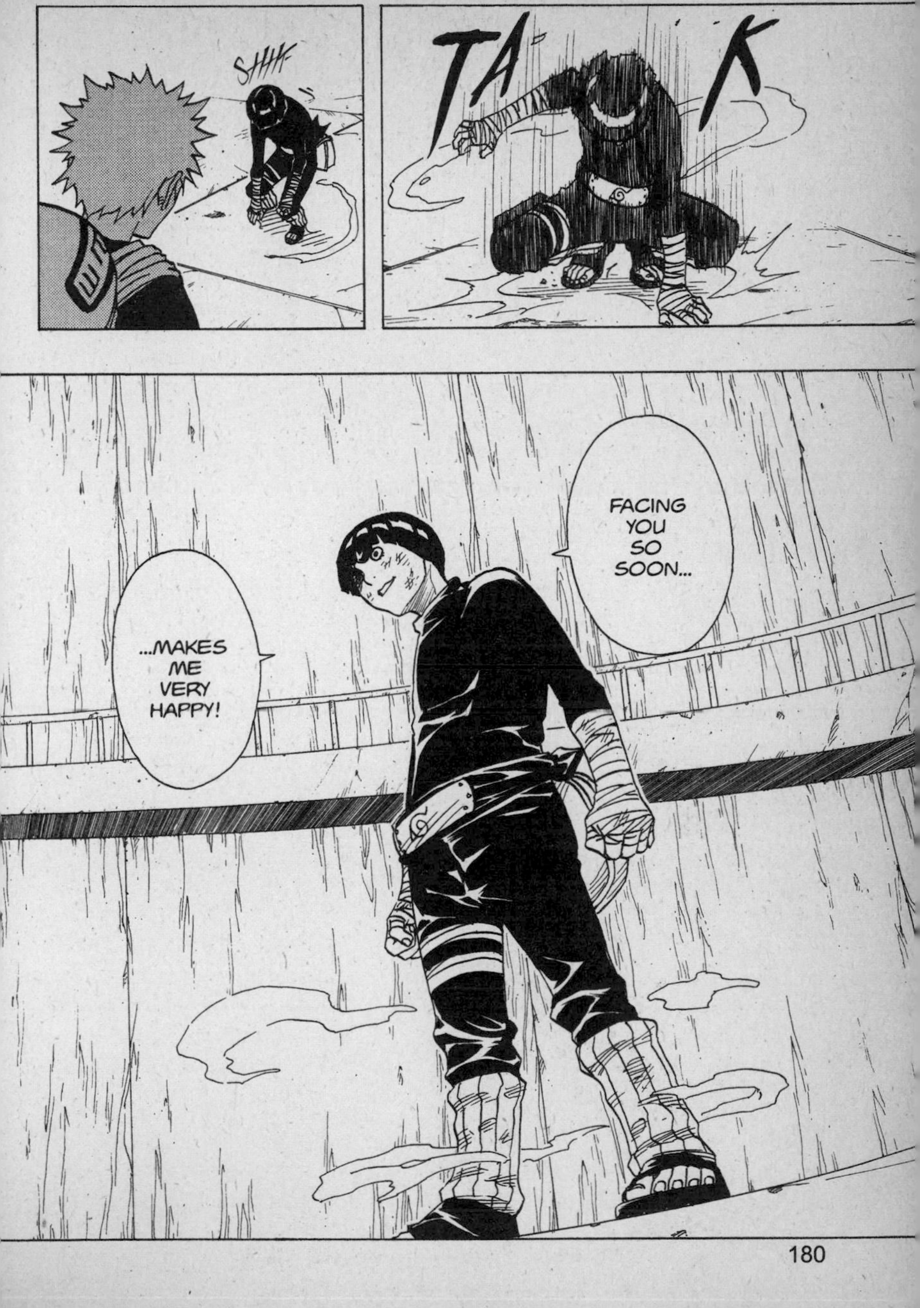
TA-K
SHHK
FACING YOU SO SOON...
...MAKES ME VERY HAPPY!

READ THIS WAY

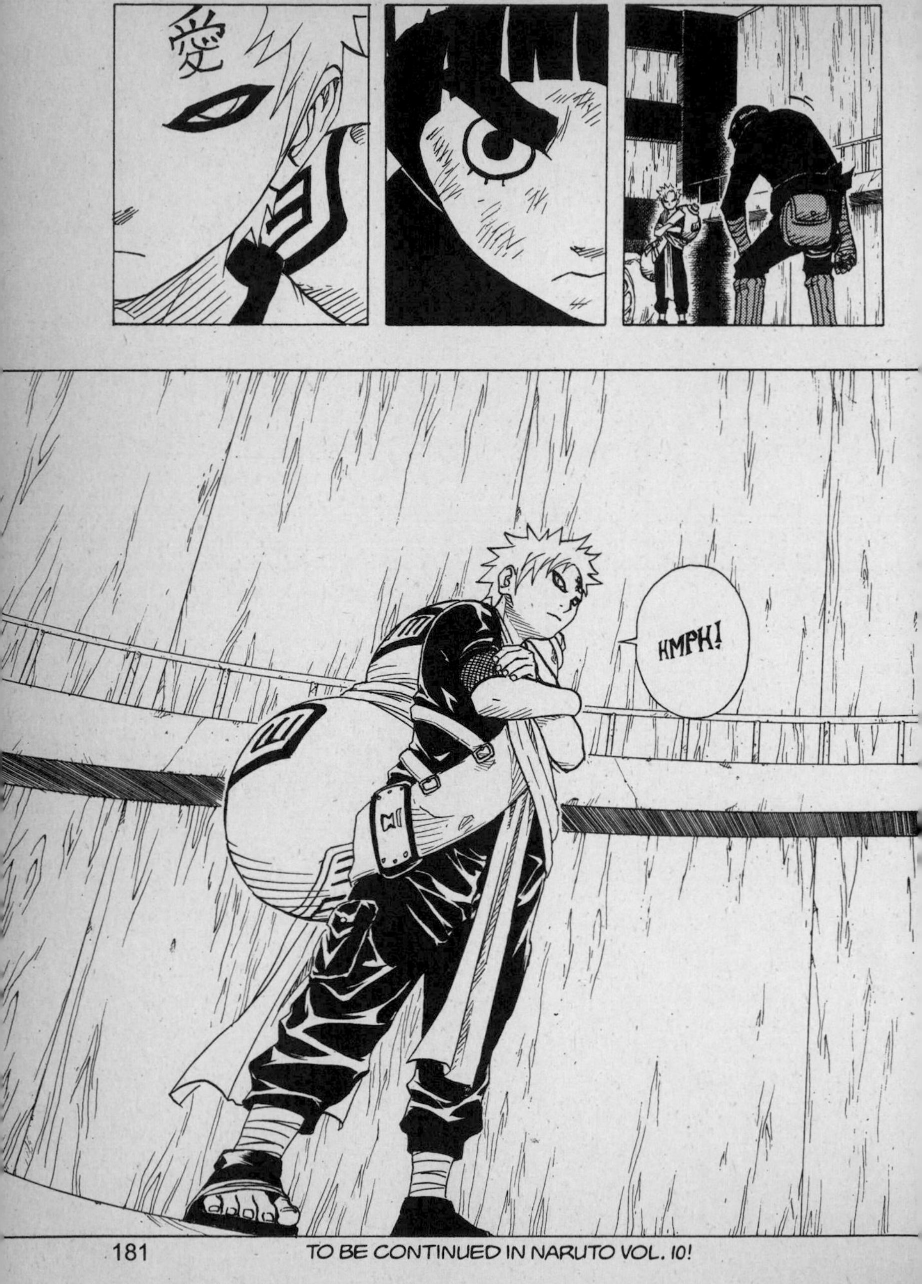
愛
HMPH!

TO BE CONTINUED IN NARUTO VOL. 10!

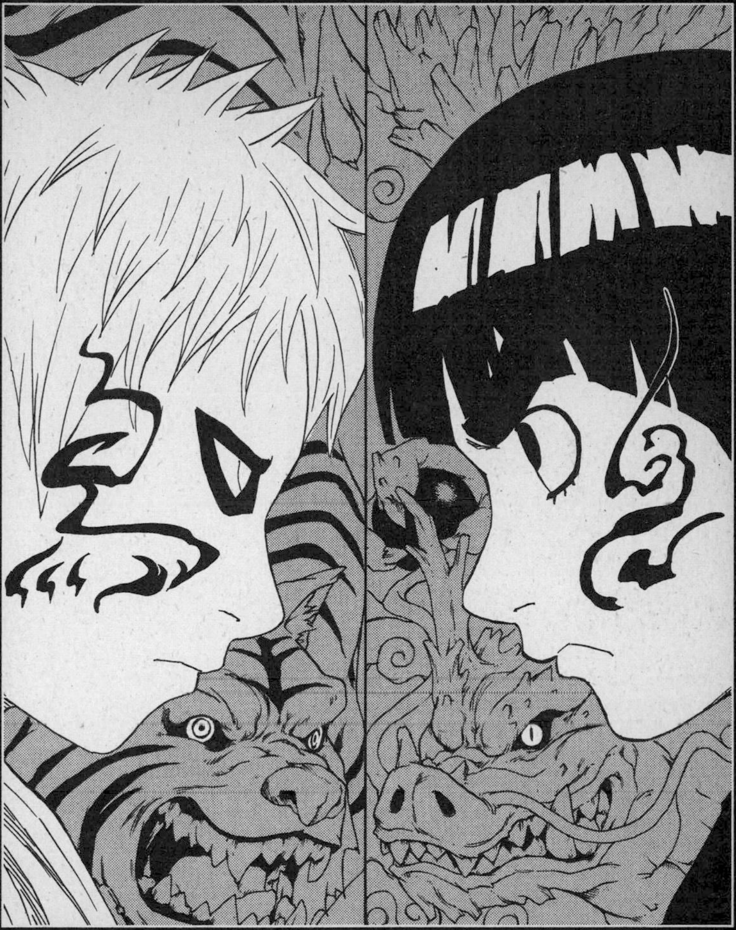

IN THE NEXT VOLUME...

The one-on-one battles heat up to the boiling point when creepy, mysterious Sand ninja Gaara takes on bushy-browed Konoha ninja Rock Lee. Will Gaara's bloodlust and his strange powers of sand manipulation make him too much for Lee? Or could Lee's dedication and amazing work ethic be enough to let him win? The preliminaries conclude with a bang! Who will move on…and what comes next?!

AVAILABLE NOW!

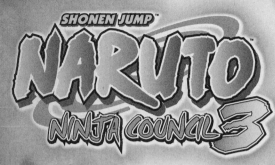

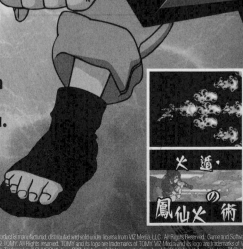

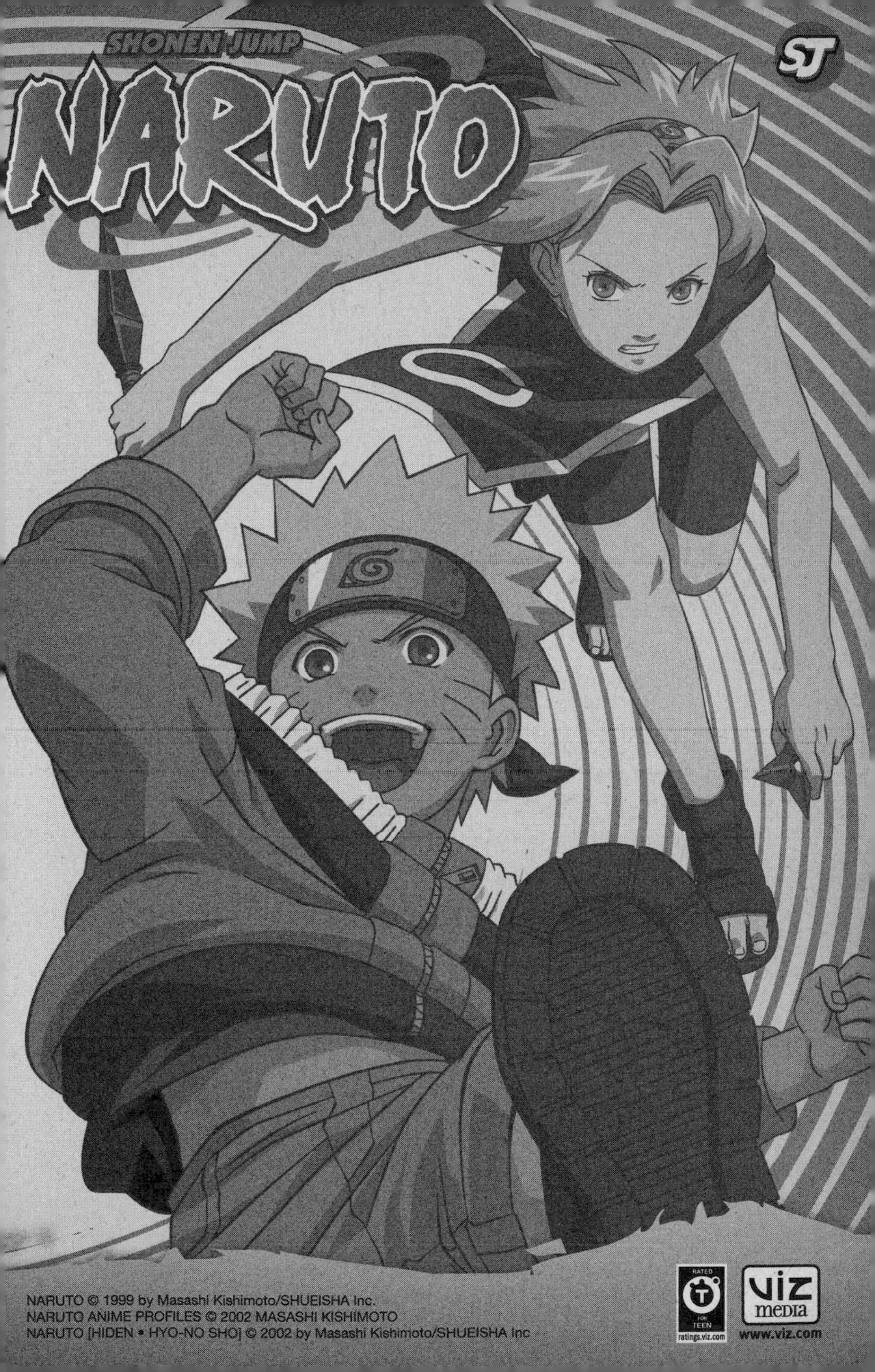
SHONEN JUMP
NARUTO
SJ

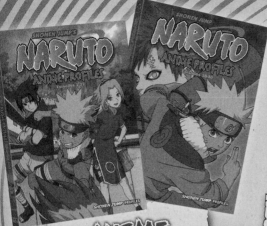
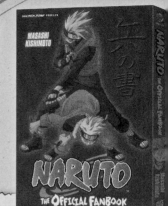
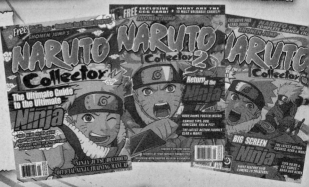
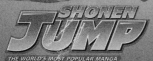

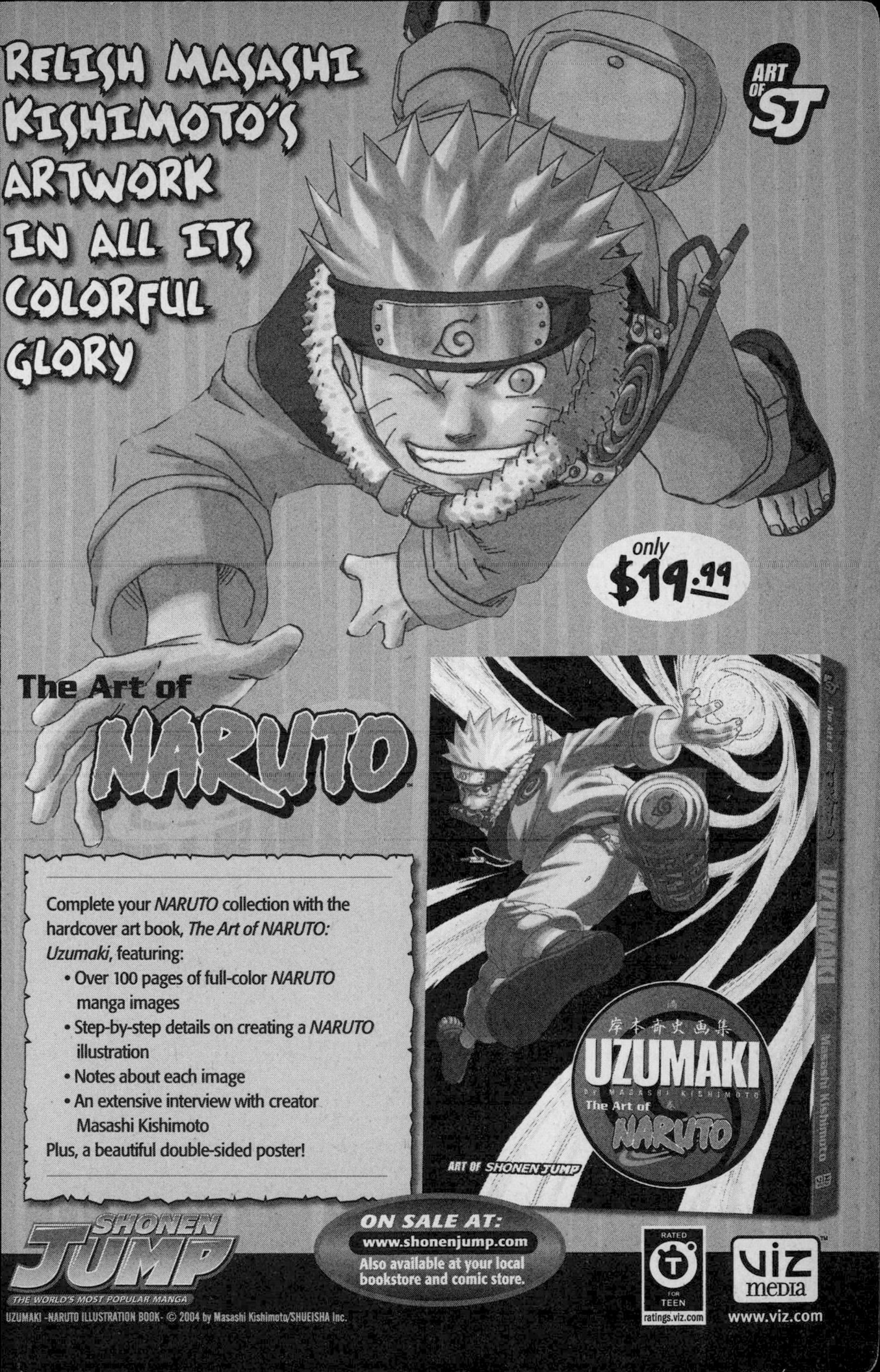
RELISH MASASHI KISHIMOTO'S ARTWORK IN ALL ITS COLORFUL GLORY
ART OF SJ
only $19.99
The Art of NARUTO
Complete your NARUTO collection with the hardcover art book, The Art of NARUTO: Uzumaki, featuring:
• Over 100 pages of full-color NARUTO manga images
• Step-by-step details on creating a NARUTO illustration
• Notes about each image
• An extensive interview with creator Masashi Kishimoto
Plus, a beautiful double-sided poster!
岸本斉史画集
UZUMAKI
The Art of NARUTO
ART OF SHONEN JUMP
SHONEN JUMP
THE WORLD'S MOST POPULAR MANGA
ON SALE AT:
www.shonenjump.com
Also available at your local bookstore and comic store.
RATED T FOR TEEN
ratings.viz.com
viz media
www.viz.com
UZUMAKI -NARUTO ILLUSTRATION BOOK- © 2004 by Masashi Kishimoto/SHUEISHA Inc.

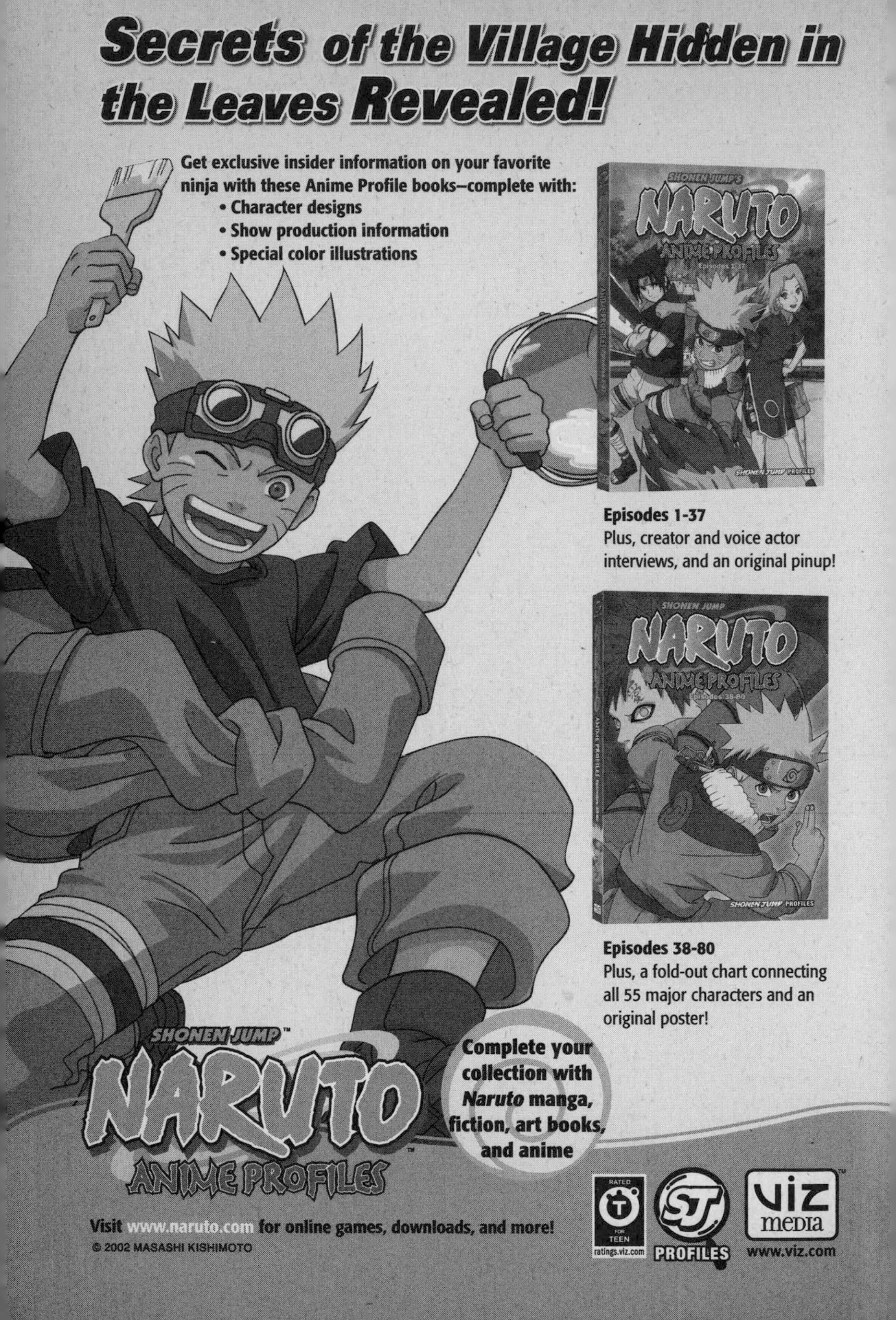
Secrets of the Village Hidden in the Leaves Revealed!
Get exclusive insider information on your favorite ninja with these Anime Profile books–complete with:
• Character designs
• Show production information
• Special color illustrations
SHONEN JUMP'S
NARUTO
ANIME PROFILES
SHONEN JUMP PROFILES
Episodes 1-37
Plus, creator and voice actor interviews, and an original pinup!
SHONEN JUMP
NARUTO
ANIME PROFILES
Episodes 38-80
SHONEN JUMP PROFILES
Episodes 38-80
Plus, a fold-out chart connecting all 55 major characters and an original poster!
SHONEN JUMP™
NARUTO™
ANIME PROFILES
Complete your collection with Naruto manga, fiction, art books, and anime
Visit www.naruto.com for online games, downloads, and more!
© 2002 MASASHI KISHIMOTO
RATED T FOR TEEN
ratings.viz.com
SJ PROFILES
VIZ MEDIA™
www.viz.com

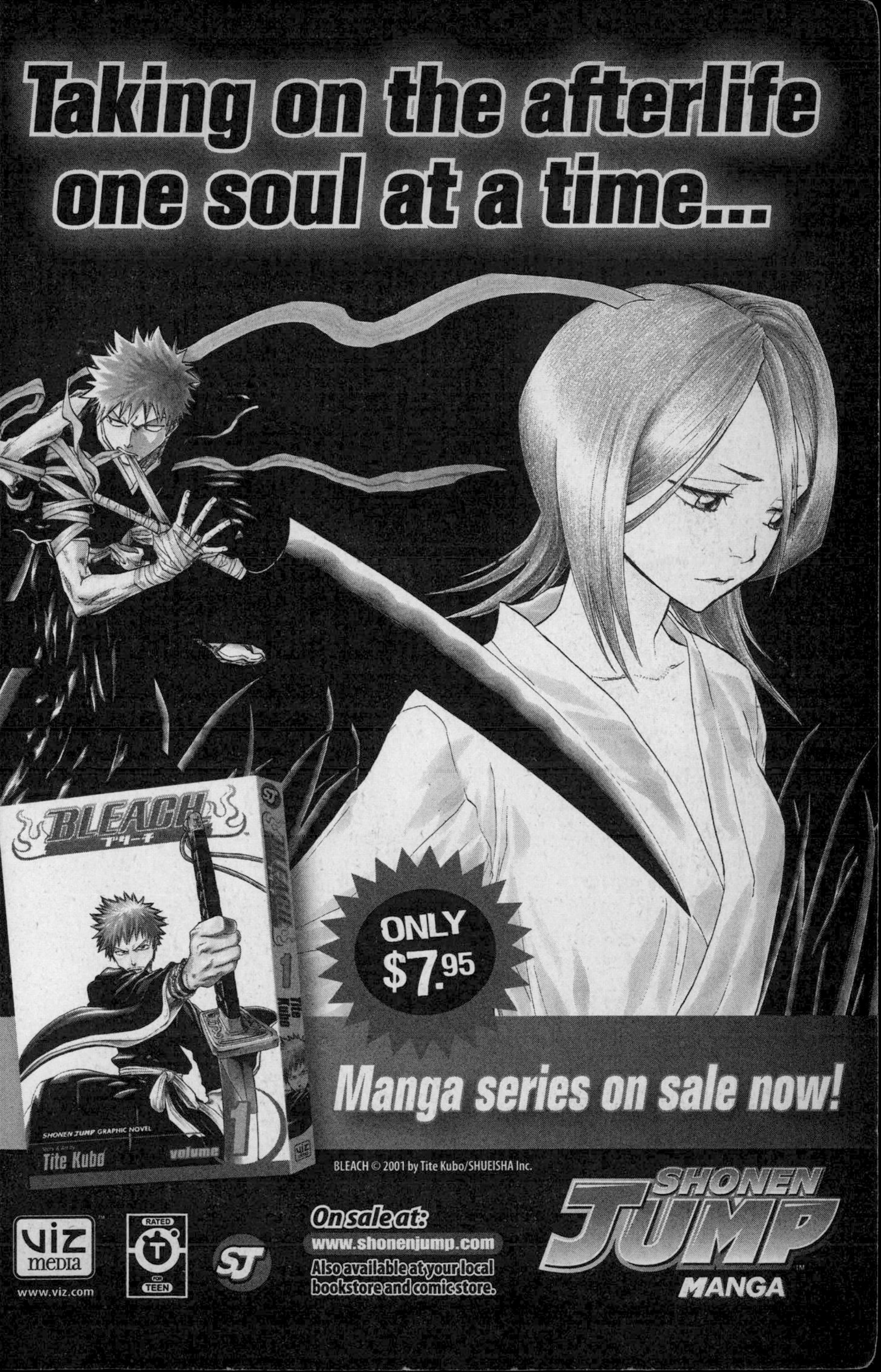
Taking on the afterlife one soul at a time...
BLEACH
ONLY $7.95
Manga series on sale now!
SHONEN JUMP GRAPHIC NOVEL
Tite Kubo
volume 1
BLEACH © 2001 by Tite Kubo/SHUEISHA Inc.
viz media
www.viz.com
RATED T FOR TEEN
On sale at:
www.shonenjump.com
Also available at your local bookstore and comic store.
SHONEN JUMP MANGA

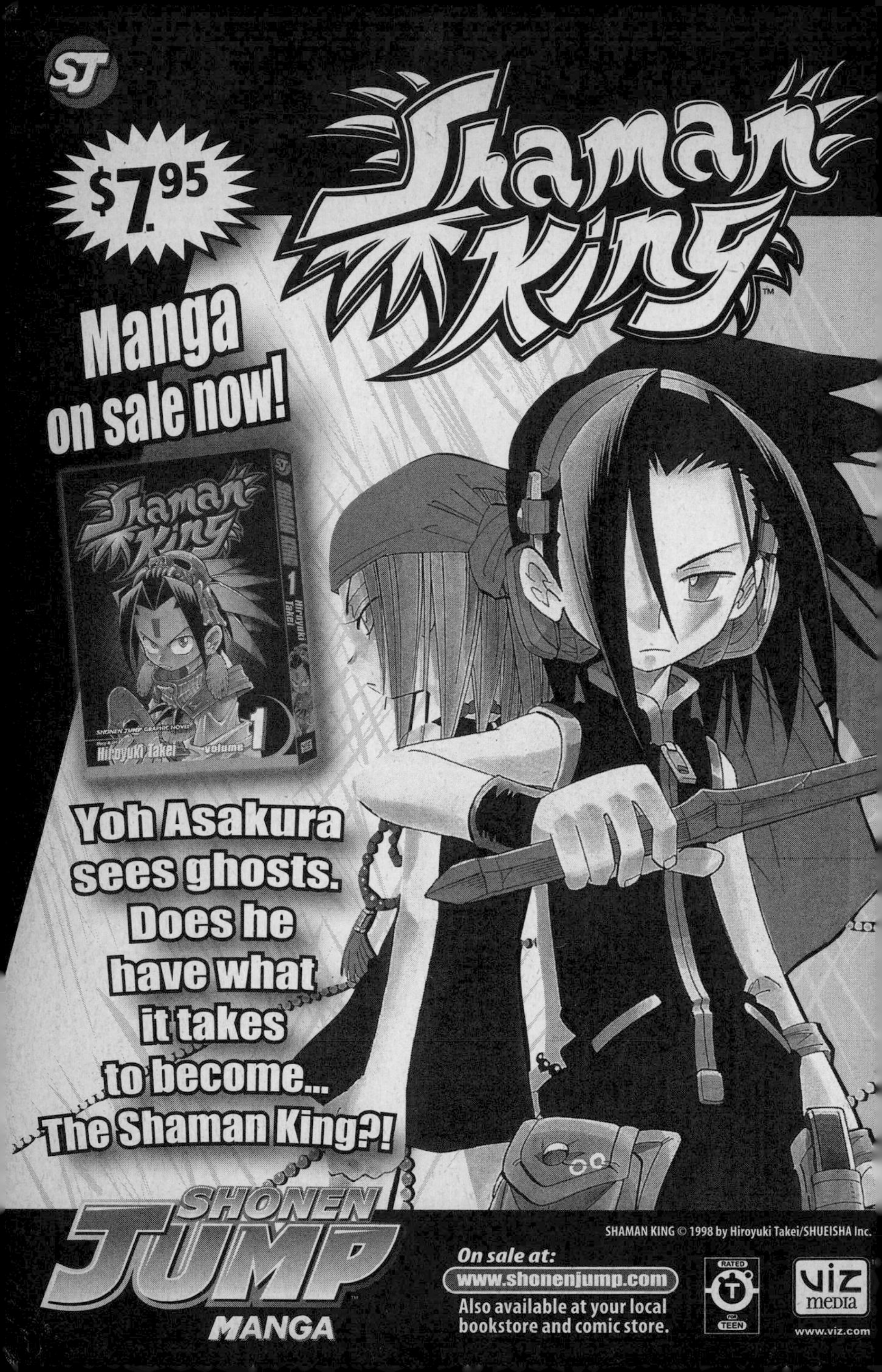
SJ
$7.95
Shaman King™
Manga on sale now!
Shaman King
Hiroyuki Takei
volume 1
Yoh Asakura sees ghosts. Does he have what it takes to become... The Shaman King?!
SHONEN JUMP MANGA
SHAMAN KING © 1998 by Hiroyuki Takei/SHUEISHA Inc.
On sale at:
www.shonenjump.com
Also available at your local bookstore and comic store.
RATED T TEEN
VIZ media
www.viz.com